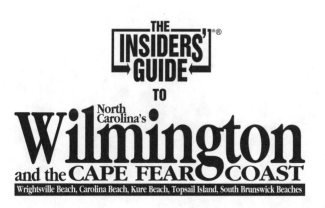

THE INSIDERS' GUIDE®

TO

North Carolina's Wilmington

and the CAPE FEAR COAST

Wrightsville Beach, Carolina Beach, Kure Beach, Topsail Island, South Brunswick Beaches

9 780912 367484

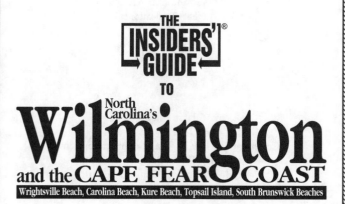

THE INSIDERS' GUIDE®

TO

North Carolina's
Wilmington
and the CAPE FEAR COAST

Wrightsville Beach, Carolina Beach, Kure Beach, Topsail Island, South Brunswick Beaches

by
Bill DiNome
and
Carol Deakin

By The Sea Publications Inc.

Published and distributed by:
By The Sea Publications, Inc.
P.O. Drawer 860
Beaufort, NC 28516
(919) 728-1860

•

First Edition
1st Printing
Copyright 1994 by By The Sea Publications, Inc.
Jay Tervo, Publisher
Printed in the United States of America

•

This book is produced under a license granted by:
The Insiders' Guides, Inc.
P.O. Box 2057
Manteo, NC 27954
(919) 473-6100

•

•

ISBN 0-912367-48-2

Preface

To some, it seemed a long time coming, perhaps overdue. But here it is, the very first *Insiders' Guide to Wilmington and the Cape Fear Coast*, the most in-depth, most comprehensive guide to the Azalea and Treasure Coasts available. Some may say its arrival is overdue because of Wilmington's historic preeminence as the state's only deep-water port, as the state's first true political and cultural mecca and as the state's largest city until well into the early 20th century. As the cliche goes, timing is everything. And the timing of the *Insiders' Guide*'s 1994 arrival, if nothing else, is indicative of the "quiet" boom of resurgence the region is experiencing (quiet compared to recent media hoopla about the Southwest, Seattle and certain other Southeastern cities). This boom is apparent in the steady influx of population and industry; the flourishing of the arts, higher education and restaurants; the proliferation of tourist accommodations and recreational attractions; and the availability of goods, housing and services — all bespeaking a healthy economy that has shown little inclination to participate in the country's recession blues.

The idea behind all the *Insiders' Guides* grew from a spark of recognition back in 1979 among some long-time residents of the Outer Banks that their coastal refuge had much to offer tourists and new residents. And who better to relate inside information than residents? Since then, other *Insiders' Guides* have sprung up, every one written by residents of the region featured.

This guide is not a shopping list of things to do or places to go. Rather, it is designed to give you a sense of the character of the region and its offerings. It makes no attempt to include everything there is to enjoy on Cape Fear. However, it does include everything we feel comfortable recommending to our own friends and families. It is the result of painstaking research, verification and firsthand experience. We've tried to include information that will prove useful, not only to short-term visitors, but also to newcomers who plan to stay. Even longtime residents and natives may gain new perspectives and tips. Interspersed throughout the book are insightful vignettes, interviews and histories about the places, people and events that have shaped the Cape Fear coast.

The *Guide*'s usefulness is enhanced by its functional structure. Chapters are arranged according to activities and subjects such as restaurants, night life, arts, volunteer opportunities and golf. Within each chapter, the topic is divided by locale, starting with Wilmington, then spinning off toward the outlying beaches and communities. The order in which the locales appear in every chapter is the same as in the Area Overviews. Within each locale, listings are alphabetized by their common names.

We'll recommend places to hear a symphony, mosh to rock 'n' roll, charter a dive trip or shop for antiques. You'll find out where to rent a jet ski, study yoga, store your boat and repair your bike or car. Those relocating here will find the chapters on real estate, retirement, medical care and schools invaluable.

The Service and Information Directory will assist you in locating emergency services, subscribing to a newspaper, reserving a taxi, securing utility services and preparing for hurricanes. Keep in mind that the region's new area code is 910. All phone numbers listed in this book share the 910 area code unless otherwise noted.

Every attempt has been made to present accurate, up-to-date information. Of course, things change; businesses come and go; hotels renovate. Even the shoreline moves. Let us know about any information you read here that is at variance with what you find out there. Even feedback about a job well done would be greatly appreciated. Necessary changes will be incorporated into upcoming editions.

Welcome to Wilmington and the historic Cape Fear coast!

— B.D. and C.D.

Photo: Scott Taylor

Walking the beach is the number one favorite pastime.

About the Authors

Bill DiNome came to Wilmington, sight unseen, in the summer of 1990 and immediately fell in love with it. It may have been his first dolphin sighting that helped him decide to stay. Or, it may have had something to do with the exotic Spanish moss, or the clean, uncrowded beaches. The decision may have been helped by his childhood fascination with legendary pirates who sailed into myth along these very shores. He did stay. Behind him lay some (extremely) modest accomplishments as a native New York City musician and as an award-winning copywriter in the publishing industry. He also left behind a few unpaid parking tickets and a mother concerned about his eating habits.

In 1991, he took time out (four months) to wander, alone, over the back roads and hiking trails of America before returning to the Port City and tapping into *The Beat*, the music magazine of the Carolina coast. He soon became contributing editor. Settled again, he immediately dived headlong into the history, culture and club scene of the Lower Cape Fear. Meanwhile, he penned a series of pseudonymous novels published by Berkley/ Putnam, and his eating habits improved dramatically. He continues to contribute articles to several publications and works as a free-lance editor, copywriter and author.

His greatest accomplishment is his marriage to a longtime Wilmington resident who, along with her son, has become an invaluable insider informant. His many interests include history, backpacking, travel, film, birds, mucking about in caves, reading, music and deciding whether there are any alligators left in Greenfield Lake.

Carol Deakin is a free-lance writer and artist who made Wilmington her home in the summer of 1986 after coming to the realization that she wanted to spend her life at the edge of the land.

A Georgia native who has lived throughout the South for 43 years, she describes Wilmington as the "most Southern city" in which she has lived. She has come to the conclusion that writers Tennessee Williams, Carson McCullers and Truman Capote would have all been very happy to spend their days in Wilmington.

In order to immerse herself in the rich culture of the region, she became a resident of the downtown historic district, living just a block from the Cape Fear River and in walking distance of cafes, galleries and theater, where there are many interesting people to see. Her home is a modest Victorian cottage that was built in 1898, and she currently is researching its history in order to qualify it for an historic designation plaque. Research to this point reveals nothing of particular interest, but it's a very cute house.

Carol is a 1973 graduate of the University of North Carolina at Greensboro. She has worked as a public relations and marketing director in theater, the public schools and nonprofit organizations. Eventually, she decided to leave the confines of regular employment and work independently.

She is a pen and ink cartoon artist and a partner in Watermark Publishing, which specializes in cruising guides to waters of the southeast. She is also a free-lance writer for local and regional publications. Her interests include sailing, cooking and, of course, talking and writing about Wilmington.

Acknowledgements

Garlands of Martian fire flowers to Deborah Flora, my wife, best friend, comic relief and reality check. Throughout this project, she hung tough to the promise that we would reacquaint ourselves when it was done (Hi!) and proved invaluable in the meantime since she knows every third person in the phone book. Her son, Taj, deserves monster props for his superhuman effort in putting up with me. Fanfares, knighthood and all their favorite chocolates to the many folks who fielded my questions, held my hand and generally helped me wrestle this beast to the mat. They were great teachers all. To Michelle Burch at *Encore Magazine* who didn't have to but did, Michael Byrd at Wordwright Publishing who gets me read, Ren Brown at St. John's Museum of Art, Caronell Chestnut, Betty Parks, Betty Polzer of Topsail Beach, John Taggart of the NC National Estuarine Research Reserve, Harry Warren at the Cape Fear Museum, Bubba who got me around, and all the others who helped flesh out the bare bones I started with — you know who you are! Special thanks to Jay Tervo.

— B.D.

The Insiders' Guide would not have been possible without the generous help of many people in the Cape Fear area.

My sincere thanks goes to publisher, Jay Tervo, for his soft-spoken, sensitive and steady guidance throughout the process of writing this guide. Thanks to the Cape Fear Museum, most notably Executive Director Janet Seapker, who offered great leads for historical information. Carolyn Soders of The Cape Fear Council of Governments, Jane Peterson of the Cape Fear Coast Convention and Visitors Bureau, Linda Pearce of Elderhaus, artist Claude Howell, Thalian Hall Executive Director Tony Rivenbark, the staff in the North Carolina Room at the New Hanover County Public Library, Bonnie Pierce and Betsy Perkins of the Arts Council of the Lower Cape Fear, Betty Kennedy of Bland & Associates Realtors, Laurel Pettys of Intracoastal Realty, Deanes Gornto and Larry Cranford of Harbour Associates, Amy Hamme of the Child Advocacy Commission, Dianne Avery of the New Hanover County Schools, and hundreds of helpful folks from Topsail Island to Sunset Beach were very generous with their time and information.

The Greater Wilmington Chamber of Commerce was very helpful in providing a manufacturer's guide and a thick packet of information on the impact of business on the Cape Fear area. Paul Laird of the chamber made special efforts to provide the insider with accurate information. Staff at the City of Wilmington, New Hanover County, Brunswick County and Pender County consistently were able to answer questions and offer suggestions for sources.

Thanks to cruising guide author Claiborne Young for an on-the-water research trip into marinas and the benefit of his considerable knowledge.

Special thanks go to my dear friend Elizabeth Darrow who served as unpaid editor before the real ones got ahold of my scribblings, and provided much support, encouragement and constructive advice throughout the duration of this project.

I also thank the editors, artists, layout people and everyone else who worked so hard to create this book and didn't get their faces on the cover. I thank Bill DiNome, speaking of faces on the cover, for being such an outstanding partner in writing this guide.

— C.D.

I wish to gratefully acknowledge Carol Deakin and Bill DiNome for the incredible amount of hard work they both did to make this book possible. Thanks go also to Jane Peterson at the Cape Fear Coast Convention and Visitor's Bureau for helping in so many ways, and to Louise McColl, Allison Ballard and Rhonda Coleman at Jordan-McColl for advertising sales. Photo credits belong to Curtis Krueger and Scott Taylor, and the good folks at Insiders' Guides International deserve kudos for yet again another fine showing — thanks Beth, Michael, Gina, Giles, Theresa, Mike and Julie! And to be sure, thanks to the *Wilmington Star News* for sponsoring this first edition of a long line of *Insiders' Guides to Wilmington and the Cape Fear Coast.*

— J.C.T.

STATE OF NORTH CAROLINA
OFFICE OF THE GOVERNOR
RALEIGH 27603-8001

JAMES B. HUNT, JR.
GOVERNOR

Dear Friends:

As Governor of the State of North Carolina, it is indeed my privilege to welcome you to the Cape Fear Coast – Historic Wilmington, Wrightsville Beach, Carolina Beach, Kure Beach, Topsail Island and the South Brunswick Islands.

Tourism is the area's number one industry. With its beautiful beaches, fishing, boating, water sports, and golf, there is something for every sports enthusiast. Additionally, such major attractions as the Battleship North Carolina, North Carolina Aquarium, and Fort Fisher State Historic Site, just to name a few, draw visitors by the thousands every year. And no matter where you go, you will experience Southern Hospitality at its very best.

Of equal importance is the area's inviting business climate. With the completion of I-40 and its connection with I-85 and I-95, the Cape Fear Coast is now easily accessible by highway. Wilmington continues to be a busy port city with its access to both the Cape Fear River and the Atlantic Ocean.

On behalf of all our citizens, I again welcome you and invite you to enjoy all that the Cape Fear Coast has to offer.

My warmest personal regards.

Sincerely,

James. B. Hunt Jr.

Table of Contents

Preface v
About the Authors viii
Acknowledgements x
Getting Around 1
Area Overviews 7
Restaurants 39
Accommodations 73
Vacation Rentals 103
Camping 110
Shopping 119
Attractions 137
Annual Events 172
Nightlife 179
Water Sports and Rentals 195
Sun, Sand and Sea Tips 215
Fishing 223
Marinas and the Intracoastal Waterway 239
Sports, Fitness and Parks 248
Golf 271
Ferry Services 283
The Arts 287
Places of Worship 301
Service Directory 309
Real Estate 325
Schools and Child Care 347
Retirement and Senior Services 360
Volunteer Opportunities 368
Hospitals and Medical Care 377
Higher Education and Research 384
Airports 396
Commerce and Industry 399
Daytrips 407
Index of Advertisers 417
Index 418

Directory of Maps

Regional Overview .... inside front cover
Wilmington and The Cape Fear Coast xiv
Topsail Island to Calabash xv
Downtown Wilmington xvi

Wilmington And The Cape Fear Coast

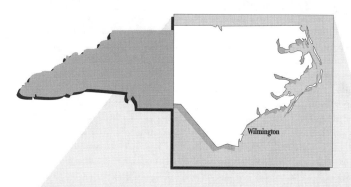

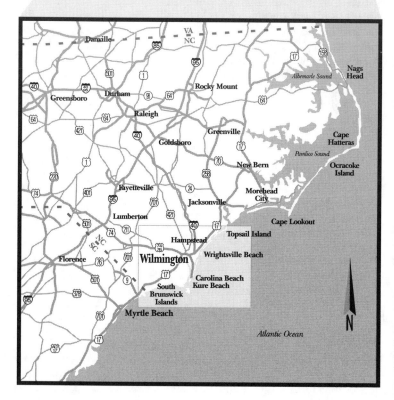

Topsail Island To Calabash

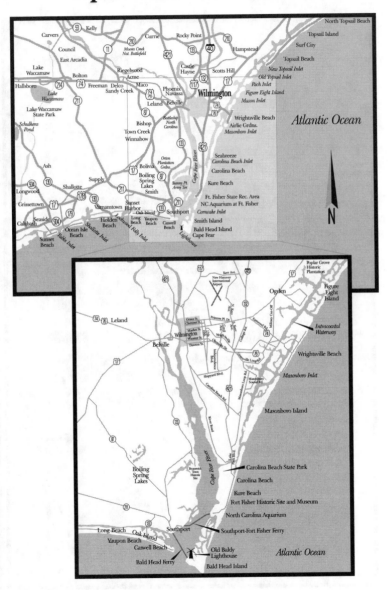

Downtown Wilmington

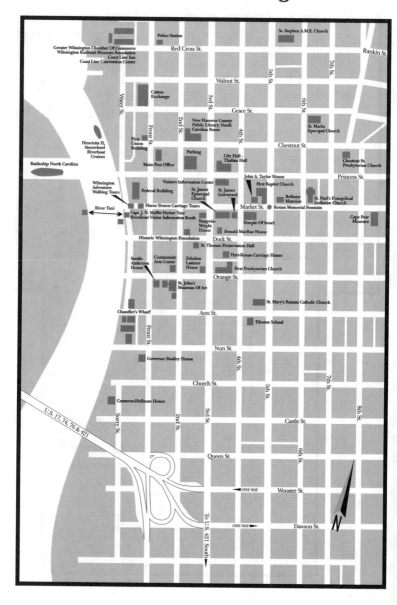

St. Stephen A.M.E. Church

Police Station

Greater Wilmington Chamber Of Commerce
Wilmington Railroad Museum Foundation
Coast Line Inn
Coast Line Convention Center

Red Cross St.

Rankin St.

7th St.

5th St.

Walnut St.

Water St.

Cotton Exchange

3rd St.

Grace St.

6th St.

2nd St.

New Hanover County
Public Library, North
Carolina Room

St. Marks
Episcopal Church

4th St.

First Union Building

Front St.

Parking

Chestnut St.

Henrietta II,
Sternwheel
Riverboat
Cruises

Main Post Office

City Hall -
Thalian Hall

Chestnut St.
Presbyterian Church

Battleship North Carolina

Princess St.

Wilmington Adventure Walking Tours

Visitors Information Center

John A. Taylor House
First Baptist Church

Federal Building

St. James Episcopal Church

St. James Graveyard

Bellamy Mansion

St. Paul's Evangelical Lutheran Church

River Taxi

Horse Drawn Carriage Tours

Market St.

Kenan Memorial Fountain

Cape Fear Museum

Capt. J. N. Maffit Harbor Tour
Riverfront Visitor Information Booth

Burgwin-Wright House

Temple Of Israel

Donald MacRae House

Historic Wilmington Foundation

Dock St.

St. Thomas Preservation Hall

Hart-Kenan Carriage House

Smith-Anderson House

Community Arts Center

Zebulon Latimer House

First Presbyterian Church

St. John's Museum Of Art

Orange St.

St. Mary's Roman Catholic Church

Chandler's Wharf

Ann St.

Front St.

Tileston School

Nun St.

Governor Dudley House

4th St.

Church St.

5th St.

7th St.

8th St.

Cameron-Hollman House

Surry St.

2nd St.

3rd St.

Castle St.

6th St.

U.S. 17, 74, 76 & 421

Queen St.

ONE WAY

Wooster St.

To U.S. 421 South

ONE WAY

Dawson St.

N

Getting Around
Wilmington and the
Cape Fear Coast

Congratulations! By virtue of the fact that you're reading this chapter, consider yourself among the luckiest, if not the most sagacious, of travelers for having chosen Wilmington and its environs as your destination. Getting into the area by air, sea or land is easier than ever before. New Hanover International Airport's new, full-service terminal serves three major airlines. The recently-completed Interstate-40, which has its western terminus some 2,500 miles away in Barstow, California, is the fastest automotive link to the rest of the nation. And water, the region's dominant physical feature, makes the Cape Fear coast particularly accessible to boaters from Canada or the Keys.

New Hanover International Airport, located off North 23rd Street, 2 miles north of Market Street, is the prime entry point for most people flying into the area. It and the Grand Strand Airport in Myrtle Beach, South Carolina, are nearly equidistant from Shallotte (pronounced "shuh-LOTE") and the South Brunswick Islands. For detailed information on flying to Cape Fear, see the chapter on Airports.

Boaters enjoy two options for getting to Cape Fear by water: sail-

Early morning waters are calm at a local harbor.

Photo: Curtis Krueger

The Battleship USS North Carolina participated in every major engagement in the Pacific in World War II.

ing "outside" through open ocean waters, or "inside" via the Intracoastal Waterway (aka "the Ditch"). From New River Inlet at the northern tip of Topsail Island (that's "TOP-sull") to the South Carolina border, 42 marinas are at your disposal along nearly 90 miles of protected waterway. Refer to the chapter on Marinas for complete information.

Cruising the asphalt can be as much fun as any other way of getting here, especially given the many places to visit en route. But first, some bearings:

Situated at the eastern terminus of I-40, Wilmington is about 12 hours from New York City (599 miles) by interstate, given the quickest of pit stops; seven hours from Washington, D.C. (374 miles); four hours from Charlotte, NC (197 miles); 3 1/2 hours from Charleston, SC (169 miles); and about 1 1/2 hours from Myrtle Beach (72 miles). The interchange between I-40 and I-95 at Benson, NC, is 1 1/2 hours from Wilmington (about 75 miles). Driving from Raleigh will take almost 2 1/4 hours (127 miles), while driving from Chapel Hill will take almost 2 3/4 hours.

If you're coming long distance, I-40 is most folks' road of choice, although it's a long, dull ride (as are most interstates). Choosing second-

Insiders' Tips

One of the most beautiful times to visit the Wilmington area is during "off season" in the winter.

2 ·

ary roads will enrich your ride with local flavor without adding very much travel time. If you prefer the interstate, be sure to have enough gas to last two hours or more at 65 mph between I-95 and Wilmington. Services along that leg of I-40 are limited, are located several miles out of your way, and all close early in the evening. Within that stretch of tall pines and farmland is only one rest area, about an hour outside Wilmington. Facilities are restricted to well-kept rest rooms, phones, water fountains, junk-food vending machines, a picnic area and a dog walking area.

I-40 enters Wilmington from the north, converging with Route 132 and assuming the name College Road. College Road passes over Market Street (Route 17/74), which stretches downtown to the right (west) and left toward the ocean (east).

From Charlotte, U.S. 74 is a direct link to downtown Wilmington. (Watch your speed around Whiteville!) That road links with U.S. 76 out of Florence, SC; Route 211 from Southport; and Highway 17 from the south.

The main roads between Wilmington and Wrightsville Beach form something of a crooked triangle, the apex being the drawbridge into Wrightsville Beach (Causeway Drive). The northern leg of the triangle consists of Market Street and Eastwood Road (Route 74), a 55 mph two-lane road about 5 miles long that intersects Market Street immediately east of the College Road overpass. The southern leg of the triangle is Route 76. It runs directly

from the Cape Fear Memorial Bridge downtown (as Dawson Street), becomes Oleander Drive, then overlaps Wrightsville Avenue at the traffic light where Airlie Road and Military Cutoff Road intersect and Oleander ends. (The white stucco church of St. Andrews Episcopal is your landmark.)

The main arteries leading south into Pleasure Island (Carolina, Wilmington and Kure beaches, Fort Fisher) form another triangle. At Monkey Junction, College Road (132) meets U.S. Highway 421 (Carolina Beach Road), which extends from S. Third Street downtown.

From Calabash to Topsail, there's basically one road to remember: U.S. Route 17. They don't call it Ocean Highway for nothing. Like the spine of coastal Carolina, Highway 17 parallels the ocean and intersects every main route to the sea. Still a 45 mph two-lane road along some of its length, the highway is undergoing improvements to accommodate the increasing traffic flow. However, construction seldom creates appreciable delays.

Entering the region from the south, Highway 17 intersects NC Route 179, which veers seaward through Calabash. Route 179 hugs the Intracoastal Waterway, giving access to the picturesque pontoon bridge to Sunset Beach (Sunset Blvd.) and to the Ocean Isle Beach high span (NC Route 904) before leaning northward into Shallotte, where it rejoins Business 17. In Shallotte, Bus. 17 intersects NC 130 (Holden Beach Road), a direct route to that beach community.

Continuing north, Highway 17

Photo: Curtis Krueger

Eye to eye with a great white heron.

joins NC 211 near the town of Supply. NC 211, which brings you directly into the picturesque old village of Southport, is named, appropriately enough, the Southport-Supply Road — possibly because there were just no more interesting names left. The Fort Fisher ferry, which connects Southport to the south end of Pleasure Island, has its terminal on Southport's northeast side, at the foot of — did you guess? — Ferry Road. The 25-minute ride across the Cape Fear River is a wonderful way to visit historic Fort Fisher (see the chapter on Ferries).

Northward again, Highway 17 joins routes 87, 74 and 76, then crosses the Cape Fear Memorial Bridge into downtown Wilmington. Highway 17 joins Market Street as it exits town from the northeast. It then passes through Ogden, Scotts Hill, Hampstead and Holly Ridge. State routes 210 and 50

Photo: Scott Taylor

A great white heron in flight is art to behold.

both lead to Topsail Island, converging at the bridge into Surf City (Roland Avenue). (Until last year, this intersection boasted Topsail Island's only traffic light. Now there's a flashing light in Topsail Beach, too. Time marches on.) On Topsail Island, Route 50 turns south toward Topsail Beach, while Route 210 runs north through North Topsail Beach then back onto the mainland across the New River Inlet bridge, which affords a breathtaking view of the Intracoastal Waterway. Route 210 rejoins Highway 17 a few short miles beyond, just minutes from Jacksonville.

Drivers take note: speed limits at the beaches can be a test of patience, and they are as strictly enforced as the laws of nature. Throughout Wilmington at night, patrol cars often idle in darkened parking lots, awaiting unwary speeders. Relax, take it slowly, and enjoy.

To get around Wilmington and its immediate area, pick up a copy of the Guide Map put out by the Cape

Fear Coast Convention & Visitors Bureau. It's a great street map and is available free at the Visitors Information Center (in the Old Courthouse at Third and Princess Streets), at many hotels, and from the Chamber of Commerce. Realtors' maps are also handy and very detailed.

Cyclists may want a copy of the Wilmington Bike Map, available at those same places and from local bike shops. It's an exhaustive treatment of all major bike routes, side streets, and riding conditions.

Public transportation in Wilmington consists of six bus lines linking outlying neighborhoods, the university and shopping centers to downtown. One-way fare is 60 cents, 30¢ for seniors and the handicapped. Discount ticket books are available from any bus driver. There is no bus service on Sundays and major holidays. The Wilmington Public Transit Guide has a handy map and table of schedules. Ask for one at the Visitors Center.

Inside
Wilmington and
Cape Fear Coast

The story about Wilmington and adjacent barrier islands and river communities begins with the water. The history of this region, at least from the European viewpoint, began with the discovery of a river.

When Giovanni da Verrazano poked the bow of his ship into an unnamed river in 1524, he ushered in a new historical period that eventually would lead to the development of the area.

There is some dispute about the original name of the river. It may have been Cape Fair. Verrazano's first description of the area suggests the possibility: "The open country rising in height above the sandy shore with many faire fields and plaines, full of mightie great woods, some very thicke and some thinne, replenished with divers sorts of trees, as pleasant and delectable to behold, as if possible to imagine."

While residents and visitors still would agree with Verrazano's description of the area, Insiders know that the river appropriately was named the Cape Fear River.

The Cape Fear River is a curiously formidable body of water that has both encouraged and resisted development of the communities along its shores. Throughout the establishment of both permanent and temporary settlements along its banks, the Cape Fear has figured prominently in the best and the worst things that happened to residents at different points in time.

In the days before cars, trucks and trains, the river was the ideal route to prosperity for settlers. The river gave rise to the area's early success as a major port, since water transportation of goods, both for export and import, put Wilmington in the right location for profit.

The positioning of the City of Wilmington on a bluff 30 miles north and 5 miles east of the Atlantic, together with the curvature of the shoreline created a port relatively safe from storms.

Frying Pan Shoals at the river's mouth posed some difficult navigational challenges and many a ship went aground in that treacherous spot. Even Gentleman Pirate Stede Bonnet went aground on the shoals, was captured and taken to Charleston, South Carolina, where he was executed.

In both the Revolutionary and Civil Wars, the Cape Fear River was a highly defensible and vital link to supplies for residents and much of the area.

However, when the residents weren't prepared for conflict, the river sometimes allowed attackers to come up the river and wreak havoc on various settlements.

One of the earliest settlements in the region was on the river's western bank. In 1622, settlers from the Massachusetts Bay Colony found the area inhospitable; they were replaced by a group of English settlers from Barbados who named the settlement Charles Town or Old Town.

This settlement existed until 1667, and archaeological evidence suggests that the colonists spent many a wistful day staring in futility down the river for signs of a supply ship from England. Pirates who found shelter in the river didn't contribute to the pleasure of living in Charles Town, and evidence also suggests that the local Indians weren't entirely friendly. The colony left and founded the City of Charleston in South Carolina.

Queen Elizabeth opened the area to English colonization as early as 1662, but obstacles, such as piracy and the resistance of Native Americans, created large gaps between colonization efforts. The Town of Brunswick was founded by English settlers on the west bank of the river in 1725 but withered away as more strategically located Wilmington, on the east bank, began to prosper. Wilmington was founded in 1732 and incorporated in February 1740 by an act of the North Carolina General Assembly.

Previously named New Carthage, New Liverpool, Liverpool, New Town and Newton, this dominant east-bank settlement was named Wilmington by Governor Gabriel Johnston to honor his friend Spencer Compton, Earl of Wilmington, in 1739. By 1780, Wilmington was the largest city in North Carolina, with a population of 13,500 in-city residents and an overall county population of 28,000.

Wilmington prospered as a major port, shipbuilding center and pine forest products manufacturing center. Tar, turpentine and pitch were central to the economy; lumber from the pine forests was also a lucrative economic resource. At one time, Wilmington was the site of the largest cotton exchange in the world. The waterfront bustled with sailing ships, and steam ships crowded together to pick up or unload precious cargo.

The Cape Fear River gave rise to the city on the bluff, created its economy, protected it and sometimes gave it up during times of war. It contributed to the tenacity that is so much a part of the local attitude.

The city motto is "Persevere." It

Cape Fear Coast
Convention & Visitors Bureau

★ INFORMATION CENTER
★ VIDEO PRESENTATION
★ BROCHURES
★ MAPS

Wilmington · Wrightsville Beach
Carolina Beach · Kure Beach

CAPE FEAR COAST CONVENTION & VISITORS BUREAU

24 North Third Street
Wilmington, North Carolina 28401

800-222-4757
910-341-4030

Photo: N.C. Travel and Tourism

A colonial gentleman's town residence — the 1770 Burgwin-Wright House.

seems to say something about the character of the early settlers as well as the people who reside here today. The city symbol is a beehive. Although the origin of this symbol is unclear, it seems appropriate for the city's past, present and future. There is always a sense of activity in Wilmington.

The downtown riverfront has seen extreme ups and desperate downs during the 252 years of its development. The city has a history of being plagued by fires, some the unfortunate consequence of volatile naval stores operations and others caused by lightning. As many as 300 buildings have been reduced to cinders by one fire.

In the 20th century, the city has experienced bleak economic and social problems just as damaging as fires in the 19th. While it was trying to recover from the Great Depression in the 1930s by promoting ship building and other enterprises tied to the business of World War II, other problems loomed.

One of the mainstays of the economy, along with the State Ports located just a few miles south of downtown, was the railroad. In 1841, the Wilmington and Weldon Railroad was built. It created a profitable business for the next century. The 161-mile long railway system was the largest in the world at the time. The railroads employed thousands of people directly and indirectly provided employment for thousands of others who sold them goods and services.

In 1955, the Atlantic Coast Line closed. By 1960, 4,000 families were relocated to Jacksonville, Florida, a pivotal event that sent the economy spinning downward.

Then, there were obstacles to overland transportation caused by poor roads that increasingly isolated Wilmington from commerce in the rest of the state. While the Triad and Triangle areas of North Carolina thrived in a network of interstate highway systems, Wilmington increasingly felt like the distant cousin a hundred miles removed.

Highway 421 was traveled by tourists on the way to area beaches, but business needed the speed and ease of an interstate. A two-lane blacktop was a liability.

Compounding a slipping local economy, Wilmington erupted in the 1970s with race relations problems that put the city on the map of the world as home to the Wilmington Ten. The city on the river literally reeled from the impact of the riots and bad feelings. White flight from downtown to the suburbs kicked the economic supports out from under the struggling downtown area.

Downtown was largely abandoned, both by residents and businesses. Tourists ignored it. Beautiful homes fell into disrepair because the neighborhoods were regarded as unsafe. Forlorn, vacant buildings stared blankly over the river; crime was rampant; and much of downtown's commerce came to revolve around seedy bars and unsavory dealings.

Fortunately, the story has a happy ending that is actually a new beginning. It was the river that called Wilmingtonians back to reclaim their heritage and make yet another start. Wilmington reminded itself to persevere.

In the early 1970s, a few voices began to question why this beautiful and special city should be lost. The Wilmington Historic Foundation questioned why such valuable architecture should be allowed to rot. City government cast an eye on the situation and determined to do something about it with the creation of the Historic District Commission. Diehard merchants banded to-

Get fresh vegetables at Wilmington's recently reopened City Market. The market began in the same spot in the late 19th century, and some of its ghosts still linger.

Insiders' Tips

The Kenan Memorial Fountain, at the intersection of 5th and Market, was installed in 1921 and designed by architects Carrere and Hastings.

gether in the establishment of the Downtown Wilmington Association. DARE, the Downtown Area Revitalization Effort, was organized.

It would take volumes to describe each organized group that has contributed to the renewal of downtown Wilmington. There are thousands of people responsible for putting downtown back together once more. Some of them worked through organizations, but many have worked alone in pursuit of private dreams that would form a collective vision.

The efforts have resulted in the restoration and maintenance of a national treasure. Wilmington boasts one of the largest districts on the National Historic Registry, with homes dating from as early as the middle 1700s. Meticulously restored Victorian, Georgian, Italianate and

Antebellum homes, from grand mansions to cottages, attest to the previous and current perseverance of the citizens to maintain the special charm of the neighborhood.

The grassroots movement that drew attention to the area for renewal is still very much the work of the people who live there. This is not a museum; the 200-block neighborhood is home to real people who do real things to make a living. The neighborhood wasn't merely restored for the sake of remembering the past; it's a place where life goes forward.

The $23-million expansion of the New Hanover County International Airport in September of 1990 and the linking of Wilmington with Interstate 40 in June of 1991 were significant events. These structures have already brought about dramatic

Photo: Scott Taylor

Ships are seen frequently all along the Carolina coast.

Photo: N.C. Travel and Tourism Division

The Battleship North Carolina *and downtown Wilmington offer endless opportunites to learn and explore.*

changes in accessibility, population growth and economic opportunities for the entire Cape Fear region. Their impact on downtown Wilmington and its suburbs, as well as area beaches, is obvious.

Wilmingtonians are fiercely proud of their city's history and are pleased to share it with visitors, although the sudden influx of visitors is a bit startling for locals. The downtown neighborhood isn't actually a tourist town. Everyone appreciates the benefits of Wilmington's new accessibility and enjoys the obvious admiration that outsiders express. But, feelings are, to be honest, a little mixed.

It's like inviting a couple of people over for Sunday dinner and, upon opening the door, seeing that they've brought a dozen friends with them. All are welcome in a Southern home, of course; it can just give someone a

case of the vapors for a moment. (One must also, metaphorically speaking, run out into the yard to kill another chicken.)

Wilmington graciously welcomes visitors as honored guests in the best Southern tradition. Perhaps the attitude that tourists are, in fact, guests instead of customers is based on a personal awareness that this is our home, and we are welcoming people into it.

Home pride is good news for the visitor. The restaurants, shops and businesses cater to locals, so prices for dining and entertainment are extremely reasonable. (Reservations for fine dining are definitely recommended.) There is not, in this insider's opinion, any venture that resembles a tourist trap downtown. On the contrary, there is much to be had for very little. Community pride is contagious, and locals look to each other to present the area to visitors in a good way.

In the latter decade of the 20th century, the Cape Fear River has come to serve as a focal point of the city's booming tourist industry. Hotels and restaurants situated on its banks enjoy brisk business all year long and have built outdoor dining and bar areas for patrons to enjoy the view of the river.

Wilmingtonians gleefully show off their restored city, and the visitor can expect questions to be responded to in enthusiastic detail. Various tours, including walking, horse and carriage and boat tours, are available for nominal fees at the foot of Market Street by the river and provide lively narratives of the history of the area.

Shops in the downtown area are largely specialty shops that are personally overseen by their owners. Gifts, clothing, hardware, jewelry, film, imported items, toys, bath items, furniture and flowers are abundant in the anchor shopping centers and along Front Street and adjacent streets downtown. The Cotton Exchange and Chandler's Wharf are both restored clusters of buildings with shops that sell interesting wares for both the visitor and the resident.

Night life is abundant, and it is safe to say that virtually any kind of bar crowd can be found downtown. Dance clubs, jazz bars, karaoke, rock 'n' roll, rhythm and blues and much more can be found in the 55-block area of downtown's commercial district.

The arts make their home in the neighborhood, too. Thalian Hall, home to the oldest community theatre in this country, has been refurbished in a grand manner in recent years and is the site of traditional and experimental theatre, including national touring companies, a dozen local theatre companies and more. The Arts Council of the Lower Cape Fear is located downtown, as well as St. John's Museum of Art and a few commercial galleries. Many artists live in the residential area downtown and frequent cafes, as do film and television stars who are in the area for productions of the local movie studio.

To this insider, the nicest thing about downtown Wilmington is its pleasant walkability. The Riverwalk, with its view of the Battleship *North Carolina* moored on the western shore, is a pleasant place to stroll, grab a delicious hot dog from a street vendor, listen to free music and gaze at the river.

Because Wilmington is a prominent international port of call, it's likely that a stroller will see an occasional ship being escorted by tugs

A stroll on the Riverwalk downtown is a cheap and romantic date.

up the river. Military ships from other nations frequent the city, and there is a service, "Dial-A-Sailor," that allows residents to invite sailors into their homes for dinner for cross-cultural exchange. The HMS *Bristol*, hailing from England, drops into town now and then, much to the excitement of locals who throng the docks to greet the crew. As a courtesy, this ship and others offer free tours of their ocean-going quarters.

A walk through the residential area lush with live oaks draped in Spanish moss, beautiful azaleas and native oleander is a plant enthusiast's delight. Most of the homes downtown have private gardens that are occasionally opened to the public during special events, such as the Azalea Festival in the spring and Riverfest in the fall.

Historic homes marked with informative plaques and friendly neighborhood people working in their yards provide a delightful and absolutely free experience that appeals to insiders as much as visitors.

The film industry, too, lends an exciting opportunity for spotting the occasional star or just watching the enormity of the process of making movies. "Matlock" has done a significant amount of filming in downtown Wilmington, as have dozens of other productions. The Carolco Studios facility is not available for touring, but the frequency of filming activity throughout the Cape Fear region greatly increases the chances that a visitor will stumble upon a production in progress.

In brief, the city on the river has emerged as a vital and vibrant place in the last decade of the 20th cen-tury. Although tourism is important, it's also important to note that downtown is the center of government for New Hanover County. The financial, wholesaling and services of the Central Business District downtown create a combined economic impact of half a billion dollars a year on the local economy.

Wilmington often has a seductive effect on her visitors and, be forewarned, even one visit has been known to cause responsible people to go back home and pack up the moving van. Many people are being lured to Wilmington right now, responding to the curious energy of the place.

Wilmington: The Suburbs

As Wilmington eventually sprawled toward the beaches, so must this guide. With the advent of technology that allowed people to easily move longer distances over the land, the boundaries of Wilmington increasingly pushed toward the sea in two directions: south and east.

With the dawn of the 20th century, the car and an electric trolley system allowed Wilmingtonians to make use of the surrounding land in large numbers. Wilmington radiates out from its urban center through diverse neighborhoods in a crazy quilt of suburban areas. The would-be resident can choose from modest to grand neighborhoods nestled among live oaks or pines. There is a neighborhood for every taste and budget.

Market Street is the best indica-

Photo: William Russ, N.C. Travel & Tourism Division

Children learn firsthand about life as a Civil War soldier at Fort Fisher.

tor of the changes that happen as the city spreads out to meet the beach. There is consensus among locals that a drive from the river on Market Street to the sea (which requires turning onto Eastwood Road near the city limits) reveals a bit of everything that Greater Wilmington has to offer.

Downtown Market Street is a straight road running past interesting architecture, fountains and monuments as it leaves the river. (There is a shocking swerve around the Kenan Memorial fountain at Fifth Street, so don't gawk too much if you're the driver.) Beyond the Museum of the Lower Cape Fear, a must stop if you want an historical overview of the area (that includes, but is certainly not limited to Michael Jordan's uniform and Olympic gold medal), you'll pass New Hanover High School where football greats Sonny Jurgensen and Roman

Gabriel played as teenagers.

Beyond the school, the trees crowd in to create a canopy over the suddenly very narrow road. This is the Mansion District, which was once the affluent suburbs and is still a highly stable and attractive neighborhood. As downtown housing prices have skyrocketed with the popularity of the area, the Mansion District has enjoyed renewed interest, and the quiet, shady streets off Market Street are a favorite location for families with children.

Next up is venerable Forest Hills, a large, well-manicured neighborhood of homes built largely in the 20th century. On the other side of this neighborhood is Independence Mall, with all the modern day shopping conveniences of Belk, J.C. Penney and Sears. Past Forest Hills, the signs of commercial enterprise spring up in profusion. Now, you can say to yourself as you see all of the hotels, motels and restaurants along the strip that you are in touristland.

Where Market Street meets Kerr (pronounced "car") Avenue, the scene erupts with all the familiar commercial businesses that thrive in every city in America. If you veer off to South College Road, expect the largest retail-inspired traffic snag in all of the Lower Cape Fear. The giants of retail are all there, as are restaurants, specialty shops, strip centers and more.

In the middle of all of this commercial activity stands the University of North Carolina at Wilmington. It is surrounded by a broad expanse of grass and the occasional pine tree, as well as live oaks and magnolias. If you do not leave Market Street and take the first right under the overpass, you hit Eastwood Road on the approach to Wrightsville Beach. It is approximately a 20-minute drive from the river to the sea on a regular day.

The approach to the beach takes you past upscale neighborhoods that are, in several cases, walled from view. Landfall, a private community built around outstanding golf courses and a tennis facility, is behind a wall and guardhouse on your left. The next sight is the bridge over the Intracoastal Waterway to Harbor Island and Wrightsville Beach.

Greater Wilmington: An Overview

Before crossing the bridge to the barrier islands, it seems appropriate to pause and relate some facts about Greater Wilmington.

Wilmington occupies most of New Hanover County. Geographically the smallest county in the state, New Hanover had a population of 120,284 as of 1990; Wilmington proper had a population of 55,530. County population density is more than 600 people per square mile, which is in stark contrast to neighboring Pender and Brunswick counties with 33 and 60 people per square mile, respectively.

Population projections raise the New Hanover County population by more than 15,000 additional residents by 1995. The explosion in population in the entire Cape Fear area is fueled by many factors, including easier accessibility by land and air, an extremely pleasant four-season climate, scenic beauty, entrepreneurial opportunities, the discovery of the area by the film industry and much more.

Educational opportunities also draw people. The University of North Carolina at Wilmington, long a relatively dormant institution, has taken off in the past decade. Chancellor James Leutze, host of the popular Public Television series "Globe Watch," lends a visionary style of leadership to the university that emphasizes international awareness. The 650-acre campus is among the fastest growing universities in the 16-campus UNC system. It offers degrees in 58 areas of concentration, including a marine sciences program that ranks seventh in the nation.

The public school system prides itself on innovation. With a 76 million dollar budget, the system devotes 70 percent of the total budget to direct instructional costs. There are 30 schools in the New Hanover County Public School System organized as K to 5, 6 to 8 and 9 to 12. There are nearly 20,000 students in the system.

Employment in the area is concentrated in the services sector and wholesale/retail trade. These two areas account for half of the employment in the county. Manufacturing only accounts for slightly more than 15 percent of the jobs. The retail sales business is something of a phenomenon in Greater Wilmington, placing the area in sixth place in retail sales within the state.

Tourism, of course, is a vital industry. Direct tourism and related industries are significant economic factors in the Cape Fear area. At this writing, more than 60,000 people visit the Cape Fear Coast Convention and Visitors Bureau annually in downtown Wilmington. An estimated 1.3 million visitors a year chose to vacation on the Cape Fear Coast.

People who may be considering a move to the area should understand something very important about the local economy: wages are generally low. The median family income in 1991 was $34,000, the same as the average for the state of North Carolina, but much lower than some of North Carolina's inland cities and, certainly, lower than wages in other areas of the nation. One suspects, especially this insider, that salaries are going to change in the near future because the area is becoming more attractive to many people. The film industry, for example, has already brought a different perspective to the area in terms of salaries.

Retirement is coming to figure significantly in the attraction of the area. People who would have gone to Florida to retire find the Cape Fear area immensely appealing because of the climate and the relatively inexpensive cost of living.

Recreational opportunities are abundant. Some of the finest golf courses and tennis courts in the country are located within New Hanover County. Boating, sailing and in-the-water recreation are readily accessible. Fishing is both an industry and a serious sport, with the purses as large as $25,000 for the biggest fish in the U. S. Open King Mackerel Tournament.

The climate is moderate compared with a continental standard. The growing season for plants is long, averaging 244 days. Some types of plants grow all year with temperatures averaging 47 degrees in January and 79.8 in August. The maritime location makes the climate of Wilmington unusually mild for its latitude.

Wrightsville Beach

Wrightsville Beach is a special place for both the resident and the visitor. It is quite unlike the commercial beaches that often come to mind when one thinks of the coast. This is not a carnival atmosphere; there are no Ferris wheels or gaudy displays of beach merchandise, no bumper boats, no arcade. Instead, Wrightsville Beach is primarily an affluent residential community that has its roots in Wilmington. For nearly a century, Wrightsville Beach has been the main retreat from summer heat for residents of Wilmington. Many of the homes are owned by city residents whose families have maintained ownership through the decades.

Wrightsville Beach was incorporated in 1899 as a resort community. The Tidewater Power Company built a trolley system from downtown to the beach, providing the only land access to the island until 1935. The company, which owned the island, was interested in development and built the Hotel Tarrymore in 1905 to attract visitors and revenue. Later named The Oceanic, this grand hotel burned down in 1934, along with most structures on the northern half of the island. Lumina, a beach pavilion, was also built by the Tidewater Power Company to attract visitors. Located on the site of the current Oceanic Restaurant at the south end of the beach, Lumina offered a festive place where locals gathered for swimming, dancing and outdoor movies. The building was demolished in 1973.

Development of the beach continued steadily until 1954 when Hurricane Hazel, a monster of a storm, came ashore and wreaked devastation over the island's homes and buildings. Hazel also shoaled the channel between Wrightsville Beach and adjacent Shell Island. Developers, seeing an opportunity for expansion, filled in the remaining water and joined the islands together. Today, the area is the site of the Shell Island Resort Hotel and numerous condominiums and large homes.

Today's Wrightsville Beach is a very busy and prosperous place. The area is still a stronghold of long term residents who summer in family homes built to catch the ocean breeze. The permanent residential population is approximately 3,000, but that figure swells considerably in the summer. Surprisingly, brisk commercial development in the form of marinas, restaurants and other services has not seriously changed the residential orientation of the island.

There are a few businesses that stock an assortment of water toys, beach chairs and tropicwear, but most of the island's enterprises center around accommodations, musical entertainment and, of course, dining. Drawing heavily on local patrons, these establishments offer good service and reasonable prices.

A visitor to Wrightsville Beach is bound to be impressed by the clean and uncluttered nature of the place. The residential atmosphere ensures a dedication to keeping the beach clean. Lifeguards oversee the safety of swimmers in the summer season, and the beach patrol keeps an eye on the area to make sure laws are obeyed. Alcohol and glass containers are not allowed on the beach. If you have some questions, just ask one of the friendly lifeguards.

Boaters, sun worshippers, swimmers, surfers and anglers will find much to appreciate and enjoy about the setting. Public access points, liberally sprinkled across the island, make a day in the sun a free experience for daytrippers — with the notable exception of parking. Always an issue at Wrightsville Beach, the parking situation was exacerbated by the completion of Interstate 40 in 1991 and the expansion

of the airport. In 1993, traffic counts indicate that 70,000 cars pass over the bridge on a summer or holiday weekend. Insiders know that the island is extremely crowded during peak summer weekends and are therefore more inclined to leave those times to visitors. On those weekends, visitors are advised to arrive early in the morning and bring plenty of quarters for the parking meters. Parking lots at area restaurants and hotels are vigilantly guarded, and residents are not inclined to allow unknown cars to occupy their driveways. Towing is strictly enforced in no parking zones.

There are many opportunities for water-related sports and entertainment on Wrightsville Beach. Some of the Cape Fear area's nicest restaurants are located on Harbor Island and Wrightsville. The most luxurious marinas along the North Carolina coast are clustered around the bridge at the Intracoastal Waterway and offer a full range of services.

Charter boats, both power and sail, are available in abundance. Jetski rental, windsurfing, kayaking and sailing lessons are there for the asking. Bait, tackle, piers and more than enough advice on the best way to fish are all easy to find. Visitors who bring their own boats will appreciate the free boat ramp just north of the first bridge on the ICW.

For vacation house renters, there are all the comforts of home. Robert's Grocery, an astonishingly well stocked and reasonably priced local grocery store on the island, caters to local residents. This makes it much more attractive to visitors. There is also a public laundromat in the center of the island, although most rental homes have washers and dryers.

The island's very pleasing shoreline, bounded on the east by the Atlantic Ocean and on the west by the equally appealing channel and Intracoastal Waterway, invites visitors to relax. The beach, regularly renourished to combat erosion, is a smooth stretch of tan-colored sand. The shells that arrive on the shore are not as varied or intact as shellseekers would prefer, but one can stumble upon an occasional treasure.

A visit to Wrightsville Beach, whether for a day or for a vacation, is bound to be a memorable experience that will be repeated time after time. Since this is a year-round community, it can be experienced and enjoyed almost any time of the year. Vacation home renters have the luxury, generally, of reserved parking, so just park the car and forget about it until it's time to leave. The island is wonderfully walkable, and you can find everything you need there for a comfortable vacation.

Wrightsville Beach Reflection

New Yorker and professional dancer Dorothy Nesbitt moved to Harbour Island at Wrightsville Beach in 1956. She and her husband, Joe, moved from New York to build the house in which they still reside today. Mrs. Nesbitt is regarded widely as an authority on dance, a proponent of the arts and a strong voice on social justice issues. Dorothy has reflected candidly on her life in and opinions about Wrightsville Beach:

"We moved down here because Joe was born here and brought up on Bradley Creek. We used to come for visits; you know, we would come here on vacation. When we were living in our apartment in New York City, when our daughter was 1 1/2 years old, we were afraid she would climb up and fall out the window. We began to think of doing something else.

Joe really liked it here, and I always liked the beach. I was brought up on Long Island. Long Island had gotten too populated, though; there was less beach — there was less wild beach. We came down here because the wild beach was still left. That was about all we had to go on. We came down 2 years after Hurricane Hazel, and the whole area was washed over. When we first moved in, there was nothing around our house. We paid $1,000 for this lot; thinking back, we should have bought two of them. We tried later, but they were already gone. Now, we have these houses 7 1/2 feet away from us.

A friend of mine always says you can't buy a view, and I guess that's true. The interesting thing about Wrightsville Beach is how it has evolved over the years. Initially, it was just for certain things. Most of the houses were just summer homes without heat. When Wrightsville Beach started out, it was for the more affluent members of Wilmington to have houses here. They only had a trolley coming across to the beach. They had Lumina with name bands; and this was a real occasion for people to go to the dance.

Photo: Ciccone Newport

Dorothy Nesbitt

Joe remembers this. He was born in Wilmington, and his father was the public health officer from 1911 to 1917. They moved away, but returned in the 1930s. They had a house on Bradley Creek; he loves sailing, fishing, the beach — you know, what Wrightsville Beach really offers.

They had hotels and boardwalks. This was all before Hazel. Then, when we got here, it was pretty much all washed off. People weren't too keen to come out here and build because a lot of them got wiped out. Also, this was when the Coast Line — "THE job" in the area — was about to move to Jacksonville.

When we first came down here, there was a real sense of community; there was a center. I could go and sit where Newell's (Department Store) used to be — where Wings is now — and wait for my laundry to dry in the laundromat next door. The post office was in that hot dog stand. Later, the bank came along. Everybody who lived on Wrightsville Beach would come there, and we would greet each other.

They used to have the Crest Theater with movies; and Lumina was a center where people would dance and spend their evenings out. Well, the Crest showed regular movies; but it started showing adult movies, and everyone got very indignant. It was replaced with a teen arcade, but people didn't like all that racket. Now, it's a fitness club. The Lumina, of course, was torn down.

They used to have The Wit's End and The Palm Room. These were places to find a nucleus of Wrightsville Beach people socializing together. That kind of place almost doesn't exist anymore.

I think Robert's Grocery is the only place left where locals can meet. Robert's Dorothy Roberts lives right across the street from us. The store is the only networky part of Wrightsville Beach now, at least for the old beach and the old people. Robert's has good food, good vegetables and fruits; and these are friendly people who keep in touch with what's going on.

There is still a very insular attitude, but, you know, this isn't the same family beach it used to be. Young local families have a hard time getting their part of the beach; many residents are retirees from outside; and, of course, there are people who rent vacation homes.

Of course, you know about the whole to-do at Seapath. A lot of locals formed an organization to protest when the developers were going to put up four buildings. They made such a fuss that only one building was allowed. People around here could see Miami Beach in those plans, so they really stopped it in that case.

The beach is geographically limited; there's only going to be so much development. Parking is a problem they're never going to solve, and I don't think another bridge is any kind of solution. There's just a limited amount of growth that Wrightsville Beach itself can handle, and I think we're there.

Something very good is the recreation park. To me, that's a supreme achievement. It gives a lot of people opportunity to participate in everything under the sun. They have excellent programs going on for everyone all the time. Excellent programs for children. To me, it's the only thing that has kept pace with the development of the beach. **"**

Masonboro Island

Located between Wrightsville Beach and Carolina Beach is Masonboro Island. One of the last and largest pristine barrier islands remaining on the southern North Carolina coast, this island is accessible only by boat. While parts of the island belong to private landowners, no development is allowed. Masonboro is a component of the North Carolina National Estuarine Research Reserve. The island is home to gray foxes, cotton rats, a variety of birds, river otters and several species of aquatic life.

Carolina Beach

Just down the road from downtown Wilmington on Highway 421 is a beach with a very different atmosphere from Wrightsville Beach. The difference in these two New Hanover County beaches ensures that virtu-

EYEWITNESS NEWS 3

Coverage You Can Count On!

5:30, 6:00, and 11:00 p.m.

ally anyone can find coastal happiness in this area. Established in 1857 when Joseph Winner planned the streets and lots for the 50 acres of beach property he had purchased, the island's only access was by water. In 1866, a steamship carried vacationers down the Cape Fear River to Snow's Cut, and a small railroad took them the rest of the way into Carolina Beach.

Carolina Beach is the major beach community on the narrow slip of land that is pressed between the Cape Fear River and the Atlantic Ocean. The island, dubbed Pleasure Island a few years ago as part of a marketing plan (a name that is controversial among the residents and may or may not be the name of the place), has several communities, but only three are readily distinguishable: Carolina Beach, Fort Fisher and Kure Beach. All share wide, clean beaches and boast some of the finest fishing along the Cape Fear coast. All are heavily residential in character. Two have restaurants that specialize in the preparation of fresh seafood. But at this juncture, the similarities cease.

Carolina Beach developed a reputation as a rough and rowdy party beach, not without reason in years past. That reputation is in the midst of a tremendous change since there is a popular and governmental movement to improve the image of this community. Recent years have seen the cultivation of pleasant landscaping, the passing of an abundance of wholesome ordinances, attention to zoning and tangible citizen action. The Boardwalk, long a place with a questionable reputation, is experiencing a revitalization with an increase of family-oriented establishments.

In 1993, the powers-that-be decided to restrict alcohol at a yearly beach festival in an effort to further alter the image of the community. The festival was considerably less festive, much to the relief of most of the town's residents. Previous crowds numbered in the tens of thousands; the 1993 festival attendance was much lower. Despite a reduction in alcohol sales, food sales were actually up. Overall, the drastic change in character of the event has been met with only a whimper from the opposition. One suspects Carolina Beach is well on its way to becoming the family beach it means to be.

A drive through Carolina Beach reveals a pleasant 1950s style beach of modest cottages, a few upscale dwellings and an abundance of three-and four-story condominiums. Unfortunately, these structures were built on the oceanfront and tend to obscure the view of the sea for sev-

Dramatic coastal beaches attract visitors to the Cape Fear Coast throughout the year.

eral congested blocks on the north end. Clearly, tourism is the mainstay of the town's economy, and there are several stores that cater to their customers' beach needs. There is an amusement park, Jubilee Park, which is only one of two such attractions on the Cape Fear coast. It is a quaint park that offers a family good value in a wholesome setting. Nearby, there are also the obligatory waterslides, mini-golf courses and other things that appeal to the kids. There is also a movie theater in town, as well as grocery stores and bait shops.

Anglers will find a kind of paradise at Carolina Beach. The surf promises wonderful bounty all year long; there are plenty of tackle shops and piers, as well as the opportunity to experience deep-sea fishing from the sterns of a number of charter boats. Several yearly events are based on the abundance of mackerel, and one may win, for a nominal entry fee, as much as $25,000 for the winning fish.

At the extreme northern end of the island, the beach is open to four-wheel drive vehicles. While there is a certain allure to driving right off the street onto the sand into this very expansive space, don't do it if you are in a car. Getting stuck in the sand is as easy and frustrating as being stuck in the snow. Carolina Beach also offers one of the few state parks in the region. For a modest fee, one can camp and enjoy the wonders of nature. There is also a marina. The Venus Flytrap, a carnivorous plant, is abundant in the park. This plant, a relic from prehuman existence on the planet, only grows within a 100-mile radius of Wilmington.

Away from the bustle of the center of town, this is a quiet community of almost 4,000 regular residents. It is growing in appeal to locals from Wilmington for one reason: it isn't crowded. There is plenty of elbow room on the beach; there is no problem finding parking; and some of the best vacation rental deals are here. Many a Wilmingtonian has given Wrightsville Beach over to visitors for the summer in the past few years and turned to Carolina Beach for a quiet spot on the sand.

Kure Beach and Fort Fisher

Carolina Beach dissolves into the Town of Kure Beach to the south. Kure Beach, a younger community, is overwhelmingly residential and dotted with modest cottages, new houses and several old-style beach motels. Several apartment buildings cluster together in one spot, but there is little else in the way of tall buildings on Kure because condominiums are not allowed. You'll find neither arcade nor amusement park here. A permanent population of only a few more than 600 residents makes for a very close community. This is the American small town in a beach setting.

There is one pier jutting its way out into the Atlantic where anglers can be seen any day of the week trying for sheepshead, Spanish mackerel, trout, flounder and the fish that sounds like a frog, the croaker. If you're looking for peace and quiet in a friendly setting, Kure Beach is the place to go.

Farther south, toward the point where the Cape Fear River and the

Atlantic Ocean finally converge, the summer homes increase in size and opulence. Twisted live oaks cover the landscape and increase in density until, at last, natural flora overtakes architecture. There are several spots of interest near the end of the island. Fort Fisher, an earthworks fort of significance during the Civil War, appears on the right. The North Carolina Aquarium at Fort Fisher, a fine facility that boasts a touch tank and a close-up encounter with live sharks, comes up on the left. Near the aquarium is a four-wheel drive beach where fishermen flock to take in the bounty of the waters. At the end of it all is the Fort Fisher-Southport Ferry, possibly the best $3 cruise in the world.

All in all, Pleasure Island offers 7 1/2 miles of very pleasant vacationing and living.

Topsail Island

After exploring Carolina and Kure Beaches, turn north to examine Topsail Island. Topsail got its name from pirates who would hide in the coves awaiting a view of the top of a sail. Once a ship was seen, it could be easily ambushed in the channel and relieved of its cargo. Eventually, merchant ships learned to look for sails, and pirating went on the skids.

In 1946, Topsail Island was taken over by the US Navy to begin "Project Bumblebee," a missile program that was a predecessor to Florida's rocket program at Cape Kennedy (now called Cape Canaveral). The first supersonic missiles in the country

were tested on this remote island. It was, technically, a secret project, although residents in the mainland area must have noticed the launching of 200 prototype missiles between 1946 and 1948.

Remains of the project are readily observable on the island. Seven concrete missile observation towers, including two that have been converted into homes, remain on the island. The launch pad is now the patio for the Jolly Roger Hotel.

Topsail is another fishing community. Topsail Inlet is subject to shoaling, a constant concern. Commercial fishermen with considerable experience traverse the tricky inlet; pleasure boaters are strongly advised to go south to Masonboro Inlet at Wrightsville Beach for sure passage into the Atlantic. The island is a haven for sea turtles, and the residents are vigilant in their protection of these creatures. The Topsail Turtle Project dedicates itself each season to preservation and protection of sea turtles.

Topsail Island is a residential community that offers vacation home rentals, a few restaurants, two marinas and a full-service pier. There are two resorts at the northern end of the island where the road comes precariously close to the Atlantic Ocean. The primary beauty of this island is the seemingly unaggressive rate of development, although that

Photo: Curtis Krueger

*This baby loggerhead is a member of a species that nests along
the Cape Fear Coast.*

picture is sure to change in the near future. There are three municipalities on this 27-mile island. Topsail Beach, Surf City and North Topsail Beach separate the island into distinct neighborhoods.

North Topsail has a fishing pier that is regarded as one of the best in the area. There is a golf course on the island, as well as two large resort centers.

Surf City is the "big city" of the island, located at its center and connected to the mainland by a 39-year-old swing bridge. Although this is a modest, small town by anyone's standards, it serves the island with restaurants, a grocery store and other commercial enterprises.

Topsail Beach, located at the southern end of the island, is a residential beach community that may seem to exist in the 1950s. There is a first-class marina, Topsail Marina, but the area is almost exclusively given over to private homes. There are piers about every mile, so fishing is the number one activity.

Figure Eight Island

Figure Eight Island is a private, oceanfront resort community. There are no commercial enterprises on the island. It is, in the strictest sense, a highly restricted residential island of extremely expensive homes. The development includes a yacht club, marina, tennis courts and boat ramp. The island is connected to the mainland by a causeway bridge, and a guard will only let you onto the island if you've called ahead to someone on the island — such as a friend or a Realtor — and are on the list at the gate. Unless prior arrangements have been made, you'll be denied access.

There are opportunities to rent vacation homes by calling Figure Eight Realty at (919) 686-4400. Some of the larger Wilmington real estate companies may also handle properties on this exclusive island. See Vacation Rentals in this guide.

The Brunswick Beaches: Oak Island to South Brunswick

In historical and geographical terms, the Cape Fear area extends south to the South Carolina line. The Brunswick Beaches, a region made up of six beach communities, offer some of the most pleasant coastal living and vacationing on the eastern seaboard.

Caswell, Yaupon, Long, Holden, Ocean Isle and Sunset Beaches present special opportunities for both the resident and the visitor. These beaches are overwhelmingly residential in character and, in terms of commercial development, are quite sparse. Since the configuration of the North Carolina coastline here has an east-west orientation, each of these beaches offers a sunrise and sunset over the Atlantic Ocean.

There are three beach communities on Oak Island: Caswell Beach, Yaupon Beach and Long Beach.

Caswell Beach is the site of Fort Caswell, a military stronghold that dates from 1826. Fort Caswell is now owned by the North Carolina Baptist Assembly and welcomes visitors of all denominations each year. There are some summer homes, but the area is mostly permanent residences.

Yaupon Beach is a haven for live oaks and is named for a species of holly that grows in the area. Known as a family beach, Yaupon consists mostly of permanent residents, most of whom are retirees.

Recreational areas include a championship golf course, nine beach access points, a picnic area on the Elizabeth River estuary system and fishing piers. As the name implies, Long Beach occupies the longest stretch of beach on Oak Island. There are 52 beach access points for both the local and the visitor who appreciate absolutely uncrowded beaches. There are a few restaurants and motels; for the most part, however, a visitor will enjoy renting a house for an extended vacation here. Vacation rental is the liveliest business on the beach with approximately 14 rental companies operating on Oak Island.

The South Brunswick Islands: Holden Beach, Ocean Isle Beach and Sunset Beach (Featuring Calabash and Shallotte)

Of the three islands in the group known as the South Brunswick Islands, Holden Beach is the longest. Stretching 11 miles along the Atlantic, it is a jogger's paradise. There are about 600 permanent residents, and there are a host of opportunities for visitors to assimilate themselves into this exceedingly quiet family community. The beach and the sea are the central attractions in this town that prides itself on a serene quality of life.

Ocean Isle Beach is the center island, offering 8 miles of beach with a total resort experience. There are restaurants, specialty shops, public tennis courts, access to all water sports and a waterslide. This beach has the only highrise on the South Brunswick Islands. Home to 550 full-time residents, Ocean Isle welcomes visitors to a peaceful place.

Sunset Beach, described as a diminutive island gem, is only 3 miles long. Reachable by a one-lane pontoon bridge, which sometimes makes for a bit of a wait in the high season, the island is well worth the pause in getting there. Again, this island is residential in character. Some of the best bargains in vacation rental are here, and the visitor who wants a quiet coastal place will do very well to book a house on this beach. As with all of the beaches on the Cape Fear coast, quality golfing is available on the mainland. For fishermen, there is a full service pier. Sunset Beach offers a special delight: a walk to Bird Island at low tide. Bird Island is completely untouched by development at this writing. A walk through the shallow inlet is easy for children, as well as adults. Frequently, there are informal, guided tours, announced by posters attached to street markers on the beach, so it's easy to hook up with locals who are pleased to share their knowledge of the island with you. The environment is purely natural and is a deeply comforting place where people of the 20th century can experience life as it was before the development of the land.

Just a few miles from Sunset Beach is the town of Calabash. This charming seaport is known widely as the "Fried Seafood Capital of the World," full of restaurants serving battered and fried shrimp, fish and oysters in a style that is indigenous to North Carolina. There are some health-conscious changes in the oil used by Calabash restaurants these days, but the taste is still authentic Calabash-style.

The town of Shallotte serves as the hub for services for these beach communities. In fact, it is perhaps best known as the commercial Mecca of Brunswick County. Because of its mainland location and island proximity, it offers residents and visitors the convenience of larger town living and services.

Recalling Hurricane Hazel

Ann Reardon is a Brunswick County native whose family has been on this part of the coast since the middle of the 18th century. She experienced the onslaught of Hurricane Hazel in 1954. After the storm came through, she moved from the waterway between Ocean Isle and Sunset Beach to Wilmington. She now owns and operates a fragrance and bath shop called The Linen Closet in the Cotton Exchange in downtown Wilmington.

"I recall when there was nothing . . . not any buildings on Ocean Isle Beach . . . We used to take a passenger ferry over there and look for sea turtle eggs when I was young because it was a fun thing to look for the tracks. Over the years, the beach was gradually built up with mostly cottages and vacation homes.

When Hurricane Hazel came, and that's the first hurricane I remember in my life, we were down at the inland waterway where my in-laws had their business. We knew it was going to storm, but there was no such thing as hurricane tracking in those days. It isn't like now when we have so much advance notice and can prepare.

My husband and my sister's husband at that time, they were brothers, went off rabbit hunting, and I was cooking breakfast. My sister and I knew the wind was blowing. It was a cloudy day, and it was raining. My husband and his brother went down to the water, and I remember looking down the road as I stood at the kitchen window and I saw, you know, a lot of people used kerosene back then, anyway, they used to store it in a tank that sat on top of the ground. Well, I looked out the window and I remember seeing my neighbor's kerosene tank just floating right toward me. The water was rising so fast from the waterway that I couldn't believe it. It was a shocking sight. The next thing people said we had to get out of that place in a hurry, so we just got away immediately. There was no time to gather anything up. We just left as fast as we could.

There was a man that lived directly across from us in a two-story cinderblock house. His name was Charlie Milligan. He lived there by himself. Well, in the excitement of everybody down there trying to get out, nobody thought that we hadn't told Charlie to go inland with us to Shallotte. We were at Shallotte school in a shelter when we remembered about Charlie. We felt terrible, but there was nothing we could do. The storm was so bad that we couldn't go back. When it was over, the National Guard would let no one in except for families who belonged there.

When we got back, we couldn't believe what had happened to our house and everyone else's. We had nothing. I mean, it was flat where homes had stood just hours earlier. The water just washed it all away. Our home that was built from good lumber from the Army barracks nearby, they let people have the wood after the war and the barracks closed, was turned over and the roof sat on the bottom.

We couldn't believe that so much damage had happened. Then, we noticed Charlie Milligan's house. He was the only one who stayed behind, and his was the only house that was still standing. This was on Somerset Landing between Ocean Isle and Sunset Beach. Of course, we were relieved for him, but we were also sad for ourselves.

I think if we had stayed another hour, we would not have made it because where we had lived was gone. I mean it was totally gone for us. We came back; we looked; and I cried. All of us cried. Some people had tried to tie things down before they left for shelter, but it didn't work. There was nothing to do but go.

After Hazel was over, there didn't seem to be much point in staying down there. Since my husband worked in Wilmington, we just decided we would go there instead of starting over on the water. **"**

Southport

Southport is reachable by both ferry and scenic highway. Leaving Wilmington, take the Cape Fear Memorial Bridge and hang a fast left onto Highway 133 just off Highways 17, 74 and 76. If you miss it, you can also take Highway 87, although the 133 route is very beautiful and offers several attractions, including Orton Plantation, the Carolina Power & Light Nuclear Plant and Brunswick Town, site of the first European colony in the region.

The city of Southport, located in Brunswick County, is steeped in history. This 200-year-old coastal community saw the establishment of North Carolina's first fort in 1754: Fort Johnston. A small community of river pilots, fishermen and tradesmen grew up around the fort. In 1792, the town of Smithville was created. In 1808, Smithville became the county seat of Brunswick County. When, for the remainder of the century, the town created plans to link rail service with the existing river traffic to make the community a major southern port, it was renamed Southport.

The town is widely regarded as the Fourth of July Capital of North Carolina. Southport celebrated the Fourth of July just after the signing of the Declaration of Independence in 1776. History records that in 1795, citizens gathered at Fort Johnston and observed a 13-gun military salute to the original 13 states. In 1813, a Russian warship was in the harbor and fired a 13-gun salute. On this day, fireworks were used for the first time to close the celebration. In 1972, the Fourth of July Festival was chartered and incorporated as the official North Carolina Fourth of July Festival, and it has become a tremendously popular four-day event for residents and visitors.

Southport, listed on the National Register of Historic Places, is ranked by both Rand McNally and Kiplinger as one of the most desirable places in the United States to retire. The live oak tree-lined streets, charming architecture, quaint shops — most notably an abundance of antique shops — as well as year-round golf, boating and fishing seasons, create an enormously pleasant environment for the residents of the town. This is the place to go for people who genuinely want to kick back and relax in a place with beautiful coastal scenery.

Bald Head Island

Just off the coast of Southport and the mainland, at the mouth of the Cape Fear River, is the pristine island of Bald Head. The island is easily identifiable in the distance by the wide-based Bald Head Island lighthouse, a structure built in 1817 and retired in 1935. Once a favorite hiding spot for pirates such as Blackbeard and Stede Bonnet, Bald Head Island is now a private and extremely affluent residential community that can only be reached by private ferry or personal boat.

It is probably safe to say that this is one of the most unspoiled beach and maritime forest areas on the North Carolina coast. Despite residential development, as well as a few commercial amenities such as a restaurant, general store, marina, golf course, specialty store and electric cart rental business, the island's natural beauty is fiercely protected. Developers have appreciated the island's natural environment and have gone to considerable pains to introduce humans into nature in a way that will not disturb the environmental situation.

There are 14 miles of beaches, unspoiled dunes, creeks and forests. There are 2,000 acres of land surrounded by 10,000 acres of salt marshes. The Bald Head Island Conservancy, a nonprofit organization, was formed to ensure that the unique natural resources of the island are maintained and preserved.

The Sea Turtle Program, featured on Public Television, is a program that protects and monitors these wonderful creatures. Turtle nesting on Bald Head Island accounts for 30 to 50 percent of all eggs laid in North Carolina. Due to the many species of birds found on the island, the Audubon Society conducts an annual count here as part of its national program.

Something quite special about

Photo: Curtis Krueger

This stone lighthouse on Bald Head Island was built in 1817 and stands 109 feet high. It served as a radio beacon during World War II.

the island is the absence of cars. Gasoline-powered engines are forbidden. The residents, as well as visitors who rent lovely homes, all drive electric carts or ride bicycles. In the latter decade of the 20th century, the reduction of noise and pollution is one of the finest features of the place. A visitor can come for the day by private ferry service from Indigo Plantation in Southport. The cost is $15. Day parking in Southport is $4. For a longer stay, there are many rental units on the island. The cost, compared to rental on most of the mainland, is high; but so is the experience for the visitor who wants to really get away from it all.

Despite Bald Head Island's private status, the welcome mat is out for visitors. There are several daytripper packages available that include lunch or dinner, historic tours and ferry service. For information on these trips, call Bald Head Island at (800) 234-1666.

Nuss Strasse Cafe

Authentic European Cakes and Pastries
Imported Wurst, Sauerbraten and Roladen
Fresh Strudel Daily
Real German Rye Bread
Available by the Pound

- Lunch -
Seven Days a Week

- Dinner -
Tuesday through Saturday

(910) 763-5523

Cotton Exchange · 1st Level · Wilmington

Inside
Restaurants

Folks on Cape Fear exhibit a much greater than average propensity for dining out, according to recent food-service industry reports. The proof is in the lively business done by the region's huge number of restaurants and in the increasing variety of quality restaurants and international and gourmet cuisines available here. When it comes to dining out, Cape Fear has no shortage of places to choose from. Restaurateurs might even say there's a surplus.

Restaurateurs also agree that the coastal Carolina waters are by far the most pristine in the east, yielding consistently high-quality seafood. Practically every restaurant worth its

salt offers fresh daily catches that may include grouper, mahi mahi, shark, swordfish, mackerel, triggerfish, or any of a host of other common species. While frying has traditionally been the most common preparation method, nowadays grilled, poached, broiled, steamed and blackened fish are available almost everywhere.

Of course, the traditional regional specialties still comprise the heart and soul of Cape Fear dining. The famous Calabash-style seafood is ubiquitous. It gets its name from the Cape Fear town heralded as the seafood capital of the world for having at least 30 seafood restaurants within a square mile area. While

Photo: Scott Taylor

These blue crabs are on their way to someone's dinner table.

most native chefs are secretive about the particulars of their recipes, Calabash-style is a well-known combination of seasoned corn meal batter and deep frying. Calabash-style has also become synonymous with "all-you-can-eat," and restaurants typically serve a huge variety of piping-hot seafood in massive quantities. But that's not all there is to regional cuisine.

Low-country steam-offs are buckets filled with a variety of shellfish, bivalves, potatoes, corn and Old Bay seasoning. When fresh oysters are in season in the fall, oyster roasts abound, indoors and out, and are typically accompanied by jalapeno corn bread and plenty of beer. While crab (aka peelers, jimmies, steamers, soft shells) is popular, it seems that crab dip attracts more attention in these parts, and competition among restaurants boasting the best dip is stiff. New Year's Eve dinners commonly include collards and black-eyed peas, symbolic (some say) of paper money and small change, to ensure prosperity in the year to come. These and okra, sweet potatoes, grits, turnip and mustard greens and kale are all regional favorites. Hushpuppies, those delicious deep-fried dollops of sweet cornmeal dough that come in a variety of shapes, take the place of bread on most coastal tables. Based on black-eyed peas and rice, Hoppin' John is a hearty dish seen in many variations. Boiled peanuts (pronounced "bawled" in these parts) are popular, and nowhere does pecan pie taste better. Iced tea flows freely, in most places by the pitcher-full, and locals prefer it very sweet.

Country-style barbecue, while not a coastal creation, is a piquant Southern specialty that's well represented on the Cape Fear coast. Recipes for pork barbecue are sources of pride and the foundations of many businesses. The marinated meat is typically served chopped (shredded) either on a sandwich roll with homemade cole slaw or on a plate accompanied by Brunswick stew, baked beans and slaw. Most barbecue restaurants also serve beef and chicken barbecue, and the ambience is only as formal as plastic utensils and Formica tables allow. A notable exception is **Sims Country Bar-B-Que** in Grissettown (southern Brunswick County), a joyous all-you-can-eat barn-style barbecue feast. Every barbecue restaurant has its own recipe, so consider sampling other notable establishments such as **Jackson's Big Oak Barbecue** (920 S. Kerr Avenue, Wilmington) or **Merritt's House of Bar-B-Que** (1510 N. 4th Street, Wilmington) as well as others not listed here. Always watch for pig pickin's sponsored by fire departments, churches, clubs and charity organizations as fund-raisers. There will always be at least one hearty gentleman, wearing long black rubber gloves, shredding the meat by hand as fast as it can be served.

International cuisines now available on the Cape Fear coast include Chinese (Szechuan and Cantonese), Thai, Greek, Italian, German, Japanese, Indian (on occasion), Middle Eastern, Caribbean, French and Australian. The several restaurants serving Mexican food are good places to advance the perpetual quest for the perfect margarita, but by no means does the search end there.

A welcomed development in the region is the rebirth of the coffee house, an institution with a distinctly English pedigree. Wilmington hosts two coffee houses. **Cape Fear Coffee & Tea**, 24 South Front Street, is a popular downtown spot for the morning cup o' joe, fresh muffins and pastries, newspapers, magazines and locally produced artwork. It carries coffees by the pound and related paraphernalia and is open 7 AM to 7 PM seven days. **Kona's Coffee Beanery**, Plaza East Shopping Center, Wrightsville Beach, offers java by the cup or pound plus an assortment of unusual foods such as avocado toast and hot vanillas. Local movie crews like the chocolate-covered espresso beans for that caffeine buzz without having to worry about spilling stray cups of coffee on the set.

Perhaps due to the influx of northerners, the Wilmington area is experiencing a pizza renaissance, too. Since the crust is at least as important as the sauce, which pizzeria you prefer may depend on crust alone. The following family-owned pizzerias are all worth a try: **Elizabeth's Pizza** (4304 Market Street): thin, crisp crust; **Krazy Pizza & Subs** (two locations: 417 S. College Rd. and Shipyard Boulevard at 17th Street): soft, crisp crust; **Numero Uno** (204 Princess Street): soft, doughy crust; **Vito's Pizzeria** (8 North Lumina Avenue, Wrightsville Beach): thin crust; and **Roberto's Pizzeria & Restaurant** (Holden and Ocean Isle beaches): thick, crisp crust. Well-known national franchises such as Domino's and Pizza Hut have several area locations. All these shops except Elizabeth's offer free delivery.

The Carolinas rank highest in the nation for per-capita consumption of fast food, but this is misleading because the hordes of tourists who come here are figured into the stats. Fast-food joints are concentrated along the busier commercial routes on the outskirts of Cape Fear towns. Market Street, South College Road and Oleander Drive are the main fast-food strips in Wilmington. In Southport, the River Run Shopping Center at highways 133 and 211 offers McDonald's, Pizza Hut and Subway. Kentucky Fried Chicken sizzles across the street.

In keeping with the area's resort character, dining generally is very casual. While you might feel out of place dressed down for a sumptuous dinner at Cafe Atlantique or The Pilot House, casual dress is commonplace practically everywhere else. Wearing shorts during the summer, even at the better restaurants, is simply practical and not frowned upon.

Planning and Pricing

The descriptions that follow are not intended to be the last word on dining in the Cape Fear region. Rather, these restaurants are tried and true, offering a variety of cuisines, ambience and price range. Because of the rapidly-changing restaurant scene, it makes sense to call individual restaurants to verify hours and reservations. You may want to inquire about early bird specials and senior citizen discounts. You can expect to find waiting lines at the most popular restaurants throughout the summer (especially on weekends), on holidays and during festivals. Waits are generally brief with few exceptions (such as Caffe Phoenix during Azalea Festival and Riverfest). Wine and beer are available at all restaurants on the Cape Fear coast, and most serve mixed drinks as well.

Unless otherwise noted, the listed hours of operation are for the summer season. Winter hours are frequently curtailed, and some restaurants close entirely during the off-season. Most places also remain open later on Friday and Saturday nights than during the week.

The price code that follows is based upon a mid-priced dinner for two consisting of one appetizer, entrees, desserts and coffee. For restaurants not serving dinner, the code reflects a mid-priced lunch. Keep in mind that these codes represent averages; less expensive and more expensive meals are available at any given location, even when ordering the same number of items. The codes, however, do not reflect the state's 6 percent sales tax or gratuities. Major credit cards are accepted by most restaurants listed here. Reservations are generally not required unless your party consists of six persons or more, but most restaurants will accept them.

The price code used in the descriptions is as follows:

Under $20	$
$21 to $35	$$
$36 to $50	$$$
$51 and up	$$$$

Wilmington

CAFE ATLANTIQUE
Near the foot of Market St.   763-8100
$$$$

Since 1987, Chef Scott Fisher has been presenting "new bistro country-style" French cuisine that has quietly put Cafe Atlantique on the map as one of the premier gourmet restaurants in the entire southeast. He has done this so quietly that not even the establishment's address appears in phone listings. He uses almost all organic vegetables, homemade pasta made with the finest ingredients available (such as truffle oil), and top-quality meats and seafood. Chef Fisher creates completely new menus, usually on a daily basis. Everything here is perfection, from the softly lit, early-Deco ambience to the meticulous, world-class presentation. Chef Fisher is an avowed "ambassador of wine," and his wine lists, while matching the impeccable quality his cuisine demands, present several surprisingly affordable domestics. A menu "degustation" (chef's choice) is available upon request for those who wish to witness Cafe Atlantique's full artistic expression. Chef Fisher's professional interests lean toward range-fed chicken, squab, mallard and other fowl. Dining at Cafe Atlantique is by reservation only. Seatings are from 6 PM Tuesday through Saturday. Private parties are welcomed.

CAFFE PHOENIX
9 S. Front St.   343-1395
$$

High ceilings, candlelight, original art, an interior balcony . . . what

Photo: Irv Hooper

This boat may be bringing back your fresh seafood dinner.

the Phoenix offers the eyes is more than complemented by a menu of consistent quality that makes it one of the most appealing and affordable dining experiences on Cape Fear. Situated in an old glass-front building downtown, the Phoenix is also a popular meeting place. The room can become noisy with conversation but that detracts little from its chic allure.

The regular menu exhibits an Italian accent. The Crostini al Pesto or the Apples and Curry Dip appetizers will whet any appetite. Portions are generous and presented by servers dressed in black. Dressings and sauces are all-natural and made fresh. Their special seasonal offerings are inventive. Classical, jazz, Brazilian and other styles of recorded music add to the ambience.

Caffe Phoenix serves lunch from 11:30 AM to 3 PM, light fare between 3 and 5 PM, and dinner from 5 until 10 PM Sunday through Thursday (until 11 PM Friday and Saturday). Mixed drinks, a selection of

coffees and excellent homemade desserts are served until closing. The two plush easy chairs on the far left offer a cozy spot for a romantic night cap. Reservations are not accepted.

CARIBBEAN CAFE
4102 Oleander Dr.   395-0225
$$

Borrowing some of the best of the Caribbean's varied recipes, the Caribbean Cafe succeeds in creating an exotically-spiced menu and a lively atmosphere. Authentic dishes, such as Jamaican jerk chicken, are served to the sounds of reggae and soca music. Seafood combinations, lamb, veal, beef and pork tenderloin and a large selection of vegetable sides are offered along with Jamaica's Red Stripe, Mexico's Pacifico and Negro Modelo, and several other beers. Watch for the seafood combination specials served in the Cafe's tasty black bean sauce. Their oysters "Rockyfeller" are heavenly. Caribbean Cafe has all ABC permits. Its parking lot entrance is located on 41st Street. Lunch is served from 11:30 AM to 2 PM Monday through Friday; dinner from 5:30 to 10 PM Monday through Saturday.

CROOK'S BY THE RIVER
138 S. Front St.   762-8898
$$

Those who thought grits and hush puppies were the high-water mark of Southern cooking owe it to themselves to visit Crook's. A spin-off of Crook's Corner in Chapel Hill founded by the late Bill Neal, it sports a similar pink pig above the entrance. Crook's is a fine amalgam of traditional Southern ingredients, cosmopolitan touches and some elusive magic. The Shrimp & Grits and the vegetarian Black Bean Cakes are wonderful. Be sure to try the Mt. Airy Chocolate Souffle Cake, which looks as deep as chocolate can get but practically floats off the plate it's so light.

Crook's recently added an outdoor deck overlooking the Cape Fear River. There is live music in the lounge on Thursdays all year. Menus change frequently, and the Sunday brunch is superb. Crook's serves lunch Monday through Friday, 11 AM to 2 PM and dinner 6 to 10 PM (10:30 PM weekends). Reservations are accepted.

ANNA THERESA'S PIASTA CAFE
317 N. Front St.   762-2030
$$$

This warm little restaurant in the Cotton Exchange serves southern Italian cuisine for lunch and dinner, and it recently opened for breakfast, too. Lunch selections include stuffed breads, sandwiches and specialty pizzas. Dinner is more elaborate, offering seafood, pasta and chicken entrees. Breakfast consists of Italian-style biscuits (with prosciutto, cappicola and other imported cuts), frittata (Italian omelets) and Anna Theresa's fine desserts, muffins and pastries. The connoli are quite good since the crisp pastry shells are left unfilled until you order. Among Anna Theresa's newest additions is live music on Friday and Saturday evenings. Anna Theresa also imports a variety of Italian delicacies, all available at the restaurant. Breakfast is served beginning at 8 AM, lunch at 11 AM and dinner from 5 to 10 PM every day.

ELIJAH'S
Chandler's Wharf, Water St.   343-1448
$$ to $$$

No one can say they have been to Wilmington without trying Elijah's crab dip. Overlooking the Cape Fear River, Elijah's offers genuine low-country fare, such as the enormous Carolina Bucket that is served with a complete "tool kit" that includes shucking knife, clam fork and lemon wedges, or fancier fare such as the delectable Oysters Rockefeller and Cajun-spiced New York Strip steak.

Elijah's is two restaurants in one: the Oyster Bar that includes outdoor deck seating, and the enclosed dining room that features a slightly more formal presentation of seafood, poultry, pasta and choice beef. Nautical artwork is reminiscent of the building's former incarnation as a maritime museum. The ambience is casual, and the western exposure makes it a great place for a sundown toast. Elijah's is open seven days during the summer but is closed Mondays after Labor Day. Lunch and Sunday brunch are served 11:30 AM to 3 PM, dinner 5 to 10 PM. The Oyster Bar remains open until midnight. Reservations are accepted only for parties of eight or more.

FLIP'S BAR-B-QUE HOUSE
5818 Oleander Dr.   *799-6350*
$

Recently rated best barbecue in the coastal Carolinas by local media, Flip's has been a Wilmington landmark since 1950. Perhaps the enormous stuffed bear rearing up in the dining room (among several other stuffed trophies) has something to do with it. Hushpuppies, Brunswick stew, chopped and sliced ribs, fried and barbecued chicken and various other regional specialties are made fresh daily. Foods are available for takeout and can be shipped anywhere in the country. Flip's is open everyday for lunch and dinner.

J. MICHAEL'S PHILLY DELI
Hanover Center, Oleander Dr.   *763-6466*
$

J. Michael's is famous for the hands-down best Philly cheese steaks in Wilmington and excellent onion rings. The bulk of the menu is less impressive. The dining room has the feel of a sports bar, complete with wide-screen TV. Appetizers such as the fried mozzarella sticks and fried mushrooms are popular, but it's the cheese steaks and beer that keep J. Michael's on the map.

K-38 BAJA GRILL
5410 Oleander Dr.   *395-6040*
$$

"See you at K-38!" became a common farewell among Southwesterners who meet at a scenic seaside spot 38 kilometers south of the border in Baja, where the natives prepare their traditional dishes in roadside shanties. Some of their recipes and inspirations for new ones were brought to Wilmington by Josh Vach, along with many authentic ingredients. The result is K-38's excellent pallet of flavors and textures that stand out among those of most other Mexican restaurants. You'll find all the standard offerings — tacos, burritos, quesadillas, etc. — all done well. But K-38's specialties truly impress, particularly the Camarones Barbacoa (barbecued shrimp). All meat entrees are grilled. K-38 demands a stop by seekers questing for the perfect margarita. The place itself is attractive and atmospheric, and a small room on the right is perfect for larger parties (reserve it in advance.) K-38 is open for lunch Monday through Friday 11 AM to 2:30 PM and for dinner at 5 PM nightly.

Insiders like to drop by Caffe Phoenix in historic downtown for a memorable chocolate cappuccino after the theater.

Insiders' Tips

NUSS STRASSE CAFE

316 Nutt St. 763-5523
$$-$$$

The old brick and exposed rafters of the Cotton Exchange are fitting for this cozy establishment that serves authentic German cuisine in a setting reminiscent of a Bavarian country inn. Seating is divided among three small rooms on different levels. Servers in traditional garb offer a variety of national German dishes, including bratwurst, wienerwurst and Polish kielbasa, as well as hearty thick sandwiches, hot German potato salad, toothsome homemade breads, an incredible host of pastries and, of course, excellent German beer. Lunch is served from 11 AM to 3 PM daily and dinner from 5:30 to 10 PM. Nuss Strasse has all ABC permits and ample parking.

PADDY'S HOLLOW

The Cotton Exchange 762-4354
$-$$

Stepping into Paddy's is like stepping into a friendly Victorian pub, complete with the glint of brass and etched glass. While their large burgers are renowned, the menu includes such hearty fare as flounder stuffed with crab meat, quiche and freshly cut steaks, plus traditional pub offerings such as Welsh Rarebit. Weather permitting, meals are also served on the outdoor patio. Paddy's serves mixed drinks and concocts a fine Irish coffee. Their beer selection includes Guinness Stout by the pint. The bartender will gladly pour it "black and tan" if Stout alone is too much for your palate. Hours are 11:30 AM to 11:30 PM most days. Paddy's presents local musicians after dinner

hours on weekends when it stays open until 2 AM. The restaurant is closed on Sunday.

THE PILOT HOUSE

2 Ann St. 343-0200
$$$

The Pilot House is among the preeminent dining establishments in downtown Wilmington. Overlooking the Cape Fear River at Chandler's Wharf, the restaurant occupies the warmly decorated and historic Craig House (c. 1870) and strives for innovations on high-quality Southern regional cooking. Their large menu, featuring sauteed and chargrilled seafood, pasta, heart-healthy selections and a delectable roster of appetizers, changes at least every other week, so space repeat visits accordingly. The kitchen staff even grows its own herbs in an herb bed in front of the building. The style of service is semiformal, with linen, Wilton pewter and teamed servers, but the management successfully steers for middle ground. You will see everything from Bermuda shorts to tuxedoes among the guests (lunch is more casual than dinner.) The wine list is carefully chosen and well-rounded, and there is a lounge adjoining the dining room. The Pilot House features additional outdoor seating, weather permitting. It serves lunch from 11 AM to 3 PM and dinner from 5 to 10 PM Monday through Saturday. Sunday brunch is served seasonally. Reservations are recommended.

P.T.'S GRILLE

4544 Fountain Dr. 392-2293
$

Once everyone tastes P.T.'s freshly-

grilled sandwiches, fast-food restaurants become passe. P.T.'s stays crowded during peak lunch and dinner hours, and the reasons for that (aside from its proximity to the UNCW campus) are obvious. Every menu item here is a package deal that includes a sandwich (whopping 1/2-pound burgers, tender chicken breast, 8 oz. hot dogs, fresh roast beef and more), spiced french fries (skin-on) and a soft drink (refill included). Prices are unbeatably low and quality high, and all the ingredients are fresh. You place your order by filling in a user-friendly order form and dropping it through the window when eating on the outdoor deck. Your meal is generally ready in 10 minutes,

prepared to order — fast food without tasting like fast-food. P.T.'s Grille is located west of South College Road, across a parking lot from a frozen yogurt shop. It's a short walk or drive from College Road Cinemas for after-dinner entertainment. Take-out orders are welcomed and may be habit-forming.

RUCKER JOHN'S
RESTAURANT AND MORE

5511 Carolina Beach Rd.   455-1212
$$

Casual, comfortable and providing friendly service, Rucker John's serves a wide section of salads, beef, poultry, pasta and fish seven days a week for lunch and dinner. Salads can be made to order and dressing are made fresh on the premises. Burgers, ribs and grilled seafood are consistently well done, and croissant sandwiches offer a welcomed change of pace. Lunch and dinner specials and drink specials change daily. The restaurant offers comfortable banquette and table seating in a setting warmed by oak, carpeting and soft lighting. It is the 1 1/2 year-old sister establishment of 10 additional tables, televised sports and a horseshoe-shaped bar that remains open until midnight. It's becoming something of a neighborhood bar. Rucker John's possesses all ABC permits and is open 11 AM to 10 PM every day. The kitchen serves later on Friday and Saturday nights. Be sure to include Rucker John's in your eternal quest for the perfect margarita. It is located in the Myrtle Grove Shopping Center at Monkey Junction (where Carolina Beach and College roads meet, about 7.3 miles south of downtown Wilmington).

SZECHUAN 132
419 S. College Rd.   799-1426
$$

Recently expanded, Szechuan 132 stands above most other Chinese restaurants in Wilmington but especially in terms of the personalities of the staff and the proprietor, the engaging Joseph Hou. Much of the menu is actually Cantonese, but Szechuan items such as the Hot and Sour Soup and Szechuan Pan-fried Noodles live up to their names. Mr. Hou continues to expand and re-

vise his wine list (mostly domestics). His decor is attractively plain and contemporary, done in rose hues. Comfortable banquettes and high-backed chairs invite diners to linger. Mixed drinks are available. Everyday, Szechuan 132 offers excellent lunch specials averaging $7 and gladly accepts take-out orders. It is located in the University Landing Shopping Center, and reservations are recommended for dinner. Lunch is served 11:30 AM to 2:30 PM and dinner from 5 to 10:30 PM Monday through Friday. Meals are served all day on Saturday and Sunday from noon to closing.

TRAILS END STEAK HOUSE
Trails End Rd.   791-2034
$$$

There's nothing better than an old restaurant with a history. And when it comes to steaks, most locals agree, there's nothing better than Trails End. Located on the Intracoastal Waterway near Whiskey Creek, at the end of a road that lives up to its name, Trails End is best known for three things: steaks, beef and red meat. All their steaks — real sirloin, filet of tenderloin, prime rib, Delmonico and more — are broiled over hardwood charcoal. Every entree is served with hors d'oeuvres and salad bar. Trails end's colorful history, dating to 1965, is related on the back of every menu and through news articles and memorabilia on the walls near the entrance (the front door handles are horseshoes from the Budweiser Clydesdales, a gift to the restaurant's founder from Mrs. August Busch).

DISCOVER THE LURE OF THE BRIDGE TENDER VILLAGE

- **The Bridge Tender Restaurant & Marina**
  Award-winning food, wine and waterfront views
- **Fish House Grill**
  Fresh seafood in a waterfront cafe setting
- **The Fisherman's Wife**
  Fanciful fish gifts from folk art to finials

Historic Airlie Road on the Intracoastal Waterway

Trails End is reputable for the longevity of its staff (a waiter retired last year after 26 years of continuous service), and the dedication of its clientele. The original building was something of a shack that had no windows. Rebuilt in 1987, the existing building recalls much of the old atmosphere. It is not a large place (seating less than 90), but now there are large windows yielding a marvelous waterway vista. Reservations are strongly recommended. Trails End Road is about 7 1/2 miles south of Wilmington. To find it, take Pine Grove Drive south from Oleander (at Hugh MacRae Park). Turn right onto Masonbroro Loop Road. Make the first left onto Trails End Road, 1/10 mile after the Whiskey Creek bridge, and proceed beyond the "End State Road" sign until the scent of fine, broiled beef stops you in your tracks.

The grill is open Monday through Friday from 6 PM until 10 PM and on Saturday from 5:30 PM until 10 PM.

WATER STREET RESTAURANT
5 Water St.   343-0042
$

Housed in a former peanut warehouse called the Quince Building (1835) located on the riverfront, the Water Street Restaurant offers inexpensive, offbeat and healthful meals from 8 AM to 10 PM every day in an open, casual space shared by shopkeepers selling tourist novelties. Breakfast and brunch selections include shrimp and grits and banana French toast. A large array of salads (tabouli, shrimp, falafel, fruit, etc.), burgers (including chicken and veggie), burritos and pita pockets (turkey, shrimp, hummus, baba ganouj, etc.) are typical of Water Street's flair. "Square Meals" are served after 5 PM. Water Street Market is a favorite place to stop for ice cream, frozen yogurt or a cold beer (imported and domestic). Many salad items are available to go. The sidewalk seating is in full view of the river, and live piano music is provided almost every night of the year. Free parking is available in the lot at the corner of Dock and Water streets.

Wrightsville Beach

BEACHES
2025 Eastwood Rd.   256-4622
$$

Decorated with pastel colors and local art, Beaches offers an attractive setting, casual presentation and good quality. The menu is relatively restrained, but what Beaches does, it does well. As you would expect, fresh local seafood comes in a delicious variety of preparations. The coconut shrimp appetizer is a tasty twist on the old Calabash-style, and their seafood chowder is an award-winning recipe. But Beaches' reputation stands most firmly on the excellence of its charcoaled beef dishes, particularly its steaks. The variety of domestic and imported wines and the full bar offer something for everyone. Most wines cost less than $20 a bottle. Beaches' lounge has become a well-known night spot for conversation and televised sports and, on Thursdays, for live music, usually acoustic. There is also limited outdoor seating suitable for drinks or light meals. Beaches is open for dinner from 5 to 10 PM on weekdays and until 10:30 PM on weekends.

THE BRIDGE TENDER RESTAURANT
1414 Airlie Rd.   256-3419
$$$

The Bridge Tender's tremendous local following is testimony to its consistent, high quality and flexibility in pleasing its customers. Situated on the Intracoastal Waterway within full view of the Wrightsville Beach drawbridge, this small, 18-year-old establishment excels in preparing fresh seafood and in its nationally recognized, multiple-award winning domestic wine list. From lamp-lit tables beneath a high, raftered ceiling, the view of the waterway marinas is romantic. All of the Bridge Tender's offerings are fresh and made from scratch, and they serve only certified Angus beef. Specials change daily, making repeat visits worthwhile. Some of its specials include the Mixed Grill, the Maryland crab cake appetizer and Cajun-spiced shrimp served over rice. The adjoining lounge offers the same excellent scenery as well as hot and cold appetizers from Monday through Thursday. The Bridge Tender has all ABC permits and serves lunch Monday through Friday from 11:30 AM until 2 PM. Dinner guests are seated from 5:30 to 10 PM.

Photo: Scott Taylor

A perfect example of art in nature.

A fishing trawler returns home with a day's work.

DOXEY'S MARKET & CAFE

Landfall Shopping Center   256-9952
$

Aside from being one of the area's preeminent outlets for natural groceries and products, Doxey's serves all-natural, high-quality foods at its cafe. The salad bar and hot bar offer fresh vegetables (mostly organic), homemade salads, bean cuisine and several soups. Sandwiches and daily specials are also available. Patrons may dine on the premises or take their meals to go.

EDDIE ROMANELLI'S

5400 Oleander Dr.   799-7000
$$$

Romanelli's offers a high-toned atmosphere suffused with the richness of dark wood, red brick and full carpeting. The recently expanded menu emphasizes American regional dishes, many with a distinctly Italian accent. Among the house specialties are superb crab dip and the homemade 10-inch pizzas, some of which are rather innovative, such as the Barbecued Chicken Pizza and Philly Steak Pizza. The menu offers a variety of appetizers (try the Pesto Cheese Toast), sandwiches, salads with fresh-made dressings and Italian baked specialties. Lunch and dinner menus are essentially the same, with dinner portions being larger and including soup and salad. Adjoining the restaurant, with its high, raftered ceiling, skylights and handsome sectional seating, is the bar that was voted "Most Popular After-Hours Night Spot" by the readers of *Encore Magazine* earlier this year. Menu and drink specials are offered every day. Romanelli's is open seven days a week from 11:30 AM to 11 PM. A late-night finger food menu is served at the bar from 11 PM to 1 AM (until 11 PM on Sundays).

FISH HOUSE GRILL

1410 Airlie Rd.   256-3693
$

Fast, friendly service in a colorful, casual waterside atmosphere makes the Fish House Grill more of a pleasure than it would be if it had only good, inexpensive food going for it. The restaurant is situated on the Intracoastal Waterway and offers brightly-colored indoor seating and deck seating at shaded tables. The same menu items are available for lunch and dinner. These include the zesty Fish House Stew, nachos, slow-roasted barbecued pork, ribs, fish sandwiches, fresh seafood and items from the raw bar. Portions are generous and beer and wine are available. Adjoining the restaurant is a gift shop, The Fisherman's Wife. The Fish House Grill is open from 11:30 AM to 10 PM Tuesday through Sunday. Off-season hours may be somewhat curtailed.

GARDENIAS

7105 Wrightsville Ave.   256-2421
$$$

Last year's opening of Gardenias, located just west of the draw bridge, was another quantum leap for the culinary arts in the Cape Fear region. "Fresh concepts" is the theme, reflected in fresh cut flowers and floral-print table linens, entirely fresh ingredients and an eclectic, innovative menu. Even the garnishes are fresh flowers, all of them edible. Designed by Chef Gail Tolan, the menu exhibits New American blends of traditional dishes and local ingredients with imaginative sauces. To the accompaniment of soft jazz in an inti-

mate room, semiformal servers present local seafood, certified Angus beef, fresh pasta, vegetarian selections, freshly baked breads and incredible desserts. Presentation is artful and picture-perfect. The wine list, chosen by multiple-award-winning wine connoisseur Patricia Dudding, offers 28 wines by the glass, allowing diners to sample unfamiliar varietals and vintages. She seeks out the very best wines as well as the very best values in each category, striking a balance between affordability and quality. A variety of microbrewery beers is also stocked, and every house pour for mixed drinks is top-shelf. Candlelight, custom-blended coffees and consistent hospitality complete the Gardenias experience. Gardenias is open for dinner seven days a week from 6 to 10 PM (11 PM on weekends). Reservations are accepted but not necessary.

GIUSEPPE'S GOURMET ITALIAN RESTAURANT

Plaza East   256-9600
$$$$

Giuseppe's offers very fine Italian specialties in an Old World setting. When it comes to importing Old World style, there's a fine line between ambience and cornball, and Giuseppe's comes dangerously close to crossing it, particularly where the statuary is concerned. But the good

Insiders know they can find breakfast-all-day places, which serve up meals complete with grits and biscuits, all over the Cape Fear area.

Insiders' Tips

They're hoping for a good catch.

food more than makes up for the decor. The menu includes pasta dishes that serve well as a main course, but if you prefer a traditional high-style Italian dinner, smaller portions make a fine second course to follow the antipasto and precede the main course. Seafood entrees such as the Grouper Florentine and Veal Giuseppe's Style are delightful. Homemade soup is offered to preface the meal. Giuseppe's wine list includes some fine selections and prices, and the restaurant has all ABC permits. It's easy to overdo it here, so save room for dessert. The zuppa inglese is quite good, especially with a demitasse of espresso. Giuseppe's seats for dinner from 5:30 PM to 9:30 on weeknights and until 10:30 on weekends. The bar closes at 2 AM.

KING NEPTUNE

11 N. Lumina Ave.   *256-2525*
$$

King Neptune has been in business since the '50s, outlasting its original owners but never wearing out its appeal. From soups and chowders to steamers, platters and hearty specialties that include steaks and pizza, King Neptune focuses on seafood and does it well. Owners Pam and Bernard Carroll have added distinctive new menu items with an island flair, such as the trigger fish with rum-mango sauce, the spicy Voodoo Snapper and traditional Jamaican jerk chicken. The dining room is large and bright, decorated with photographs of the aftermath of Hurricane Hazel and local art. After dinner, the adjoining Ol' Nep's Lounge is popular and offers perhaps the widest selection of rums on the North Carolina coast as well as an international selection of beers (not to mention an endless supply of entertaining sailing and fishing photographs). King Neptune serves dinner seven days a week from 5 to 10 PM and offers senior citizen discounts. The lounge remains open until 1 AM. Free parking is available

Big Daddy's

"SEAFOOD AT ITS BEST"

⚓ SEAFOOD

SPECIALIZING IN FRIED OR
BROILED OCEAN FRESH SEAFOOD
LOBSTER TAILS
ALASKAN SNOW CRABS
CHAR-BROILED FISH STEAKS
- Major Credit Cards Accepted -

⚓ STEAKS & PRIME RIB

CHOICE
WESTERN BEEF

ALL ABC PERMITS

™

458-8622

206 K AV. IN THE HEART OF KURE BEACH

in the lot across the street.

THE OCEANIC RESTAURANT
703 S. Lumina Ave.   *256-5551*
$$$$

There are few dining experiences as fulfilling as dining on the pier at the Oceanic. As pelicans kite overhead and the surf crashes below, you could be enjoying a chilled drink, fresh blackened swordfish, or some of the region's most acclaimed crab dip. Should the weather turn angry, the Oceanic's two floors of indoor seating offer panoramic views. The Oceanic does nothing innovative, but their tried-and-true menu items are satisfying and affordable. Heart-healthy menu items abound. Juices used in mixed drinks are all squeezed fresh daily. Those seeking the perfect margarita should dowse here. The decor never strays from the theme, and the historic photographs are attractions in themselves. Top off your meal with a walk on the pier or beach. Sunday brunch begins at 10 AM, and breakfast is served all day on week-

ends. Lunch is served 11:30 AM to 4 PM and dinner from 4 to 10 PM. The third-floor banquet room is available for private parties. Reservations are accepted for groups of six or more, and there is ample parking.

Carolina Beach

BIG DADDY'S SEAFOOD RESTAURANT
202 K. Ave.   *458-8622*
Kure Beach
$$$

A Kure Beach institution for three decades, Big Daddy's serves a variety of better quality seafood and combination platters. Seafood can be broiled, fried, chargrilled, steamed or made Calabash-style. These and choice steaks, prime rib and chicken are offered every day in a family-oriented, casual setting. Highlights of Big Daddy's menu include all-you-can-eat, low county, family-style dining ($14.95), an all-you-can-eat salad bar ($2.95), special plates for seniors and children, and the sizeable Surf and Turf Supreme (beef tenderloin with split Alaskan king crab legs, $18.95). An after-dinner walk along the beach or on the Kure Beach fishing pier (both a block away) further adds to Big Daddy's appeal. Because the restaurant consists of several carpeted rooms, all with a nautical decor, the total size of the establishment comes as something of a surprise (it seats about 500 people.) Rare and unusual maritime memorabilia make for entertaining distractions. Entrance to the restaurant is through a colorful gift shop offering novelties and taffy. Patrons frequently make secret wishes and cast coins into the fountain there. Located at the only stop light in Kure Beach, Big Daddy's has all ABC permits, and there is ample parking in front of and across the street.

BOWMAN'S AT THE BEACH

911 N. Lake Park Blvd.   *458-6292*
$

Bowman's is a small, laid-back diner-style restaurant with a dedicated local following. Serving seafood plates, flounder, shrimp, oysters, whiting, "bar-b-que," fish sandwiches, chicken strips, beer and wine, Bowman's also delivers locally for free ($5 minimum order). They are open year round from 11:30 AM until 9 PM every day except Monday.

HARBOR MASTERS
RESTAURANT & LOUNGE

315 Canal Dr.   *458-7013*
$$

Harbor Masters serves decent, wholesome food that won't bowl you over, but its excellent location overlooking the Carolina Beach Marina goes a long way toward explaining the long-term dedication of its regular clientele. Situated on the opposite side of the building from the lounge, which features live music on weekends, the restaurant serves up regional seafood and meat specialties for dinner after 5 PM. Specialities include lobster tails, steaks and low-country fish entrees. Breakfast is served from 6 AM and lunch thereafter.

Topsail Island

DINE ASHORE

710 N. Shore Dr.   *328-3661*
Surf City
$$

The Dine Ashore (pun intended) occupies a historic building once used as an officers' club during World War II when Topsail Island was an Army firing range. The restaurant is adjacent to Barnacle Bill's Fishing Pier. Complementing its ocean view, the Dine Ashore provides a variety of shellfish and fresh local catches ("Reel Fresh Fish") served with chowder, slaw and hushpuppies, as well as "Dry Dock Dinners" of steak, prime rib and chicken, and "Reef and Beef" combinations. The decor is strictly nautical right down to the netting draped above the windows. Dine Ashore offers a salad bar, a breakfast buffet and a Luncheon-By-the-Sea on weekends and holidays. Reservations are accepted.

Totally informal, inexpensive breakfasts, lunches and dinners are served in Barnacle Bill's Grill adjoining the Dine Ashore. The Grill offers indoor and ocean deck dining with table service and is the pre-

GOOD FRIENDS
GOOD FOOD
GREAT RADIO

WMV

NEWS/TALK   AM 980

ferred eating spot for those fishing from the pier. The panelled walls are chock-full of interesting old odds 'n' ends. Seafood combos, pasta, burgers and subs are the staples. You don't need to be extraordinarily brave to sample the Turtle Eggs, jalapenos stuffed with Monterey jack, lightly battered and deep-fried, $3.95 a half-dozen. They're not as hot as you may expect, so go ahead.

CAMP DAVIS RESTAURANT

Hwy. 50   *329-2151*
Holly Ridge
$-$$

A meal at this historic landmark is a journey back to the World War II era when Camp Davis was an antiaircraft training base. It is in Holly Ridge, one block west of the intersection of Highways 50 and 17, just a few minutes from Surf City. The restaurant is in the former Administration Building and is replete with vintage photographs and memorabilia that include facsimiles of Germany's and Japan's surrender treaties, NASCAR collectibles and crafts. It is now something of a social center in Holly Ridge, which has a population of about 800. Politics and tourists are frequent topics of discussion at the lunch counter.

The restaurant has four wood-paneled rooms, each seating about 50 people. One room is available for private events. Breakfast, lunch and dinner consist of basic, well-prepared fare — sandwiches, burgers, seafood, steaks — served daily except Sundays. Candlelight at dinner is incongruously pleasant. The prices can't be beat — breakfasts can be as low as $1.99, dinner specials $5.95. Phone-in and take-out orders are welcomed. The restaurant is open 6 AM to 10 PM Monday through Saturday. (For a sidelight on the history of Camp Davis, see the oral history on Operation Bumblebee.)

HOLLAND'S
SHELTER CREEK RESTAURANT
Hwy. 53   259-5743
Near Burgaw
$-$$

Local color is seldom as brilliant as at Holland's. From the moment you step in the door and come face to face with a stuffed buck, you know you're in for a country-style treat. Situated over the banks of Holly Shelter Creek, the restaurant adjoins the sport and tackle shop where you can rent canoes, buy hunting supplies or inspect photographs of proud anglers and their prize catches. Popular among sportsmen and campers, Holland's serves shrimp, oysters, clam strips, flounder and catfish, plus a variety of standard grill fare in a friendly backwoods atmosphere. Holland's is a good 30 miles north of Wilmington (a tad longer from Surf City) on Highway 53 north of the Holly Shelter Game Land. From I-40, travel about 7 1/2 miles east, toward Jacksonville. You will find it on the right-hand side next to Holland's Family Campground. The restaurant is open every day from 11 AM to 9:45 PM.

JIMMY'S DELI
Hwy. 17
Hampstead   270-3223
$

Located in Hampstead Plaza (behind Ace Hardware) at the northwest corner of the junction of Highways 210 and 17, Jimmy's comes highly recommended by tourists and Insiders alike. It's a casual, New York-style deli serving Italian specialties with tasty homemade sauces, cold cuts, great subs, full dinners, wine, beer and mixed drinks by the glass (Jimmy's was among the very first in Pender County to do so.) Jimmy's Deli is open seven days a week from 7 AM to 9 PM except Sundays when it operates from 9 AM to 2 PM.

OCEANSIDE RESTAURANT
Foot of Roland Ave.
Surf City   328-0619
$-$$

As in many places along the Cape Fear coast, the Oceanside is the kind where greetings are readily exchanged between strangers. Overlooking the beach, the Oceanside is a popular family eatery, especially

Insiders' Tips

Enjoy an overhead view of sand volleyball and a panorama of the Atlantic Ocean from the pier at The Oceanic.

on Sundays, and serves breakfast, lunch and dinner seven days a week. The preferred seating is naturally along the windows facing the ocean, while larger groups are better accommodated on the inland side. The Hungry Man Breakfast is aptly named and a bargain at $4.50. Burgers, burritos, and sandwiches (including soft shell crab in season) are typical of the lunch offerings, while seafood (including combination platters), chicken and a limited choice of steaks round out the evening menu. Beer, wine and desserts are available on request, and there is ample parking. The Oceanside is open weekdays from 7 AM to 9:30 PM and on weekends until 10 PM.

THE RUSTY SCUPPER
Hwy. 210
North Topsail Beach   *328-2780*
$$

Located on the beach opposite Rogers Bay Campground, the Rusty Scupper is about the only eatery between Surf City and the resorts of North Topsail. Much of the restaurant's seafood is brought in fresh on owner Glenn Gore's two fishing vessels. The decor is an entertaining medley of nautical whatnots, antique photos, shark jaws, surfing memorabilia and sailors' esoterica. There may not be two matching lanterns in the entire building. The menu is basic: seafood (mostly fried or broiled), appetizers, fresh-cut steaks and chicken. The split-level oceanfront deck is a popular place to dine when the weather is cooperative. Waits of 45 minutes for a table are not uncommon in the summer. Wednesdays in season are Steamers Nights from 7 to 10 PM. The lounge has all ABC permits. The Rusty Scupper caters, is available for private parties and is handicapped accessible. Its summer hours are 4 to 11 PM Monday through Friday, 11 AM to 11 PM Saturdays and 1 to 10 PM Sundays.

SOUNDSIDE
209 N. New River Dr.
Surf City   *328-0803*
$$$

Warm ambience, attentive service and quality cuisine make Soundside an above-average dining experience. Established in 1981 and formerly located in Topsail Beach, Soundside is situated on an inlet over which sunsets enhance evening meals. Swaths of deep-colored cloth canopy the ceiling. Tables are all dressed with fresh flowers, handsome tablecloths, oil lamps and black china. Service is semiformal (the tuxedoed servers may forgo the jacket). The newly-completed upstairs bar has its own exterior balcony facing the water.

Soundside's menu, predominantly seafood, includes unusual dishes such as the Smoked Salmon with Pesto Cheesecake ($6.25). Highlights among the entrees include Jumbo Shrimp Bach (sauteed shrimp baked with tomato salsa and feta) and Parmesan Crusted Lemon Chicken. Grilled items, prime rib, soups and salads, and domestic and imported wines are also available. Reservations are requested for dinner. The excellent Sunday Brunch ($9.95) requires no reservations. Soundside seats for dinner 5 to 10

Photo: Scott Taylor

Grilled, steamed, baked, fried, sauteed, poached — any way you want them, they're always fresh.

PM. The restaurant closes during the month of January and is handicapped accessible.

When you want something more casual, step next door into The Market, a gourmet food and gift shop where you can enjoy all Soundside's non-entree menu items and wine by the glass at candlelit salon tables on a screened-in porch overlooking the water. The Market is open 10 AM to 10 PM seven days a week during the warm season. It's a great place for late-evening dessert and coffee with a loved one.

SUNSETS

Foot of Florida Ave.
Topsail Beach   *328-1883*
$$

Sunsets is an ambitious new culinary addition to Topsail Island, its theme being "fine cuisine from islands around the world." A verdant walkway leads to the entrance. Overlooking the Topsail Sound fishing pier, Sunsets strives for the exotic. Guests can sample satay, the Indonesian skewer of grilled shrimp or beef; a zesty Jamaican lentil soup; Key West-style snapper topped with a walnut brown sugar sauce; or Cuban-style shrimp and scallops served over angel hair pasta. Imported beers include Jamaica's Red Stripe, the Philippines' San Miguel Dark and Ireland's Guinness Stout. Be sure to leave room for the Hummingbird Cake, a melange of pineapple, nuts and bananas.

Sunsets seats for dinner 6 to 9 PM and offers a fixed-rate Early Bird Special ($18.75). There are also special "Island Feasts" each week and healthy, affordable children's selections. Private parties can be accommodated. Sunsets serves Tuesday through Sunday during the summer, three days a week in May and October and closes during the off-season. Reservations are recommended.

TOPSAIL VIEW RESTAURANT

New River Inlet Rd.   328-0463
North Topsail Shores
$$-$$$

Commanding a seventh-floor view of the Atlantic and most of Topsail Island from the top of the St. Regis Resort, the Topsail View is a sophisticated setting for dinner and private parties. Tables seating up to 180 are formally set, and the menu offers an elaborate selection of seafood and steaks, imported beer and domestic wines. The raised center of the nearly octagonal room serves as a dance floor for weddings. Dinner is served from 5 PM to 10 PM daily. Room service and Sunday brunch ($7.95) are available. The restaurant prepares certain items for takeout and delivery. Telephone orders are accepted from 11 AM to 10 PM (the in-house phone number is 150).

Oak Island

DEL'S RESTAURANT

6302 E. Oak Island Dr.,   278-3338
  Long Beach
$

Pleasant, small and casual, Del's specializes in Italian-style seafood and regional dinners, pizza, subs and sandwiches. Spaghetti Buckets yielding two to eight servings are an innovation you won't see everyday, except at Del's. The friendly staff serves beer, wine and wine coolers, as well as a smattering of Cajun-style meat dishes. Call-in orders can be picked up at the drive-through window, and local delivery is also available after 5 PM (call

278-1912). Del's hours are 11 AM to 9 PM Monday through Thursday, 11 AM to 10 PM Friday and Saturday, and noon to 9 PM Sunday.

JONES' SEAFOOD HOUSE

6404 E. Oak Island Dr.   278-5231
Long Beach
$$-$$$

Jones' Seafood House affords patrons a casual dining experience in a friendly atmosphere. The menu offers all the most popular regional specialties including fresh crab meat patties, trout filet and grilled shrimp-and-scallop skewers. Meat lovers won't be disappointed by the variety of steaks, chicken and pork and a selection of surf and turf combinations. Dinner specials and a children's menu are available and the restaurant has all ABC permits. All menu items are available for takeout. Jones' Seafood House and the lounge are open Monday through Saturday from 4 PM. Lunch is served on Sundays beginning at 11 AM.

MARGE'S
RESTAURANT & WAFFLE HOUSE

5700 E. Oak Island Dr.
  Long Beach   278-3070
$

Among Long Beach residents, Marge's is one of the most popular diner-style eateries for breakfast and lunch. No matter how crowded it gets, the food is served hot, fast and with a smile, and no one will rush you. Table-to-table conversation comes easily as folks dine on large omelets, flaky biscuits, pasta, grilled foods, fried seafood and local specialties such as hushpuppies, okra and beans. Marge's is open from

5:30 AM to 2 PM daily, and serves breakfast all day. Take-out orders are welcomed.

WINDJAMMER
RESTAURANT & LOUNGE
1411 E. Beach Dr.
Long Beach   278-7740
$$

Recently spruced up, the Windjammer continues to improve its already good reputation for fine dining on Oak Island. Through enormous oceanfront windows, the view overlooking the Ocean Crest Pier is stunning. The menu emphasizes a variety of seafoods served Calabash-style, sauteed or broiled. Freshly cut steaks and chicken make limited appearances. The Windjammer is the only place on the island where you can try the enormous Bloomin' Onion. The jalapenos stuffed with crab meat ($4.95) are, as owner Wade Goin puts it, "Right famous." In a fairly large, bright room seating 120 people, the Windjammer features occasional live entertainment during the high season and offers breakfast and lunch buffets. It is open six days a week in the summer and has all ABC permits. Dinner is served from 5 to 10 PM.

Holden Beach

CAPT. WILLIE'S RESTAURANT
Holden Beach Causeway
Holden Beach   842-9383
$$

Formerly Reaves Fish Camp, Capt. Willie's is now owned and operated by one of the area's grand old families. They specialize in fresh country cooking featuring a wide variety of seafood plus a few steak, chicken, pork and barbecue dishes. Their lunch buffet and evening seafood buffet are worthwhile bargains, and the ambience is as casual and friendly as one would expect from an older establishment. Capt. Willie's is open from 11 AM to 10 PM during the busy season and is located next to the Water Slide Ice Cream shop.

ROBERTO'S PIZZERIA & RESTAURANT
Jordan Ave.
Holden Beach   842-4999
$

The Roberto family hails from Philadelphia, so not only is their hand-tossed pizza authentic Italian-American, but their Philly cheese steaks are also right on the money. They operate at two locations. The Holden Beach restaurant (the only restaurant on the island) closes from November through March, and the Ocean Isle Beach location at 6773 Beach Drive, Southwest Highway 179, 579-4999, is open all year. Their pizza crust is crisp outside and soft inside — a nice balance. Specialty dinners, hoagies (Philadelphia's name for subs or "heroes"), burgers, nightly specials, beer and wine are available to eat in, take out or have delivered locally. Roberto's is open seven days, 10 AM to 11 PM during the summer.

Ocean Isle Beach

THE ISLANDER RESTAURANT
Causeway Dr.
Ocean Isle Beach   579-6474
$$

One of Ocean Isle's highlights is

the Islander's daily lunch buffet. For less than the price of a movie you can feast to capacity on regional specialties such as fresh corn bread and biscuits, traditionally-prepared collards, country ham, crispy fried chicken and pudding. Your server will leave a pitcher of iced tea on your table, and you're likely to hear patrons being asked if they got their second helpings. Dinner at the Islander can be crowded but is always marked by quality and good service. Seafood, steaks and a salad bar comprise the core of the dinner offerings. Breakfast is almost as popular as dinner and is served from 6 AM. The adjoining cocktail lounge hosts live entertainment on weekends. The Islander is a casual, family-oriented restaurant replete with down-home courtesy and style.

SHARKY'S PIZZA & DELI

Causeway Dr.
Ocean Isle Beach   579-9177
$

When owners Al and Ray traded their power suits for bathing suits and opened Sharky's in '91, their goal was to provide a good place to eat with a great view. They have succeeded. The food at Sharky's isn't fancy but is well-priced and can be enjoyed indoors or on the handicapped-accessible deck overlooking the waterway. You can tie up your boat at Sharky's 150' dock. Thor-

oughly casual and fun for the whole family, Sharky's offers Lite Bites (wings, chicken tenders, etc.), thin-crust pizza, a nice selection of hot and cold subs, beer, soups and salads. Occasionally, Sharky's hosts family-oriented holiday parties with live music, volleyball and plenty of food. There's even a rooftop band stand. Most days, the stereo pumps lively rock, country and beach music. Ray describes his clientele and staff as "a laid-back, fun-loving, music-loving bunch." Sharky's also provides free local delivery. It is located next to the ABC Store at the foot of the bridge.

Sunset Beach

CRABBY ODDWATERS
RESTAURANT AND BAR

310 Sunset Blvd.
Sunset Beach   579-6372
$$

If the food weren't so darn good, this upstairs restaurant would still be worth a visit just to read the story of how it got its "damp and crawly name" (a story told in one easy-to-remember sentence of barely more than 400 words). This is a small, handsome restaurant with an enclosed deck overlooking a waterway. The tables have holes in the center where you can pitch your shucked shells and, despite the plastic uten-

Insiders who yearn for car-side wait service can visit Merritt's Burger House on Carolina Beach Road for a trip into the past.

Insiders' Tips

sils, the ambience and cuisine are high quality. Local seafood of all types is the focus, featuring the unusual shrimp, scallop or combo "KaBillbobs" and wonderful nightly specials (ask about the spicy Seminole Snapper). A limited choice of landfood (and, sometimes, hot jambalaya) is offered. Crabby Oddwaters is located above Bill's Seafood — which is owned by a guy named Joe — on the mainland side of the pontoon bridge. It is open for dinner from 4 PM all year.

TWIN LAKES SEAFOOD RESTAURANT
Sunset Blvd.
Sunset Beach   579-6373
$$

Twin Lakes stands rooted in the region's long-standing culinary tradition, having family connections linked to the earliest seafood days of nearby Calabash. With its exterior painted in tropical colors, surrounded by banana trees and overlooking the waterway and the Sunset Beach pontoon bridge, Twin Lakes is an attractive family restaurant that stays busy. Indoors, floral table coverings and local art stand out amid the aquamarine and pink decor. There is little here for the dedicated meat eater. Seafood, vegetables and pasta comprise the bulk of the menu. Specials change daily and seafood, which may be fried, sauteed, grilled, broiled or blackened, is only hours out of the water. Seafood salads, stir-fry and pasta combinations are all nicely done. Early Bird Specials are available Sunday through Friday, 4 to 6 PM and include an entree and a side dish for $7.95 or less.

SIMS COUNTRY BAR-B-QUE II
Barbecue Rd.
Grissettown   287-3505
$

If you eat at a Southern-style barbecue joint only once in your life, this is the place to go. For $9 (children under 12, $4) you can eat all the smoky chicken, beef and pork barbecue you can handle, along with plenty of other country-style fare, served on cardboard plates. Everyone sits together on long benches which fill half the barn. The other half accommodates the live bluegrass bands, cloggers, square dancers and diners who come from miles around for the nightly hoedowns that begin at 7 PM. It's a pity this place is only open Thursday, Friday and Saturday in the summer (Friday and Saturday in spring and fall) and that it closes from November through March. Beverages are extra, and no alcohol is permitted. Grissettown is north of Sunset and Ocean Isle beaches near Highway 17. To get to Sims from Hwy. 17, take Route 904 north for 1.4 miles; turn right onto Russtown Road; 1.4 miles further, turn right down unpaved Barbecue Road and park on the lawn.

Calabash

LARRY'S CALABASH SEAFOOD BARN
Hwy. 179   579-6976
$$

Unless you insist on having a view of the docks at the foot of River Road, Larry's is one of the better choices for Calabash-style seafood on the other side of town. The all-you-can-eat seafood buffet, which often includes crab legs, and raw bar

are frequently cited by insiders as reasons for repeat visits. Much of the seafood served here is caught using the restaurant's own boats. Despite it's name, Larry's bears little resemblance to a barn. Rather, it is clean, bright and spacious and even features rocking chairs on the front porch. Larry's also serves steaks and mixed drinks and offers golfers' specials, a children's menu and discounts to large groups.

THE ORIGINAL
CALABASH RESTAURANT

On the waterfront   579-6875
$$

Whether this is actually the first original Calabash restaurant is sec-ondary to the fact that it's a decent place to try Calabash-style seafood. (Insiders say Beck's "Old Original Calabash Restaurant," established 1940, was the first.) The hamburgers, steaks and chicken seem like distant afterthoughts on a menu outbalanced by seafood including everything from oyster stew and Teriyaki shrimp to stuffed flounder in Hollandaise and soft shell crabs. The Original Calabash stands at the foot of River Road in a large parking area rimmed by several of their competitors, but you can't miss it. As you drive in, it's the one straight ahead with all the flashing lights. Welcome to Calabash.

THE ORIGINAL ELLA'S OF CALABASH

1148 River Rd.   579-6728
$$

Ella's is among the stalwarts of Calabash that remain open most of the off-season, and they've been doing so since 1950. This is also one of the less flashy establishments, preferring to draw their patrons with good food, affordable prices and a casual, friendly atmosphere rather than with excessive pre-fab nautical ambience. Ella's offers a worthwhile lunch special (choice of two seafoods plus slaw, hushpuppies and fries) — a bargain at $3.95. Steaks, chicken, oyster roasts (in season), mixed drinks and a children's menu are also available. Ella's opens at 11 AM daily and is located almost midway between the waterfront and Highway 179 (Beach Drive).

Southport

THE CHART HOUSE

832 N. Howe St.   457-4777
$

Genuine home-cooking in an informal, no-frills setting makes the Chart House a popular breakfast and lunch spot for area locals. Standard American breakfast items and Belgian waffles are complemented by Southern-style biscuits, country ham and grits. Breakfast is served all day. Daily lunch specials are hearty and inexpensive. Seafood offerings can be fried, grilled or blackened, and grilled meats, homemade barbecue and fish sandwiches are available. Lunch is served from 11 AM to 2 PM.

THE CROW'S NEST GRILL

105 E. Moore St.   457-6393
$

You may recognize the Crow's Nest's storefront from the movie "Crimes of the Heart" starring Sissy Spacek. It was in the wake of that filming that local natives Rodney and Cathy Potter Melton opened this casual little eatery boasting Southport's "finest hamburgers and hot dogs," a believable claim in a locale dominated by seafood restaurants. You can have your burger any number of ways, enjoy a fresh local fish sandwich ($2.75) or have one of the several vegetarian offerings. It's not hard to enjoy a decent meal here for less than $4 a person. Top off your lunch with an apple turnover a la mode ($1.19) or a milk shake. The fast-food outlets on the outskirts of town sell poor approximations of what the Crow's Nest does best and with mostly fresh ingredients. Call-in orders are welcomed. The Crow's Nest Grill is open 10 AM to 7 PM Monday through Friday and 10 AM to 5 PM Saturday.

LUCKY FISHERMAN

4419 Long Beach Rd. SE
(Hwy. 133)   457-9499
$

Owned and operated by the Wells family, this lively establishment offers a huge all-you-can-eat seafood buffet every night from 5 to 10 PM for a mere nine clams (children 12 and under, $3.95). There are usually more than 30 hot items to choose from, made from old low-country recipes modified to accommodate low-cholesterol and reduced-sodium diets. The salad and dessert bars are equally impressive, and nightly specials keep the offerings varied. Entrees are available a la carte and include fresh fried or broiled fish, lobster tails, crab legs and steaks. Early bird specials and senior citizen discounts are available. A separate children's menu offers popular kid-sized meals for under $3. Lucky Fisherman is open every day and accepts take-out orders. Reservations and special parties are welcomed.

THE PHARMACY
110 E. Moore St.   457-5779
$$$

Consensus indicates that, while there is room for improvement in the Pharmacy's menu offerings, the ambience is hard to beat. This quality establishment exudes old-world style, from the green awning, potted flowers and benches outside, through the splendid arched doors and into its cozy interior. Green trim adds to the warmth of the bare brick walls, embossed tin ceiling, soft old-fashioned lighting, old signs and artwork. The menu emphasizes steaks, seafood and prime rib, with burgers and a good selection of soups also represented. The British Beef and Dip ($5.25) is a worthwhile, inexpensive treat served with au jus and horse radish on the side. The Pharmacy has all ABC permits and is located next door to the Antique Mall. Its hours are 11 AM to 2:30 PM and 5 to 10 PM Monday through Saturday. It is closed Sundays.

PORT CHARLIE'S
317 W. Bay St   457-4395
$$

With a harbor view from practi-cally every seat, Port Charlie's is many insiders' first choice for quality seafood, steaks, pasta and consistently fine service in Southport. If too much fried fish has jaded your palate, Port Charlie's can revive it with a variety of salads, Cajun-spiced seafoods and meat, chargrilled steaks and sauteed veal. Situated next to Southport's yacht basin, Port Charlie's features limited screened-in porch seating and an attractively rustic dining room, as well as docking facilities for customers (come by boat!). Free snacks are occasionally served in the Marker One Lounge that also offers darts and a juke box. Port Charlie's possesses all ABC permits, serves dinner seven days, 5 to 9:30 PM, during the summer and provides ample free parking and senior citizen discounts.

THE ROUND TABLE
St. James Plantation   253-7495
Hwy. 211
$$$

This is a place for long, leisurely, multi-course feasts savored beneath a high chandelier and served by an attentive, tuxedoed staff. With years of high-end food-service experience accumulated in New York, Hilton Head and other cities, proprietors Mark and Janet Coster are adept at devising elegant repasts. Expect to find escargot, caviar and paté among the appetizers. A regular dinner menu is offered on Fridays and Saturdays for which reservations are required. Among its offerings are roast stuffed pork loin with apple cider raison sauce, grilled filet mignon and boneless roast capon stuffed with chicken mousse, pimentos, spinach and prosciutto. The Costers also offer homemade desserts, a varied wine list of domestics and imports, and a veritable catalog of gourmet courses available by prior arrangement. Located in the Club House at The Gauntlet Golf & Country Club (2.5 miles from the gate house), the Round Table also serves Sunday brunch, 11 AM to 3 PM, complete with carving station. Relatively lighter lunch fare is offered Monday through Saturday. While the "medieval flair" the restaurant boasts is limited almost entirely to the names of the specialties such as Lady of the Lake and Merlin's Steak, the Round Table continues the age-old tradition of sumptuous feasting.

SANDFIDDLER SEAFOOD RESTAURANT
Hwy. 211   457-6588
$$

With its high-pitched roof, plainly set tables and nautical decor, the Sandfiddler offers rustic ambience and affordable low-country cuisine. Lunch specials, served with hushpuppies, slaw and fries, start as low as $3.75, and landlubbers will find plenty of landfood to choose from, including steaks and pit-cooked pork barbecue. Most of the regional seafood staples are available, including deviled crabs, fried fantail shrimp stuffed with crab meat, and a good selection of combination platters. Carry-out orders can be accommodated. The Sandfiddler's lunch hours are 11 AM to 2 PM Monday through Friday; 11:30 AM to 2 PM Sunday. Dinner is served from 5 to 8 PM Monday through Thursday and until 8:30 PM Friday and Saturday. The restaurant is lo-

cated on the outskirts of Southport near Rt. 87.

SEA CAPTAIN RESTAURANT AND HARBORSIDE LOUNGE
608 W. West St.   457-5075
$-$$

These two establishments are affiliated with and located next to the Sea Captain Motor Lodge near Southport's old yacht basin. The Sea Captain Restaurant serves affordable, Southern-style breakfasts and lunches in a casual atmosphere. Guests may design their own omelets. Breakfast is served weekdays 5:30 to 11 AM and until 2 PM on weekends. Egg substitutes are available for patrons on restricted diets. Lunch specialties include Cajun-style blackened treats such as beef or shrimp burgers and chicken breast, and the home-cooked lunch special of meat, two vegetables, rolls or hushpuppies. Lunch is served 11 AM to 2 PM daily. The newly re-opened Harborside Lounge serves drinks and dinner beginning at 5 PM and offers a partial view of the harbor.

THAI PEPPERS
115 E. Moore St.   457-0095
$$

Unique among the restaurants in the Lower Cape Fear, Thai Peppers demands a visit. Typical of Indochinese cuisine, Thai foods are influenced equally by China and India, so you will find familiar appetizers, soups and stir-fried entrees from China but also delicious Thai hybrids. Such Thai specialties as satay (skewered meat), ajard (cucumber salad), tom kha gai (chicken coconut milk soup), and a wide variety of stir-fries, rice and curries are available. Meals are often served with contemporary Thai music in the background. Those who shy away from curry may become true believers once they sample the several varieties offered here. The Fried Basil Leaves with Meat (chicken, beef or pork), the Stir-Fried Ginger with Meat, and the Green Curry ($6.95 each) are not to be missed. Thai food tends to be spicy, but Thai Peppers will adjust the heat of any dish to taste, avoiding pepper spice entirely if you wish. Any menu item can be prepared without meat. Founded by Voravit "Tic" Hemawong, a native of Bangkok, Thai Peppers is small and casual and offers seating outdoors. The best bargains are the Lunch Specials (appetizer, soup, entree and rice, $4.50) which change every day. Iced Thai coffee, a customary Thai beverage, or Thailand's own Singha beer are excellent accompaniments. Thai Peppers serves lunch from 11 AM to 2:30 PM Monday through Friday. Dinner is served from 5 to 9 PM Sunday through Thursday and 5 to 9:30 PM Friday and Saturday. Carry-out orders are welcomed, and reservations are recommended for parties of more than five.

Bald Head Island

THE BALD HEAD ISLAND CLUB
$$$ 457-7300

Refined yet somewhat relaxed, the Club dining room is a warm atmosphere in which to enjoy a fine selection of seafood, chargrilled steaks, pasta, poultry and fresh desserts. The wine list offers some of the better domestic vintages. The weekly gala buffet, a sumptuous fixed-price feast, is a deservedly-popular summer event for which reservations are required. Set in a building reminiscent of coastal New England architecture, the room is toned by wood, carpeting and floral wallpaper and commands a fine ocean view. No T-shirts or cutoffs are allowed, but dress shorts are permitted during the summer. Entry to the Club requires at least a temporary membership, which is included in accommodation rates for all properties leased through Bald Head Island Management, Inc. Temporary memberships may also be arranged for day-visits and group tours through the management office. The Club dining room serves dinner 5 to 10 PM Tuesday through Sunday, Memorial Day to Labor Day. It is closed for the month of January and open on weekends during February. Call for information on spring and fall schedules. Reservations are always preferred.

ISLAND CHANDLER DELICATESSEN
$ 457-7450

This is really no more than the deli counter at the Island Chandler grocery store, but the well-prepared ready-to-eat foods (cold salads, sandwiches, cheeses, seafood, etc.) can be enjoyed at the tables on the patio overlooking the marina. Be sure to ask for some plastic utensils.

RIVER PILOT CAFE
$$ 457-7390

Boasting the finest ocean view on the island, the River Pilot Cafe and its adjoining lounge serve breakfast, lunch and dinner in a more casual setting than the Club dining room. Nonetheless, the expanded wine list and fine linen provide an upscale tenor to a menu that includes soups, excellent salads and burgers, as well as daily meat and seafood specials. In summer, the Cafe serves the island's best breakfasts. It's also a superb vantage from which to view stunning sunsets over the ocean while enjoying a meal or drink. The River Pilot is open from 8 AM to 10 PM daily during the summer, and reservations are requested for dinner.

Minnie Evans Painted for Her Life

On Good Friday, 1935, a domestic servant with a fifth-grade education named Minnie Evans experienced a vision from God. Many years later she recalled, "God talked to me. I didn't talk back to him, I know, but he talked to me. He gave me that guarantee: 'The light that you see shall shine around all of you.'" That day, Minnie created two small drawings filled with cryptic scrawls that resembled

Photo: Wilmington Star-News

Minnie Evans

Chinese inscriptions, runes, or even the voodoo charms. Five years passed, and her dreaming continued. Around 1940, Minnie began creating vast numbers of paintings at a relentless pace, all of them inspired by visions.

Using common media such as pencil, ink, crayon, poster paint and, in later works, oil paint, Minnie committed her dreams to paper, even on discarded U.S. Coast Guard stationery. She discovered the techniques of color, composition and form entirely on her own. Her dream world was populated by angels and demons, griffins and unicorns, but-terflies, flowers, exotic plants, rainbows and feathers. Eyes abound in her compositions, eyes within eyes. Some are winged or share more than one face. Many paintings are strongly symmetrical and have complex mandalas. In all her work, the light that she sees shines with exuberant color — pink skies, blue flowers, yellow earth. Golden sunrises and vermillion sunsets sometimes appear in the same work.

"My whole life has been dreams," she once said. Describing the creation of her painting entitled "A Dream," Minnie explained, "I just seen those prophets in the air. And they sang a beautiful song to me, not that I could

This untitled work by Minnie Evans hangs at the St. John's Museum of Art.

understand any of their words, but it was the most beautifulest song I have ever heard. And I just stood there and smiled and looked up there, and they just — they stayed there a good while, and they was singing and waving and they were talking or saying something to each other. Looked like there might have been a lot of feathers blowing, blowing, you know . . . turnin' all over and over to each other. . . . So after while they all go together and started off, and the last one that stayed, before he went up, he dropped his hand down and waved bye-bye to me and went right on up — in the air. But not any words that I understood, you know, what they said or even the song. But the beautifulest song that they sang! Very beautiful . . . . The next day I started on it [the painting] because I didn't want any of it to leave me."

To Minnie, the message of her dreams was explicit and clear: "They said, 'Draw or die!'"

"I wish all artists felt that way!" says Ren Brown with a chuckle. The Director of St. John's Museum of Art in Wilmington and a friend of the artist, Brown says that's why she painted thousands of works. "It was a forced issue, and not a pleasant issue for her to have to make these works."

One of her early visions took place in the middle of the night, explains Ren. "Angels hit her on the bottom of her feet and woke her up . . . and her shock that this is happening! At first she thinks it's one of the children that had gotten up and is being bad. But it's an angel. Then she's told that she has to do this artwork, that this is a command. . . It was such a mission that she had to take [the paintings] with her every single day, wherever she went. . . . Her son George takes her to work every day for 19 years, and she takes every one of these works with her everyday, all rolled up. Then one day she doesn't bring the works with her. He questions her and she says, 'Well, I'm not bringing them today,' with no more excuse than that. On his way there, the truck he's driving catches fire and he just gets her out alive. The cane, the coat, the lunch that she had with her, that all goes with the truck, but George just kind of whipped her out. Of course, the works would have been lost."

Minnie Jones was born in a log cabin in Long Creek, Pender County, NC, on December 12, 1892, the descendent of a Trinidadian slave whom young Minnie knew through old family stories. At age 16 Minnie married Julius Evans, a body servant to wealthy Wilmington landowner Pembroke Jones. She worked as a domestic at the Jones' Airlie estate until 1948 when she became gatekeeper at Airlie Gardens. There, Minnie would draw and paint, often piling her paintings around the gate. She sold them to visitors for as little as 50 cents apiece.

"If you bought one, she was so thrilled that you liked them, she gave you two, " Brown says. Some people used them as postcards. She was most prolific, especially in the 1950s and 60s. Minnie never counted or dated her works, producing literally thousands of pieces during her lifetime. Her work tapered off as she grew into her 80s and shows some loss in technical ability. But, says Ren, "her use of color and composition make up for it."

In 1962 she was discovered by photographer Nina Howell Starr who brought Minnie and her paintings to New York City. Minnie's artwork has since been exhibited at the Whitney Museum of Art, the American Museum of Folk Art and the Museum of Modern Art in New York; The Smithsonian Institution in Washington; the Portal Gallery in London; the Los Angeles County Museum; the North Carolina Museum of Art in Raleigh; the St. John's Museum of Art in Wilmington and dozens of other museums and galleries. In 1983, nine years after failing health ended her employment at Airlie Gardens, a short film entitled "The Angel That Stands By Me" preserved not only Minnie's voice and personal warmth but also vignettes of her three sons and her mother, who died soon after filming at age 102. In 1986 the stage production "Praise House," based largely on Minnie's experience premiered at the Spoleto Festival then came to Wilmington's Thalian Hall to coincide with an exhibit of her work here. St. John's Museum of Art now possesses 13 original masterpieces by Minnie Evans, Wilmington's most famous artist.

She is called an "outsider artist" because she learned and practiced her craft outside mainstream academic art circles. She is not considered a folk artist, but simply a visionary whose work is informed by her heritage, her dreams and her deep religious feelings. Although she escaped being labeled an eccentric or a crackpot suffering hallucinations, her family was somewhat reticent about her zeal, masking perhaps a tinge of embarrassment or fear. Only her son George accepted her completely. But even Minnie was quick to admit, "My art is as strange to me as it is to others."

Minnie Evans died in Wilmington in 1987. A traveling retrospective exhibit of her work is due to visit Wilmington in 1996.

Inside
Accommodations

Accommodations on the Cape Fear coast vary widely in price, style and amenities. The widest selections are available in Wilmington and Carolina Beach. Bed and breakfasts, resort hotels, efficiency apartments and simple motel lodging abound, offering visitors styles to match their personalities, interests and budgets.

Recalling the days when a candle in the window was a symbol of welcome, many bed and breakfast innkeepers in the region continue to adorn their windows according to tradition — even if the candles today are electric — and preserve the ancient code of hospitality by welcoming travelers into their homes. It's the personal touch of the innkeeper that stamps each B & B with its individual character. Some are as casual as a pajama party. Others are like museums filled with antiques and steeped in Victorian elegance. Most B & Bs do not allow pets, smoking indoors or very young children (unless by prior arrangement). The innkeepers are generally knowledgeable about the area and will assist their guests in making reservations for shows, meals, charters and golf packages, or just by answering questions. Many B & Bs make picturesque settings for weddings, receptions and small meetings, and most

provide corporate discounts. Bed and breakfasts attract people who enjoy people. Guests should respect the fact that they are staying in the homes of their hosts. What develops at the breakfast table is the magic of the B & B. Long talks after meals frequently blossom into long-term friendships, and the return rate of B & B guests is remarkably high.

Full-service resort and business hotels are strategically located in desirable areas such as Wilmington's riverfront and on the beach strand at Wrightsville Beach. In the smaller towns such as Surf City, Carolina Beach, Yaupon Beach, etc., lower-priced oceanfront motels are more common. In Wilmington, the "motel strip" is Market Street west of College Road with some overflow around the intersection of College Road and New Centre Drive. Motels of every price range are there, from the budget Motel 6 to the relatively pricey Ramada. Carolina Beach practically teems with small, family-run motels concentrated within a small area. No fewer than 15 motels line Carolina Beach Avenue North within 1/3 mile north of Harper Avenue. In general, beach motels, especially the older ones, are not known for their stylish decor, just great locations.

Accommodations on Bald Head Island consist of real estate rentals, some available for stays as short as a weekend. But there are no hotels or motels. For information on rental property on Bald Head, see the chapter on Vacation Rentals.

We have listed here a cross-section of accommodations — inexpensive and expensive, elegant and down-scale, busy and peaceful. Of course, there are many more than what's listed. But what they all share is the kind of quality we feel comfortable recommending to our own friends and family.

Rate Guidelines

Since prices are subject to change without notice, we provide the following guidelines to make comparison shopping easier. This system is based on double occupancy per night during the summer but does not reflect state and local taxes. Most establishments offer lower rates during the off-season. Always confirm rates and necessary amenities before reserving your accommodations. It may also pay to inquire about corporate, senior or long-term discounts where applicable, even if such discounts are not mentioned in the descriptions below. Most establishments accept major credit cards — Visa, MasterCard, Discover and, increasingly less frequently, American Express — and personal checks (especially when making payment in advance). Be aware that cancellations, even when made with the required notice, may incur an administrative fee, although you'll find most innkeepers in the region to be reasonable and fair.

$25 to $52	$
$53 to $75	$$
$76 to $99	$$$
$100 and up	$$$$

Wilmington

CATHERINE'S INN ON ORANGE
410 Orange St.	251-0863
$$	(800)476-0723

Catherine's Inn is one of the best bed and breakfast bargains available. The Italianate home, built in 1875, stands behind a picket fence in the shade of a live oak in the heart of Wilmington's historic district, less than five blocks from the Cape Fear River. In the Victorian parlor opposite the fireplace a piano stands awaiting musically gifted guests. The four elegant bedrooms are meticulously maintained and cozy, each with fresh flowers, local artwork and a complimentary liqueur at bedtime. Every room has a fireplace, telephone, king-size or double bed and private bath (two with claw-foot tubs.) Bedside step stools for the high four-poster in the large Lounsbursy Room add a touch of traditional convenience. The Corporate Room is favored by business people for its intimate scale and desk space.

Coffee is delivered to each room before breakfast, which is always a delicious, hearty affair graced by homemade fruit syrups, fresh-squeezed juices, silver and crystal. Innkeeper Catherine Ackiss serves at a long table that is positioned in the high-ceilinged dining room at a curious angle — the idiosyncratic

touch of a charming hostess who has been unofficially adopted as mother by many a repeat guest. Complimentary beer and wine are always available. A minimum 72 hours notice is required for cancellations.

COAST LINE INN

503 Nutt St.   763-2800
$-$$$

If motels could be elegant, the Coast Line Inn might be a model. Located on the Riverwalk at one end of the historic Coast Line Center, the Inn has 50 warmly-decorated rooms, each one with a river view. The decor is rich and masculine — deep colors, antique art prints — and the rooms are meticulously well-maintained. Complimentary continental breakfasts are placed in baskets outside the rooms, if desired, and laundry service is available. The Rivers Edge Lounge on the fourth floor is a great place to enjoy a sunset or live entertainment on Wednesday and Friday nights. The lounge opens at 5 PM Monday through Sat-

urday. The Coast Line Inn is within easy, safe walking distance of many fine restaurants and the Greater Wilmington Chamber of Commerce. Computer/modem hookups are also available.

COMFORT INN EXECUTIVE CENTER

151 S. College Rd.   791-4841
$$-$$$ *(800)444-4841*

The Comfort Inn, although considered "budget" accommodations, provides excellent amenities for the price. It is a 146-room facility located midway between downtown Wilmington and the beach. Laundry and valet services, complimentary beverages in the lobby lounge, free local phone calls, outdoor pool and a Nautilus center contribute to the Comfort Inn's appeal. Continental breakfasts and daily newspapers are available each morning in the lobby, and there is no extra charge for children under 18 staying with their parents. There are also rooms specifically designed for handicapped guests. If you forget any personal toiletries, the Inn will provide them free.

THE CRICKET INN

4926 Market St.   791-8850
$-$$ (800)274-2537

Offering weekly and monthly rates, the AAA-approved Cricket Inn is a good budget bargain. Free local calls, complimentary continental breakfast, satellite TV and an outdoor pool are available, and children under 18 stay free when lodging with an adult. Nonsmoking rooms, handicapped access and use of a copy machine are also provided. The 123 rooms have exterior entrances convenient to parking.

GRAYSTONE INN

100 S. 3rd St.   763-2000
$$$-$$$$

If Bellamy Mansion stands as the epitome of Civil War-era elegance, Graystone Inn must be its 20th-century successor. This palatial mansion, built in 1906, is the most imposing structure downtown, a historic landmark with a semicircular Ionic portico rising almost three stories. The vast interior spaces are models of restrained decor punctuated by antique treasures, many older than the house itself. The study, where cable TV is available to guests, is a masterpiece of masculine warmth paneled entirely in mahogany and graced by a marble fireplace. The stark Chinese-influenced music room boasts a baby grand piano and luxurious Chinese Chippendale settees. From the foyer, a grand Renaissance-style staircase, made of solid hand-carved red oak, rises three stories with terrace landings on each floor. The stairs culminate in the former ballroom, now a recreation room featuring a century-old Brunswick billiard table. Innkeeper Wanda Cranford also extends this incomparable setting to wedding parties, banquets, corporate meetings and film shoots. Ms. Cranford creates varied full American breakfasts on weekdays and continental repasts on weekends. Breakfasts are served on silver trays in the enormous formal dining room. Beverage service is available throughout the day. At night, wine and sherry are offered, and occasionally you'll find homemade desserts.

Each of the five rooms is as large as many suites in four-star hotels. All have private full baths and come with every modern amenity, including separate telephone lines and central air conditioning. Intercoms between rooms are a special convenience to large parties and corporate guests. Graystone Inn is ideally located for walking to all of downtown Wilmington's attractions. Cancellations require 48 hours notice.

Insiders' Tips

Downtown Wilmington has a dozen bed and breakfast accommodations.

A peg-legged fowl in flight.

THE GREEN TREE INN

5025 Market Street   799-6001
$ (800)225-ROOM (7666)

Centrally located between the beach and downtown Wilmington, the Green Tree Inn is an extremely affordable 123-room motel located just minutes from fine restaurants and attractions. Free American breakfasts are provided on weekdays at the Ramada, and golf packages and laundry service can be arranged. Rooms feature cable TV (with HBO and ESPN) and children may stay free with parents. A major appeal is the adjoining Yellow Rose Saloon, Wilmington's premier country music club, where patrons can enjoy live entertainment on weekends, dancing and dance lessons most days, and free buffets on Tuesdays and Wednesdays. Cover charges fro admission to Club Rio and the Yellow Rose Saloon are waived for guests. The Green Tree Inn offers group rates, handicapped-accessible and nonsmoking rooms, check-cashing services and kitchenettes. Ice, vending machines and newspapers are readily available.

HAMPTON INN

5107 Market St.   395-5045
$$ (800)HAMPTON (426-7866)

The Hampton provides its guests with an outdoor pool in season, coffee 24-hours a day and a free continental breakfast. The 118 rooms conform to national-chain standards, and there are meeting facilities for up to 25 people. The Hampton operates according to a 100-percent-satisfaction-guaranteed policy. Guests with a sweet tooth will find the hotel's proximity to Dunkin' Donuts either a blessing or a curse.

WILMINGTON HILTON

301 N. Water St.   763-5900
$$-$$$$ (800)HILTONS (445-8667)

Situated directly on the Riverwalk, the Hilton is downtown Wilmington's premier full-service hotel and corporate meeting cen-

Photo: Curtis Krueger

ter. Every one of its 178 rooms and suites overlooks the Cape Fear River and the Battleship *North Carolina*. On Friday evenings in the summer, the outdoor pool deck is the scene of live-music parties known as the Sunset Celebration. Complimentary beverages are served to guests on the Concierge Level in the evenings and in-room continental breakfasts are included. The guest rooms meet the Hilton's typically high standards and include terry robes. Compton's on the Riverwalk is a fine restaurant and lounge featuring grilled steaks, fresh seafood, a wide selection of domestic wines and Sunday brunch. The workout room and whirlpool are popular amenities. There is no charge for children, regardless of age, who share rooms with their parents. Eleven meeting rooms, including the Grand Ballroom, can accommodate up to 800 persons with full food service. Courtesy vans are available as well as various other amenities and services.

HOLIDAY INN

4903 Market St.   *799-1440*
$$-$$$

With 230 guest rooms, this is Wilmington's largest hotel, providing full-service amenities, such as coffee and newspapers, each morning. Other amenities include guest laundry and valet service, room service, a courtesy van, banquet space (up to 100 people), a restaurant and lounge on premises, cable TV and the chain's "Forget Me Not" program that provides personal toiletries to guests who forgot their own. The Holiday Inn boasts an outdoor Olympic-size swimming pool and the popular dance club, Motions, next door.

HOWARD JOHNSON PLAZA-HOTEL

5032 Market St.   *392-1101*
$$-$$$ *(800)654-2000*

Featuring all the standard amenities of this national chain's full-service hotels, the Plaza is located 3 miles from downtown and 7 miles from Wrightsville Beach. It is especially well suited to corporate travellers, having courtesy airport transportation, telephone-computer jacks in the 124 guest rooms, available office equipment and meeting facilities accommodating up to 500 people. Other amenities include an indoor heated pool and whirlpool, sauna, fitness center, laundry and valet service, premium cable TV, electronic card lock room keys, three suites and a full-service restaurant-lounge adjoining the main building.

THE INN AT ST. THOMAS COURT

101 S. Second St.   *343-1800*
$$$$ *(800)525-0909*

The St. Thomas is a wonderfully-designed and sophisticated accommodation located just two blocks from the Cape Fear River. The forthright decor of the rooms ranges from country French to Southwestern to antebellum and embraces tasteful artwork, replica antique furnishings, handsome rugs over wide-planked floors and modern conveniences. Some rooms are fully equipped with kitchenettes and washer/dryers and are suitable for long stays. Wet bars and microwaves are available in others. The recent addition of a small fourth building bordering the gar-

JAMES PLACE
Bed & Breakfast

Located in historic downtown Wilmington;
just a short stroll from
waterfront dining & shopping.

Start the day with elegant coffee,
followed by a delicious full breakfast
in the dining room.

After a long day, enjoy a relaxing dip in
the hot tub located in our private courtyard.

Nine South 4th Street
Wilmington, NC 28401
(910) 251-0999
J.W. Smith, Proprietor

---

den court brings the number of units to 34. Second-floor terraces have comfortable chairs for each room. Ample off-street parking is available. The attentive staff can arrange golf and tennis packages and clinics, sailing charters and lessons, and secretarial services.

JAMES PLACE
9 S. 4th St.   251-0999
$$

A stay at James Place is like a visit with your favorite uncle. Innkeeper Jim Smith maintains an extremely casual atmosphere, with TV, telephone and radio only in the common rooms downstairs and eclectic, unpretentious decor throughout his turn-of-the-century B & B. A full breakfast is served to all guests together in the dining room at 8:30 AM (Jim admits meal time is negotiable) with soft classical music on the stereo. The three guest rooms are plain and comfortable, each with two robes in the closet and central air conditioning. Candies, reading

material and beverages are available outside the rooms. There are two bathrooms upstairs, one being semiprivate, but Jim can usually accommodate special needs. An outdoor hot tub is available in the enclosed courtyard. Off-street parking is ample. Cancellations require seven days notice.

MARKET STREET BED & BREAKFAST
1704 Market St.   763-5442
$$ (800)242-5442

Jo Anne Jarrett's large, prewar brick home is blessed with more than an acre of well-kept grounds and solid construction, which contribute to the surprising level of indoor quiet despite being at a very busy midtown crossroads. The off-street parking in rear is a boon, and guests are supplied with a house key to come and go as they please. One of the three nicely appointed rooms is a two-room suite with four-poster bed and lace canopy. Ruffles, lace curtains, tiled private baths and area rugs are all tastefully done. The cozy top-floor room is popular among honeymooners (despite the twin beds). The full breakfast (home-made breads and muffins, meat and eggs) is not served in the rooms. Rather, it is formally served in the dining room. Television and snacks are available in the summery ground-floor sun room. For private phone calls, a booth is available near the foot of the beautiful ter-raced staircase. Furnishings are con-temporary and of a high quality, but the home is not museum-like regardless of the full-size spinning wheel in the living room. The grounds are verdant in summer with ferns, flowering vines and dog-woods. Mrs. Jarrett requests ten-day notice for cancellations. Corporate discounts are available.

McKay-Green Inn

312 S. 3rd St.   *762-4863*
$$$-$$$$

Innkeeper Jeff Youngblood's love for his work is as obvious as his love for antiques. With partner Kory Brimmer, he has crafted a AAA-rated bed and breakfast of lavish adorn-ments, formal perfection and full-service amenities for visitors who appreciate the finer things. Located within walking distance of everything downtown, the historic McKay-Green residence exhibits Italianate and Queen Anne architectural de-

tails. Outside, brick paths loop around fountains beneath the two-story front porch. Period carpets, bay windows and two fine sitting rooms lend an air of bygone grace. A full Southern breakfast by candle-light is served in the formal dining room or on the porch outside each room on request. Services provided by Jeff and an attentive evening host-ess include continuous beverage ser-vice, light hors d'oeuvres and assis-tance with booking reservations, tee-times for golfers and private boat charters.

Each of the four rooms features fully-stocked private baths; one bath is within the guest room itself, in the European tradition. The Victo-rian rooms are all furnished with authentic period pieces, including magnificent bedroom suites with hand-carved headboards, welcom-ing settees and armoires. Ice buck-ets with sparkling water, compli-mentary mints, and fireplaces con-tribute to the air of elegance. Rates fluctuate seasonally. Corporate and long-term discounts are available. Cancellations require a minimum 48 hours' notice.

Ramada Inn Conference Center

5001 Market St.   *799-1730*
$-$$

Full services and affordability make the Ramada an excellent

choice for businesspeople and tourists alike. Situated about midway between downtown Wilmington and Wrightsville Beach, the 100-room establishment provides top-notch amenities in keeping with corporate-chain standards. These include airport transportation, room service, valet and laundry service, color cable TV with HBO and an outdoor pool. Most beds are doubles, with king beds optional, and the spacious rooms include lounge chairs and writing desks. An executive suite features a board room with refrigerator and wet bar, conference table and adjoining rooms. The Ramada can accommodate banquets for up to 150 people and offers 3,000 square feet of meeting space. There is no charge for children under 18 staying with parents. The adjoining Club serves full dinners seven days a week, and is among Wilmington's more popular mature nightspots, featuring karaoke, top-40 dance music, salsa music on Sundays and shagging.

SAVAGE-BACON HOUSE
114 S. 3rd St.   763-1338
$$$

Still in the midst of renovation, this B & B is distinguished by ornate marble fireplaces (non-functioning) in every room, leaded glass details, pocket windows on the ground floor, high ceilings and large backyard with an Ionic-columned pergola. The building (c. 1850) is classic Greek Revival, with a wraparound front porch and a handsome interior staircase with pulpit landing. Downstairs rooms include a parlor with a vintage upright piano, a large common dining room with egg-and-dart moldings and an extra half-bath. A semi-formal full breakfast is served in the dining room or in the garden. Of the three guest rooms (king, queen or full beds) one has a private bath and all are furnished simply and tastefully. A 24-hour cancellation notice is required.

TAYLOR HOUSE INN
BED AND BREAKFAST

14 N. 7th St.   763-7581
$$-$$$$ (800)382-9982

This stately home's unassuming exterior conceals an interior of surprising grandeur. Built in 1908, the Taylor House was acquired two years ago by innkeepers Ray Higgins and Jim Long. The home is blessed with vast ceilings, enormous rooms, rich oak woodwork, parquet floors, ten fireplaces (two are regularly used) and a magnificent open staircase. Downstairs, a library with a century-old rosewood baby grand piano, and a separate parlor, offer ample room to relax with the nightly wine and cheese socials offered by the innkeepers. Ray's full English and American breakfasts are served by candlelight with Waterford crystal, linen napkins and bone china. The dining room is adorned with unusual antique furnishings and art objects.

Of the five large bedrooms, two comprise a suite decorated with English and Oriental touches. A decanter of sherry is set in every room. Each room has a large private bath, most with antique tubs. Furnishings exude warmth and tradition: mirrored armoires, Chesterfield sofas, and four-poster beds.

Convenient to downtown Wilmington, the Taylor House is located on a brick-paved street just off Market Street. Discounts apply to stays of three nights or more. A seven-day notice is required for cancellation.

THE WORTH HOUSE

412 S. 3rd St.   762-8562
$$$-$$$$

The Worth House is an impressive Queen Anne-style turreted house, scrupulously restored, with a wraparound front porch and classic cast-iron fence in front. The interior exhibits a tastefully simple elegance distinguished by lace, oak wainscots and floral motifs. Special touches are provided by working wood-burning fireplaces used during the winter months in each of the five guest rooms, complimentary beverages appropriate to the season (delicious iced drinks in summer, warm drinks in winter), fax, and a large backyard with ponds and herb gardens. Innkeeper Sharon Smith occasionally surprises guests with fresh-baked treats. Full homemade breakfasts are sumptuous, beautifully presented, yet informal and may be enjoyed in one's room, in the dining room, or anywhere else on the premises, including the verandas and gardens. Guest rooms are large, some graced with four-posters, and each has a private bath. Ask about the Azalea Room with its private glassed-in veranda, or the Hibiscus Room with a breakfast nook nestled in the corner turret. The Worth House welcomes children over 8. Cancellations require seven days notice.

Wrightsville Beach

BLOCKADE RUNNER RESORT HOTEL
275 Waynick Blvd.   256-2251
$$$$

The Blockade Runner is a top-quality oceanfront resort. All rooms have water views, either oceanfront or soundside, and are bright and comfortable. Amenities include beach furniture for guests, a complete health spa, and the fine Ocean Terrace Restaurant, which hosts the Comedy Zone on Thursday evenings. The oceanside deck has a tropical feel with its Quarter Cabana Bar adjoining the heated indoor/outdoor pool and the beach access. Complete room service, tennis and bicycles are available, and a sailing center on Banks Channel offers various water craft rentals and lessons for which packages can be arranged. Children's activities and golf packages are also available. Conference facilities and banquet services make the Blockade Runner appealing for corporate and large social events.

HOLIDAY INN WRIGHTSVILLE BEACH
1706 N. Lumina Ave.   256-2231
$$$$

From the private balconies, every room has at least a partial oceanview. This oceanfront Holiday Inn boasts the island's largest pool and patio deck (complete with Tiki Bar) with live entertainment on weekends from Memorial Day to Labor Day. The Oceanside Cafe serves breakfast, lunch and dinner and provides room service. Children under 18 stay free when they share a room with their parents. Discounts and special programs are offered to seniors, frequent business travelers and corporate accounts.

ONE SOUTH LUMINA MOTEL
1 S. Lumina   256-9100
$$$$ (800)421-3255

This is among the rare efficiency motels fitted with full-size appliances, including washer and dryer, rather than the motel-size appliances standard elsewhere. Balance this with the fact that One South Lumina is a small establishment with only 21 rooms, each a one-bedroom suite with queen-size bed. Oceanfront suites are slightly pricier than oceanview suites, and all are rented by the night or week during the summer. Monthly rentals are available during the off-season. Utilities costs are extra and 48 hours notice is

Appreciate the value of shoes at the beach. The asphalt is very hot; there are sandspurs; and daysailing in Banks Channel is often over oyster beds.

Insiders' Tips

• 83

requested for cancellations.

SHELL ISLAND RESORT HOTEL
2700 N. Lumina Ave.   *256-5050*
$$$$ *(800)8456701*

Shell Island — the building complex itself — is operated by two separate rental management corporations that handle reservations separately. The exact number of units managed by either company varies from time to time. But all of the 169 rooms are privately owned and rented to hotel guests by the corporations on the owners' behalf. Place inquiries with both corporations when seeking a rental and compare. The facilities are the same and well worth looking into.

Situated at the quiet north end of Wrightsville Beach, Shell Island is an all-suite hotel, and every suite has an ocean view. Each suite can accommodate six persons and consists of a living area with a queen sleeper sofa, a bedroom with two double beds, one full and one half bath, a kitchenette and a small balcony. While not extremely spacious, the suites are comfortable. A wide array of services is provided, including baby sitting, bell staff, a courtesy van, pool deck services, room services and valet. Lunch may be enjoyed during the summer season beside the two pools (one indoor and one out). Sauna, whirlpool, health club, convenience store, cable TV, public fax and conference facilities add to Shell Island's comprehensive package. Captain Tony's Blue Marlin Restaurant & Bar offers a commanding view of the ocean and serves a varied menu of seafood and meats in a nautical atmosphere. The Kids Club provides activities for children on and off the premises, including educational field trips. Shell Island Resort is approved by AAA and AARP and welcomes guests by the night or with a variety of package deals for longer stays.

SHELL ISLAND ALL-OCEANFRONT SUITES
Wrightsville Beach   *256-8696*
$$$$ *(800)689-6765*

All facilities are the same as described above, but reservations for an average of 115 suites are handled separately. Yes, it is confusing, but what's a little confusion compared to 3,000 beautiful feet of private beach and excellent resort amenities?

SILVER GULL MOTEL & APARTMENTS
20 E. Salisbury St.   *256-3728*
$$$-$$$$ *(800)842-8894*

Situated directly on the beach near Johnny Mercer's pier at one of the most popular beach accesses, all 32 rooms at the Silver Gull have at least partial, if not full, oceanviews. The decor is down-scale basic, but the rooms are comfortable and the

Insiders' Tips

There's a lot to watch downtown at night, especially on weekends when all kinds of people show up for the evening.

management attentive. Each room is equipped with a small kitchenette, cable TV, private balcony, room-controlled heat and A/C, and phones. Daily maid service is provided. Rooms with connecting door and roll-away beds are available. Shaded parking is limited, but coffee isn't. Cancellations require 24-hour notice.

SUMMER SANDS MOTEL

104 S. Lumina Ave.   256-4175
$$$$

This is a comfortable 32-room efficiency motel located in the heart of "downtown" Wrightsville Beach within a short walk of restaurants, shopping, laundry facilities and the strand. Guest rooms all have balconies, and the ones facing Banks Channel (the sound) provide the better view, especially at sunset. During the summer guests enjoy the enclosed outdoor pool. Monthly stays are available off-season only.

SURF MOTEL SUITES

711 S. Lumina Ave.   256-2275
$$$$

Calling itself the first and largest "motelminium" on the island and open year round, the Surf has offered resort-quality accommodations since 1981. All 45 rooms are two-room suites with separate bedrooms, full bath, dining areas, queen-size sleeper sofas, cable TVs, telephones and private oceanfront balconies. Amenities include an outdoor pool and sun deck on the oceanside of the building, full maid and linen service and a conference room. Commercial rates are available.

Carolina Beach

ATLANTIC TOWERS

1615 S. Lake Park Blvd.   458-4844
$$$$ (800)458-8313

This ten-story resort-style motel offers comfortable (if somewhat small) suites with attractive feminine decor, separate bedrooms and new full kitchens. Each suite can accommodate six to eight guests. In some rooms, built-in bunk beds increase sleeping space. All 137 rooms are oceanfront with telephones, cable TV, private balconies, exterior terrace entrances, maid service and elevator service. The outdoor pool deck is in view of the ocean and stands beside a gazebo where guests may picnic. The very informal Sandpiper Lounge on the ground floor will provide catering service on request.

BEACH HARBOUR RESORT

309 Canal Dr.   458-4185/9937
$$$-$$$$

Consisting of privately owned time shares, Beach Harbor invites short-term guests to its clean one- and two-bedroom suites. Rooms vary, but all have balconies, living and dining areas, full kitchens, cable TV, sleeper sofas and washer/dryers. Local calls are free. There is an outdoor pool and picnic area and the parking area is shaded. Beach Harbour is directly across from Harbor Masters Restaurant & Lounge and the Carolina Beach Marina.

CABANA DE MAR MOTEL

31 Carolina Ave. N.   458-4456
$$$-$$$$ (800)333-8499

One of the most attractive and well-appointed motel accommodations in Carolina Beach, Cabana De Mar resembles a condominium complex more than a motel. Its 71 one- and two-bedroom suites are small yet pleasant, with complete furnishings, cable TV, elevator access and daily housekeeping service. Some rooms face the oceanfront and have modest private balconies. Street-side suites are the best value. Laundry rooms are available, but some rooms are equipped with washer/dryers. The motel is located within convenient walking distance of central Carolina Beach's attractions and restaurants. Seventy-two hours notice is requested for cancellations.

KING'S MOTEL
318 Carolina Beach Ave. N.   458-5594
$$-$$$$

Highly practical, if not aesthetically sophisticated, the rooms at King's include basic motel lodgings as well as fully-equipped efficiencies. (There is no division between the twin double beds and the kitchen area in the efficiencies.) All are well-maintained and sanitary and include cable TV, A/C and heat, dinettes and full bath. Many of the 42 rooms (distributed between two buildings) have oceanviews and balconies. The oceanside pool is equipped with a slide. King's is owned by the same family that owns the Surfside Motor Lodge, 458-8338, and Paradise Inn, 458-8264, down the street, both of

which offer similar accommodations and value.

SEVEN SEAS INN
130 Ft. Fisher Blvd.
Kure Beach   458-8122
$$-$$$

Entirely refurbished since it changed ownership, the Seven Seas is a family-oriented establishment now in prime form. Comprised of two buildings — one oceanfront, the other oceanview — Seven Seas offers 37 very clean, comfortable rooms. Large and small efficiencies and motel accommodations are newly carpeted and roomy. They are equipped with double beds, telephones, cable TV, individual A/C and heat, microwave ovens and sleeper sofas. The grounds are well-kept and include beautiful pool facilities with shaded cabana, benches and beautiful cactus beds. A game room is available to children and the beach is just yards away. When entering Kure Beach by the main road (2nd Avenue/Highway 421), look for the enormous agave plant on the ocean side of the road.

Topsail Island

GILLIES' BED & BREAKFAST
1507 N. Shore Dr.
Surf City   328-3087
$$

Bill and Dotty Gillies run a different kind of B & B than is typical in the region. Their home at the north end of Surf City is "a beachy thing," as Bill says, with a view of the ocean from either of their two elevated decks. Their style of accommodation is exceedingly casual, laid back to the point that they may leave guests to fend for themselves almost entirely. Or they may invite them to share meals, snacks or drinks at any old time of day, depending on the interaction established among guests. Each of the three nonsmoking guest rooms is accessible by exterior entrances and comfortably furnished in a clean, contemporary beach-house style. All have private baths. The room downstairs is equipped with what Bill calls a Pullman kitchen and queen-size bed. Guests are welcome to help themselves to beverages in the sun room, to the Gillies' bicycles and to their coolers when heading for the beach. They request that guests leave their own coolers at home, but bring their own beach towels. The Gillies provide bath towels and all else, including cable TV, a full American breakfast on weekends and lighter morning fare during the week. The Gillies do not accept credit cards and request a two-night minimum stay on summer weekends. Cancellations require a one-week notice, and long-term discounts are available.

THE JOLLY ROGER MOTEL
Foot of Flake Ave.
Topsail Beach   *328-4616*
$$-$$$ *(800)633-3196*

From rooms with one double bed each to apartment suites, the Jolly Roger offers a wide variety of room sizes and amenities. Amenities include daily maid service, cable TV, fully equipped kitchens and baths and room-controlled A/C and heat. Fully-carpeted efficiency apartments and two-room suites also feature sleeper sofas. Rooms on the second and third floors of the large new annex provide the best oceanviews and balconies (which offer no privacy), but rates for rooms facing inland are substantially cheaper. The hotel office is located at the Jolly Roger Fishing Pier next door where you can also arrange deep-sea fishing trips. A seven-day notice is required for refund of deposit.

OCEAN FRONT INN
512 S. Shore Dr.
Surf City   *328-SURF (7873)*
$$-$$$

Don't let the street-side facade of the Ocean Front discourage you. This old establishment's best side faces the ocean, and its current owners stress cleanliness, friendliness and ongoing renewal. The single-bed motel units are somewhat claustrophobic, but the two-bed units, efficiencies and suites are comfortable and convenient. The suites feature full kitchens. All the rooms are fitted with large one-way windows: you can leave your curtains open for the view, and no one can see inside. There are four buildings, two ocean-front decks with showers, handicapped accessible facilities and a game room. Weekly rates are available as are four-day packages for stays spanning Sunday through Wednesday nights. The Ocean Front is located on the quiet south end of Surf City and is open year round.

St. Regis Resort

New River Inlet Rd.   328-0778
North Topsail Shores   (800)682-4882
$$$$

Each of this resort's 225 privately-owned units offers oceanview balconies, two full baths, fully-equipped kitchens and washer-dryer facilities. One-, two- and three-bedroom suites are clean and modern, and even the one-bedroom suites can accommodate up to six people. Some include Jacuzzi. The resort comprises three seven-story buildings fronted by a private beach. Two pools are available, one enclosed by a solarium. Whirlpools, sun deck, fitness center, tennis courts, chipping and putting green and volleyball facilities will satisfy almost every style of vacation. The Topsail View Restaurant commands an unbroken island-and-oceanview from the heights of the resort, and the Quarterdeck Lounge hosts karaoke and dancing three nights a week. New River Inlet Road branches off New River Drive (Highway 210) before the high-span bridge. The Resort requires a 21-day notice for cancellations.

Sea Vista Motel

Foot of Florida Ave.
Topsail Beach   328-2171
$$ (800)732-8478

Most of the Sea Vista's business consists of regular guests. Some of the reasons for that may be its location at the quiet southern end of the island, where undeveloped tracts of land still surround the motel property, and its large, bright rooms with full-size appliances, cable TVs, balconies and individually controlled air conditioning. Within an easy walk are the Topsail Sound fishing pier and a restaurant. Since individual rooms are privately-owned, the decor and furnishings vary, so repeat guests often request certain rooms. But all 35 rooms are comfortable and clean. They consist of eight efficiencies, five mini-efficiencies and two apartments, which do not enjoy a direct oceanview. The honeymoon suite is an efficiency with private balcony perched atop the center of the oceanfront building. Discounts apply for seniors and seven-day stays, and children stay free. Cancellations require 48 hours' notice.

The Topsail Motel

1195 N. Anderson Blvd. (Hwy. 50)
Topsail Beach   328-3381
$$-$$$ (800)726-1795

Consisting of one- and two-bed oceanfront rooms with kitchenettes, two- and three-bed efficiency suites and oceanfront apartments with full kitchens (30 units in all,) the Topsail Motel offers basic motel amenities and a superb dune-front location. Ground-floor rooms have enclosed patios, and second-floor rooms a deck balcony. Rooms are equipped with cable TV and individual A/C-heating units. A lawn area with chairs and a panoramic view fronts the property and crossovers give access to the ocean. Weekly rates offering a one-night discount are available, and 48-hours notice is required for refunds. Rates are highest on weekends. The motel is located 5 miles south of the Surf City stop light.

VILLA CAPRIANI RESORT

1 N. Topsail Shores	*328-1900*
$$$$	*(800)934-2400*

Reminiscent of the grand resorts of the French and Italian Riviera, Villa Capriani is a beautifully-landscaped complex that offers on-site dining, tennis and entertainment. The building is of sand-colored stucco with terra cotta roofs and archways. Enclosed balconies overlook a multi-level courtyard featuring two ocean-front freshwater pools, waterfalls, hot tubs, tanning decks and an elevated cabana bar that offers a fine oceanview. All the privately-owned guest rooms overlook the courtyard and enjoy oceanviews as well. Guests may choose among one-, two- and three-bedroom suites, fully-appointed with full kitchens, one bath per bedroom, washer/dryer and individually-controlled air conditioning. Some rooms have sleeper sofas. The rooms are well-kept, fully carpeted and furnished in modern contemporary style. Palliotti's Restaurant is located off the courtyard opposite a handsome, small lounge where local musicians are often featured on weekends.

South Brunswick Islands

DRIFTWOOD MOTEL

604 Ocean Dr.	
Yaupon Beach	*278-6114*
$$	

This attractive two-story motel offers an oceanfront location, out-

• **89**

door pool, laundry facilities, outdoor grills and picnic tables, plus refrigerator, phone and cable TV in every room, all at reasonable cost. The second-floor verandas provide wonderful views, especially at sunset, as well as deck chairs and tables for relaxing in the ocean breeze. Recently remodeled, the Driftwood offers neat, carpeted rooms, each with its own A/C and heat, and a shared full kitchen available to all guests. Adjoining the kitchen is an outdoor play area for children. The Driftwood is open year round.

ISLAND RESORT

500 Ocean Dr.
Yaupon Beach   278-5644
$$-$$$

This motel resort provides at least partial oceanviews from most of its 22 neat rooms, plus the option of a freshwater pool and outdoor hot tub. There are ten motel rooms and eleven efficiency apartments consisting of one and two bedrooms and mini-kitchens. Amenities include laundry facilities, handicapped access, and a private oceanside gazebo with grills. The Island Resort is open all year.

SOUTH WINDS MOTEL

700 Ocean Dr.
Yaupon Beach   278-5442
$-$$$$

From singles and doubles to efficiency suites and a two-bedroom luxury penthouse, South Winds is an older, well-run mom and pop operation offering guests several options to choose from. It is ideally-situated across the street from the beach strand, the Yaupon Beach Fishing Pier and two restaurants. Rooms are quaint and equipped with cable TV, air conditioning and telephone. Some are handicapped accessible. The larger accommodations feature fully equipped kitchens, sleeping sofas and double beds. Cribs and rollaways are available at a small cost. A cabana adjoins the pool and a tennis court. An outdoor grill and picnic area are available to guests. Senior citizens qualify for discounts.

OCEAN CREST MOTEL

1411 E. Beach Dr.
Long Beach   278-3333
$-$$$

Since Wade Goin took ownership of this 30-year-old establishment, it has blossomed to become one of the premier oceanfront motels in Long Beach. Streetside rooms

The Matriarch of Ocean City Beach: Caronell Chestnut

Caronell Chestnut has something to be proud of. She and her family will forever be remembered for helping to create the first oceanfront development in North Carolina available for ownership by African-Americans: Ocean City Beach on Topsail Island. She is a woman of gracious charm, to whom a laugh comes as easily as a smile. And she laughs readily when recounting the tale of Ocean City Beach:

Photo: Bill DiNome

Caronell Chestnutt and her family helped create the first oceanfront development in North Carolina available for African-Americans.

"Back during the war years, this particular area down there called Ocean City was a tract of land that was owned by a lawyer, his name was Edgar Yow. At that time, blacks had no place on the Atlantic Ocean to live — that was during segregation — so he was interested in selling a part of that land so that blacks could have a place to own land on the ocean. He had a black client who had just come to Wilmington to practice medicine, a Dr. Gray, and this idea was given to Dr. Gray.

Well, Dr. Gray wanted to just devote all of his time to his practice. But he was a good friend of my husband, Wade H. Chestnut II, and his two brothers, who had an automobile service business here in Wilmington called Chestnut Motor Service, Inc. and Chestnut Sales and Service. The idea just stuck with my husband. Eventually my husband sold out his part of the business and was interested in developing that particular area. When he came to me to tell me about it, he carried me up there and he was talking about 'This could be the business area, this could be the residential area,' and all I could see was the sky and the water and the land. I didn't have the vision. But he had all that vision, and it has succeeded so much. We had two little boys then, one was 3 and one was 5, and all I could see was taking everything we had and investing it in this land and losing out. And what would happen to my boys? But anyway, it worked out very, very well.

We just started from scratch. There was just nothing there. It was really a forlorn place. The only way you could get over to the island was over one of these pontoon bridges. When the tide is low you go down; when the tide is high you go up. The lots at that time were so cheap, but blacks didn't have money nor the confidence in investing money because it was a new thing altogether for our race of people. We had an area called Seabreeze out of Wilmington, but that was not where you would build your homes and have land-ownership. That was the only place where we could go to have any joy. You could buy clam fritters for 5 cents and take the boat over to the ocean side. It was black-owned, and you could go down to the restaurants. But you couldn't buy land. There was a place in South Carolina called Atlantic Beach — it's now called North Myrtle Beach — but that was a very small area.

As time went on, the land was blocked off and surveyed, and we started building the homes. Well, on the land there was one tower [left from Operation Bumblebee]. So my husband remodeled the tower and opened a business there, a restaurant [the Ocean City Terrace]. There was no fishing pier at the time. In 1949 we remodeled the tower, and then we started building a home, which was the first home built in that particular section of the island. There were three homes that went up at the same time, but we got into ours first. We had to rush the contract because he was working there, and there wasn't a place to stay.

There was just one road. It didn't go all the way to [New River] inlet but just went some of the way. This one road was very narrow. It was hard to even park because you would get stuck in the sand. But we had some fun though, because we would go down as far as we could and go crabbing in the inlet. Crabbing was just great there! We just had such a good time! So the neighborhood, they would all get cars and go down crabbing, but you'd have to walk about a mile to get to the inlet where the crabs were really biting. The bad part about it was, you would catch all of these bushel baskets of crabs, but coming back, try to bring them back to the car! It was a lot of fun, but it was a lot of heavy work. But we enjoyed that.

My son says that he remembers as a little boy we were all over there, the neighborhood had filled up everything we carried with crabs — and they were continuing to bite — and I made him take off his jeans and tie the ends of them so we could bring the crabs back in them! All of that's just completely changed now because all that area's developed. St. Regis is down there and all those condominiums. It's just a different place completely. This was back in the '50s.

We now have over a hundred families in that particular area, and there's certain restrictions. We wanted no trailers in there. The whole area is just houses that have to be built from the ground up, and they have to be put on pilings so that if the storms come, at least they'll be protected.

Now in 1954, that was the big one, that was Hazel. Things were just really jumping, as the slang goes, but it just knocked us out for a while in '54. So our home, the first home that we built, was completely destroyed. The water came over and just carried everything over in the sound. We had to learn how to build, because we were not on pilings at that time, and the water just knocked it right off. We formed a council among ourselves with officers and what not, and we got our goals that we wanted for the community. And it continues to function even now. It's called the Ocean City Beach Citizens Council. That has helped a lot with the knitting together of the community.

[The community] isn't as close as it was when we started. One of the reasons is that people who started, more of us taught and our husbands would move us down there when the schools would close. The wives and children stayed from the day school closed until after Labor Day when school opened again. And that's when the community was very close together. The husbands would come in every weekend regardless of where they lived, whether Charlotte or Goldsboro, all around, but they would come every weekend after they'd go to their particular jobs. However, my husband stayed there because he had the restaurant. Now everybody goes home on Sunday night and comes back Friday night. But still we're very close.

We started a little camp there. My husband and I are Episcopalians by religion, and there was one Episcopal camp for whites up near Little Washington, but at this time in the 50s, blacks were not allowed to go there. So we had a minister who came to the church, his name was Father Edwin Kirton, and he rented for the first two years, 1953 and 54, a camp, Camp Baskerville, down on Pawleys Island. So we sent children there for the camping sessions. And in 54, when Hazel came, Pawleys Island was destroyed as well. So then my husband closed up everything and let the campers come [to Ocean City] for those weeks. He let them meet in the dining hall and fed them. They slept over in the little motel. The children hadn't any camping experiences before, and it was just a great experience for them. So as a result, the bishop provided the money; we provided the land, to build a dormitory . . . and a dining hall and a priest's cottage. It was called Camp Oceanside. The first building that was built was a chapel because we are Episcopalians, and we wanted the chapel there. This chapel was called St. Mark's Chapel at first, and then after my husband died, they changed the name to the Wade H. Chestnut Memorial Chapel. It's still there. And that's an interesting chapel because that is the only Episcopal chapel on the island, and it's an integrated congregation. Every Sunday we have a different congregation. Whether they are Baptists, Methodists, Presbyterians, whatever they are, we consider them Episcopalians on Sunday morning. After having operated for a number of years, the diocese of East Carolina, the Episcopal diocese, closed Camp Oceanside, and we had a completely new camp built down on Emerald Isle. It's called Camp Trinity.

I've seen the whole thing develop. It was black out there, black at night! But we finally got some street lights, and the community paid for them by the month. And many years later we got a telephone, and we thought we had really arrived then! We donated money for the rescue squad down in Surf City because we wanted to be covered with that and the volunteer fire department. All that came through the council. We even had Surf City's mosquito sprayer to come through because the mosquitoes were awful at that first time! They're not as bad now.

"You made your own entertainment. You just get together, but nothing structured. Dining and talking, playing cards. That was the main thing we did. We liked to have company come in, and people always enjoyed coming down to visit, spending the days on weekends. You made your own fun. The neighborhood, the closeness of the community . . . The children could play on the ocean. We'd never let our children go down to the water unless some adult was with them. All of that's changed now, but at that time, any of the children who wanted to go in the water would go to somebody's house and ask, 'Miss, would you please go down to the water so we could go in the water?' Even the cooking would be real funny. If you cooked something, you wanted to share it with a neighbor because it was just a close community. And that's some of the things that I miss now because you couldn't do that now. You have your little group of people, but it's not like it was with everybody then. 99

Caronell's husband Wade died in 1961, but not before seeing some of his dreams and hard work come to fruition. "We're just continuing to be there," she says about Ocean City. "And most of the original homeowners have passed on. There's just about, I guess, five or six of us left."

The beach community they helped organize celebrates its founding every 10th year with a gala program of activities in July and a souvenir booklet filled with congratulations, memorials and hope for the future epitomized in the smiling faces of the grandchildren of the original community members.

Caronell Chestnut has a perspective only time can give. As an educator, she is still acquainted with her first students who are now septuagenarians themselves. Throughout her life she has also found time to volunteer for service organizations while sitting on the boards of many prestigious institutions, including five different specialty hospitals, New Hanover Memorial Hospital (now New Hanover Regional Medical Center), United Way and Family Service. She remains involved in her church and the YWCA. "Born right here in Wilmington, I been here all my life. Worked here, retired here, continue to live here. I've been very, very busy," she says with a chuckle.

offer the best value for up to four guests per room. All oceanfront rooms feature private balconies, and you can choose between one- and two-bedroom units with kitchenettes or efficiencies. The carpeted rooms are clean and bright and tastefully furnished. All are equipped with in-dividually-controlled A/C and heat, cable TV and private phones. The Ocean Crest adjoins the fishing pier of the same name and the Windjammer Restaurant. The complex includes a handsome oceanfront townhouse on the premises featuring gas fireplace, two private balco-

Photo: Curtis Krueger

Nature lovers will enjoy the preservation and variety of beach flora.

nies, full kitchen, two bedrooms, laundry and 2 1/2 baths. Seven days notice is required for refunds.

GRAY GULL MOTEL

3263 Holden Beach Rd. SW
Holden Beach   842-6775
$

Don't be fooled by the low rates. This family-owned motel, the only one at Holden Beach, is very well-maintained and courteously run. Each of the 17 carpeted rooms is provided with cable TV and telephone and has easy access to the outdoor pool and picnic tables. There is one efficiency available. The Gray Gull is on the mainland side of the Intracoastal Waterway, just minutes from the beach. The office is located in the hardware store next door where anglers can also buy tackle. Cancellations require 24 hours notice.

COOKE'S INN MOTEL

I Causeway Dr.
Ocean Isle Beach   579-9001
$-$$

Cooke's offers 37 very clean rooms (three handicapped accessible) with individual A/C and heat, twin beds, telephones, refrigerators and cable TV. The outdoor pool and sun deck are situated too close to the parking lot, but with the beach only 200 yards away, it's not the number-one attraction anyway. Cooke's, a family-owned and operated business, is also convenient to dining and entertainment, some of which are within walking distance.

ISLAND MOTEL

Causeway Dr.
Ocean Isle Beach   579-3599
$$

Located above the offices of Island Realty in Ocean Isle Plaza, the Island Motel offers ten simple and neat double-occupancy rooms and one two-room suite. All have air conditioning, views of the waterway, TVs and telephones and may be rented by the night or by the week. Island Realty can also provide vacation rentals requiring stays as short as two nights in a condominium setting when the motel is booked. Nearby boat slips are also available for rent. When calling after hours, dial 579-6019.

OCEAN ISLE MOTEL

37 W. Ist St.
Ocean Isle Beach   579-0750
$$$-$$$$ (800)352-5988

This 50-room motel features private oceanfront balconies and tranquil soundside views of the marshes and Intracoastal Waterway. The outdoor pool and deck overlook the ocean and have access to the beach, while bathers can use the indoor heated pool and hot tub all year long. The carpeted rooms are carefully maintained and handsome. Each is equipped with refrigerator, cable TV and phones, and daily maid service is provided. Some rooms connect. Handicapped facilities and elevators are also available. Guests are entitled to complimentary continental breakfasts and can purchase golf packages offering a choice of play on more than 65 area courses. The Ocean Isle Motel's conference space offers quiet, "off the beaten path" facilities for business meetings.

THE WINDS
CLARION CARRIAGE HOUSE INN

310 E. Ist St.
Ocean Isle Beach   579-6275
$$$-$$$$ (800)334-3581

This oceanfront resort is an excellent choice for its range of accommodations and prices. Studios, mini-suites, deluxe rooms, one- and two-bedroom suites and separate houses are all richly-appointed and comfortable. Many have indoor whirlpools, and all have kitchen facilities. The grounds are fastidiously landscaped to resemble the tropics with palms, banana trees and flowering plants nestling a series of boardwalks and decks. The heated outdoor pool is enclosed in winter. Choose among sauna, mallet pool, outdoor jacuzzi, exercise room, ping pong, beach bocci, shuffleboard, volleyball and tennis (nearby) to pass the time. Sailboat and bike rentals are available on the premises. In addition to the wide array of honeymoon and golf packages (available on 73 championship courses,) summer programs are also provided for children. Some rooms are handicapped accessible and complimentary continental breakfasts are available.

Southport

RIVERSIDE MOTEL

103 W. Bay St.   457-6986
$

This small eight-room establishment commands an excellent waterfront view of Southport's harbor with Bald Head Island to the left and Fort Caswell to the right. Situated between the Ship's Chandler Restaurant and the Cape Fear Pilot Tower, the Riverside is one of Southport's two multiple-unit accommodations downtown. The cozy double-occupancy rooms are equipped with two double beds, microwave ovens, cable TV, refrigerators, coffee-makers, toasters and

telephones (local calls are free). The rooms are small and reasonably well-kept, and nearly everything in Southport is a short walk away.

SEA CAPTAIN MOTOR LODGE

608 W. West St.   457-5263
$-$$ (800)554-5205

The Sea Captain is the largest motel accommodation in Southport, located near the old yacht basin, just a short walk from historic Howe Street. All 96 units are modern, well-kept and equipped with a refrigerator, telephone and color TV. Accommodations include single motel rooms, efficiencies and two-room efficiency apartments with separate sleeping areas. An Olympic-size outdoor pool and shaded gazebo are centrally located among the lodge's four buildings, and there are two adjoining dining facilities: the Sea Captain Restaurant for breakfast and lunch and the Harborside Lounge, serving dinner only.

Top Secret: The Sand Spit and the Bumblebee

Everyone who spends any time at all on Topsail Island notices the towers. You can't miss them. They're concrete, painted white, about 35 feet tall and square. Some might say they're ugly — in a handsome sort of way. The locals all knew the towers had something to do with Camp Davis during World War II, but exactly what, no one was sure. Then along came resident Betty Polzer and local historian David Stallman, and before long the mystery of Topsail Island's towers became an object of hometown pride.

"It was curiosity that started what turned out to be a crazy, crazy pursuit," says Betty. "Fortunately I met up with David Stallman who had the time and wherewithal to chase the research. The thing that opened the door for us was his trip to Johns Hopkins to get some information for his book *A History of Camp Davis.*"

Prior to the war, Topsail Island was a desolate place with less than a handful of residents, something of a cooperative fishing village. Farmers on

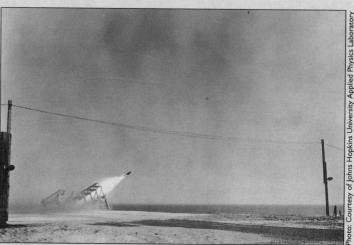

Photo: Courtesy of Johns Hopkins University Applied Physics Laboratory

A missile blasts off over Topsail Island.

the mainland were known to herd cattle across the waterway and graze them on the island where they could be watched from the tops of the dunes. There were no roads on Topsail back then, no electricity, no running water. And that wasn't so long ago!

Then the war came, and it came in a big way to Holly Ridge, a hamlet about 5 miles inland. The government leased land to build Camp Davis, an anti-aircraft training facility, and in two years Holly Ridge rocketed from 28 residents to 110,000. Nearly 1,000 buildings were erected, a complete water system installed and more than 30 miles of roads put down. One road led across an old pontoon bridge to the "Sand Spit," which was used as a test-firing range. The Sand Spit was Topsail Island.

When the war ended, the Army withdrew from Holly Ridge. Camp Davis was used briefly as a separation center for the Marine Corps and would undoubtedly have been declared surplus then, had it not been for a top secret Navy project. For several years the Navy had been conducting secret guided-missile tests at sites in New Jersey and Delaware. Before long, these sites became unsuitable. The Navy sought a new place with few residents, limited access and a firing range of 20 miles or more. The Sand Spit fit the bill on every count and the Navy moved in. Through resourceful salvaging, many of Camp Davis' buildings were reworked to accommodate nearly 500 personnel. As the East Coast Guided Missile Test Range, the island became home to as many as 200 people. This would be the proving ground for supersonic guided missiles.

The launch site was located near the southern end of the island. The launching platform, a concrete slab 75 feet by 100 feet by 1 foot thick, overlooked the ocean with crude launch ramps of wood and steel. A bomb-proof observation room with 14-inch-thick walls and a slit window stood beside it. Down an inclined roadbed coming from the platform was the control tower, and at the far end of the road stood the Assembly Building, hardened against explosions and lightning strikes. This is where the missiles took shape.

Eight observation towers were built at precise distances from one another along the island to allow precise tracking of the missiles. The towers housed photographic and timing instruments and maintained two-way radio contact with the control tower for telemetric communication. Designed to withstand vibration and heat from wind and sun, they were constructed of reinforced concrete on platforms with pilings at least 20-feet-deep. Their open frames were covered with plywood. Many other support buildings were constructed: a mess hall, sleeping quarters, repair and welding shops and a photographic lab. The entire range was completed in one year. Two patrol boats and a 65-foot cruiser made sure local fishing boats were warned of upcoming tests and that no unauthorized landings were made on the Sand Spit.

It was Johns Hopkins University's Applied Physics Laboratories that directed the project, and the rockets they tested on Topsail Island were of a new breed. The name for the project came from an aphorism hanging on the wall in a captain's office which read: "The bumblebee cannot fly. According to recognized aerotechnical tests, the bumblebee cannot fly because of the shape and weight of his body in relation to the total wing area.

Photo: Courtesy of Johns Hopkins University Applied Physics Laboratory

This rocket is being readied for transport from the Assembly Building to the launch pad..

BUT, the bumblebee doesn't know this, so he goes ahead and flies anyway." Operation Bumblebee was born.

Many rockets were two-stage, with a solid-fueled booster to send aloft the Navy's most advanced prototypes. The second stages carried radar equipment and something totally new on the scene: the ramjet engine. Some missiles were made from the 6-inch-thick tailpipes of Navy Thunderbolt airplanes and were called Flying Stovepipes. From the first firing in the fall of 1946 to the site's decommissioning in spring of 1948 more than 200 missiles were launched. They flew at speeds averaging 1500 mph in a northeasterly direction and ranged in size from 3 to 13 inches in diameter and 3 to 13 feet in length. The tests directly resulted in the development of the Terrier and Talos missiles, the Navy's first supersonic missiles.

Soon the Navy needed a larger range without the humid, often stormy weather of Cape Fear. So the project was moved to three other locations, including White Sands, NM, and Cape Canaveral, FL. Camp Davis was put into surplus, and Topsail Island was returned to landowners and developers.

It would be tidy to say, "And the rest was history," but it wouldn't have been history had it not been for Betty Polzer. She knew the Assembly Building was worth preserving, and she had the gumption to achieve it. Betty envisioned the old building as a community center, but funding the idea met with initial skepticism. Known locally as the Arsenal Center, the Assembly Building had been used as a restaurant, bar and shops.

"The place had left a bad taste in people's mouths," Betty says. "At one time it was called The Bald Pelican, a nightclub, a riotous nightclub and a noisy nightclub! And there were fights in the parking lot, and the police had to be called. We found out that IBM owned it, had taken it over for a defaulted loan. But they wanted $400,000 for it. The roof leaked like a sieve. It had been vandalized. But the building was there, solid as can be."

Town and county budgets had nothing to spare, so Betty began selling the idea to the public through her column in the *Topsail Voice*. She arranged meetings at her home. She spoke to everyone who would listen and created a wish-list of uses for the proposed community center. She worked with local historian Ed Turberg who researched the history of the building in order to propose its inclusion on the National Register of Historic Places. Architectural experts were brought in, and they were not entirely surprised to find the Assembly Building to be one of the most intact historic structures in the east.

Nonetheless, snags of all kinds cropped up. IBM threatened to wreck the building. Someone claimed asbestos was exposed inside. Others worried that there were buried explosives nearby. Negotiations with IBM resulted in a purchase agreement — provided the Topsail Historical Society and the Topsail Beach Economic Development Council (TBEDC) could prove themselves capable of affording it.

"I figured, 'I've got to go out and start begging,'" Betty recalls. "Somebody had divided it into a bunch of shops and stores. We had that all torn out. The place was filthy, the wiring wasn't safe, none of the plumbing worked. Well, I got a gathering of a wonderful group of people around here, and each one of them pressed the right button."

Electricians and plumbers brought the building up to code. Cadres of residents appeared with brooms and mops to clean. The city donated two dumpsters that were immediately filled with debris. A nearby restaurant sent beer and hot dogs. Betty smiles. "I was so thrilled! Surf City Hardware store donated 90 gallons of paint and paint brushes. The firemen said, 'Have no fear, we'll paint for you.' And this is how we went."

"One man came up to me at the first meeting I had at my house and said, 'Betty, it will never work. You're foolish, forget it.' And he fought me every step of the way. The day of the dedication, he came up to me, whispered in my ear, 'You've sold me,' and gave me a check for $500. And I respected that man because somebody's got to play the devil's advocate. We're still the best of friends."

The first event at Topsail's new community center was held in September 1992, and space is consistently booked for concerts, classes, festivals and private occasions. It plays a major part in Autumn With Topsail, TBEDC's annual festival. Betty Polzer has since passed on stewardship of the Assembly Building, now an official National Historic landmark, and it is thriving.

Eight towers remain standing in varying degrees of preservation. Three have been converted into homes. One is part of a fishing pier facility. One fell into the sea. But they aren't all that remains of Operation Bumblebee. The patio of the Jolly Roger Fishing Pier is built upon the launch pad, and the bombproof bunker is part of its motel basement. Over in Holly Ridge, the Camp Davis Restaurant occupies the camp's former Administration Building, and it, too, is now a National HistoricLandmark.

The importance of Operation Bumblebee can hardly be exaggerated. The ramjet engine is to jet aviation what the Wright Brothers' airplane was to propeller flight. So, when someone asks you about North Carolina's license plates that say, "First in Flight," remember the Sand Spit and the Bumblebee.

Photo: Scott Taylor

Two coastal residents out strolling for a bite to eat.

Inside
Vacation Rentals

There are seemingly endless opportunities for vacation home rental in the Cape Fear area. Nearly a hundred rental offices between Topsail and Sunset Beach suggest the tremendous scope of the business. From Topsail Island in the north to Sunset Beach in the south, it's safe to say that there is a vacation home for any taste and budget. Whole houses, duplexes, condominiums and apartments are readily available for families, couples and individuals.

The distinctive characteristics of each of the beaches make it easy to choose one that is just right for you. People who want some nightlife and the conveniences of a nearby city will gravitate toward Wrightsville Beach, Carolina Beach and Kure Beach. Vacationers who don't mind limited shopping and entertainment opportunities and are searching for more remote spots will head for Topsail and the Brunswick beaches. The quietest communities on the coast, without question, have to be charming Sunset Beach and beautiful Bald Head Island. For the visitor who wants to temporarily become a resident, there is no better way than to rent a home for a week or two on any of our area beaches.

Renting a home will put you inside the neighborhood. Many area beaches have year-round residents who anchor the community in ways that are comfortingly familiar. Since these are generally small communities, it doesn't take long to settle in and get to know some of the folks on each island.

Renting a vacation home is very different from checking into a hotel. There's no room service; an unmade bed in the morning will still be unmade when you get back from a romp in the surf; and there's no restaurant downstairs to call for room service. You take care of your own needs, which is actually the most fun part of this kind of beach vacation. It's your schedule, the opportunity to enjoy your own home cooking away from home and a sense of absolute privacy that simply isn't part of the hotel experience.

In most cases, vacation homes are someone's special investment, second only in importance to their regular homes. The owners may visit their homes several times a year, and it is apparent, in many cases, that the homes bear distinct imprints of the owners. There may be photo albums of the host family and guests. There will likely be a guest book of visitors.

Fitting into someone else's second home, you may discover, is an intimate experience that often leads to friendships. Despite the money that changes hands in this agreement, there is also an exchange of trust. Some of the more desirable homes develop a list of regulars, and getting into line for these can be a bit of a wait. Once on the list in a favorite spot, you'll be able to count on it for many years to come and be regarded as a member of an extended family you may never actually meet.

ACCOMMODATIONS AND LOCATIONS

You can have any kind of place you want. The only limitation is your budget. Large, contemporary homes on private lots, small cottages, ordinary apartments, comfortable condominiums, fishing trailers, middle class homes, and more are available to the renter.

Generally, the closer a place is to the ocean, the higher its price. The benefits of an oceanfront house or apartment include an unobstructed view of the ocean, a short walk for a swim in the waves and the ability to keep an eye on the kids from the house as they play on the sand.

Oceanside housing may still have a view, and you may not have to cross a road, but there may be a bit of a walk to reach the sea. Several rows back, the prices drop. The walk gets longer, and a view of the water is often just a glimpse. These locations generally have decks built on the rooftops, and there seems to be a competition among homeowners to see who can build the highest.

Soundside housing is on the Intracoastal Waterway or adjacent channels and sounds. If you have a powerboat and the house has a pier, this can be a very exciting location. Soundside housing with this amenity is a bit more expensive than housing in the center of each island.

A FEW RULES

It is important to note that vacation home rental has rules and regulations that reflect the family orientation of this kind of arrangement. The rental agency's primary allegiance is to the homeowner. The agency maintains the properties for the owners and assumes responsibility for renting homes to reliable tenants.

There is an age requirement for renting most vacation homes through real estate management companies. Generally, the primary renter must be at least 21 years old, although some companies require the primary renter to be 25. An exception to this may be marital status. If you're 24 and married, you probably qualify, but companies will differ. Individual inquiry is recommended. Some companies that don't have an actual age requirement take a long, hard look at younger customers and make decisions to rent based on what seems to be intuition.

Most rental agreements forbid house parties on the premises, especially in the quieter beach communities. Rowdiness is very much unappreciated on all area beaches, and a noisy party may cause you to forfeit your rental agreement without a refund. Most homes have a written maximum occupancy regulation, and you are required to honor it.

Photo: Scott Taylor

Do we have to go tomorrow?

PETS

Pets are not allowed. If Fido must come with you, check the service directory in this guide for the location and services of local kennels. Since your pet is not allowed on most beaches in the summer season, you might want to leave him at home in friendly surroundings. Also, please note that this region has a seasonal flea problem, which, more than anything else, dictates this policy. As a local Realtor has written in a brochure, "it only takes two fleas" to cause a flea problem in a house. If you smuggle in a pet and the housekeeping staff that follows you discovers fleas, be assured that your deposit will be used to pay for fumigation.

FURNISHINGS AND AMENITIES

In the majority of rental homes, expect to find most of the comforts of home. Most homes will be air-conditioned, will have full-service kitchens, including coffeemakers and microwaves, and will usually have cable TV.

In most cases you'll need to bring a few housekeeping items. Linens may be your responsibility; if the house has linens, you may be required to do a bit of laundry before your departure.

There is a general expectation, too, that you'll leave the house as clean as you found it. Some rental agencies will provide cleaning service and linens for a fee if you are not particularly inclined toward domestic concerns on your getaway. If you don't clean up and haven't made arrangements for maid service, your deposit will be applied toward this work. Minimally, this charge is $50.

Cleaning supplies are usually in the house because a prior vacationer bought them and left them there. It's a nice gesture on your part to do the same, even if current supplies seem ample; and it's essential for you to provide cleaning supplies if some haven't been left for you. Owners supply vacuum cleaners, mops and brooms. You are responsible for putting out the garbage — just like at home! Some beaches have recycling programs, and you'll be instructed in the event that yours does.

Most homes have telephones, and you're on your honor not to use them in any way for which the owners would be charged. If your vacation home doesn't have a telephone, most rental companies will arrange to get emergency messages to you.

RATES

Houses may run from $300 to $3,300 a week, depending upon your choice of beach, luxury factor and season. Bald Head Island has the priciest rates on average for vacation rentals, along with Figure Eight Island, followed by Wrightsville Beach. Topsail has among the lowest rates. The Brunswick Beaches are among the most reasonable in terms of overall rental rate. Most agencies will require a deposit, and there are various stipulations in the agreement with which you should familiarize yourself. A state tax of 6 percent and county room tax of 3 percent are added to the cost. Rental rates are subject to change without notice, and the following rates are only intended as a general guide. Winter rates may be as much as 30 percent less. A deposit of 50 percent is generally required to confirm reservations. Major credit cards are accepted, but other methods of payment are available depending upon the agency's policies.

The following rental agencies are among the best of the hundreds of companies from which you may choose. Select the beach of your choice, and contact the local Convention and Visitor's Bureau or local Board of Realtors for the names of other rental companies. Chambers of commerce also carry brochures about rental companies.

Wrightsville Beach

BRYANT REAL ESTATE
1001 North Lumina Avenue
Wrightsville Beach,   256-3764
N.C. 28480   (800)322-3764
This is the oldest vacation rental agency on Wrightsville Beach and it handles approximately 200 diverse properties.

INTRACOASTAL REALTY CORPORATION
534 Causeway Drive
Wrightsville Beach,   *(800)346-2463*
N.C. 28480

This company offers approximately 100 properties, from condominiums to single family homes, primarily on Wrightsville Beach.

FRAN BRITTAIN REALTY
98 Waynick Boulevard
Wrightsville Beach,   *256-2224*
N.C. 28480   *(800)362-9031*

More than 50 properties are handled by this company that rents exclusively on Wrightsville Beach.

Carolina Beach, Kure Beach and Fort Fisher

WALKER REALTY
501 North Lake Park Boulevard
Carolina Beach, N.C. 28428   *458-3388*

Carolina Beach, Kure Beach and Fort Fisher are the locations of more than 80 properties handled by this company.

CAROLINA BEACH REALTY
307 Lake Park Boulevard   *458-4444*
Carolina Beach, N.C. 28428   *(800)222-9752*

These homes and condominiums, approximately 85, are located on Carolina Beach, Kure Beach, and Fort Fisher.

UNITED BEACH VACATIONS
1001 North Lake Park Boulevard   458-9073
Carolina Beach, N.C. 28428   *(800)334-5806*

This large company manages 200 rental units including condominiums and single family homes on Carolina Beach, Kure Beach, and Fort Fisher.

GARDNER REALTY
P.O. Box 2125   *458-8503*
Carolina Beach, N.C. 28428   *(800)697-7924*

Gardner Realty offers a selection of rental properties including apartments, condominiums and single family homes on Carolina Beach, Kure Beach, and Fort Fisher.

COASTAL CONDO-LET
P.O. Drawer 2150
Carolina Beach, N.C. 28428   *458-4203*

Properties range the island from Carolina Beach in the north to Fort Fisher in the south for this larger company that handles 125 condominiums, cottages, apartments, and larger homes.

Topsail Island

LEWIS REALTY
412 Roland Avenue
Surf City, N.C. 28445   *(800)233-5211*

This small rental agency has about 20 rental properties in Surf City on Topsail Island. The properties are mainly single-family cottages.

TOPSAIL REALTY
712 South Anderson Boulevard
Topsail Beach, N.C. 28445   (800)526-6432

This large company handles 180 properties that are mostly single-family homes on Topsail Island. There are some townhouse/duplex rental units at the south end of the beach.

JEAN BROWN REAL ESTATE
P.O. Box 2367
Surf City, N.C. 28445   *(800)745-4480*

Relatively new to the vacation rental business, this small company offers about 25 diverse properties along Topsail Island.

CENTURY 21 ISLAND REALTY
200 North Shore Village
Sneads Ferry, N.C. 28460   (800)334-4848

This company handles about 300 properties located primarily on the north end of Topsail Island.

Brunswick's Oak Island:
Caswell Beach, Yaupon Beach, Long Beach

COLDWELL BANKER
SOUTHPORT-OAK ISLAND REALTY
1030 North Howe Street   278-6011
Southport, N.C. 28461   (800)243-8132

Weekly resort rentals are available through this large company that has 400 cottages, duplexes and condominiums on Oak Island.

MARGARET RUDD &
ASSOCIATES, INC., REALTORS
210 Country Club Drive   278-6523
Yaupon Beach, N.C. 28465   (800)733-5213

There are 210 rental properties managed by this company on Oak Island, most of which are single-family homes and condominiums.

RED CARPET, DOROTHY ESSEY &
ASSOCIATES, INC., REALTORS
6102 East Oak Island Drive   278-RENT
Long Beach, N.C. 28465   (800) 849-2322

Up to 400 diverse properties are offered for rental on Oak Island, in Southport, and Boiling Spring Lakes.

SCRUGGS & MORRISON REALTY
4324 East Beach Drive
Long Beach, N.C. 28465   278-5405

This company handles about 100 single-family homes and duplexes on Oak Island.

SHANNON'S SERVICES, INC.
4902 East Beach Drive
Long Beach, N.C. 28465   278-5251

The oldest rental agency on the beach, this company handles rentals of single-family homes and duplexes on Oak Island.

South Brunswick Islands:
Holden Beach, Ocean Isle Beach, Sunset Beach

ALAN HOLDEN REALTY
128 Ocean Boulevard, West   842-606
Holden Beach, N.C. 28462   (800)720-2200

This busy agency manages 375 rental properties that are mostly cottages and duplexes, as well as a few condos, on Holden Beach.

SLOANE REALTY
16 Causeway Road   579-6216
Ocean Isle Beach,   (800)843-6044
N.C. 28469

The largest and oldest vacation rental business on Ocean Isle Beach has 375 condos and cottages available.

Insiders' Tips

Keep a stock of mosquito repellant handy in the summer. Citronella candles are a must for outdoor entertaining.

CENTURY 21
ISLAND REALTY VACATIONS
Ocean Isle Plaza, Suite 1
Ocean Isle Beach, N.C. 28469   579-3599

This company offers 150 cottages and condominiums exclusively on Ocean Isle Beach.

R.H. McCLURE REALTY, INC.
24 Causeway   579-3586
Ocean Isle Beach,   (800) 332-5476
N.C. 28469

Approximately 115 single-family homes and duplexes are handled by this company on Ocean Isle.

THE ODOM COMPANY
428 Sunset Boulevard
Sunset Beach, N.C. 28468   (800) 446-3435

This company has 165 homes, all privately-owned, available on Sunset Beach. The largest house on Sunset Beach overlooking Bird Island is handled by this agency.

SUNSET PROPERTIES
419 Sunset Boulevard
Sunset Beach, N.C. 28468
In State: (800) 446-0218
Out of State: (800) 525-0182

This large company handles the rental of 215 vacation homes and duplexes exclusively on Sunset Beach.

Bald Head Island

BALD HEAD ISLAND MANAGEMENT, INC.
P.O. Box 3069   (800)234-1666
Bald Head Island,
N.C. 28461

At this writing, there are 42 rental properties on this pristine island. Each rental includes the use of one four-passenger electric golf cart for transportation around the island because cars are not allowed.

Cape Fear Coast
Camping

These ever-changing shores of Cape Fear have witnessed an epic succession of campers, including the ancient Siouan and Algonquian gatherers, whose shell middens littered the coast; the ill-fated English settlers, who were driven out by native force; and today's tourists, who play the nomad on soil once thick with plantation rice and cotton. Despite the fact that most of the finest tracts of coastline have been built over, campers can live a simpler life still — if only for a few days — here on Cape Fear amid the quiet spectacle of the bright Atlantic.

For the most part, there isn't much "roughing it" when camping here. Campgrounds nearest the beaches are generally crowded with RVs and provide ample amenities. So, if you'd like to take the kitchen sink along, you may as well take your electric bug-zapper, too. But, if you wear your home on your back and have the use of a small boat, leave the parking-lot style camping behind for the pristine isolation of Masonboro Island. In the off-season, your only neighbors could be the pelicans that nest there. Either way, camping the Cape Fear coast is ideal for visitors on a budget, anglers who want to walk to the water's edge, and anyone for whom recreation is "re-creation."

As the Boy Scouts say, "Be prepared," especially for blistering sun, sudden electrical storms with heavy downpours, voracious marsh mosquitoes and insidious "no-see-ums" in summer. Temperatures in the region generally are mild, except for the occasional frost in late-winter.

Sunscreen is essential. Hats and eye protection are wise. Be prepared for rain in any season. For tent camping, a waterproof tent fly is a must. Always pack a slicker or nylon poncho. A tarp or dining fly is handy when cooking. To withstand high wind, use longer tent stakes or specially-designed sand stakes. Stay abreast of weather reports, especially during hurricane season. Bring a radio.

To combat insects, consider mosquito netting for your sleeping and dining areas. Avon's Skin So Soft is effective for most people (not all) in warding off mosquitoes, but something more lethal is required to fend off ticks and chiggers. Cutters is a good choice. Those who shy away from chemical repellents may consider using the oil from crushed fern leaves, a moderately effective repellant used by natives of old.

Bicycle campers will find available campsites spaced about a day's ride apart, except in the Wilmington

A great lumbering live oak stands guard over campers.

vicinity where campgrounds are more numerous. A lightweight camp stove and cookset will come in handy when restaurants aren't convenient and at sites where fires are prohibited. Plan each leg of your journey in advance, and try to arrive at camp sites in daylight.

The primary animal hazard is poisonous snakes, which are prevalent in forested areas. Raccoons and other small nocturnal creatures are seldom more than a nuisance. It's wise never to feed any animal. Normally, the animals posing the greatest threat are human, which is why open fires and alcoholic beverages are restricted in most campgrounds. Beware of poison ivy, poison oak and poison sumac in brushwood and forests.

Naturally, the highest rates at private campgrounds apply during the summer and holiday weekends, averaging from about $13 to $22. Tent sites are cheaper than RV sites. Some campgrounds charge less, others more. At most private grounds, weekly rates often discount the seventh day if payment is made in advance. Monthly rentals or longer are extremely limited from April to August. Some campgrounds offer camper storage for a monthly fee.

Wilmington

CAMELOT CAMPGROUND
7415 Market St.   *686-7705*

Twenty minutes from downtown Wilmington, Camelot is better situated for getting to the local attractions than for getting away from it all. Moreover, owners Fred and Shirley St. John have endowed their establishment with plenty of its own resort quality. Camelot is Woodall-rated (the most recognized approval among private campgrounds). The tree-shaded grounds include a large swimming pool, playground, volleyball, horseshoes, outdoor stage, fishing pond, pull-throughs and separate tent sites (totalling 87), a dump station, full and partial hookups, group camping and an adjoining miniature golf course. The lodge has clean, tiled rest rooms, hot showers, a laundromat, grocery and supply store, game room and mail service. There is even a TV lounge. A convenience store and gas station near the campground entrance further add to Camelot's tourist appeal. Weekly and monthly rates are available. Reservations are accepted.

CAROLINA BEACH FAMILY CAMPGROUND
9641 River Rd.   *392-3322*

This wooded, shady, 103-site campground is conveniently situated for cyclists touring the Ports of Call Route and the Cape Fear Run. The large RV-and tent-sites are complemented by a swimming pool, hot showers, laundry, game room, a limited grocery store and easy access to many area attractions. Partial and full hookups are available as well as A/C, electric and heat. The campground is located about 1/2 mile from Highway 421 (Carolina Beach Road) on the Wilmington side of the Snow's Cut bridge.

Masonboro Island

Accessible only by boat, Masonboro Island is the last and largest undisturbed barrier island remaining on the southern North Carolina coast. It is the fourth component of the North Carolina National Estuarine Research Reserve and deservedly so. This migrating ribbon of sand and uphill terrain about eight miles in length offers the camper a secluded, primitive experience in possibly the most pristine environment left on the Cape Fear coast. It is also used by anglers, bird watchers, hunters, students and surfers (who prefer the north-end). Everything you'll need must be packed in, and everything you produce must be packed out.

Of the reserve's more than 5,000 acres, about 4,400 acres are tidal marshes and mud flats. So most folks land at the back sides of the extreme north or south ends, on or near the sandy beaches by the inlets. Pitch camp on the back side of the dunes only. While the NC Division of Coastal Management hopes to limit its involvement and preserve the island's traditional uses, it does prohibit polluting the island and camping on the front of the dune ridge.

Wildlife here is remarkable and fragile. Endangered peregrine falcons are rare seasonal visitors. Masonboro Island is one of the most successful nesting areas for loggerhead turtles (threatened) during the warm months. Piping plovers, also threatened, feed at the island in

Insiders' Tips

When hiking or camping in the Cape Fear region, check yourself and your family for ticks every day. Lime disease, which is on the rise, is not likely to be transmitted in less than 24 hours.

winter. Keep your eyes peeled on the marshes for river otters and, at low tides, raccoons. Gray foxes, cotton rats and tiny marsh rabbits all frequent the small maritime forest. The marshes, flats and creeks at low tide are excellent places to observe and photograph great blue and little blue herons, tricolor herons, snowy and great egrets, oystercatchers, clapper rails and many other flamboyant avians. Brown pelicans, various terns and gulls, American osprey and shearwaters all live on Masonboro, if not permanently then at least for some part of their lives.

Be sure to bring netting and/or insect repellent, trash bags and plenty of sun protection. Camp stoves are recommended on this windswept barrier island. Keep in mind that much of the island is still privately owned, especially the north end. The University of North Carolina at Wilmington conducts an ongoing visitor-impact study that attempts to assess the continued viability of camping here. Together, visitors' behavior and scientific scrutiny will have some influence on whether Masonboro Island is preserved or developed. For further information, see Cape Fear Coast Islands in the chapter on Attractions.

The simplest boat is adequate for getting here, especially if you approach the island from the calm sound side. If you don't have your own boat, refer to the chapter on Attractions for information on the Masonboro Island Taxi & Sunset Cruises which run out of Banks Channel at the Blockade Runner Resort Hotel.

The Beaches

CAROLINA BEACH STATE PARK
P.O. Box 475   458-8206
Dow Road, Carolina Beach, 28428

Once a campsite for the so-called "Cape Fear" Indians, colonial explorers, and Confederate troops, Carolina Beach State Park remains a gem among camping destinations on Cape Fear. Water sports enthusiasts are only minutes away from the Cape Fear River, Masonboro Sound and the Atlantic. There is a full-service marina with two launching ramps. Need we mention the great fishing? Also, 5 miles of hiking trails wind through several distinct habitats, home to carnivorous plants. The even terrain includes maritime forest, pocosin (low, flat swampy regions) and savanna. Hikers on the Sugar Loaf Trail pass over tidal marsh and dunes and along three lime-sink ponds. Cypress Pond, the most unusual, is dominated by a dwarf cypress swamp forest. The park is a bird-watcher's paradise and is home to lizards, rare frogs, and occasionally to alligators, opossums, gray foxes and river otters.

Dense vegetation lends the camp sites a fair amount of privacy. Each site has a table and grill, and sites are available on a first-come basis ($9 per site). Drinking water and well-kept rest rooms with hot showers are close by. There is a dump station for RVs, but no hookups. Ranger-led interpretive programs deepen visitors' understanding of the region's natural bounty. Unleashed pets and possession of alcoholic beverages are prohibited. The park is located 15 miles south of Wilmington, one mile north of Carolina Beach just off Highway 421 on Dow Road. From Wilmington, make your first right after crossing Snow's Cut bridge. (Also see Parks in the Sports and Fitness chapter.)

PINEWOOD CAMPGROUND

Hwy. 50   329-1618/1534
Holly Ridge

Because of its low rates and proximity to the waters around Topsail Island, Pinewood usually stays booked during the entire summer season. Anglers set up long-term camps here, so the sparsely wooded grounds are dominated by RVs and boat trailers. Weekend, weekly, monthly and yearly rates are available, as well as long-term storage. Facilities include a bath house, a fish house for cleaning the day's catch, a small game room with a pool table and video games. Extra refrigerators and freezers are for rent. Pets are not permitted. The entrance is down the 10 mph, dirt road adjacent to the Hitching Post night club, about 3.2 miles from Surf City.

ROGERS BAY FAMILY CAMPWAY

Hwy. 210   328-5781
North Topsail Beach

This colossal camp city (520 sites) is remarkable for its shaded and manicured grounds, its recreational offerings and its superb location across the road from the sparsely populated beach of north Topsail Island. Rabbits make frequent visits to the lawns and beneath the old, gnarly live oaks. Open all year, this Woodall-rated facility features a fine in-ground swimming pool, teen recreation room, playground, complete hookups, dump station, three air-conditioned bathhouses, a convenience store, propane refills, camper storage and a laundry room. A popular seafood restaurant stands directly across the road. Nearby are attractions such as miniature golf and a fine full-length golf course. Weekly, monthly and yearly stays and storage are available. Weekend reservations require a minimum two-day stay (with $10 deposit); three days are required for holiday weekends. Camp fires are prohibited, and pets must be leashed at all times.

SURF CITY FAMILY CAMPGROUND

Hwy. 210   328-4281
Surf City

All that separates Lonnie and Beulah Smith's sun-drenched campground from the beach is a dune and some buildings. Open seasonally from April to November, this location offers 72 sites suitable for RVs, mobile homes and tents. Hookups, bath houses, full rest rooms, picnic tables and a small store are among the amenities. Alcoholic beverages are tolerated when kept out of sight. Sunday church services (Baptist) take place on the beach. The owners welcome holiday stays, recommending reservations at least one month in advance. Surf City Family Campground is well situated for taking advantage of all that central Topsail Island has to offer. The off-season mailing address is Route 1, Box 254, Holly Ridge, NC 28445.

Long Beach Family Campground

5011 E. Oak Island Dr.   278-5737
Long Beach

Boasting access to the beach and the active night life of east Oak Island, and located just minutes from historic Southport, this campground is understandably popular all year. Few of the 157 sites enjoy any shade, but the separate tent area is grassy and commonly hosts foraging sea birds. Full and partial hookups are available, as are flush toilets, hot showers, sewage disposal, tables, public phone, ice, and seasonal lease sites. Look for coupon discounts, good for weekday stays, at the campground office and various tourist information locations.

Holden Beach Pier
Family Campground

441 Ocean Blvd. W.   842-6483
Holden Beach

Why these 55 sun-baked sites remain jammed all summer with campers living cheek-to-jowl may be explained by their location next to Holden Beach Pier. This campground is recommended to budget

vacationers who insist on living at the beach and nowhere else. All sites have water, electric hookups and shaded tables, and the grounds essentially comprise an RV village. Pets on leashes are allowed. The adjacent Holden Beach General Store is a full-service grocery and beach-supply store.

Campground by the Sea

1113 Ocean Blvd. W.   842-6306
Holden Beach   (800)822-0948

Stretching from the beach strand to the Intracoastal Waterway, Campground by the Sea succeeds on all counts as a place the entire family can enjoy at an extremely modest price. The 159 treeless sites located 4.5 miles west of the Route 130 high span are well-maintained, Woodall-rated and efficiently run by the affable proprietor William Williamson. Highlights include a second-floor swimming pool overlooking the ocean, free docking on the Intracoastal Waterway, clean rest rooms with tiled showers, planned cook-outs and activities (in season), a TV lounge and a game room. The on-site grocery store stocks propane, supplies and novelties. Each site has a sheltered table on a small deck. Occasional live entertainment is provided on the pool deck. The pier on the Intracoastal features a fish-cleaning table and gives access to a nearby picnic area.

Campground by the Sea is open all year. Weekly rates offer discounts, and monthly rates are available. A limited number of camper homes, 24-35 feet in length, are available for rent ($30-38 per night in season). Senior citizens discounts apply.

SEA MIST CAMPING RESORT
Devane Rd., Ocean Isle Beach 754-8916

In itself, Sea Mist's panoramic view of Shallotte Inlet and the ocean is enough to entice any camper, but owners Nellie and Baker Harrel don't depend on view alone. (They will probably own oceanfront property soon due to erosion of Ocean Isle Beach's east end.) Visitors love Sea Mist's pool, reputedly the largest in Brunswick County, with its shaded deck and surrounding picnic area. Volleyball, basketball and tetherball are among the activities available. Guests with boats may use the concrete boat ramp at no extra charge. This large, Woodall-rated resort has 246 relatively spacious RV- and tent-sites with tables. Most have full hookups. Guests may choose among shaded sites and sites in full sun along the waterway. The clean rest rooms, bath houses and the well-stocked camp store offset the lack of a laundry on the premises. (Bring your laundry to Shallotte, about a 15-minute ride). Leashed pets are permitted. Perhaps best of all, Sea Mist is only ten minutes from the many attractions of Ocean Isle Beach. Weekly, monthly and annual rates and storage are available. Reserve early.

Sea Mist Camping Resort is located on the Intracoastal Waterway opposite the east end of Ocean Isle Beach. From Shallotte, follow Route 179, which changes its name from Village Road to Brick Landing Road, past picturesque forgotten farm buildings. Remain on Brick Landing as it diverges left from Route 179. Continue almost to the Intracoastal to unpaved Devane Road on the left. Devane passes through the Waterway Campground before ending at Sea Mist Camping Resort. (Waterway Campground, 754-8652, is less desirable than Sea Mist, but makes a tolerable second choice in the event Sea Mist is booked.) If you're coming from Sunset or Ocean Isle Beach, follow the camping signs on Route 179 that direct you to turn right onto Goose Creek Road. This road intersects Brick Landing Road.

LAKE WACCAMAW STATE PARK
Bella Coola Development   669-2928

It wasn't until the age of aviation that thousands of huge elliptical depressions were noticed dotting the Carolinas' coastal plain. All the depressions are oriented along parallel northwest-southeast axes. Some are lakes. Locals came to call them "bays," not referring to bodies of water but to the abundance of bay trees — red, sweet and loblolly bays — that flourish at the rims of the depressions. About 400,000 Carolina bays exist, ranging in size from a fraction of an acre to more than 5,000 acres. (One

Insiders' Tips

Enjoy the nature walk behind the N.C. Aquarium at Fort Fisher at Kure Beach.

lies within Wilmington city limits.) Most are seasonal wetlands filled with fertile peat. Their origin is still a mystery. Scientists first suspected an ancient meteor shower or meteoric explosion, but this hypothesis collapsed under scrutiny. The most widely accepted theory now posits strong winds blowing across a sandy landscape or shallow sea during the last Ice Age as the cause. Lake Waccamaw, named after the region's tribal natives, is the largest Carolina bay.

Lake Waccamaw's shallow waters support 52 species of fish. Three types of fish and five species of shellfish are found nowhere else in the world. The lake water is also curious in that it has a neutral pH; most bay lakes are acidic.

Visitors may explore Lake Waccamaw's environs if they're willing to rough it a bit. The park is undeveloped, with no more facilities than pit toilets, tables and grills. Three primitive group campsites (no water) are available by reservation and, if not reserved, to individuals and families on a first-come basis. Permits may be obtained at the ranger station that, in keeping with the bays' puzzling nature, keeps no regular hours beyond closing at 6 PM. If you're lucky, you may contact a ranger by phone, 646-4748. Fees are $5 per site or $1 per person, whichever is higher.

The park is located in Columbus County about 7 miles south of U.S. 74/76 and 35 miles inland from Wilmington. Highly visible signs lead the way.

Discover The Cotton Exchange

Anna Theresa's
The Basket Case
Bear Mountain
Beckley Place
The Candy Barrel
Cape Diablo
Down To Earth
East Bank Trading Co.
Endless Impressions II
Fidler's Gallery
Folklore Amazonas
FoxChase
The Golden Gallery
Key West Aloe
The Kitchen Shoppe
Kringles Korner

Kuts Hair Salon
The Linen Closet
Makado Gallery
Nuss Strasse Cafe
Olde Wilmington Toy Co.
Outrigger Boutique
Paddy's Hollow
The Petite Quarter
R. Bryan and Company
The Sand Dollar
The Scoop
Sweet Nuthins
Top Toad
Two Sisters Bookery
T.S. Brown Jewelry
The Whittler's Bench
The Write Place

33 SHOPS AND RESTAURANTS
Across from the Hilton in Historic Downtown Wilmington.

Open Mon-Sat 10-5:30
Many Open Sunday 1-5

Restaurants Open Evenings
Free On-Site Parking

Inside
Shopping

The Greater Wilmington area is the sixth largest retail center in North Carolina, and there are abundant opportunities to spend your money here. Since retail is such a big part of the area's economy, it comes as no surprise that quite a number of noteworthy shops won't be listed in this section because it would take an entire book to discuss the shopping possibilities. A browse around the area's large and small shopping districts promises wonderful opportunities to purchase interesting items.

There are three primary shopping areas in Wilmington: the downtown historic neighborhood, Oleander Drive near Independence Mall and the massive shopping corridor along South College Road from Market Street to Monkey Junction (at the intersection of South College and Carolina Beach Road). Dozens of smaller, appealing shopping centers are spread throughout the Cape Fear region.

Downtown Wilmington

The Historic District shopping options will tug at your traveler's checks and credit cards in a fierce way. For the most part, downtown stores are independent specialty stores operated by owners whose personal taste is very much reflected in the merchandise. Downtown has some of the most fun shops in the region, as well as some of the finer stores that carry upscale merchandise. This is not a shopping district with national names on illuminated signs. There are no big discount chain stores selling the necessities of daily life. Instead, this retail area specializes in unusual items that appeal to shoppers in the mood to pause and ponder their selections. Art, antiques, fine clothing, jewelry, gifts, toys, gourmet items, wine, imported goods, glass, china, and more await the discerning downtown shopper.

Part of the charm of this shopping district is its very personal nature. In most cases, the store owner will be helping you with your selections because these stores are small, independent operations. As you may well imagine, the quality of customer service is very good in this friendly retail setting. Residents make friends with the owners of the stores where they regularly shop, and visitors may sometimes find themselves waiting for a conversation to conclude before they can make purchases. Because downtown is really a small town unto itself, the conversations can be very colorful and interesting, and no one minds if you can't help but eavesdrop.

Downtown shopping is separated into three entities that seem to be merging into one in recent years. Viewed as an extended, outdoor mall, downtown is anchored by two large centers at the northern and southern perimeters of the central shopping district. The Cotton Exchange is a shopping/dining/office complex at the northerly end of the river. Chandler's Wharf, a smaller but definitely big-on-charm operation, occupies the southern end. The area between these shopping meccas is Front Street, a busy corridor lined with restaurants, galleries, banks, services, and stores. Streets that cross Front offer many shopping possibilities as well.

The Cotton Exchange, 321 North Front Street is a 36-store and restaurant center overlooking the Cape Fear River. This center was the site of the first renovation of downtown Wilmington in the early 1970s. The Cotton Exchange was named in honor of its onetime status as the site of the largest cotton exporting business in the country. Shoppers can enjoy a bit of history as they stroll the mall's three-level space where displays of cotton bales, weighing equipment, and photographs tell the story of the center's evolution.

Enjoy four restaurants and shop in the **Sanddollar Shell Shop**, **Sweet Nuthin's Lingerie**, the **Makado Gallery**, **Fidler's Gallery**, **Golden Gallery**, **East Bank Trading Co.**, **Bear Mountain**, and many others. There are many interesting stores within the Cotton Exchange, and a visit will reveal all of the fascinating shopping possibilities available on three levels in seven buildings.

As usual, the best stores are the ones that appeal to both locals and visitors. **R. Bryan and Company**, 763-6860, is probably one of the nicest clothing stores anywhere. Quality is impeccable. Service is second to none. The store appeals to conservative tastes — one could call it classic. It leans toward traditional cuts, rather than Italian. Owner Richard Bryan and his well-trained staff make shopping in this store a very comfortable and satisfying experience. Exclusive brand name clothing and accessories for both men and women include Burberry, H. Freeman, Robert Talbott, Pringle, and Bobby Jones.

The **Olde Wilmington Toy Company**, 251-1404, is presided over by owner Stephanie Carr. Ms. Carr is a hands-on owner who loves her merchandise in a very personal way and is likely to be caught on her hands and knees showing a child a toy in action. Touted locally as the "noseflute expert" of the Cape Fear region, she is always enthusiastic in demonstrating her products to interested parents and children. The store features educational, old-style, and entertaining toys that rarely use batteries. If you're on the second level of the Cotton Exchange and you hear a hearty laugh, it's Stephanie.

T.S. Brown Jewelers, 762-3467, is a fine jewelry store that isn't afraid to also offer costume items. The store specializes in gemstones (with more than a thousand loose stones on display) and settings. Handcrafted jewelry in original designs by twenty artists makes this a special place to look for unusual items. Owners Tim and Sandy Brown provide a high level of personal customer service and train their staff to do the same. Tim and Sandy are also jewelry designers and will be glad to create a custom piece for you.

The **Candy Barrel**, 762-3727, is a delicious place to browse and settle upon a decision. Chocolates are homemade and include several varieties of fudge. This store sells all kinds of chocolate-covered nuts, white and dark chocolate-covered pretzels, hard candies, taffies, toffees and fresh popcorn. If you have a weakness for homemade truffles, indulge here.

The **Kitchen Shoppe**, 762-1919, is a luscious assortment of items for the accomplished and new cook. Calphalon, cookbooks, gadgets, grill items, glassware, cookware, and spices make up the dazzling array of items in this special store. Owner Liz Kirby usually has a pot of coffee on for customers. The store also sells

fresh coffees and a variety of peppercorns.

The **Outrigger Boutique**, 343-0405, has all kinds of fascinating natural fabric clothing for the woman who enjoys more playful fashions. While resortwear has been a theme at this store in the past, the shopper will find a broad selection of unusual garments and accessories that are right for many occasions.

The **Write Place**, 343-0617, a card and stationery store, may well qualify for a Guiness record. It is the tiniest store imaginable, crammed with thousands of cards, gift items, buttons, T-shirts and giftwrapping. When you look for merchandise in this store, you should expect to be shoulder to shoulder with other customers who will jockey with you for space and, certainly, a big laugh because owner Jim Fountain goes to extremes to find really funny stuff for his customers.

A discussion of the Cotton Exchange would not be complete without mentioning **The Basket Case** on the lower level. The first store in the complex, it opened in 1979 when the very notion of a shopping complex on the site (then overlooking a dirt parking lot) was a shocking idea. Owner Jean Hanson has steadily expanded this unusual gift store, stocking it with Department 56, Byer's Choice, Sandicast, Snowbabies, and, of course, elaborate plush puppets. Mrs. Hanson delights in animating her puppets for customers.

Chandler's Wharf, 2 Ann Street, has many appealing shopping opportunities. This center has evolved over time, but it began as a ship's

The Cotton Exchange is a charming complex of specialized shops, boutiques and restaurants in historic warehouses on the Wilmington waterfront.

Photo: N.C. Travel & Tourism Division

chandler. There are still some marine artifacts scattered about the grounds — including an old tugboat, an enormous anchor and other reminders of its origins. Cobblestone streets, plank walkways, attractive landscaping and a gorgeous view of the Cape Fear River are some of the features that make shopping at Chandler's Wharf such a pleasant experience. This shopping center was created by Thomas Henry Wright, Jr., in the late 1970s and is flourishing today with some of Wilmington's most delightful stores.

This center also boasts two of the best restaurants in Wilmington — **The Pilot House** and **Elijah's** — and the pleasure of dining in either one is heightened by having the option of enjoying lunch or dinner on outdoor decks right on the water. Shop a while, then take the time to dine at either restaurant. Each one features a covered

deck overlooking the Cape Fear River.

A discussion of Chandler's Wharf shopping must begin with **The Saucepan**, 763-6430. Whether you cook or love a cook, this store is jampacked with an outrageous assortment of the best items on the market for the kitchen, galley, dining room, and breakfast nook. Calphalon, Krups, Henckels and other quality brands dominate the shelves. Cookbooks, a generous assortment of imported and domestic wines, gourmet pastas and sauces, chocolate, coffee and tea, and kitchen gadgets are just some of the items available. This store is also blessed with a top-notch staff of serious cooks who really enjoy sharing their enthusiasm for the merchandise with customers.

A Proper Garden, 763-7177 (800) 626-7177), has everything for your garden that you never knew you needed — until you walk in the door and find yourself wanting it all. Birdhouses, chimes, gazing globes, fountains, lawn ornaments, swings, hammocks, and umbrellas are just some of the things you'll want. Something special about this store is the extremely soothing environment created by bird sounds, splashing water, and light streaming in softly from a large window overlooking the wooded area behind the center. Some customers have become so relaxed they've actually climbed in the hammock display and fallen asleep.

Rebecca's Lingerie, Ltd., 763-4720, has everyday undergarment items as well as lounging attire and special occasion lingerie. This store also specializes in mastectomy needs. Discreet and sensitive service is a hallmark of Rebecca's, where state-of-the-art fitting is matched with a genuine desire to help women during and after the postsurgical transition. For other lingerie needs, Rebecca's is also simply a great place to shop for oneself or for someone special.

The **Quarter**, 762-0970, has classic to contemporary dresses, sportswear, and accessories for women in sizes 4 to 18. This store has been selling fine clothing in this location for eight years, and recently opened **The Petite Quarter** at The Cotton Exchange for women 5'4" and under. Lots of linens and linen blends — the best fabric to wear in the Cape Fear area most of the year – are available in many appealing styles.

Scentsational, 762-2626, a 14-year old store in Chandler's Wharf, sells marvelous scents in every imagin-

able configuration. Air sprays, scented candles, environmental oils, soaps, shower gels, aroma-therapy products, and more are available in the wonderful scents of Crabtree & Evelyn, Scarborough, French fragrances, and others. Scentsational also sells French and antique linens. Essentially, this little store is bulging with items intended to make a person — men, women, and children — feel good. Just the aroma wafting through the door is enough to lift anyone's spirits.

Salon Deja Vu, 762-4106, has been serving residents since 1981. Sad to say, the services of this exceptional salon are not readily available to area visitors who are in town for only a brief vacation. Locals know it takes a bit of a wait to get on Norma Norwood's list of clients, and once people are there they make sure to remain on it. The wait is well worth it. People say Norma runs a tight ship, which is very happy news for her clients. The appointment you set (usually at the conclusion of your current one) is the one you get. If Norma plans to see you at 1 PM, then you will be in the chair at 1 PM on the dot. Hair care services are great, the conversation is likely to be intellectually stimulating, and prices are extremely reasonable.

The **Brass Lantern** is located in the section of Chandler's Wharf outside the main building. Adjacent to Elijah's Restaurant in the cobblestoned area, this is a gift store that specializes in delightful gifts for the distinctive home. Herend porcelain and pottery, Ceralene Raynaud, and Richard Ginori are some of the offerings of this interesting store. Owner Ernie Barbee's high level of personal service to his customers has established The Brass Lantern as one of Wilmington's finest gift stores during its fifteen years of operation. A bonus: Ernie has great jokes, and he can be easily persuaded to tell one.

Water Street Bakery, 762-4157, creates breads and pastry well beyond the expectations of anyone with a sweet tooth. Ask about the Caribbean Fudge Pie if you crave chocolate. The Key Lime Pie is also great. Enjoy the large cinnamon rolls for a nice break in the morning or afternoon.

Downtown Shopping Corridor

On and adjacent to Front Street, Downtown Shopping Corridor has many stores that will attract both visitor and resident to a potential shopping frenzy. Antique stores rapidly are becoming one of the primary retail operations downtown, and there are approximately 20 stores specializing in valuable antiques and interesting old things. Most of these stores are located along Front Street.

There are also numerous import shops downtown. The nearby State Port allows for convenient importing of goods from all over the world. **Down Island Trader**, 111 South Front Street, 762-2112, specializes in imported items from Bali. The clothing, decorative accessories, jewelry, and other handcrafts are reasonably priced — actually, very inexpensive — and there is almost always something new to peruse.

The **Compass Rose Import Company**, 16 Market Street, 763-2302, specializes in old world imports. Exotic eastern imports including rugs, furnishings, decorative accessories and things that defy categorization crowd the large space.

Next door, located in the same building as Compass Rose, is **Anasazi**, 762-8044. This fascinating store features southwestern folk art, Native American crafts, Mexican antiques, hand blown glassware, and wrought iron. Check out the used cowboy hats and leather boots.

Designs on You is a vintage fashions shop with two locations on Front Street in downtown Wilmington. The stores, located at 271 North Front, 251-0770, and 16 South Front, 251-1133, have an incredible selection of clothing, shoes, hats, and accessories that date from the Victorian era to the seventies. These stores provide costumes to the local film industry. The North Front Street store, a three-level vintage extravaganza, offers costume rentals for groups and individuals. Bulk buyers are invited to visit by appointment outside of regular hours.

The **Old Wilmington Florist**, 19 Market Street, 763-5558, is a wonderful full-service florist that offers extremely sophisticated arrangements at very reasonable prices. Live plants, cut flowers, arrangements, and more are available on a moment's notice. Tropicals are a specialty of this florist, and everyone in Wilmington can instantly identify the beautiful work of the Old Wilmington Florist.

Island Passage, 4 Market Street,

Patt Noday *Kim Kopka*

GOOD MORNING CAROLINA

Weekdays 6:00 a.m. WWAY TV 3

Coverage You Can Count On!

762-1911, and 8 Market Street, is actually two stores that offer fashions at one, and shoes and gifts at the other. These stores are owned by Harper Peterson, a downtown entrepreneur who also owns the **Wilmington City Market**, 122 South Market Street and **Water Street Restaurant** (a cafe) at 5 South Water Street. The Wilmington City Market, a reincarnation of the century-old farmer's market in downtown Wilmington, is the place to find baked goods, local vegetables, plants, flowers, and crafts.

Some of the old-timers in downtown Wilmington — stores that have stood the test of time and responded with quality products and service for a long while — are still here because they're great places to shop.

Kingoff's Jewelers, 10 North Front Street, 762-5219, a downtown jeweler since 1919, offers fine jewelry, watches, the famed "Wilmington Cup," china and repairs. **Tom's Drug Store**, 1 North Front Street, 762-3391, is an authentic old-style drug store that has been a landmark in downtown Wilmington since 1932. The store has a complete pharmacy and offers free citywide delivery. You can also get lots of opinions on current affairs at Tom's.

Finkelstein's Jewelry and Music Company, 6 South Front Street, 762-5662, has been in business since 1906.

This combination music store/jewelry store/pawnbroker is a must stop for the visitor or resident who is drawn to any of these services. **Barefoots and Jackson Furniture**, 21 South Front Street, 763-1609, has been selling Broyhill and Lexington furniture downtown for half a century.

Hilda Godwin's, 105 Market Street, 762-4472, is a unique women's clothing shop that features fine sportswear, dresses, and accessories. While this lovely little store is wonderful for year-round shopping, things really get exciting around the holiday party season. **The Julia**, 277 North Front Street, 762-3175, is another regular stop for locals who want unusual and quality fashion.

A relatively new store downtown deserves a remark or two. **Bristol Books**, long established at The Galleria near Wrightsville Beach, has opened at 120 South Front Street, 251-3770. This outstanding little bookstore has a full selection of fiction and nonfiction, magazines, out-of-town newspapers, cards and calendars, books-on-tape rental, and a monthly potluck featuring regional cooking.

Parking to shop downtown is somewhat limited, especially during the lunch hour on weekdays. If you circle for fifteen minutes, you will probably find a one-hour space if you are willing to persist. There is a

parking deck on Second Street and this may be your best bet for finding a place to leave your car for several hours. The Water Street/Front Street deck is largely occupied during the week by people who work downtown, although there are a few spaces reserved for visitors. The deck is open and free for anyone on weekends. Many downtown merchants also will validate your parking ticket when you shop in their stores.

Parking along downtown streets is free with the exception of some metered areas next to the post office. If you are willing to walk half a dozen blocks—a very pleasant stroll in fascinating surroundings — you may find a space on the residential blocks on the perimeter of the central business district. Downtown shopping centers have their own free parking lots, and this is a nice feature. In 1993, sidewalks all through downtown were refurbished to accommodate wheelchairs, so individuals with physical handicaps will appreciate the rela-tive ease of movement through downtown.

DOWNTOWN ANTIQUE STORES

There is an Historic Downtown Wilmington Antique Dealers Association, and most of the stores will provide you with a map that pinpoints the other shops. Needless to say, it is easy to plan a whole day around antique-ing in downtown Wilmington. Park the car anywhere along Front Street or adjacent streets, and set off on foot to discover these stores.

Moore Antiques, 20 South Front Street, 763-0300, occupies a building with **Hollingsworth American Country**, 675-3322. These businesses complement each other with Moore's collection of collectibles, toys, and furniture, and Hollingsworth's reproductions.

Elizabeth Lowe Antiques and Interiors, 110 Orange Street, 392-1009, is one of the oldest antique stores downtown. **Virginia Jennewein Antiques and Appraisals**, 143 North

Photo: William Russ, N.C. Travel & Tourism Division

Chandler's Wharf offers a look at Wilmington's waterfront as it existed in the 19th century.

Front Street, 763-3703, is also one of the longest established shops **downtown**. **Woodcolt & Company**, 1008 Princess Street, 762-0171, has salvaged, recycled, custom designed and painted furniture, as well as what the owner describes as "serendipitous finds."

About Time Antiques, 30 North Front Street, 762-9902, has pottery, glassware, French and Victorian furniture, and linens. **The Antique Gallery**, 107 South Front Street, specializes in period English and French furniture, porcelains, silver, crystal, china, and collectibles.

Oleander Drive and Independence Mall

Wilmington has a full-service mall filled with all of the national and regional stores that shoppers all over America have come to expect in a city.

Independence Mall, 3500 Oleander Drive, has nearly a hundred stores in a climate-controlled environment. **Sears**, **J.C. Penny**, and **Belk** anchor this complex of fashion, music, computer, art supplies, food, jewelry, sporting goods, and shoe stores.

Naturally, the anchor stores are the main draw for malls. Belk-Beery has undergone what must certainly be described as a drastic upgrading in 1993, and it has emerged as a department store that is on par with stores in much larger metropolitan areas. For Wilmingtonians, the newly renovated Belk store is a long-overdue shopping upgrade that this coastal area has long desired. J.C. Penny underwent a similar renovation, although on a much less grand scale, in recent years. Sears is . . . well . . . Sears, with everything that anyone expects when they visit this vanguard of American department store shopping. Sears also has a full-service automotive center.

There are one-hour photo developing stores, sporting goods shops, nine jewelry stores, half a dozen shoe stores, a cinema, music stores, apparel dealers in large quantity, restaurants, a store where everything is a dollar, beauty salons, a tobacco shop, import shops, and banking services. This mall offers just what customers have come to love in their area malls. It's the place to go when you have a lot of needs and want to find them under one climate-controlled roof. Parking is free and ample at Independence Mall. The mall is entirely handicapped-accessible as well.

The area around the mall bustles with shopping possibilities as well. **Hanover Center**, 3501 Oleander Drive, is a strip center that has grown increasingly stronger in recent years, and is a nice complement to Independence Mall. It houses **Rose's**, 763-5105, a discount department store, **Eckerd Drugs**, 763-3367, and **Sherwin-Williams** home decorating center, 763-1119. Some of the smaller stores that bear mentioning are **Temptations**, 763-6662, a gourmet foods store with a cafe, and **Patricia's Shoes**, 763-2234, the main shoe store in town for really unusual women's shoes.

In the next strip to the east, is a store that people in business will really appreciate. The enormous selection, low prices and superior customer service at the **Office Depot**, 3727 Oleander Drive, 392-9013, can't be beat. Despite the cavernous size of the store, one must only look

slightly perplexed to receive the attention of helpful, friendly sales staff members. This store has a large selection of computers, accessories, paper supplies, copier services, and much more. If you have a business, you would do well to visit this store that describes itself as the largest office supply store in the world.

A special strip mall that needs to be mentioned is **Audubon Center** in the 1400 block of Audubon Boulevard just a bit east of Independence Mall on the other side of Oleander. This small center houses some very nice clothing stores. **H. Neuwirth Men's Wear**, 452-3860, **Country Vogue**, 791-3082, and **The Wonder Shop**, 799-4511 are all reliable places for traditional Cape Fear fashion. **Kingoff's Jewelers**, 799-2100 (also located downtown), has been serving area jewelry needs since 1919.

South College Road

This is the part of Wilmington that is home to the mega-stores. **Sam's**, **Wal-Mart**, **KMart**, **Lowe's**, **Brendle's**, **Best**, and **Phar-mor** are some of the big stores you need for appliances, home improvements, auto parts, and — well, you know what you need. All over America, these stores are just the same. Discount prices, high volume, and national brands are hallmarks of these stores that dominate South College Road. These are the places where, in many cases, your neck starts to hurt from looking up.

It's a very popular area jammed with traffic. Fortunately, the developers anticipated lots of customers and built expansive parking lots.

There are also some smaller, interesting stores interspersed among these retail giants. Furniture is a large business in town, and many of the large ones — as well as small ones — are on or near this road.

Sutton-Council Furniture, 421 South College Road, 799-9000, is probably the dominant furniture store in the entire Wilmington market. There are more than 40,000 square feet of showroom space in this store that retails such brands as Pennsylvania House, Henredon, and Hickory Chair. **Murrow Furniture**, 3514 South College Road, 799-4010, at the other end of the street, has 65,000 square feet in its showroom and sells such traditional brands as Council Craftsmen, Drexel Heritage, Thomasville, Henredon, and others. These stores are Wilmington's High Point connection. In case you don't know, High Point, North Carolina is the home market of North Carolina's furniture industry.

Montie's Cheese Works, 415 South College Road, 799-0600, is a dream come true for cheese lovers. This is the place to go if you crave a hard-to-find cheese or want an expert to guide you in your selection of something new and unusual. There is also a selection of wines, crackers, entertainment accessories, and other neat things in this store. For an even broader selection of wine, drop by the **Wineseller**, 1207 South Kerr Avenue, 799-5700, just off South College. This is one of the very few wine specialty stores in the region with regular wine tastings, home winemaking systems, and a wine club.

While it is impossible to name all of the great stores throughout the Cape Fear area, there are some stores that don't fall into highlighted shopping areas but deserve special mention here.

The **Sun and Moon Bookshop and Boutique** near Wrightsville Beach, 7110 Wrightsville Avenue, Crosspoint Plaza, 256-9131, is a combination specialty bookstore and boutique. In addition to colorful clothing, gifts, jewelry, cards, and fine crafts, this store offers an abundance of "feel better" books, lectures, and classes.

Paula's Health Hut, 3405 Wrightsville Avenue, 791-0200, has Wilmington's largest selection of vitamins, health foods, diet, and all-natural products.

Now and Then, 5001 Wrightsville Avenue, 395-1785, is a consignment shop for women's clothing. There are incredible bargains to be had in this marvelous little store that has very strict standards regarding its consignment wares. There are many top-brand ensembles, great sales, impeccably high quality items and cleanliness in this store. They don't take anything on consignment unless it is of excellent quality and newly dry-cleaned. A Bergdorf-Goodman outfit suitable for any fancy occasion can sometimes be had for less than a hundred dollars. This store has clothing for every possible event or use, ranging from jeans to party dresses.

Carolina Beach

Any Carolina Beach resident will remark that shopping opportunities are somewhat limited on the island, so folks generally go to Wilmington for many of their shopping needs. There are several major stores just up the road on Highway 421 toward Wilmington at a spot called Monkey Junction. This is where Highways 421 and 132, the extension of Interstate 40, come together. **Myrtle Grove Shopping Center**, just southeast of this intersection, is home to **Wal-Mart**, **Winn-Dixie**, **Radio Shack** and **Smash Video**. The northwestern corner is the site where KMart and Wilson's Supermarket are located. A few miles toward Carolina Beach is the small **Masonboro Commons** center that offers **Revco** for full-service drugstore needs, as well as **Food Lion**.

Carolina Beach is largely dominated by restaurants, motels and arcades, but there are several places to shop for specific merchandise. **Wings**, 807 North Lake Park Boulevard, 458-4488, is the ultimate beach goods store. Whether you want boogie boards, beach clothing for the family, windsocks, beach toys or T-shirts made your way, Wings is the place to find whatever you need.

Island Tackle & Hardware, located at 15 Federal Point Shopping Center at the first light coming into Carolina Beach from the Snow's Cut bridge, is a fisherman's first stop. This combination hardware and tackle store sells bait, offshore lures, rods and reels, line, coolers — everything a fisherman needs and then some. For damage done to reels by the big fish off the Carolina Beach shores, Island Tackle & Hardware, 458-3049, also does reel repair.

Women will find a nice selection of sportswear, career and party clothing at **Linda's**, 201 North Lake Park Boulevard, 458-7116. This small store has a wide assortment of costume jewelry and other accessories.

Wrightsville Beach

Truth be told, there is not a lot of shopping on this primarily residential beach. A store that should be mentioned, though, is **Redix**. It is on the causeway into the beach, just to the right after you cross the bridge over the ICW. Redix is partly a beach goods store but the larger part of it is devoted to quality clothing. If you need a sweater, this is definitely the place to go in Wilmington. When Redix has sales, there are great bargains to be had on Liz Claiborne, Jones of New York, and other name brands.

Back on the mainland side of the bridge, **The Fisherman's Wife**, 1410 Airlie Rd., 256-5505, specializes in decorative accessories and gifts with a "fishy" theme, including home accent pieces. **Whiting & Co.**, 6800

Two-steppers can find heaven at the Yellow Rose Saloon on Market Street in Wilmington.

Insiders' Tips

Wrightsville Ave., The Galleria, 256-3993, offers casualwear for women and men in brands such as Nautica and Kenar. Look to this store for hard-to-find linen clothing that is best-suited to Wilmington's summer days. **Island Passage**, Crosspoint Plaza, 7110 Wrightsville Ave., 256-6990, has fun, casual clothing and accessories for women. This is the largest of what may be described as the "Island Passage Empire," a group of stores that includes two downtown and one on Bald Head Island in addition to the Crosspoint Plaza location. **J. Nicholson**, 1319 Military Cutoff Rd., Landfall Center, 256-2662, sells women's clothing and accessories including Criscione, Al Bates, AKA and Bettina Riedell. While you're in the Landfall Center, check out **Doxey's Market** for health foods, natural beauty aids, organic vegetables and an extensive line of Japanese cooking products.

Topsail Beach

Again, there is not much in the way of shopping on this island that is mostly occupied by homes, a few restaurants, and some services.

The **Gift Basket**, 702 South Anderson Boulevard, (800) 424-7245, specializes in 14 K gold jewelry and fine gifts. It also has the largest selection of flags in the area.

Spinnaker Beach Center, 111 North Shore Drive, Surf City, 328-2311, has kites and windsocks, surfing apparel, resort wear, rollerblades, and Jimmy Buffett/

Carribean Soul T-shirts. **Island Treasures**, 627 South Anderson Boulevard, 329-4487, carries sportswear, T-shirts, gifts, jewelry, pottery, and beach supplies.

Southport

Antiques dominate the shopping scene in historic Southport. The **Antique Mall** has 25 dealers located in three buildings. The mall, located at 108 East Moore Street, 457-4982, has an abundance of furniture and collectibles. It is open Monday through Saturday from 10 AM until 5 PM. **Northrop Mall**, 111 East Moore Street, 457-9569, has 24 antique and collectible dealers under one roof.

Other antique dealers include the **Country Crafters**, 814 North Howe Street, 457-4703; **Curiosity Shop** (Southport's Original Antique Shop), 113 North Howe Street, 457-6228; **Harbor View Antiques**; 800 East Moore Street, 457-6805, **Parr Antiques and Collectibles**, 113 South Howe Street, 457-6938; as well as others. As you may note, one may simply park the car and walk to many stores that specialize in antiques in downtown Southport.

Brunswick Beaches

One does not go to the Brunswick Beaches necessarily to shop, but there are several shopping experiences available to those who want to buy something.

Sabra's Gifts, 223 Norton Street, Yaupon Beach, 278-1643, has a wide selection of gourmet foods, fruit baskets and specialty gift baskets. The **Oak Island Senior Citizens Shop**, 5610 East Oak Island Drive, Long Beach, 278-5224, has supplies for artistry, basketry, quilting, tole-painting, cross stitch, and stenciling. It also features handmade crafts and paintings.

Need some sand dollar hardener? Maybe you never thought you would need this particular item but that's probably because you've never had such an opportunity to find whole sand dollars like you will on the Brunswick Beaches. The **Cockle Shell**, Holden Beach Causeway, Holden Beach, 842-6030, not only has this mystical ingredient but also sells live hermit crabs, coral, a wide variety of seashells, books, jewelry and lamps.

Carson Cards and Gifts, Twin Creek Plaza, Shallotte, 754-9968, has shelves of collectibles such as Tom Clark Gnomes, Hummel, Porcelain Birds by Andrea, and more.

Shopping in the Cape Fear area is an increasingly satisfying experience. Retailers are becoming more savvy as time passes. They are taking note of the influx of outsiders from larger cities who expect a higher level of choice, quality and price than has been traditionally offered in this area.

At this writing, there are dozens of new shopping experiences of all kinds in the works. If the current trend continues, you can expect Greater Wilmington to continue to rise from its sixth-place retail position in the state to a higher spot. Bring your traveler's checks and credit cards when you visit — the combination of quality products and personal service is bound to be irresistible.

The Maco Light

Cape Fear is aptly named and not just for its treacherous shoals. Many a strange tale has been told and retold about inexplicable events and eerie sights occurring well inland amid moss-hung forests or on the fog-laden rivers. Some of Wilmington's older homes have long been known for unearthly visitations. One such building is the Price-Gause house on Market Street, built upon the antebellum Gallows Hill, where for many years criminals were executed and buried. Even gracious Thalian Hall has had its share of phenomena — stage lights snapping on with no one at the controls, for instance, and the apparition of a woman wearing a gossamer gown seen walking through the upper balcony. But no mystery is as enticing or better known than the Maco Light.

Back in 1888, President Grover Cleveland was traveling by rail through the Cape Fear region, campaigning for reelection. As his train approached Maco, a town about 15 miles west of Wilmington in Little Green Swamp, the President noticed that the train had two lanterns lit. His questioning elicited from the conductor the tragic tale of Joe Baldwin.

Joe Baldwin was a flagman who, after fighting in the War Between the States, worked the rail lines serving Wilmington. One dark, foggy night in 1867 not far from the Maco station, Joe was riding in the caboose of a slow freight train when a clattering sound startled him. He noticed that the train suddenly grew quieter, the click-clack of the wheels on the tracks slowing down. He went to the front of the car to investigate. To his fearful surprise he discovered that the coupler pin had fallen away, and the caboose in which he rode had separated from the train. Looking down the midnight track ahead, he could see the dim lights of the train dwindling in the darkness, soon to vanish. The caboose continued to coast, slackening in speed as it went.

Alarmed by the screech of a steam whistle, Joe spun on his heels. Through the window at the back of the caboose, he saw a light looming over the track. The whistle screamed again. Hardly believing his eyes, he ran to the rear door. What he saw was the lantern of a speeding passenger train approaching the caboose, which was standing nearly stock-still on the same track.

Quickly Joe fetched a lantern, lit the wick and raced to the platform at the rear of the caboose. He swung it back and forth in desperate hopes that the approaching engineer would see the light and brake in time — but all was in vain. At a trestle over the swamp, the train slammed into the caboose, killing Joe Baldwin instantly. Hours later, in the early morning fog, rescuers struggled to recover Joe's crushed body. To their horror, his head had been severed and, even after days of clearing the wreckage, search as they might through the densely grown swamp, they could not find it. Joe Baldwin was buried headless.

Over the years since then, many people reported seeing, on dark, desolate nights, a single swaying light along the track where the incident occurred. It was seen to rise and fall, to swing back and forth. Some said it seemed to brighten as if moving forward along the track, and when it came to within several yards of the trestle, it would flash brilliantly only to fade again and recede into the darkness. Many Wilmington residents living today can attest to it. Some say it was Joe Baldwin looking for his lost head. And many a train running down that track at night kept two lanterns lit on the locomotive so as never to be mistaken for Joe Baldwin's light.

In 1964, the renowned parapsychologist and ghost-hunter Hans Holzer came to investigate the Maco Light. Without doubt, he confirmed that the light was a psychic phenomenon and that it behaved as if someone were giving warning of impending danger. He confirmed it to be a ghost at the heart of the mystery, although he never asserted that it was, in fact, Joe Baldwin; only that it was the troubled soul of someone who had met a ghastly demise at the Maco crossing.

Finally, in 1977, the Seaboard Coast Line Railroad ceased operations in the region and tore up the track at Maco. The light was seen no more. Some folks speculate that Joe Baldwin no longer needed to warn oncoming trains. In any case, the story had so impressed President Cleveland that he referred to the Maco Light in subsequent speeches, bringing it to national attention.

Star-News History

THE MORNING STAR.

On the front page of the first edition of the Wilmington 'Morning Star,' publisher William H. Bernard explains his decision to switch from afternoon to morning publication, three weeks after founding the 'Evening Star.'

What is now one of the most respected newspapers in North Carolina began life above a grocery store at 3 S. Water Street, Wilmington.

The *Morning Star* was owned by William H. Bernard, a Confederate veteran. In the aftermath of war, he saw the need for courageous leadership in the South.

The first issue of the *Star*, a four-page evening newspaper, appeared on Sept. 23, 1867. The following month the Wilmington *Morning Star* made its first appearance, replacing the evening paper.

In the 1920's, the *Star* began publication of the afternoon *Evening News*. The corporation then published the *Star*, the *News*, and the *Sunday Star-News*.

The company was bought in 1975 by the New York Times Company. Publication of the News ceased that same year, leaving the *Morning Star* and the *Sunday Star-News* as the surviving papers and explains the split personality in the names.

The *Morning Star* is today the oldest daily newspaper in continuous publication in North Carolina.

**Morning Star
Sunday Star-News**

Inside
Attractions

Two things have shaped the types of attractions that flourish on the Cape Fear coast: history and geography. The area's rich historical legacy, more than four centuries in the making, manifests itself in museums, monuments and living structures that speak eloquently of our inherited past. The proximity to the sea of a culturally vibrant, major city and its satellite settlements lends a distinct resort quality to the entire region.

Downtown Wilmington and its environs naturally "grew" historic attractions that might even be called organic because they are so integral to the identity of Cape Fear. Historic sites such as Brunswick Town, Fort Fisher, and Topsail Island's Assembly Building convey specific eras and events as no textbook or commemoration can. This region is so rich in history it would be impossible to list every historic attraction in a book of reasonable size. So, as you travel to such places as Southport's Old Smithville Burial Ground, stay alert for other sites with similar stories to tell, such as Southport's old Morse Cemetery (near downtown) and the John N. Smith Cemetery (on Leonard Street off Herring Drive). Memorials are so abundant you may miss the one at Bonnet's Creek

(Moore Street north of downtown Southport), at the mouth of which the Gentleman Pirate Stede Bonnet used to hide his corsair. Other memorials bear more silent testimony to the past, such as a few shipwrecks that are awash at low tide and may still be spied from the beaches (for example, the blockade runner *Vesta*, run aground Feb. 4, 1864 south of Tubbs Inlet in about 10 feet of water; the blockade runner *Bendigo*, run aground Jan. 11, 1864 one mile southwest of Lockwood Folly Inlet in about 15 feet of water).

Downtown Wilmington itself practically groans under the weight of its own history and presents the most varied single attraction in the area. By foot, by boat, or by horse-drawn carriage, you can explore the historic district for years without tiring. By 1850, Wilmington was the largest city in North Carolina. As a port city, it was nearly on a par with other great southern ports such as Galveston and New Orleans. But when the Atlantic Coast Line Railroad pulled out of Wilmington in the 1950s, the city went into such a rapid decline that even its skyline was flattened. Downtown was all but deserted until a core of local entrepreneurs fought to revitalize and restore their hometown. By 1974, downtown Wilmington became the state's largest urban district listed in the National Register of Historic Places. Many of the images of Wilmington's bustling past are preserved in the Public Library's North Carolina Room, which is open to the public. Likewise, the Cape Fear Museum interprets the region's history in several far-reaching exhibits. Together, they are excellent resources for interpreting what you see today and for exploring further.

The Cape Fear coast might have been only half the resort it is were it not for its superb beaches. Excellent fishing and fine seafood dining depend on them as do the many cruise opportunities available at Carolina Beach Marina and at marinas from Topsail to Calabash. But no beach resort would be complete without a water slide, go-cart track or batting cages. So take note of the Surf City Water Slide on North Shore Drive (Topsail Island), the Magic Mountain Water Slide in Holden Beach (with five killer flumes), Jubilee Park in Carolina Beach and the Ocean Isle Beach Water Slide on Causeway Drive. Most of these attractions are open seven days a week between Memorial and Labor Days from about 10 AM 'til 9 PM. Prices are rated hourly, around $3-$4 per half-hour and up to about $7 for the day, with discounts for longer sessions.

Such amusements as these, plus miniature golf, movies and bowling, are usually concentrated within certain highly-trafficked areas in each locale. In Wilmington, Oleander Drive east of 41st Street is the predominant amusement strip with several more attractions than listed here. North of Ocean Isle Beach, Beach Drive (NC 179/904) is another strip, with its share of go-carts and miniature golf. At the foot of Yaupon Pier on Oak Island, a kiddie amusement park stands across the road from a large arcade and seaside miniature golf course. Topsail Beach and Surf City share the limelight as Topsail Island's two centers for attractions. It would be redundant to list all these places; you're bound to stumble across them as you gravitate toward each community's nerve center.

Not all local attractions are summertime flings. The world's largest living Christmas tree is decorated and lit every night during the Christmas season in Wilmington. Not the typical Christmas tree, it is actually a 400 year-old live oak located at Hilton Park a few minutes north of downtown on Highway 133 and U.S. 117. Then there's Calder Court. Insiders who entertain out-of-town guests at Christmas are fond of driving them out to the King's Grant subdivision. They drive north on Route 132 (Col-

RUSH IS RIGHT..
NOON TO 3PM
DAILY

WAAV

NEWS/TALK   AM 980

lege Road) about 1 1/4 miles beyond the Market Street overpass. Turning right onto Kings Drive, they make the next two lefts and douse their headlights. In the cul-de-sac named Calder Court is one of the most flamboyant demonstrations of Christmas illumination anywhere. Every home on the street is festooned with multicolored constellations of Christmas joy. Sometimes the cars line up all the way down the street, not one with its lights on.

Then there are the gardens for which North Carolina is rightfully famous. Perhaps a legacy of our British colonial heritage, horticulture on Cape Fear is on a par with that of any other region in America. And the fact that the North Carolina Azalea Festival, to which garden tours are focal, is based in Wilmington makes a strong case for the Cape Fear coast's leadership in that field. Annual and perennial plantings are well-supported public works, as is evident at Greenfield Lake and Gardens and along many highways and byways. Two privately-owned gardens that are open to the public — Airlie Gardens and Orton Plantation — are simply spectacular in springtime. It would be difficult to overstate the importance of gardens in this region.

What follows, then, are the area's prime general attractions below which you will find a brief section on

Cape Fear Coast Islands. Wilmington's attractions have been grouped into three subsections: Downtown Wilmington, Around Wilmington and Outside Wilmington. Within each section, all attractions are listed alphabetically. Information to supplement this book can be obtained at several locations. New Hanover County Information is located at Third and Market Streets in the 1892 Courthouse building. The Visitors' Information booth at the foot of Market Street in Wilmington stocks free pamphlets and brochures for nearly every attraction operating in the area. It is open every day during the summer and is open weekends during most of the year. The folks staffing it are friendly and very knowledgeable. If they don't know the answer you need, they know someone who does. The public libraries, especially the main branch in downtown Wilmington (Third and Chestnut streets), keep many brochures on hand. In Southport, the Visitors' Center, 457-7927, is located at 107 East Nash Street. And, of course, the various Chambers of Commerce are all helpful. But you hold in your hands possibly the finest source for beginning your exploration of the Cape Fear coast's best attractions.

General Attractions

Downtown Wilmington

BELLAMY MANSION
MUSEUM OF DESIGN ARTS
503 Market St.   *251-3700*

The assertion that Bellamy Mansion is Wilmington's premier state-

ment of prewar opulence and wealth is impossible to contest. ("Prewar" here refers to the War Between the States, aka the Civil War and the War of Northern Aggression.) This four-story, 22-room wooden palace, completed in 1861, is a classic Victorian example of Greek Revival and Italianate architecture. Its majesty is immediately evident in its 14 fluted columns, which are two-stories high and crowned by Corinthian capitals. Before plans were set to renovate and restore the mansion in 1972, it hadn't been lived in since the death of Ellen Douglas Bellamy in 1946. Her memoir, *Back With the Tide* (1940), is not only a rebuttal of *Gone With the Wind* but also an eye-opening Reconstruction-era indictment by a lady of the Old South.

In its present incarnation, the mansion houses a museum of the design arts, embracing regional architecture, landscape architecture, and preservation and decorative arts. To that end, the museum was given its "soft" opening (August 93) before restoration was complete so that the process itself might stand as an exhibit.

And what an exhibit it is! Original furnishings include a Knabe pianoforte, stamped brass valences, magnificent gas chandeliers (now electrified), faux-marble fireplaces made of slate and incredible examples of the plasterer's art that are demonstrated in the elaborate cornices and ceiling medallions. Most of the craftwork is the product of African-American artisans, many of whom were granted their freedom on the steps of this very building. The museum hosts multimedia trav-

Saltwater touch tanks at the N.C. Aquarium at Ft. Fisher offer a variety of active sea life.

Photo: N.C. Travel and Tourism Division

eling exhibits and is building an in-house collection. Workshops, films, lectures, slide shows and other activities are also offered. Preservation work continuing beyond the grand opening in April 1994 will establish Bellamy Mansion as a restoration in progress. In the offing are the restoration of the original slave quarters (a fine example of urban slave housing) and the reconstruction of the carriage house that will house a gift shop.

Slide-presentations and tours take place every 30 minutes. The volunteer guides are sure to point out the glassed-in portion of a wall left unrestored to illustrate the extent of a 1972 arson, an event linked to the disfavor in which Bellamy Mansion is held by many locals as a symbol of slavery. This fact further legitimizes the Mansion's value as a historic and cultural landmark as much as its architecture and pains-

taking restoration do.

Bellamy Mansion is presently open to the public from Thursday to Saturday, 9 AM to 5 PM and on Sunday 1-5 PM, but hours will expand in step with museum activities. Fees are $5 for adults, $3 for children ages 5 through 12. The building can be rented for after-hour events. Volunteers interested in helping with anything from tours to restoration may contact Assistant Director Amy Wright for information.

BURGWIN-WRIGHT HOUSE
224 Market St.   *762-0570*

When Lord Charles Cornwallis fled his tragic victory near Guilford Court House in western North Carolina in 1781, he repaired to Wilmington, then a town of 200 houses. He lodged at the gracious Georgian home of John Burgwin (pronounced "bur-GWIN"), a wealthy planter and politician, and made it his headquarters. The home, completed in 1770, is distinguished by two-story porches on two sides (a West Indian influence) and six levels of tiered gardens. The massive ballast-stone foundation remained from the previously abandoned town jail, beneath which was an impregnable dungeon where Cornwallis held his prisoners. A volunteer for the National Society of the Colonial Dames, the building's present owners, can point out the trap door that leads to it. Underground, an old brick tunnel communicates to the river. Rumored to have concealed pirate treasure or slaves on the Underground Railroad, now it is only a drainage sluice for a stream called Jacob's Run, for which a famous nightclub down the street was named. (Jacob's Run feeds into the Cape Fear River on the south side of the old Stone Towing building at the foot of Dock Street.) The three-story kitchen shed behind the main building may have once been attached to the former jail building.

The Burgwin-Wright House is one of the great restoration/reconstruction achievements in the state (some restoration continues today), and visitors may peruse the carefully appointed rooms and period furnishings for $3. The museum and gardens are open Tuesday through Saturday, 10 AM to 4 PM. Group tours are by appointment.

CAPE FEAR MUSEUM
814 Market St. 341-4350

For an overview of the cultural and natural histories of the Cape Fear region from prehistory to the present, the Cape Fear Museum (established 1898) stands unsurpassed. The current long-term exhibition, Waves and Currents: The Lower Cape Fear Story, includes life-sized dioramas that exhibit artifacts, the early naval stores industry, a miniature recreation of the Fort Fisher battle and a remarkable scale model of the Wilmington waterfront, c. 1863. Interactive children's activities, videos, special events and acclaimed changing exhibits contribute to making the Cape Fear Museum not only one of the primary repositories of local history but also a place where learning is fun.

The museum is open Tuesday through Saturday, 9 AM to 5 PM and Sunday 2-5 PM. It is handicapped accessible. Admission is $2 for adults (18 and over), $1 for children (5-17). Children under 5 and Museum Associates are admitted free. Admission is free to all on the 1st and 3rd Sundays each month and the first day of each month.

CAPT. MAFFITT SIGHTSEEING CRUISE
Municipal Dock, 343-1611
foot of Market St. (800)676-0162

Named for Capt. John Newland Maffitt, one of the Civil War's most

Enjoy Bald Head Island for a special day trip that includes walking, biking and riding electric carts on an island where gasoline engines aren't allowed.

Insiders' Tips

Henrietta II *is docked at the foot of Market Street at Riverfront Park, the traditional "riverboat landing" in Wilmington.*

successful blockade runners, this is a converted Navy steam launch. Sightseeing cruises on the Cape Fear River with live historical narration take place at 11 AM and 3 PM daily from June through August. Sunset and moonlight cruises during those months are also offered, at 7, 8:30 and 10 PM (unless preempted by charters). During May and September, scheduled cruises leave the Municipal Dock at 3 PM only. Special fall cruises upriver are a wonderful opportunity to enjoy the crisp October air, and the Maffitt is available for charter throughout the year. Call for reservations.

The Maffitt doubles as the Battleship River Taxi during the summer (no reservations necessary). See the listing below for Battleship *North Carolina* for more information.

CHANDLER'S WHARF
Water & Ann Sts.

In the late '70s, Chandler's Wharf was an Old Wilmington riverfront reconstruction complete with ballast-stone walls, early lighting fixtures, a museum and seven historic ships moored at the adjoining docks. More than 100 years ago this had been part of the business district. The area was choked with mercantile warehouses, its sheds filled with naval stores, tools, cotton, and guano and its wharves lined with merchantmen. The disastrous (and suspicious) fire of August 1874 changed the site forever.

Today, much of the flavor of that era remains and Chandler's Wharf is again a business district — more accurately, a shopping and dining district. Two historic homes transformed into quaint shops stand along a cobblestone street lined with the rails of the former marine railway An excellent bakery, jeweller/ gemologist shop and two fine restaurants, Elijah's and The Pilot House, stand beside wooden sidewalks adorned with flowers, a small herb garden, benches and nautical artifacts. Across from the parking lot north of Ann Street, the old warehouse contains more shops. The tugboat *John Taxis*, reputed as the oldest in America, stands at water's edge. For more detailed information on Chandler's Wharf, see the chapters on Restaurants and Shopping.

HORSE-DRAWN CARRIAGE TOUR
Market St. between Water   251-8889
and Front Sts.

See historic downtown Wilmington the old-fashioned way — by horse-drawn carriage. These romantic and relaxing half-hour rides in a large, comfortable, French-top surrey are narrated by a knowledgeable costumed driver who offers interesting anecdotes about the restored homes, stately mansions and historic waterfront along the way. In busy seasons such as during Azalea Festival and Riverfest, horse-drawn trolleys are used. The tours are operated by the owners of Springbrook Farms who will also accommodate special tours and occasions. Tours operate Tuesday through Sunday from 10 AM to 10 PM from April through October. The individual fee is $7; $4 for children under 12.

HENRIETTA II
London Wharf on the Riverwalk,   343-1611
next to the Hilton   (800)676-0162

North Carolina's only true sternwheel paddleboat, the *Henrietta II* is a gaily appointed throwback to the days of the grand river boats that once plied the Cape Fear River between Wilmington and Fayetteville. From April through December, the ship hosts dinner cruises with live entertainment such as Dixieland, barbershop harmony and local blues acts. Narrated sightseeing cruises, moonlight cruises and sunset cruises also are offered. Private parties and special events can be accommodated year round. The ship is fully heated and air conditioned and features a complete bar and ample dance floor. The upper deck is an ideal vantage point for viewing the sights (such as the long-grounded tug standing in the reeds of Eagle Island opposite Chandler's Wharf).

The 149-passenger, U.S. Coast Guard-approved craft keeps a varied cruise schedule that includes 90-minute sightseeing and moonlight cruises ($8 per adult; $4 per child); entertainment dinner cruises lasting 2 1/2 hours, Thursday through Saturday during the summer ($29-$32.50); and two-hour sunset dinner cruises on Wednesday ($21 for adults, $15 per child). Special events cruises include the Sweetheart Cruise (February), the Azalea Festival (April), Fireworks Cruise (July 4), Riverfest (October), six-hour Nature Cruises and Holiday Flotilla (November), Christmas Lights Cruises and New Year's Eve Party (December). Call for schedules and prices.

OAKDALE CEMETERY
520 North 15th St.

When Nance Martin died at sea in 1857, her body was preserved, seated in a chair in a large cask of rum. Six months later, she was interred at Oakdale Cemetery, cask and all.

Her monument and many other curious, beautiful and historic markers are to be found within the labyrinth of Oakdale Cemetery, Wilmington's first municipal burial ground, which opened in 1855. At the cemetery office, visitors can pick up a free map detailing some of the more interesting interments, such as the volunteer firefighter buried with the faithful dog that gave its life trying to save his master, and Mrs. Rose O'Neal Greenhow, a successful Confederate secret service courier who drowned while running the blockade at Fort Fisher in 1864. Amid the profusion of monuments lies a field oddly lacking in markers: the mass grave of hundreds of victims of the 1862 yellow-fever epidemic. Buried here are many important Wilmingtonians whose ancestors can be traced to the days of Brunswick Town and whose descendants thrive in Wilmington today. The architecture of its monuments, its Victorian landscaping and the abundance of dogwoods make Oakdale beautiful in every season. The cemetery is open until 5 PM every day. Bicycles are not permitted.

THE RIVERWALK
Riverfront Park and wharf, along Water St.

The heart and soul of downtown Wilmington is its riverfront. At one time a crowded, bustling, gritty confusion of warehouses, loading docks and wooden sheds, all suffused with the odor of turpentine, the wharf area stretching from modern-day Chandler's Wharf to beyond the Coastline Inn was the state's most important commercial port. Experience Wilmington's charm and historical continuity by strolling the Riverwalk along Water Street. Fine dining, shopping and lodging now line the red-brick road, and regularly scheduled live entertainment enlivens the scene on Saturday and Sunday evenings from June to early August. These performances, sponsored by Wilmington Parks & Recreation and the Downtown Merchants Association, feature local talent at its best and take place at Riverfront Stage between Market and Dock Streets. Check with the Visitors' Information booth at the foot of Market Street for schedules.

Immediately north, schooners, pleasure boats and replicas of historic ships frequently visit the municipal dock. Coast Guard cutters dock beyond the Federal Court House and are often open for touring, especially during festivals. Benches, picnic tables, a fountain and snack vendors complete a colorful scene that is one of Wilmington's most popular.

ST. JAMES EPISCOPAL CHURCH & BURIAL GROUND
25 S. 3rd St.   *763-1628*

St. James is the oldest church in Wilmington in continuous use, and it wears its age well. The parish was established in 1729, but its original church wasn't completed until 1770. Taken down in 1839, some of that building's materials were used to construct the present church. The graveyard on the corner of Fourth and Market was in use from 1745-1855 and bears considerable historic importance. Here lies buried the

Photo: Curtis Krueger

Kids enjoy every part of the Battleship North Carolina.

patriot Cornelius Harnett, remembered for antagonizing the British by reading the Declaration of Independence aloud at the Halifax Courthouse in 1776. He died in a British prison during the war.

Within the church hangs the celebrated painting of Christ captured from one of the Spanish pirate ships that attacked Brunswick Town in 1748. The church was seized in 1781 by Tarleton's Dragoons under Cornwallis. Tarleton had the pews removed, and the church was used as a stable. A repeat performance of pew-tossing was enacted during the Civil War when occupying Federal forces used the church as a hospital. A letter written by the pastor asking President Lincoln for reparation still exists. It was never delivered, having been completed the day news arrived of Lincoln's assassination.

Individuals are welcomed to take self-guided tours of the church be-

tween 9 AM and early afternoon when services are not underway. Informative brochures are available in the vestibule. Groups may schedule informal guided tours with a local historian by contacting the church office.

ST. JOHN'S MUSEUM OF ART
114 Orange St.   763-0281

Even if St. John's didn't possess one of the world's major collections of Mary Cassatt's color prints, it would still be a potent force in the southeast's art culture. Housed in 3 architecturally distinctive restored buildings (one of them a former church), the museum boasts a fine sculpture garden, changing exhibits, a working studio for art classes, lectures, workshops and an extensive survey of regional and national artists working in a variety of media and styles. On display also is a fine collection of Jugtown pottery. Educational programs for children, films, concerts and a gift shop are among the museum's offerings. Admission costs $2 per adult, $5 per family and $1 for children under 18. Children under 5 may enter free, and admission on the first Sunday of every month is free to all. The museum is handicapped-accessible.

THALIAN HALL/CITY HALL

102 N. 3rd St., 310 Chestnut St.   343-3660

Since its renovation and expansion a few years back, the name is, more accurately, Thalian Hall Center for the Performing Arts. And, yes, it does share the same roof with City Hall. Conceived as a combined political and cultural center, Thalian was built between 1855 and 1858. During its first 75 years, every great national performer appeared on its stage — and some surprising celebrities, too. Lillian Russell, Buffalo Bill Cody, John Philip Sousa, Oscar Wilde, Tom Thumb, Charles Dickens and William Jennings Bryan were all among its early stars. That tradition continues as an increasing variety of national and international artists finds an audience here. Full-scale musicals, light opera and internationally-renowned dance companies are part of Thalian's consistently high-quality programming.

The renovation added the Studio Theater upstairs, as well as a modern lobby and ticket office and new elevators. Smaller-scaled productions are regularly produced in the Studio Theater by Tapestry Theatre Company and Thalian Association Community Theatre groups. Old Thalian's Corinthian columns and ornate proscenium and City Hall's elegant ballroom and high-ceilinged City Council room are a testament to its architect's classic genius. This building, listed on the National Register of Historic Places, is the only surviving theater designed by John Montague Trumble, one of America's foremost 19th-century theater designers. Historic tours cost $2.50 per person. Call for information.

BATTLESHIP NORTH CAROLINA

Cape Fear River   251-5797
opposite downtown

The Battleship *North Carolina* stands enshrined in a berth on Eagle Island and is dedicated to the 10,000 North Carolinians who gave their lives during World War II. Built in 1937 and commissioned in 1941, the 44,800-ton warship wielded nine 16-inch turreted guns among its arsenal and carries nickel steel hull armor 16-18" thick. It was this plating that undoubtedly helped her survive at least one direct torpedo hit in 1942. In fact, this "Immortal Showboat" is renowned for its relatively small number of casualties.

The Battleship came to its present home in 1961. It took a swarm of tugboats to maneuver the 728-foot vessel into its berth where the river was only 500 feet wide. Almost predictably, the bow became stuck in the mud. Unpredictably, an offshore storm, changing tides and conflicting tugboat schedules prevented Fergus's Ark, a popular floating restaurant moored at the foot of Princess Street, from quitting its mooring before the battleship arrived. When the tugboats succeeded in freeing the battleship, they failed to prevent it from swinging into the Ark. Wilmington gained a battleship and lost a restaurant.

From the first Friday in June through Labor Day, the 70-minute outdoor sound and light spectacular "The Immortal Showboat" ($3.50 adults; $1.75 children 6-11) recreates highlights of the battleship's glorious career. Music, lights, sound effects and the voices of Roosevelt, Churchill, Hitler and Truman come together in a tale beginning at the Brooklyn Navy Yard and ending in Boston, the battleship's return port. Shows commence at 9 PM.

The Battleship *North Carolina* open for tours every day of the year from 8 AM to sunset. You can drive there by way of either bridge spanning the river, but a more unusual approach is the Battleship River Taxi (see Capt. Maffitt Sightseeing Cruise, above). There are 2 self-guided tours to choose between. Both begin with a 10-minute orientation film. The full, two-hour tour takes you above and below decks to the pilot house, the turrets, a rare Kingfisher float plane, the crew's quarters and the galley. The shorter one-hour tour takes in fewer decks and eliminates much of the climbing. Only the main deck is handicapped accessible. Tours cost $6 for adults, $3 for children 6-11. Ample parking suitable for buses and RVs, and picnic grounds adjoin the berth. There is no extra charge for unscheduled appearances by old Charlie, the alligator who makes his home near the ship at river's edge.

Photo: N.C. Travel and Tourism Division

History comes alive at Fort Fisher.

WILMINGTON ADVENTURE WALKING TOUR
763-1785

Lifelong resident Bob Jenkins, the man with the hat and walking cane, walks fast but talks slowly and knowledgeably about his hometown. Pointing out architectural details, family lineage and historic events, Bob whisks you through 250 years of history in about an hour. Tours begin from the foot of Market Street at 10 AM and 2 PM daily, weather permitting. A fee is charged. Although no reservations are required, it's best to call ahead, especially in summer.

WILMINGTON RAILROAD MUSEUM
501 Nutt St.   763-2634

Wilmington's greatest transformation took place in the mid 1950s when the Atlantic Coast Line Railroad closed its Wilmington operations. Railroading had been Wilmington's chief industry for more than a century. This fact is clearly borne out by the Museum's amazing photographs and artifacts. More than that, Wilmington's Railroad Museum is a kind of fun house for people fascinated by trains and train culture. And who isn't?

For $2 ($1 for children ages 6-11) you can climb into a real steam locomotive and clang its bell as long as your kids will let you. Inside, volunteers (some of whom are walking histories themselves) will guide you to fascinating highlights. You'll learn why the 19th-century Wilmington & Weldon Railroad was called the "Well Done," or that the beheaded ghost of flagman Joe Baldwin is behind the famous "Maco Light" (which at least one volunteer claims to have

seen). Be sure to ask about the museum's *Memories* book in which visitors are encouraged to share their favorite train memories. Now in its fifth volume, it includes entries by famous actors who have made films in Wilmington. Look closely at the hanging photo of the old ACL Executive Office Building, with separate waiting rooms for whites and blacks.

The museum building was the railroad's freight traffic office and is listed on the National Register of Historic Places. In fact, the entire Coast Line Convention Center complex was a major freight terminal convenient to the bustling Cotton Exchange. Visitors can run the model trains in the enormous railroad diorama upstairs where children will also enjoy the railroad theaterette. An outdoor children's activity center, children's workshops and group discounts are available. The museum also invites you to "conduct" your birthday parties on their caboose. Rental fee includes souvenirs and a tour of the museum, and train-theme refreshments can be arranged. Museum hours are 10 AM to 5 PM Tuesday through Saturday and Sunday 1-5 PM.

ZEBULON-LATIMER HOUSE
126 S. Third St.   762-0492

This magnificent Italianate home dates from 1852 and has its original furnishings. It is headquarters for the Lower Cape Fear Historical Society which sponsors Walk & Talk Tours every Wednesday at 10 AM ($5). The tour encompasses about 12 blocks of the historic district and lasts about 90 minutes. Half-hour tours of the house are available daily until 3:30 PM ($3 adults; $1 students).

Around Wilmington

AIRLIE GARDENS
Airlie Rd.   763-9991

These spectacular private gardens located on Wrightsville Sound can be viewed along a five-mile scenic drive and on foot. With only one formal garden on the grounds, Airlie gives the impression of a dreamland forest from the moment you pass through the grand iron gate. Majestic live oaks and tall pines are hung with moss. Reflection pools plied by swans are rimmed by multicolored azaleas and camellias. Arbors, bridges and a jessamine-covered stone pergola add to the quiet grandeur of these 20 acres, much of which was once tended by a former gardener for the German Kaiser. You can view the picturesque Lebanon Chapel (1835) and one of the county's oldest cemeteries from a distance.

Airlie Gardens is open to the public from March 1 through the first weekend in October and is located 7 miles east of downtown Wilmington. When approaching by Oleander Drive, turn right at Airlie Road, where white-stuccoed St. Andrews On-the-Sound Episcopal Church stands. The entrance is a short distance on the right. Coming from Wrightsville Beach, turn into Airlie Road at the mainland side of the drawbridge (Route 74/76). A $6 fee is charged per person during the peak viewing period (March 1 to April 30); $5 thereafter. Group fees are available.

AIR TOURS

Seeing the Cape Fear coast from the air is an unforgettable experience. You may even see some surprises, like schools of dolphin offshore or the mysterious inland ellipses known as Carolina bays. All you need to do to go aloft is pick up the phone and reserve a flight with one of three fixed-based operators located at New Hanover International Airport. Very often, they'll have a plane available that afternoon or the next day. Tours are available by the 1/2 hour and by the hour and usually require a minimum of 3 passengers. Don't forget the camera.

ISO Aero, 763-8898, is your first choice because it flies high-wing Cessna 172s, which yield greater downward visibility than low-wing planes. Tours can accommodate up to 3 passengers at a time for a cost of $12 per person per 1/2 hour. ISO is located on the airport's east ramp access on North Kerr Avenue

Aeronautics, 763-4691, and its affiliate **Air Wilmington**, 763-0146, will fly 3 passengers in a Piper Warrior for $80 per hour or in a Piper Arrow for $95 per hour (both Pipers are low-wing models). Also available is a two-passenger Beechcraft Skipper in which you can cruise above the Intracoastal Waterway up to Figure Eight Island and back (a 1/2-hour flight) for $38.50. You may choose your own destinations as well, based on the same 1/2-hour fare. Both operators are located at the airport's General Aviation facility.

From the airport's main entrance on 23rd Street, make the first left onto Gardner Avenue, then bear right to General Aviation.

GREENFIELD LAKE & GARDENS
US 421 S.

In springtime, the colors are simply eye-popping. In summer, the algae-covered waters and Spanish moss recall the days when this was an unpopulated cypress swamp. In winter, the bare tree trunks thrust up from the lake in parallel vertical lines. Herons, egrets and ducks are regular visitors, as are hawks and cardinals — certainly more regular than the legendary gators rumored to skulk through these murky waters. (Every local will say there are gators here, yet none claims to have seen one. Tourists wonder if it's just a leg-pull but continue watching just the same.)

JUNGLE RAPIDS FAMILY FUN PARK
5320 Oleander Dr.   *791-0888*

This is a self-contained amusement center with water slides, bumper boats, go-carts, miniature golf, high-tech arcade, snack bar and on-site party catering all rolled into one. Jungle Rapids consists of 4 excellent water slides, including Crocodile Aisle (the fastest on the hill) and a baby slide. Lifeguards are on duty. Lockers (50 cents), picnic tables, chairs and umbrellas are available. All-day admission to the slides is $8.50 which includes one bumper boat ride. The adjoining Grand Prix Go-Cart Track is a gently banked run, which you must be at least 16 to drive. Smaller cars are available for those under 52" tall as well as two-seaters. A drive costs $4 per session, $10 for 3, or by the hour. The arcade sponsors tournaments in air hockey, video road racing and other high-profile teenage pursuits. The park is open from 10 AM to 11 PM. Water slides close at 8 PM. Inquire about the All-Day Water Park Pass ($12) which admits pass-holders to every attraction. Peak hours can be crowded. Everything except the water attractions is open all year long.

NEW HANOVER COUNTY
EXTENSION SERVICE ARBORETUM

6206 Oleander Dr.   *452-6393*

This 6 1/2-acre teaching and learning facility is technically the only arboretum in southeastern North Carolina. An extension of the University of North Carolina, the Arboretum was formally opened in 1989 and is still in the midst of ambitious development despite a shoe-string budget. What the administrators and predominantly-volunteer staff have achieved ranks among the finer theme gardens in the area. Boardwalks, brick paths, concrete walks and gravel trails wind through a profusion of plants, grasses, flowers, trees, shrubs, herbs and vegetables with plenty of shaded seating and aquatic planting pools. Several sections are sponsored by area garden clubs, such as the Herb Garden with its variety of medicinal, culinary, fragrance and tea species beside a jasmine-shrouded pergola. A variety of native habitats are re-created, and adapted transplants are abundant. The Arboretum is designed to assist commercial and private horticultural enterprises and to help residents create attractive home landscapes. This last mission is served by the Garden Hotline, 452-6396, wherein volunteer master gardeners field callers' questions about horticulture from 9 AM to 5 PM.

Many of the volunteers are graduates of various seminars, classes and workshops sponsored by or held at the Arboretum. These programs offer certificates upon completion and are reasonably priced (around $25 per class). Classes on hunting safety are offered, too. The Arboretum is free and open daily from 8 AM to dusk. Volunteer docents lead tours on request. Donations are welcomed, and badly needed. Enter the grounds from Oleander Drive (Highway 76) immediately east of Greenville Loop Road and west of the Bradley Creek bridge. And yes, the Arboretum is available for weddings.

SKATERS CHOICE

5216 Oleander Dr.   *791-6000*

Skaters Choice successfully provides good, clean fun to entire families in the context of indoor roller skating. Skaters roll to music, the styles of which change from night to night and range from current pop and disco to oldies and Christian. Jazzercise classes and after-school skating sessions are regular offerings, as well as matinee skating sessions on weekends. The rink has a large, well-stocked pro shop, game room, large snack lounge and even a parents' viewing room complete with one-way glass (you see them; they can't see you). The rink is open seven days during the summer and four nights a week in winter. The rates are extremely affordable ($2-$4 to skate, $1 for skate rental). In keeping with the management's wish to foster good moral fiber, the house rules prohibit profanity, intoxicants and anything but clean, neat, appropriate clothing. The facilities are also available for private daytime parties with skating packages included. The rink sponsors a competing speed skating team. Skaters Choice is located near the inter-

Orton Plantation at Wilmington is a fine example of Greek Revival architecture. Its gardens are open to the public and beautiful at every season.

Photo: William Russ, N.C. Travel and Tourism Division

section of Oleander Drive and Forest Park Road, five miles from downtown.

STADIUM BATTING CAGES
5570 Oleander Dr.   *791-9660*

Another indicator of a resort town is the presence of batting cages, and these are the only ones for miles around. The throwing machines are the armature type, not the kind with spinning wheels that throw wild every 3rd pitch. There are baseball and softball cages offering a variety of speeds, and the fast balls are mighty fast. Helmets and bats are available at no extra charge. One token ($1 each) gets you 12 pitches, and you can save on 72 ($5). It's a great way to practice your swing, vent some steam or spend an otherwise routine lunch hour. Hours are 2-9 PM on weekdays, 10 AM to 10 PM Saturdays and 12-9 PM Sundays.

Outside Wilmington

POPLAR GROVE PLANTATION
US Rt. 17, Scotts Hill   *686-9989*

The 1850 Greek Revival house was the focus of this 628-acre plantation that was supported by as many as 64 slaves prior to the Civil War. Today, costumed guides lead visitors and recount history. Skills important to daily 19th-century life such as weaving, smithery and basketry are frequently demonstrated. A restaurant and country store add to Poplar Grove's attraction, as do the many events held here throughout the year, including Halloween hayrides and the Medieval Festival in March. Listed on the National Record of Historic Places, Poplar Grove Plantation is located eight miles outside Wilmington on Highway 17 at the Pender County line. It is open free to the public Monday-Saturday 9 AM to 5 PM and Sunday 12-5 PM. Fees are $6 for adults, $5 fro seniors and $3 for students.

The Beaches

Wrightsville Beach

WATER WAYS CHARTERS

Wrightsville Beach   256-4282
                                 (800)562-SAIL

Captained charters and bareboat charters are available for local excursions through Water Ways, one of the area's newest sailing attractions. Owner Jerry Outlaw and his staff are all USCG-licensed captains and American Sailing Association-certified instructors. The Water Ways fleet includes a J-24, Endeavour 32 and a Hunter 33.5. Sailing instruction is also offered. For a complete listing, see Sailing in the chapter on Water Sports.

DOWNEAST ROVER

Wynn Plaza   256-4121

This handsome reproduction of a traditional 19th-century topsail schooner is one of the latest additions to Wrightsville Beach's allure. Because of its topsail rigging, it qualifies as a square-rigged "mini-tall ship." Guests are welcomed to lend a hand, take a turn at the helm or just relax. Regularly scheduled two-hour sailings during the summer depart at 11 AM and 3 PM. An extended sunset cruise sets sail at 6:30 PM. Rates for daytime cruises are $15 per adult, $12 per children under 12. Sunset cruises are slightly more expensive. The Downeast Rover and its captain are fully USCG certified. It is available for weddings and all other types of charters for up to 25 passengers. Availability off season may vary.

MASONBORO ISLAND TAXI & SUNSET CRUISES

Banks Channel   256-9463

The Lumina is a 23-passenger, USCG-certified launch that provides taxi service to the Masonboro Island preserve. Sunset cruises begin at 7 PM, and private charters are available. Daily departures for Masonboro Island are at 10 AM daily, returning at 2:30 PM ($10 per person). During May and September, the taxi runs only on Saturday and Sunday and the sunset cruises only on Friday and Saturday. Reservations are recommended for all excursions. The Lumina is moored on Banks Channel opposite the Blockade Runner Resort Hotel.

Carolina Beach/Kure Beach

CAROLINA BEACH BOARDWALK

Spanning the oceanfront in the middle of downtown Carolina Beach, the boardwalk includes the paved walks bordering a multitude of arcades, nightclubs, miniature golf, pubs, billiard parlors and novelty shops. Colorful and crowded with people in summertime, the entire area has the aura of an amusement park. But this isn't Myrtle Beach. You won't find throngs of tourists choking the boardwalk. But you will find ample clubs, pubs and attractions as well as clean, sandy beach and great surf. Dune crossovers afford beach access and car parking is within comfortable walking distance.

JUBILEE AMUSEMENT PARK
1000 N. Lake Park Blvd.,   *458-9017*
Carolina Beach

With 20 rides, 3 water slides, 3 go-cart tracks, an arcade, gift shop, picnic area and live entertainment, Jubilee Park is a seasonal mecca for family fun. Most of the rides are kiddie-size, and there is no admission fee. Buy tickets to individual rides, an all-day pass, or even a season pass.

FORT FISHER-SOUTHPORT FERRY
Hwy. 421, south of Kure Beach   *457-6942*

More than mere transportation, this 1/2-hour crossing is a journey into the natural and social history of the Cape Fear River. In certain seasons, the thrust of the screw will churn up scores of small fish, causing a cloud of ravenous gulls to follow in the ferry's wake. Excellent views of Federal Point, Zeke's Island and The Rocks are possible from the upper deck. On the Southport side, passengers get a fine view of historic Price's Creek Lighthouse standing just outside the inlet. When traveling between Southport and New Hanover County, timing your trip according to the ferry schedule guarantees that getting there is half the fun. See the Ferries chapter for schedules.

FORT FISHER STATE HISTORIC SITE
Hwy 421, south of Kure Beach   *458-5538*

Fort Fisher was the last Confederate stronghold to fall to Union forces during the War Between the States. It was the linchpin of the Confederate Army's Cape Fear Defense System, which included Forts Caswell, Anderson and Johnson. Largely due to the tenacity of its defenders, the port of Wilmington was never entirely sealed by the Union blockade until the lifelines were cut in January, 1865. The Union bombardment of Fort Fisher was the heaviest naval demonstration in history up to that time.

Today all that remains are the earthenworks, which are the largest in the South. The remainder of the fort has been claimed by the ocean. However, a fine museum, uniformed demonstrations and reenactments make Fort Fisher well worth a visit. Don't miss the Underwater Archaeology Exhibit "Hidden Beneath the Waves." The exhibit is housed in a small outbuilding beside the parking lot. Thirty-minute guided walking tours allow you to walk the earthworks and slide orientation programs take place every 1/2 hour.

The Cove, a tree-shaded picnic area across the road (U.S. 421), overlooks the ocean and makes an excellent place to relax or walk. (Swimming here is discouraged due to dangerous currents and underwater hazards.)

Since this is an archaeological site, metal detectors are prohibited. Museum hours are 9 AM to 5 PM Monday through Saturday and 1 to 5 PM Sunday. It is open all year, and admission is free. (Donations are requested.) The site, located about 19 miles south of Wilmington, was once commonly known as Federal Point. The ferry from Southport is an excellent (and timesaving) way to get there from Brunswick County. Also close by are the NC Aquarium (see below) and the Fort Fisher State Recreation Area, an undeveloped four-mile stretch of beach strand and tidal marsh (see Parks in the chapter on Sports and Fitness).

NORTH CAROLINA
AQUARIUM AT FT. FISHER
Ft. Fisher Blvd.   *458-8257*
south of Kure Beach

Housing the largest shark tank in the state, the Aquarium at Fort Fisher further distinguished itself with the recent addition of a ray and skate tank. But its touch tank seems to elicit the greatest reaction from visitors — especially those who squeamishly pick up a horseshoe crab or get squirted by a startled conch. The outdoor pond is filled with entertaining fish and turtles, and the barn swallows that nest beneath the building zoom in and out just above visitors' heads. Field trips, films and live animal exhibits are offered, and na-

ture walks loop through the grounds. The self-guided Marsh Nature Trail leads visitors to the World War II-era pillbox in which Robert Harrell, the Fort Fisher Hermit, lived from c. 1955 until his death in 1972. Shark feedings take place at 3:30 PM on Tuesdays, Thursdays and Sundays. Daily fish feedings are at 3:30 PM. There is an outdoor picnic deck and beach access nearby.

The Aquarium is located 20 miles south of Wilmington. It is open, free, 9 AM to 5 PM Monday through Saturday and 1-5 PM Sunday. Admission fees are $3 for adults and $1 for children.

Topsail Beach

THE PATIO PLAYGROUND
807 S. Anderson Blvd. (NC 50)   *328-6491*

"What is that thang?" is the common refrain of folks new to the Patio when they first lay eyes on the Gyrogym. The proprietors apparently grew tired of explaining it all season long. Now a printed handout explains that the Gyrogym is a "no-impact workout and a thrill to ride." Looking like an outsized gyroscope, the multiple steel hoops lock the rider into a whirling 360-degree environment said to yield sensations of weightlessness without the side-effects associated with motion sickness. There are some restrictions as to who may ride, no pregnant women, for example, and the ride doesn't come cheap: $5 for up to 5 minutes. With its arcade, pool tables and miniature golf, the Patio is a popular hangout for youth. Various recreational items such as bicycles, surf

Photo: Curtis Krueger

The Battleship North Carolina is open for visitors year round.

boards and umbrellas are also available for rent (see the chapter on Sports and Fitness). The Patio is located across from Jif Freez, 6.4 miles south of the bridge into Surf City.

TOPSAIL BEACH ASSEMBLY BUILDING
720 Channel Blvd.

Once the nerve center of the Navy's missile-development program code-named Operation Bumblebee, the Assembly Building only recently won National Historic Treasure status. During World War II, the U.S. lagged behind Germany in missile research. After the war, the sleepy island of Topsail was transformed into a testing and development site focused on the Assembly Building, constructed for the assembly of rockets. Recently, when residents brought in architectural experts to aid preservation efforts, it was recognized that the installations remaining on Topsail Island, the Assembly Building in particular, were among the most perfectly intact historic buildings in the east. The Assembly Build-

ing is now an active community center. Guided tours, arranged through the Greater Topsail Chamber of Commerce in Surf City, allow visitors to view the amazing original photographs of America's missile defense program in its infancy.

TOPSAIL SKATING RINK
S. Anderson Blvd. near Flake Ave.   *328-2381*

An institution for 40 years, this quaint, unpretentious indoor rink is located upstairs in a lime-green house above the tiny Post Office. It is open 7 to 10 PM 7 nights a week in the summer and on weekends during the off-season. Sessions are inexpensive ($3 to $4), and skate rentals are available. The building stands diagonally across the main road from the Flying Burrito Fish Camp within an easy walk of the Patio Playground.

TOPSAIL SCENIC BOAT TOURS
Surf City Marina, Roland Ave.
Surf City   *328-5065/2774*

The utmost in relaxation is touring the Intracoastal Waterway and adjoining inshore waters in the 33-foot pontoon boat *Kristy's Kruiser II*. It's an excellent way to view local wildlife while enjoying cool breezes and conversation. The Coast Guard-certified tours leave the Surf City Marina (the pink place near the draw bridge) at 1, 3, 5 and 7:00 PM. Tours last 1 1/2 hours and cost $15 per person, except the 3 PM tour that lasts 45 minutes ($10). Ice is furnished, and you may bring your favorite beverages or coolers. Special arrangements, such as boxed lunches, can be provided for an extra fee. Bookings are requested, and walk-ins are welcomed. Private tours can be chartered for up to 20 people ($150.00 for the first hour).

TREASURE ISLAND FAMILY FUN PARK
Hwy. 210, Sneads Ferry   327-2700

Grand Prix racing (go-carts), bumper boats, kiddie rides and an 18-hole miniature golf course are the main attractions at this park located about 10 minutes north of Topsail Island. Ice cream, snacks and an arcade may make it difficult for parents to get away cheaply, so look for discount coupons (good before 6 PM) at visitors' centers and wherever tourist information is distributed.

South Brunswick

CARTER'S STORE
Sunset Harbor Rd.   842-9352

Sunset Harbor is a destination point. That is, it lies at the end of a road (County Road 1112) that goes nowhere else, so you don't drive through Sunset Harbor, you arrive there. There's not much to see in this shady, former fishing village (which refuses incorporation) . . . except Ma and Pa Carter's variety store. It's in one of those tiny cinder block buildings with few windows. It's poorly lit, cool inside and always has an "Open" sign on the screen door even after closing. Locals come here for conversation, a cold root beer, to look at photos of the Carters' dozens of grandchildren, or for a bit of gossip from the feisty nonagenarian, Ma Carter, about how tourists and the residents at nearby River Run Plantation are changing the community. Be prepared for some sarcasm. Carter's is a true holdover from a bygone coastal Carolina. It's a stone's throw north of a more modern convenience store on Sunset Harbor Road where, you can be certain, root beer doesn't taste quite the same.

THE DECK ENTERTAINMENT CENTER
5524 E. Beach Dr. at   278-4111
SE 58th St, Long Beach

This drug- and alcohol-free entertainment facility is pure family fun. With a swimming pool, arcade, snack bar and pool tables, it's a mecca for youngsters on Oak Island. The Deck also rents beach items and sells gifts. Its location across the road from other amusement magnets such as Lighthouse Miniature Golf, water bumper rides and the Go-Dog Track (hot dog-shaped go-carts) keeps this end of Oak Island well-lit and lively.

FORT CASWELL
Caswell Beach Rd.   278-9501

Considered one of the strongest forts of its time, Fort Caswell originally encompassed some 2,800 acres at the east end of Oak Island. Completed in 1838, the compound consisted of earthen ramparts enclosing a roughly pentagonal brick and masonry fort and the citadel. Caswell proved to be so effective a deterrent during the War of Northern Aggression that it saw little action. Supply lines were cut after Fort Fisher fell to Union forces in January 1865, so before abandoning the fort, its garrison detonated the powder magazine. The citadel and surrounding earthworks were heavily damaged. What remains of the citadel is essentially unaltered and is maintained by the Baptist Assembly of North Carolina, which owns the property. A more expansive system of batteries and a sea wall were constructed during the war-wary years of 1885-1902. Fort Caswell is open for self-guided visits from Monday to Thursday, 8 AM to 4:30 PM, for a fee of $2.

OCEAN AIRE AVIATION, INC.
Brunswick County Airport
380 Long Beach Rd.   457-0710
Aviators Larry Ryan and John Martin own 2 certified aircraft used for air tours, a high-wing and a low-wing. They can accommodate up to 3 passengers at a time for a base rate of $15 per person for 15 minutes. A variety of tours lasting up to 1 hour are available within the range from Wrightsville Beach to Little River (north of Myrtle Beach, SC). Flights are available 7 days a week during the summer and by appointment off-season. See the chapter on Airports for information on other services offered by Ocean Aire Aviation.

SUMMER FUN BEACH DAYS
Long Beach Cabana,   253-4357
foot of 40th St. E.
One afternoon each month from May through September, Brunswick County Parks & Recreation sponsors live musical performances, volleyball, fun and games at the Cabana (a public beach-access facility) overlooking the ocean. Admission is free to all, and the fun begins around 1 PM. Featured musical styles tend toward island sounds as well as parrot-head (Jimmy Buffett-style) and beach music. Times and dates vary, so check with Parks & Rec for up-to-the-minute schedules.

CAPT'N PETE'S SEAFOOD MARKET
Jordan Blvd., Holden Beach   842-6675
What makes Capt'n Pete's something of an attraction is not its fresh local seafood for sale, nor its bait and tackle, gift shop, charter boats or sightseeing cruises. Nor is it the friendly people, good service or helpful advice. What sets Capt'n Pete's apart is its incredible selection of hot sauces displayed for sale beneath the fresh fish service counter. We know of no other single source for

Insiders like openings at St. John's Museum of Art not only for the art but also because of the interesting people who gather there.

Insiders' Tips

both Jamaica Hell Fire Doc's Special and Louisiana Gold Pepper Sauce, not to mention Iguana Red Pepper Sauce from Costa Rica and Louisiana's Gumbo Fil. So next time you're in Holden Beach wondering how you're going to cook up all those fine sea critters you caught earlier that day, forget the Old Bay and Crab Boil. Pick up a supply of Tennessee Sunshine at Capt'n Pete's on the Intracoastal side of the island and tell 'em we sent you. Capt'n Pete's is open seven days from 7 AM to 7:30 PM.

PYEWACKET SAILING CRUISES
Holden Beach Marina   754-0284

This graceful 34-foot Catalina sloop offers the opportunity to enjoy the South Brunswick Islands in true Cape Fear coastal tradition — on the open waters of the Atlantic. Daily 1/2-day and evening cruises ($30 per person) begin on the Intracoastal Waterway and give up to 6 passengers at a time the opportunity to lend a hand or to sit back and relax. Evening cruises are especially picturesque since sunsets along the South Brunswick Islands are over sea, not over land. Full-day cruises (9 AM- 4 PM) are also available for $50 per person (minimum 4 passengers). Departure times are approximately 9 AM and 1:30 PM for the half-day cruises and 5:30 PM for

evening cruises. Reservations are suggested. When calling after 6 PM, dial 842-3857.

MUSEUM OF COASTAL CAROLINA
3rd St., Ocean Isle Beach   579-1016

Standing on the ocean floor would be a wonderful way to experience the marine environment up close and personal. Visitors to the Museum of Coastal Carolina can do the next best thing: visit the Reef Room, an impressive undersea representation believed to be the largest natural history diorama in the southeast. Above you, sharks, dolphins, game fish and most small fish common to the region "swim in place." Meanwhile, all types of crustacean critters creep below. The remains of a shipwreck, believed to date from the 1700s or early 1800s and washed ashore by Hurricane Hugo, rest on the "sea bottom." Civil War artifacts, tide exhibits, a display of shark jaws and many other exhibits bring the natural history of the Cape Fear coast vividly to life. Admission is $2 for adults, $1 for kids 12 years old and under. Summer hours (Memorial-Labor Day) are 9 AM - 5 PM Monday through Saturday, 1-5 PM Sunday. The museum is open on weekends only in early spring and late fall: 9 AM - 5 PM Saturday and 1-5 PM Sunday.

Insiders' Tips

Clever insiders seek refuge on the high ground during Riverfest and the Azalea Festival; Roy's Riverboat landing has outside balconies on the second floor.

Southport

ORTON PLANTATION GARDENS
Off Hwy. 133 at Winnabow   371-6851

This property represents one of the region's oldest historically significant residences in continuous use. It is located at the northern extremes of "Carolina Low Country" and this coast's rice-growing range. The family names associated with it are the very root and fiber of Cape Fear's long-branching history.

Built in 1725 by the imperious "King" Roger Moore, founder of Brunswick Town, the main residence at Orton Plantation underwent several expansions to become the archetype of Old Southern elegance. It survived the ravages of the Civil War largely due to its use as a Union hospital after the fall of Fort Fisher. Thereafter, it stood abandoned for 19 years until it was purchased and refurbished by Col. Kenneth McKenzie Murchison, CSA. In 1904, the property was passed to the Sprunt family, which had been previously grafted by marriage to the Murchison family tree, and the plantation gardens began taking shape. In 1915 the family built Luola's Chapel, a Doric structure of modest grandeur available today for meetings and private weddings.

The gardens, both formal and natural, are considered among the most beautiful on the eastern seaboard. Ponds and fountains are adorned by statuary, footbridges and stands of cypress. The elaborately-sculpted Scroll Garden overlooks former rice fields and is the epitome of elegance. Elsewhere within the gardens are the tombs of Roger Moore and his family.

The best times to visit Orton Plantation Gardens span from late winter to midsummer. Camellias, azaleas, pansies, flowering trees and other ornamentals come into bloom early. Later, oleander, hydrangea, crepe myrtle, magnolia and annuals bloom. Bring along insect repellent in the summer. If you're lucky, you may catch a glimpse of Buster, the 10-foot gator that has lived in the lagoon in front of the manor house for several decades. He's been known to sun himself in front of the gardens.

Touring the gardens takes an easily-paced hour or more. They are open everyday from March through November 8 AM to 6 PM. An entrance fee of $7 is charged; $6 for seniors; $3 for children ages 6-12. Orton Plantation is located off Highway 133, 18 miles south of Wilmington and 10 miles north of Southport. Nearby are the historic sites of Brunswick Town and Fort Anderson (see Old Brunswick Town, below).

FORT JOHNSON
Davis & Bay Sts.

Fort Johnson was the first fort erected in North Carolina, established in 1754 to command the mouth of the Cape Fear River and valuable ports upriver. A bevy of tradesmen, fishermen and river pilots soon followed and so the town of Smithville was born (renamed Southport in 1887). During the Civil War, Confederate forces seized Fort Johnson, adding it to their formidable Cape Fear Defense System (which included Forts Caswell, Anderson and Fisher). The fortifications no longer stand, but the site is redolent with memories of those times. The remaining original structures house personnel assigned to the Sunny Point Military Ocean Terminal, an ordnance depot a few miles north.

"THE GROVE"
FRANKLIN SQUARE PARK
E. West St. between Howe St. and Atlantic Ave.

Shaded by centuries-old live oaks and aflame with color in spring, this is a park to savor, a place in which to drink in the spirit of old Smithville. The walls and entrances were constructed of ballast stones used by ships more than 100 years ago. Stately Franklin Square Gallery, now housing fine art in several media, was once a school house, then City Hall. The park is a place to which you'll almost certainly want to return, so why not indulge in local legend and take a drink of pure well water from the old pump — a draught that is sure to bring you back again and again.

OLD SMITHVILLE BURIAL GROUND
E. Moore & S. Rhett Sts.

"The Winds and the Sea sing their requiem and shall forever more...." Profoundly evocative of the harsh realities endured by Southport's long-gone seafarers, the Burial Ground (1804) is a must-see. Obelisks to lost river pilots, monuments to entire crews and families who lived and died by the sea and stoic poetic elegies memorialize Southport's past as no other historic site can. Many of the names immortalized on these stones live on among descendents still living in the area.

MARITIME MUSEUM
166 N. Howe St.   *456-0003*

Read Gentleman Pirate Stede Bonnet's plea for clemency, delivered before he was hanged; view treasures rescued from local shipwrecks; see a 2,000-year old Indian canoe fragment; learn about hurricanes, shark teeth, shrimping nets and much more in one of the region's newest and most ambitious museums. Many of the exhibits are hands-on, and a Jeopardy-styled trivia board is a favorite of history buffs of all ages. The museum is located in downtown Southport within walking distance of restaurants and shopping. Museum hours are 10 AM to 4 PM, Tuesday through Saturday. Admission is $2 for adults ages 16 and up. Children are admitted free.

SOUTHPORT TRAIL

This one-mile walking tour links 25 historic landmarks (some listed here), including the tiny Old Brunswick County Jail. Architectural beauty abounds along the route, revealing Queen Anne gables, Southport arch and bow, and porches trimmed in gingerbread. The free brochure describing this self-guided chain of discoveries can be obtained at the Visitors' Information Center, 109 East Nash Street, 457-7929, Monday-Friday from 10 AM to 4 PM.

WATERFRONT PARK
Bay St., foot of Howe St.

This is possibly the most relaxing and scenic vantage point in Southport. Gone are the pirate ships, canneries and menhaden boats, but the procession of ferries, giant freighters, barges and sailboats keeps Southport's maritime tradition alive. From the swings overlooking the waterfront one can see Old Baldy Lighthouse and Oak Island Lighthouse (the brightest in the nation). Take a seat on Whittlers' Bench surrounding the live oak at the foot of Howe Street, a great place to whittle, swap fish tales and imagine these gracious old streets plied by horse and buggy. Old Southport is not very far away.

Bald Head Island

"OLD BALDY" LIGHTHOUSE
457-5003

Referring to Old Baldy's authorization by Congress in 1813, a member of the family that owns the island once said, "It took an act of Congress to get the first high-rise on Bald Head Island, and it would take an act of Congress to get another." This historic landmark was put into service in 1817 and is the state's oldest standing lighthouse. It was the second of 3 lighthouses built on the island to guide ships across the Cape Fear Bar and into the river channel. The 110-foot tower has brick walls 5 feet thick to a height of 20 feet. It is open to visitors who wish to climb to the top. Several ancillary buildings nearby still stand, such as the 3 cottages called Captain Charlie's Station, registered Historic Places, all that once housed the "wickies" and their families, and the Old Boat House on Bald Head Creek.

BALD HEAD ISLAND HISTORIC TOUR & LUNCH
457-5003

This guided-tour package may be the most convenient way for a daytripper to get to know Bald Head past and present. The journey begins with a 10 AM ferry departure from Indigo Plantation. The 90-minute tour includes Old Baldy Lighthouse and Captain Charlie's Station. The fee ($29 per person; $25 children under 12) also buys parking at the ferry point, round-trip ferry and lunch, served at the River Pilot Cafe at noon. Diners may choose a specially-prepared entree and a beverage from the Chef's menu (gratuities included). You may choose between the 1:30 and 2:30 PM return ferry. Reservations are required.

State and National Parks

OLD BRUNSWICK TOWN STATE HISTORIC SITE

Off Hwy. 133   *371-6613*

On this site stood the first successful permanent European settlement between Charleston, SC, and New Bern, NC. It was founded by Roger and Maurice Moore in 1726. (They recognized an unprecedented real estate opportunity after their relative, Col. James Moore, helped clear out the native residents in the Tuscarora War, 1711-13). The site served as port and political center. Russelborough, home of two royal governors, once stood nearby. In 1748 it was attacked by Spanish privateers. The Spaniards were soundly defeated in a surprise counterattack. A painting of Christ was among the ship's plunder and now hangs in St. James Episcopal Church in Wilmington. It was at Brunswick Town that one of the first instances of armed resistance to the British crown took place, in 1765, in response to the Stamp Act. In time, the younger upriver port of Wilmington superseded Brunswick. In 1776 the British burned the town, and in 1862 Fort Anderson was built there to defend Port Wilmington.

Today, occasional church services are still held in the ruins of St. Philip's Church. The other low-lying ruins and Fort Anderson's well-preserved earthworks may not be visually impressive, but the stories told about them by volunteers in period garb are. The museum preserves thousands of artifacts that contribute to a vivid portrait of Cape Fear's influential past. Admission to the historic site is free. Hours from April 1 through October 31 are 9 AM to 5 PM Monday through Saturday and 1 to 5 PM Sunday. From November 1 through March 31, visit between 10 AM and 4 PM Tuesday through Saturday, and 1 and 4 PM Sunday. It is closed Monday during the winter season. From Wilmington, take Highway 133 about 15 miles to Plantation Road. Clearly visible signs will direct you to the site (exit left) that lies close to Orton Plantation Gardens.

Cape Fear Coast Islands

MASONBORO ISLAND

Evidence strongly suggests that the first stretch of continental American coastline ever spotted and described by a European explorer was the eight-mile-long beach now called Masonboro Island. The explorer was Giovanni Verrazzano; the year, 1524.

Masonboro's beaches were visited by the destruction of three blockade runners and one Union blockader during the Civil War. Later still came a new breed of animal, the tourist.

Before 1952, there was no Masonboro Island. In that year, Carolina Beach Inlet was cut by private enterprise after the Army Corps of Engineers deemed the project unjustifiable. That cut is what gave Carolina Beach its boom in the tourist fishing trade and created the last and largest undisturbed barrier island remaining on the southern North Carolina coast, Masonboro Island.

Masonboro is now the 4th component of the North Carolina National Estuarine Research Reserve, the other three being Zeke's Island, which lies south of Federal Point in the Cape Fear River (see below and the chapter on Fishing), Currituck Banks and Rachel Carson, both located further north on the North Carolina coast.

Masonboro is unique for a number of reasons. Its proximity to a large population center and its undeveloped condition makes it a "distant" getaway that's only five miles from Wilmington. It receives fresh water from upland runoff, not from a tidal river as most other estuarine systems do. Its plethora

of wildlife, some abundant and some endangered, and its accessibility to UNCW's marine biology program, one of the world's best, makes Masonboro an ideal living classroom for the study of habitat exposed to human impact. The island is a peaceful place where generations of locals have fished, hunted, sunbathed, swam, surfed, camped and sat back to witness nature.

The island is little more than a shifting ribbon of vegetated sand backed by 4,400 acres of salt marsh, tidal flats and creeks. The oceanfront dune is capped in places by shrub thicket and a small maritime forest of live oak, loblolly pine, red cedar and plants uniquely adapted to the infertile soils. But what impresses most is the profusion of wildlife in an essentially natural state.

Endangered loggerhead turtles successfully nest here, as do terns, gulls, ghost crabs and brown pelicans. Their neighbors include gray foxes, marsh rabbits, opossums, raccoons and river otters. Several types of heron (Great, blue and tricolor), snowy egrets, willets, black skimmers and clapper rails all forage in the creeks and mud flats at low tide. The estuarine waters teem with 44 species of fish and a multitude of clams, oysters,

A great way to get to Masonboro Island is to rent a sailboat at the Blockade Runner Motel on Wrightsville Beach — provided you know how to sail.

Insiders' Tips

snails, sponges and worms.

Small wonder Masonboro Island has always been close to locals' hearts. Accordingly, the Coastal Management Division of the North Carolina Department of Environment, Health and Natural Resources administers the island with as little intrusion as possible. Camping, hunting (within state regulations) and other traditional activities pursued here continue, albeit under constant monitoring that is intended to determine whether the island can withstand such impact. So far, so good.

The efforts to preserve Masonboro Island are spearheaded by the Society for Masonboro Island, Inc., a nonprofit, tax-exempt membership corporation organized in 1983. Much of the island's high ground, especially on the north end, remains in the hands of private landowners who could at any time alter the natural habitat or prohibit use by the public. The Society's goal is to see the island acquired for public purposes and maintained in its undeveloped state. This is accomplished by facilitating negotiations between the state and landowners for the purchase of island tracts, among other means. The Society itself has purchased part ownership in several tracts. It also sponsors public education through a newsletter, nature walks, volunteer island cleanups and a speakers bureau. Membership in the Society is inexpensive. Contact them at P.O. Box 855, Wrightsville Beach, NC 28480, 256-5777. Valuable information on Masonboro Island and barrier island habitats may also be pursued through UNCW's Center for Marine Science Research, 7205 Wrightsville Avenue, Wilmington 28403, 256-3721.

The island is accessible only by boat. If you don't own one and can't rent one, refer to the listing for the Masonboro Island Water Taxi & Sunset Cruises earlier in this chapter.

ZEKE'S ISLAND

You can walk to this island reserve in the Cape Fear River, and you need not practice walking on water. Simply drive down by the boat ramp at Federal Point (beyond the ferry terminal) and at low tide, walk "The Rocks," a breakwater first erected in 1873 that continues south of Zeke's Island for a total of 3 1/3 miles. Or you can go by boat if keeping your feet on the tricky rocks isn't your idea of fun.

This component of the North Carolina National Estuarine Research Reserve, totaling 1,160 acres, consists of Zeke's Island, North Island, No-Name Island and "The Basin," the body of water enclosed by the breakwater. The varied habitats include salt marshes, beaches, tidal flats and estuarine waters. Bottlenosed dolphins, red-tailed hawks, osprey and colonies of fiddler crabs will keep you looking in every direction. Fishing, sunbathing, boating and hunting are the primary pursuits here. Bring everything you need, and pack out everything you bring. Don't forget drinking water!

Thalian Hall

Tony Rivenbark has been overseeing the development of historic Thalian Hall since 1979. Serving as theater manager through the most ambitious renovations since the building's construction in 1858, Mr. Rivenbark has witnessed one of the most significant theatrical buildings in the country come into its own as a cultural arts center for the new century.

"I did my first play here in 1966, so it's like 27 years that I've dealt with this building. I worked briefly as one of the Thalian Hall guides when the Historic Wilmington Tour was first established in 1977. And then I was hired as a director and came back for two seasons when I was living in New York. Then, I decided not to go back to New York. In 1979, the job became available, and I was hired by the trustees.

I think one of the primary reasons that they hired me was because I had a background in the theatre. Prior to that the managers really hadn't. Interesting. Wasn't much of a job either. They didn't pay much.

But that point in time Thalian Hall was relatively underutilized and only one arts group was in here and that was the Thalian Association. Basically, it was dark most of the time. It was the headquarters for the Historic Wilmington Tour, so it was open to tourists, but it was more like an historic site than an active theatre.

There were a lot of reasons for that. And one was because the facility itself was very poor technically, even though it had been beautifully restored. So the board was at a point of trying to figure out the next step, and everybody knew there were problems with the backstage. The city administration changed a bit and, therefore, a new contract was created, which

Crowds of Wilmingtonians gathered at Thalian Hall during President Taft's 1909 visit.

made it in the interest of whoever was managing the building to try to get more use out of it because it would bring in more income. Prior to that time, the money went directly to the city, so nobody ever put forth a lot of effort to increase the use because there was no profit motive. Well, the truth is there's really no such thing as a profit in this business.

I came in directly at that point where there was a need for greater theatrical expertise, for somebody who knew the arts community here, and it was also at a time when they were looking at what direction to go in. I didn't have any great plan, but I was asked to do two things. One was to stop the smoking in the building, and the other was to increase the income. That was it. That was all I was told to do.

By paying a bit of attention to the operation of the facility and trying to make things work, encouraging people to use the building and a change in the rate, the rental in two years increased by 1,000 percent. So it didn't take long. As we were more actively pursuing people to use the building, that occurred, and the arts began to develop more in this community. There were more arts groups wanting to do things.

The real beginning or the moment that things changed was the St. Thomas Celebration of the arts in 1982. That really brought all of the arts together, it made the community aware that there was an arts community, it made members of the arts community realize that there were other people doing things. In that festival, all the arts groups were encouraged to do some kind of activity, so that created a bigger kind of energy.

In 1983 we had the 125th anniversary of the opening of the theater, we created an original musical here, Lou Cruscuolo came in, he got interested in starting a theater company. That was the same year the film industry came in with "Firestarter," and that began to create another kind of excitement. So, year after year, it got busier and busier. By 1983, the theatre was being used so much it was beginning to collapse backstage because it just couldn't handle all that, so we had to really start looking at renovation.

The last major renovation was begun in 1988, and the theater reopened in 1990 after being closed for two years. Five and a half million dollars, half a million on the stage itself — which was really the heart of the renovation — the stage floor, the fly system, all new electrical system, lighting, sound, all new curtains and drapery, an enlarged orchestra pit. Then, the next year, we added on the exterior of the building, which was about 25,000 square feet of new lobby, backspace, support space, the studio theatre.

During that time a crack was discovered in the exterior of the building. That occurred when they were putting in the pilings for the new wing. Well, it wasn't a new crack. It was an old crack that reopened. After all, this building has brick walls that go up almost 50-something feet that are 135 years old, so there's a certain fragility to this building, which is why the new backstage and fly system all rest on a steel arrangement of beams and supports that are not in any way supported by the brick walls of the building. So if the walls fell, the stage would still be there because they don't have anything to do with each other. That was all part of making the theater modern and, at the same time, not having to muck it up too much. The new wing is primarily on the back and side of the building, and that enabled us to preserve the exterior as people like it. So if people don't like the contemporary addition they can always go on the other side of the building. They can have their cake and eat it too.

There are 628 units of activity in this complex each year now. This includes meetings and rehearsal, including the City Council chamber. We're probably the only theatre group in the country that manages a City Council chamber. But it's all theater. Some people say it is.

Last year we rented to 55 arts organizations. There are nine theatre companies that use this building and, of course, we present a series of children's programs, concerts, a jazz festival. About 250 performances each year. Something happens in here every day of the year — sometimes, as many as seven things.**⁹⁹**

Cape Fear's Celebrity Roster

Wilmington and the Cape Fear coast have played well-known roles throughout the nation's history. But few people are aware of the famous and talented folks who once called the area home.

- Woodrow Wilson, 28th President of the United States
- Michael Jordan, basketball star, Chicago Bulls
- Meadowlark Lemon, basketball star, Harlem Globetrotters
- Sonny Jurgenson, NFL Hall of Fame
- Roman Gabriel, NFL Player of the Year, 1969, L.A. Rams
- Althea Gibson, Tennis Champion (U.S. Open 1957-58, Wimbledon 1957-58, French Open 1956)
- Sugar Ray Leonard, Olympic Gold Medalist boxer
- David Brinkley, TV journalist
- Charles Kuralt, TV commenta-

tor and author
- Charlie Daniels, country-rock musician
- Sammy Davis, Sr., performer
- Anna McNeill Whistler, "Whistler's mother"
- John Cheek, operatic baritone
- Caterina Jarboro, operatic soprano
- Minnie Evans, visionary artist
- Mary Baker Eddy, founder of Christian Science Church
- Robert Ruark, author and safari hunter
- William Hooper, signer of the Declaration of Independence
- Thomas Godfrey, first American playwright
- Cornelius Harnett, patriot of the American Revolution
- Edward B. Dudley, first Governor of NC elected by popular vote

Inside
Annual Events

So many festivals, so little time! But don't worry; life is slow enough on the Cape Fear coast to enjoy them all . . . time and time again. Following is a list of some of the area's most popular annual events. Should you require further information on any event, call the appropriate Chamber of Commerce for the location listed. Annual fishing tournaments are listed in the Fishing chapter. Enjoy!

January

Greater Wilmington Antique Show, Coast Line Convention Center, 763-6739.

February

EARLY FEBRUARY
The North Carolina Jazz Festival features world-class Dixieland and mainstream headliners in a cabaret setting at the Wilmington Hilton, 763-8585.

MID-FEBRUARY
Coastal Carolina Wildlife Expo and Exhibit is an elaborate two-day exhibition of wildlife art geared toward the promotion of conservation and education that takes place at Coast Line Convention Center, 763-6739.

March

The Medieval Festival includes jousting, dance, foods, revelry, medieval crafts and costumes at Poplar Grove Historic Plantation, Scotts Hill, 686-9503.

MID-MARCH
Southern Lights Festival is a week-long celebration in which Wilmington plays host to our snowbound Canadian neighbors, and others from parts north, (800) 222-4757

April

Robert Ruark Chili Cookoff, varieties of the dish that the famous author never dreamed of while cooking his own in Southport are the focus of this competitive cook-off. Arts, crafts and entertainment accompany salivating spectators as they await samples at Franklin Square Park, Southport, 457-5954.

An Easter Egg Hunt occurs at Poplar Grove Historic Plantation, Scotts Hill, 686-9503.

Greater Topsail Spring Jubilee celebrates the rites of spring with arts and crafts, volleyball tournaments, foot races, tug o' war and castle building at Topsail Island, 328-4722.

Mid-April

North Carolina Azalea Festival, the semiofficial opening of "The Season" in Wilmington, features scores of musical and theatrical performances, garden tours, and house tours throughout the city and Wrightsville Beach. A grand parade downtown kicks off a weekend of outdoor entertainment on several stages during a street fair filled with foods, crafts and people along the riverfront, 763-0905.

Don't miss the Onslow County Museum Kite Festival at Topsail Beach, 324-5008.

May

Pleasure Island Spring Festival is a day of live entertainment, arts and crafts, and a pig-cooking contest at Carolina and Kure Beaches, 458-8434.

The North Carolina Symphony makes its annual return to Brunswick Community College for its spring orchestral showcase, (800) 292-7469 or 754-6900.

Late May

Homecoming Weekend in Southport features the Black Pearl Pageant, a parade, arts and crafts, 457-6964.

Memorial Day is observed aboard the USS North Carolina Battleship Memorial. The day includes music, guest speakers and other special events, 251-5797.

Memorial Day is also observed at Fort Fisher State Historic Site, Highway 421, 458-5538.

Topsail Island also sponsors Memorial Day celebrations, 328-0666.

June

Summer Fair, food, refreshments, pony rides and hay rides take place at Poplar Grove Historic Plantation, Highway 17, Scotts Hill, 686-9503.

Mid-June

The North Carolina Music Showcase, 4 days of new rock music, featuring more than 15 bands based in North Carolina is hosted by The Mad Monk in Wilmington, 395-0280.

July

Little Miss & Tiny Miss North Carolina 4th of July Pageant takes place in Southport/Oak Island, 253-5891 or 457-1442.

North Carolina Fourth of July Festival is among the biggest and most spectacular in the state. The celebration begins on Friday of the holiday weekend on Long Beach with surfing, volleyball, sandcastle building, watermelon-eating, horseshoe tossing and tug-of-war contests. Three more days of festivities fol-

Photo: William Russ, N.C. Travel and Tourism Division

Live oaks, Spanish moss and thousands of azaleas line the driveways and lakes of Wilmington's privately owned Airlie Gardens, a former rice plantation.

low, including live music, foot races, children's field events, a street dance, a firefighters' competition, arts and crafts, antiques, a parade, and more. The celebration culminates in one of the grandest fireworks displays on the coast, Southport, 457-6964.

Fireworks over the Battleship North Carolina, on the riverfront are preceded by live entertainment, Wilmington, 341-7855.

Watch fireworks over the surf from the end of Johnny Mercer's Pier, Wrightsville Beach, 395-2965.

Fireworks will light up the night sky above Jubilee Amusement Park, Carolina Beach, 458-8434.

The Annual Wacky Golf Cart Parade features golf carts decorated according to such sober categories as "Creatures of the Sea" and "Tacky Tourist," as well as "Patriotic," "Historical" and "Environmental." Nonmember spectators are welcome, Bald Head Island, 457-5003.

Mid-July

Surf, Sun & Sand Celebration, volleyball tournaments, live music, foods, and summer-fun indulgence, Wrightsville Beach, 256-7925.

Late-July

Beach Music Festival features live beach music and shagging on the beach strand, Carolina Beach, 458-6216.

August

Feast of Pirates is 2 days of family-oriented plank-walking, sword play, swaggering, treasure hunts, Yo-Ho-Ho-ing, children's programs, live music, pirate costume contest, invitational craft sale, live music and food. The feast is an overall swashbuckling and timber-shivering bombast, inspired by an historic 18th-century pirate debauch of Wilmington. Water Street, on the first weekend of August, 762-2611.

Cape Fear Blues Festival celebrates 3 days of live performances of every type of blues imaginable. Hosted by the Blues Society of the Lower Cape Fear, the event culminates in the annual Lower Cape Fear Blues Amateur Talent Contest at the famous Ice House, Wilmington, 343-9447.

Sneads Ferry Shrimp Festival, being one of the bigger celebrations of such a small animal, kicks off with a parade, then crafts, country music, boiled and fried shrimp, carnival rides and military displays. The event takes place 20 minutes north of Topsail Island, Sneads Ferry. Admission $2, children under 12 free.

September

Labor Day Arts & Crafts Fair takes place at Middleton Park, Long Beach, 278-3708.

Piney Woods Festival, a multi-ethnic celebration of our cultural heritage, features international

The world's largest living Christmas tree is a 75-foot tall water oak in Wilmington. The tree, estimated to be more than 300 years old, is decorated each Christmas season and various groups sing carols there for visitors.

foods, music, dance, crafts and demonstrations in Hugh MacRae Park, 763-2787.

MID-SEPTEMBER

Annual Autumn with Topsail Beach Arts & Entertainment Festival gets underway at Topsail Beach, 328-9221.

Home & Garden Expo promotes the betterment of two things the historic Cape Fear region excels in. The expo takes place at Trask Coliseum, UNCW, Wilmington, 799-2611.

Big Sweep/Beach Sweep is a day for locals to clean up the area's beaches and put another tourist season behind them, 762-2611.

LATE SEPTEMBER

North Carolina Spot Festival, a fabulous feast of fish, is sponsored by the Hampstead Volunteer Fire Department in late September in Hampstead, 270-2525 or 270-4719.

David Walker Day, a day of music, guest speakers and special events memorializing a great African-American resident of Wilmington occurs in late September, 763-3972.

Marine Expo touts all the latest and greatest in vessels, equipment and accessories with which to better enjoy the Cape Fear coast. The event takes place at Coast Line Center late in the month, 452-7117.

October

Riverfest, a citywide celebration of the sea features regattas, water races (including rubber duckies), a street fair with food and crafts, concerts, live arts performances and live outdoor entertainment, 452-6862.

Octoberfest takes place at Carolina and Kure Beaches, 458-8434.

MID-OCTOBER

Pleasure Island Seafood & Jazz Festival, features seafood and live outdoor jazz and blues, games, music workshops, team softball tournament, Captain's Choice Golf Tournament and coastal awareness exhibits at the Air Force Recreation Area, Kure Beach, 458-6723 or (800) 222-4757

New Hanover County Fair consists of rides, games, agricultural contests, live music and food at County Fairgrounds, Carolina Beach Road, 251-3382.

LATE OCTOBER

Annual Chili Cookoff is a competitive feast that really does amount to a hill o' beans. You'll be able to sample winning recipes at Hugh MacRae Park, 763-6216.

North Carolina Festival By the Sea, once a low-key Halloween celebration, is now a down-home, three-day romp. Beginning on the last Friday of the month with a haunted house, carnival games and a children's costume contest, it proceeds into live music, foot races, crafts shows, an international food fair (including some regional favorites), an evening street dance, sports, kite flying, sand sculpture . . . and beautiful sunsets at Holden Beach, 754-6644.

Annual North Carolina Oyster Festival features South Brunswick Islands' favorite food, in season at this time. The NC Oyster Shucking Championship with arts and crafts, live music, a bullshooting competition (terrifically tall tales) and a fun run are also featured at Sunset Beach, 754-6644.

Halloween Festival consists of a haunted barn, spooky hay rides, a costume party and children's games at Poplar Grove Historic Plantation, Highway 17, Scotts Hill, 686-9503.

Bald Head Island Sailing Regatta is open to the public, Bald Head Island, 457-5003.

November

Bald Head Island Annual Maritime Classic Road Race, 10K and 5K

Insiders' Tips

foot races are open to the public on Bald Head Island, 457-5003.

LATE NOVEMBER

Festival of Trees, a benefit for hospice, is a dazzling display of scores of dressed Christmas trees at the Wilmington Hilton, 762-0200.

Annual Holiday Flotilla and Arts & Crafts Show features a parade of brightly lit and wildly decorated water craft of all shapes and sizes, Wrightsville Beach, 256-4303, 256-2147.

Island of Lights is a holiday parade and festival of lights at Pleasure Island that lasts through January 2. Call 458-8434.

Christmas By-The-Sea Festival is a merchant open house at Southport and Oak Island, 457-6964.

Robert Ruark Festival celebrates the famous hometown hunter and author every Thanksgiving weekend in Southport, 457-5954.

December

Old Wilmington by Candlelight Tour strolls into Christmases past and through the stateliest homes of historic downtown Wilmington; refreshments are served, 762-0492.

The Night Before Christmas Parade takes place at Carolina Beach, 458-8434.

The Christmas By-The-Sea Parade along Yaupon and Oak Island Drives featuring Santa, live bands and beauty queens, Oak Island, 457-6964.

Christmas By-The-Sea Flotilla is a lively variety of decorated and lighted vessels that sail the lower Cape Fear River by Waterfront Park, Southport, 457-6964.

Tour of Homes is a holiday ritual of congeniality on Oak Island, 457-6964.

Waterfront Home Tour is a candlelight walking tour of Southport's historic riverfront homes, 456-7927, 457-6964.

Fraternal Order of the Police Bar-B-Que takes place at Middleton Park, Long Beach, 457-6964.

MID DECEMBER

Annual Christmas Concert by the Wilmington Boys Choir features carols, hymns and popular holiday songs at St. Paul's Episcopal Church, Wilmington, 343-0669.

Walk-In Messiah Performance is a concert sing-along featuring carols and Handel's immortal classic. Scores are available for the singing public in Kenan Auditorium, UNCW, 791-9262.

The Lighting of Wilmington's Largest Living Christmas Tree, the enormous decorated live oak, takes place in Hilton Park, 762-2611.

Inside
Nightlife

The term "nightlife" can have very different meanings for locals than it does for people elsewhere, especially big-city folks. There are plenty of Cape Fear residents who spend summer nights searching the beaches for loggerhead turtle nests and helping protect the ones they find. Others prefer the night for offshore fishing. Many youngsters enjoy surprising ghost crabs with their flashlights as the little critters (the crabs) make their nocturnal runs on the beach.

Local nightlife, taken in its usual sense (which is something like "going out to be inside someplace else"), is most concentrated in Wilmington, where clubs, bars and theaters are most numerous. The outlying areas along the coast, especially the South Brunswick Islands, are famous for their unbroken peace and quiet. But "hot" spots (a relative term, to say the least) also exist at Wrightsville Beach, Carolina Beach, Surf City and Long Beach, particularly in summer.

Stroll the Riverwalk and Front Street in downtown Wilmington. There are plenty of interesting places along the way in which to pause for a toast. At Wrightsville Beach, stroll Lumina Avenue, which can be choked with people on summer nights and is just yards from the quiet beach.

Some imaginative night owls pursue less common nocturnal rituals. Billiards is one, and there are several fashionable billiard parlors that have sprung up around town. These establishments generally feature a large number of tables, drink service and sometimes short menus of bar food in softly-lit settings that are almost genteel. **Rack'M Pub and Billiards**, 791-5668, in University Landing on South College Road is such a place. **Break Time Billiards & Sports Bar**, 395-6658, is also popular. It is located in the Marketplace Mall on South College Road and features 17 professional tables as well as darts, foosball and a complete pro shop.

Bowling, too, is an endeavor that lends itself to nightlife. **Bowler's Choice**, 791-2528, on Oleander Drive is open 24 hours. **Cardinal Lanes** has two locations: 3907 Shipyard Boulevard (799-3023) and 7026 Market St. near Scotts Hill (686-4223). **Brunswick County Bowling Center**, 754-2695, located in Shallotte, hosts leagues seven nights a week, some late at night. It even features a dance floor with live music.

Browsing the Attractions chapter will reveal a variety of evening cruise opportunities that should not be overlooked. These include the sternwheeler *Henrietta II* and the **Capt. Maffitt Sightseeing Cruise** on the Cape Fear River, the **Downeast Rover** and **Masonboro Island Sunset Cruises** at Wrightsville Beach and the **Pyewacket Sailing Cruises** out of Holden Beach. Others will be found in Calabash and the Carolina Beach Marina. Some offer dinner packages.

Live entertainment is easy to find at night spots throughout the region. Every style of music is represented, with special emphasis on country, blues, beach (which most folks inland may know as R & B of the late '50s and '60s), heavy metal and rockabilly. Also frequently available are jazz, folk and various yet-to-be-labelled styles of new rock 'n' roll. For those who like to dance, take your pick from among country two-step and line dancing, free-form disco or the area's undisputed monarch of dances, the shag. You can even take in an evening of square dancing and clogging to live music (with lessons) every month at Wilmington's Community Arts Center, 341-7860, at the corner of Second and Orange Streets.

You will find many clubs throughout the region (and the state) that are private. Clubs that are not private may only serve beer and wine to the general public. In order for an establishment to serve liquor (mixed drinks) it must either earn the bulk of its revenue from the sale of food, or it must be a private club for members and their guests. Membership to most clubs is inexpensive, usually between $2 and $5 per year. Weekend visitors applying for membership should be aware that a three-day waiting period must elapse before you can become a fully-fledged member.

What follows is by no means the last word on the area's nightlife. Rather, it is a guide for many styles and tastes and many types of entertainment. Nurture a sense of adventure in your explorations, and your nightlife will be enlarged immeasurably.

Wilmington

ACME ART
711 N. 5th St.   763-8010

When the artists involved with the Acme Art collective gather a critical mass of will, they mount ambitious multimedia art functions combining visual and performing arts, the success of which is neither geared toward, nor judged by, commercial success. Recurring Full Moon shows are non-juried exhibitions open to all artists. Other occasional shows, with such names as the Ides of March and Hunter Moon exhibitions, may bring together any combination of theater, photography, painting, sculpture, poetry, music, or what have you, by artists working at Acme who consider these events to be their gifts to the public. The artists encourage those interested to visit their studios at other times as well.

BARBARY COAST
116 S. Front St.   762-8996

When you're looking for a night spot with some atmosphere, check out the Barbary Coast. It's got atmo-

Photo: William Russ

Take a pause in the past at Fort Fisher.

sphere as thick as a pea-soup fog and a crew of die-hard regulars as crusty, salty and fun-loving as the name of the place implies — and those are just the college students. The Coast is old (and looks it), small and serves only beer and wine (and plenty of it). The decor is classic flotsam and jetsam. The two pool tables are popular (when they're not supporting a makeshift stage for musicians), and the excellent juke box even more so, but the bathrooms leave much to be desired. The "Coast" raised not a few eyebrows last winter when it installed booth seating. If Wilmington were still a pirate-plagued port, Barbary Coast would be the place to find them. It's a good drinkin' bar.

BESSIE'S

133 N. Front St.   762-0003

Underground lounge lizards flourish in this low-ceilinged basement club, which is actually three bars in one. Bessie's features live rock and blues bands, dance nights and other entertainment (the Sumo Bellies Balloon Bust Tournaments are hilarious), attracting a clientele predominantly in their 20s and early 30s. Once the site of historic Orton's Billiard Parlor, Bessie's still sports five pool tables, including the one at which Willie Mosconi sank a record-breaking 365 balls consecutively in 1953. The bar sells only beer, wine and soft drinks, and you will find Guinness Stout by the pint.

An adjoining room is a small private club called **General Longstreet's Headquarters**, so named because it is co-owned by actor Tom Berringer who portrayed the bearded Confederate in the epic film *Gettysburg*.

Longstreet's is adorned with Civil War paintings, memorabilia and props from the movie. The foosball table is painted to suggest the Gettysburg battlefield, and each of its little men resembles a famous general associated with that catastrophic clash. The J.E.B. Stuart figure appropriately stands aloof, outside the playing field. The juke box packs a solid cross-section of rock music from its earliest days to the present. Longstreet's is open from noon to 2 AM Monday through Saturday and 1 PM to 2 AM Sunday. Membership includes membership to Lula's (see below).

At the opposite side of Bessie's is the **Brick Yard**, a new sports bar featuring state-of-the-art interactive sports programs by NTN Entertainment. Through this computerized system, patrons compete in fantasy games in every sport, including surfing, with other players across the nation. The Brick Yard gets its name from its original exposed brick, part of the old Orton Hotel which burned in 1949. Bessie's and the Brick Yard are open 6 PM to 2 AM Monday through Saturday (closed Sunday), and you must be 21 or over to enter.

BURRITO BOB'S

5901 Wrightsville Ave.   392-6520

Like the excellent Mexican restaurant adjoining it, the lounge at Burrito Bob's is a destination point off the beaten path between Wrightsville Beach and "town." It attracts those who seek it out. Some insiders say their relentless searches for the perfect margarita ended right here. The friendly atmosphere, excellent fresh tortillas and various bar munchies have made Burrito Bob's a perpetual favorite among locals since it opened on Columbus Day in 1981. (Burrito Bob's was the first Mexican restaurant in Wilmington.) Beware: only regulars with plenty of time on their hands dare to venture into political discussions with owner Bob Houston, an outspoken and entertaining native Libertarian.

CAFFE PHOENIX
9 S. Front St.   *343-1395*

The Phoenix has an appeal that exceeds the high quality of its food. (It is one of Wilmington's best restaurants.) With its soft lighting and regular art exhibits, it exudes both warmth and sophistication. No wonder it has become a favorite rookery for nocturnal birds of many an artistic feather — painters, musicians, models, thespians, plus its share of poseurs and tourists — who gather for a meal or cappucino, dessert and conversation. Occasionally, live musicians provide music other than the recorded selections, which typically explore the more interesting niches of classical, jazz and third-world styles. As great a place to begin an evening as it is to end one, the Phoenix is open until 1 AM and keeps a very well-stocked bar. (See also the chapter on Restaurants.)

CLUB RIO
5001 Market St.   *799-1730*

More than just a hotel lounge (it's located next door to the Ramada Inn), Club Rio is one of the more popular dance clubs among the mature singles set. Top-40, oldies, classic disco and beach music compose the play list, and shag lessons are offered twice weekly along with a buffet. For shower-stall sopranos and bathroom baritones, karaoke takes place two nights a week when admission is free. Drink specials, occasional contests, ample parking and a full bar with all ABC permits add to Club Rio's amenities.

CROOK'S BY THE RIVER
138 S. Front St.   *762-8898*

Crook's lounge is an essential stopover on the customary weekend pub-crawl along Front Street and, therefore, a popular gathering base. Trendy, perhaps, the lounge is nonetheless attractive and popular among people ranging from college-age to older boomers. The walls are decorated with colorful local artwork, and local musicians, mostly blues players, appear on Thursday nights (and sometimes Fridays). There is never a cover charge. High-quality light fare is available late into the night.

Don't drink and drive. Life here is too good — and law enforcement is strict.

Insiders' Tips

GENTLEMAN JIM'S JAZZ CLUB
23 N. Front St. 251-0330

The premier upscale jazz club in Wilmington, if not southeastern North Carolina, is located on the top floor of a classic loft building. Among the top-name artists who have graced the stage since its opening in early 1993 are Ramsey Lewis, Charlie Byrd, Stanley Jordan, Frank Morgan, Freddy Cole, Tom Browne and Dan Brubeck & The Dolphins. The regular house band's strength lies in standard bop tunes and ballads, and open jam sessions take place weekly. Entrance is by private elevator opening directly into the large, softly-lit room. Bare brick, full carpeting, tasteful photography and a handsomely-designed, well-stocked bar frame a cafe-style assemblage of intimate tables, each lit with a pyramidal Lucite oil lamp. Metal-sculpted sun- and moon-faces smile from various points throughout the room. The ceiling fan ribbed with fishing rods is a clever decorative surprise. Excellent views of downtown Wilmington and the waterfront can be had front and back. Gentleman Jim's is a private club with all ABC permits that appeals to serious jazz fans.

THE ICE HOUSE
115 S. Water St. 251-1158

A story is told about an Ice House bartender who vacationed in New York City. She and her father were walking down Wall Street one Sunday morning and a car pulled up to the curb. The driver leaned out and yelled, "Hey! Aren't you from Wilmington? You're the bartender from the Ice House!"

Few Wilmington night spots enjoy such far-flung renown. The heart of the Ice House is the large patio dominated by a tug boat pilot house and outdoor stage where visitors can enjoy live blues, jazz and folk music mere yards from the Cape Fear River, under the sun or stars, and with no cover charge. Live music cranks seven days a week. During the summer, regular lunch-hour shows feature local rock, folk and flamenco soloists. Evening shows begin as early as 5:30 PM in the high season. Musicians are welcome to the open blues jam sessions sponsored by the Blues Society of the Lower Cape Fear twice a week — amplified instruments on Tuesdays, acoustic on Thursdays. During the cold months, the music goes indoors. This place sizzles on weekends during the tourist season and can be crowded, loud and sloppy, but always a blast. It's a popular singles hangout. In many ways, the Ice House is to Wilmington what Sloppy Joe's is to Key West.

The club's colorful owners Jim Bath and Joe and Janet Carney are its heart and soul. Jim is a genuine old salt who has sailed the world. His salvage and restoration work resulted in the creation of the Seven Seas Trading Company that sells nautical hardware and curiosities at the Ice House Shops next door along with sundry other interesting merchandise. The building is an old ice house with antiquated ice-making machinery still in operation.

The Ice House has always been known for its excellent selection of beer, including several microbrewery labels and regional delights such as Blackened Voodoo and the eye-watering Chili Beer. The bar also sells wine and soft drinks. The owners recently added a steamer kitchen featuring such beer garden favorites as kilbasi, bratwurst, steamed shrimp and oysters (in season) soups and more.

KATY'S GREAT EATS
1054 S. College Rd. 395-5289

Wilmington's darts mecca, the bar at Katy's restaurant is a favorite hangout for sports fans. It's practically always buzzing with young locals who come to enjoy the games on big-screen TV and occasional live music.

LULA'S
138 S. Front St. 763-0070

Tucked away in the low-ceilinged stone-walled basement beneath Crook's, Lula's is a cozy, intimate, pub-style private club that seats only about 25 people. The tiny room is adorned with vintage photos of film and music celebrities and a huge American flag overhead. The juke box contains an eclectic selection of rock, funk, blues, Motown and even some classic Irish drinking songs. Many of the regular clientele, mostly in their 30s and younger, are familiar friends. Entrance to Lula's is through the rear of the building. Membership at Lula's includes membership at General Longstreet's Headquarters located at Bessie's (see above).

THE MAD MONK
127 S. College Rd. 395-0280

When it comes to national rock music acts, the Monk is the only game in town. Located in the Marketplace Mall, this raucous mid-sized rock club books mostly hard rock and metal bands plus the occasional rap, reggae and punk group. A smattering of local bands also appears here. General admission is open to the public, and there is an upstairs private club for members who prefer the balcony to the moshing pit. Ticket prices for national acts are on a par with those at larger big-city venues.

MICKEY RATZ
115 S. Front St. 251-1289

This is undoubtedly the most cosmopolitan, progressive dance club in the region. High-tech lighting, superior sound system, large-screen video, occasional live shows and top-notch DJs provide all the energy of a big-city disco. This private club's clientele is largely gay, but not exclusively. An outdoor patio provides a pleasant change of ambience in fair weather.

Big band jazz fans know that UNCW's 7 O'Clock Big Band is a local treasure that performs at least one concert each semester.

Insiders' Tips

MOTIONS

4903 Market St.   799-1440

Motions is a comfortable, glitzy dance club that years ago might have been called a disco. Patrons are generally mature (30s and up) and well-dressed. Perhaps because Motions also serves as the restaurant for the Holiday Inn, its Sunday buffet excels, offering all-you-can-eat crab legs, baby back ribs and fish in the dining section. A disc jockey, whose strengths lie in top-40 dance and beach music, keeps the frequently large crowds on their feet on the enclosed dance floor from Thursday through Saturday when there is no cover charge. There is a full bar with all ABC permits, plenty of parking, four TV screens (usually tuned to the current sporting event of note), a pool table and electronic darts. Motions is open from 5 PM to 2 AM and is open to the public.

NEW ZOO

Marketplace Mall, S. College Rd.   791-4778

The most popular dance club for younger well-dressed dancers is the Zoo, an enormous private establishment with excellent "disco" lighting, a large dance floor, spacious banquettes and table seating. It has a superior sound system. Featured events vary from season to season and usually include a weekly college night, various contests, giveaways and the discreetly labeled "lock-ups" for men or women wherein doors are opened only to members of one gender to enjoy Las Vegas-style dancers of the opposite sex. Live bands that appeal to the partying college audience appear periodically.

STEMMERMAN'S CLUB

128 S. Front St.   763-5552

Located in an historic building, this private club has the feel of a classic 19th-century saloon with its U-shaped balcony, turned-wood balustrade, bare brick walls and four pool tables. What sets Stemmerman's apart for its young, late-night crowd is its excellent juke box, filled with progressive rock, ska and grunge music and kept up to date by bartender Sean Drummey, a former college radio DJ. Appetizers are sold at the bar where Foster's is on tap, and the Stoli is in the fridge. Two foosball tables, electronic darts and an upstairs bar help keep the place well-attended.

SUNSET CELEBRATION AT THE HILTON

301 N. Water St.   763-5900

Every Friday evening from Memorial Day to Labor Day, the pool deck at the Hilton springs to life with the weekly Sunset Celebration, once called Wilmington's answer to The Love Boat. Featuring live rock bands, local radio DJs, free buffets, and a variety of contests, Sunset Celebrations are enhanced by spectacular sunsets over the Cape Fear River. They often become extremely crowded with folks in their 20s and 30s (most of them single) who come to meet new friends, dig the music, make silly toasts and imbibe. (Cash bars offer mixed drinks and beer.) Admission is free.

THE YELLOW ROSE SALOON
5025 Market St.   *791-2001*

Big-brimmed hats, Western boots and tight jeans are in abundance at the Yellow Rose, justifiably touted as "Wilmington's upscale country nightclub." In return for providing some of the town's finest live country music Thursday through Saturday and dancing all week, the management requires proper attire (and behavior) of its patrons. Two-step, line, and Western dance lessons for all skill levels are offered free several nights a week, and the floor can get mighty thick with boot-scootin', heel-slamming fun. Once a month, the Yellow Rose hosts a Family Night, welcoming all ages for an evening of dancing, dance lessons and recorded country music. Free buffets and ladies' nights attract regular patrons on various week nights. The Yellow Rose is located behind the Greentree Inn and is closed on Sundays and Mondays.

Movie Theaters

There are plenty of first-run and second-run theaters on Cape Fear, but "serious" films (dramas and art films) have frustratingly short runs, and controversial films seldom run

at all. It's a paradox considering the number of films shot in Wilmington. Luckily, there is **Cinematique**, the series that brings acclaimed foreign and domestic films to Wilmington's College Road Cinemas (which have the best seats in town) for three-day runs every other week. Cinematique is an increasingly popular bargain ($4 admission) and benefits St. John's Museum of Art and WHQR 91.3 FM, the local public radio station. Show times are 1:30 PM on Sunday and 7:30 PM on Monday and Tuesday.

All movie theaters in the region offer matinee showings everyday during the summer, on holidays and most weekends throughout the year at substantial savings over the average $5.50 ticket price. Since there are so few theaters outside Wilmington, we've listed all theaters together.

Cinema 6, 799-6666, 5335 Oleander Drive, is located less than 4 miles from Wrightsville Beach and offers (you guessed it) six screens.

College Road Cinemas, 395-1790, 632 South College Road, is a six-theater complex behind Swensen's and Taco Bell across the street from the UNCW campus.

Independence Mall Cinemas, 392-3333, behind Independence Mall.

Long Leaf Cinema, 799-5710, Long Leaf Mall (Shipyard Boulevard & South College Road) is a budget theater, which means the floors are sticky, but you'll get to see that film you missed at the first-run theaters. ($1.50 at all times.)

New Centre Cinema, 791-6123, 5110 New Centre Dr.

Cinema 4, 458-3444, 1020 Carolina Beach Road (Federal Point Plaza in Carolina Beach) charges $3.50 at all times.

Surf Cinemas, 457-0320, Long Beach Road Southeast, is convenient to the Southport-Oak Island area.Wrightsville Beach

Wrightsville Beach

BUDDY'S CRAB & OYSTER BAR
35 N. Lumina Ave.   *256-8966*

Home of the world's smallest dance floor, this little shack probably shucks more oysters than any other place on the beach. When it's not crammed with summer transients, it is frequented by longtime residents and former yuppies who traded burnout for beachcombing. It's so popular, owner Buddy Wiles says, "We don't have outdoor seating, we have outdoor standing!" Festooned with ships' lanterns, pulley blocks, bells, life rings, hundreds of business cards, photos and a 16th-century Seminole dugout, Buddy's also has a juke box choked with 2,000 attitude-improving songs (Embers, Buffett, Motown, Hank Jr., Garth . . .) to keep things hopping. It's a place to belly up to the bar, eat steamers and drink beer — the only place in town that serves buckets of suds (pitchers, that is) Buddy's opens at 1 PM on Sunday, 11 AM every other day and closes at no more specific time than "until."

THE COMEDY ZONE
at the Blockade Runner Beach Resort
275 Waynick Blvd.   *256-2251*

Every Thursday evening, visitors to the Ocean Terrace Room at the Blockade Runner enter the Comedy Zone. Featuring two nationally known stand-up comedians doing their thing from 9 until about 11 PM, these shows are consistently entertaining and well worth the $7 admission fee ($5 with dinner). Drinks are served throughout the performances, and the content of the shows is frequently of an adult nature.

LOCALS ONLY
(TOURISTS WELCOME)
Plaza East   *256-9600*

When it comes to live cover bands doing new and classic rock and rock 'n' roll tributes, no club does it as consistently or as well as Locals. The recently remodeled stage faces a sunken dance floor that is separated from the bar's seating area, making it possible to carry on a conversation while the bands are rocking the house. Shows generally start around 9 PM. Entrance before 8 PM is free, and limited door prizes are often featured. Patrons can partake of the pool table, foosball, pinball and ping pong table and enjoy appetizers from the bar menu. Located in the Plaza East Mall between Eastwood Road and Wrightsville Avenue, Locals is next door to Giuseppe's Restaurant. It is a private club with all ABC permits and is open Tuesday through Saturday, 5:30 PM to 2 AM.

OL' NEP'S LOUNGE
11 N. Lumina Ave.   *256-2525*

Located in the King Neptune Restaurant, Ol' Nep's is as lively as its proprietor, Bernard Carroll, who doesn't know the first thing about fishing despite all the photographs of prize catches on the walls. He'd much rather be sailing and, as you might expect of a salt, he places some importance upon rum. His "Neptune's Rum Bar" features rums from around the world, including Gosling's and North Carolina's own Outer Banks Rum. Microbrewery and imported beers are always in stock, and an inexpensive "Pub Grub" menu offers sandwiches (fish, chicken, crab cakes,) pizza, burgers, and steamers. (All items are available for takeout.) Ol' Nep's is open from 5 PM to 1 AM everyday and has all ABC permits.

Carolina Beach

CLUB ASTOR

110 Harper Ave.   *458-7883*

Located at the front of Hotel Astor, the club is technically Carolina Beach's largest nightclub, but it's not huge by any means. Rock and top-40 bands perform Thursday (9 PM) through Saturday (10 PM), and varying types of live entertainment are booked on Sundays from 8 PM The hotel also features the **Back Alley Lounge**, 458-9081, a smaller room at the back of the building (enter from the parking lot or through the Beachcomber's Restaurant) where open jam sessions take place on Saturday and Sunday afternoons, May through October (no cover).

COBB'S CORNER LOUNGE

217 Carolina Ave. N.   *458-8865*

Extremely laid-back, quiet and friendly, Cobb's Corner is a private sports bar that attracts a mature clientele, many from the nearby motels. It is located directly behind

Cabana De Mar. There is a sunny outdoor deck, and the lounge is open everyday during the high season.

HARBOR MASTERS RESTAURANT & LOUNGE

315 Canal Dr.   *458-7013*

When it comes to rock, beach and "parrot head" music, Harbor Masters stands alone in Carolina Beach. The restaurant and stage area fill separate adjoining rooms, making it easy to enjoy either side without serious distractions. Harbor Masters books popular traveling and local bands that fill the small lounge. A dance floor is surrounded by a limited number of tables and the bar (all ABC permits). Live entertainment is available from 4 PM to 2 AM on Fridays and Saturdays with headline acts taking the stage at 10 PM.

Topsail Island

THE BRASS PELICAN

2112 N. New River Dr.
Surf City   *328-4373*

The ads say this is the friendliest bar on the island. The regulars, however, say it's the coolest. The friendliness becomes apparent once they know you're here to stay, but the cool is on the surface. The Brass Pelican hosts live rock bands (some quite loud for a place this size), and offers free chow nightly from the bottomless crock pot. As in many of the night spots in these parts, a new face inevitably turns heads, so get involved in the weekly pool or dart tournaments or the occasional ping pong tourney. Enjoy the outdoor party deck draped with parachute cloth, and join in the fun. The bands play Thursday through Sunday during the summer season, often setting up outside on Sundays. Guinness Stout is the celebrity brew, and there are regular drink specials, but don't get hooked on the Tooters. The Pelican is a private club located next to Scotch Bonnet fishing pier opposite Tilghman's Square. Its coolness can be experienced from 11 AM to 2 AM.

THE MERMAID

N. New River Dr.
Surf City 328-0781

Located near the north side of Surf City, the Mermaid is a restaurant and lounge known for its live rock bands on weekends and holidays, volleyball and pool tournaments, and occasional roughhousing. Night owls can have breakfast here from 11 PM to 3 AM Friday and Saturday. On other nights, karaoke, beach bingo, cards and games help maintain the Mermaid's disputed claim as Topsail Island's "original" beach bar.

SANDPIPER

foot of Roland Ave.
Surf City 328-4040

Recently refurbished, and with its Sunday pool tournaments reinstated, the Sandpiper is something of a historic site in Surf City, the oldest watering hole on the beach. Even if it weren't revered for its age, it would still be popular because of its oceanfront location, wraparound covered deck, casual ambience and numerous windows yielding a full view of the Surf City pier and the

ocean. It's not a large place, but bright, casual and welcoming with a freestanding bar and oaken wainscots. Volleyball takes place on the beach in summer, and there's a shower to rinse off the sand.

SHENANIGANS
BEACH CLUB BAR & GRILL

2107 New River Dr.
Surf City 328-SHAG (7424)

The phone number says it all. Everything about this private club is geared toward the pursuit of fun and if the crowded dance floor on Saturday nights is any indication, they succeed. More than just a shag club (Chairmen of the Board are booked regularly), Shenanigans presents several styles of live and jockeyed music all geared toward beach-style partying, including reggae, rockabilly and old R & B with a little country, Cajun and parrot-head sounds thrown in. You can even do some line dancing now and then. Their summertime entertainment schedule is usually jammed, which goes far toward explaining the sign that reads, "Please keep animals under control."

Sporting two bars (one opens on weekends), outdoor deck, pool table, dart board and a 46-inch-wide TV, Shenanigans also takes pride in its short-menu "Snak Shak." Their "gourmet" burgers (you may wonder if they mean "gormand") bear such names as The Slam Dunk, The Long Bomb and The Slap Shot which, thankfully, do not represent most patrons' manner of eating. The kitchen serves until 10 PM on weekends, 9 PM weekdays. Shenanigans hosts volleyball tourneys and deck parties with live music in the summer. The club is located on Highway 210 in Tilghman's Square, about 3 miles north of the bridge into Surf City.

THE QUARTERDECK LOUNGE AT ST. REGIS RESORT
New River Inlet Rd.
North Topsail Shores   328-0778

Located on the seventh floor adjacent to the Topsail View, the Quarterdeck features karaoke on Thursday nights and dance music by request on Fridays and Saturdays during the high season. The lounge is not very large, quite casual and attracts a mature clientele, typically resort guests.

Oak Island

THE GALLERY
5908 E. Oak Island Dr.
Long Beach   278-9986

The Gallery has been a popular night spot for more than ten years despite a recent change in ownership. In the summertime, the Sunset Celebrations held Thursday through Saturday on the outdoor patio attract scads of people, mostly in their 20s, to dance and congregate around the "back bar." There is live entertainment on occasion throughout the year. The Gallery is a private club popular with sports fans. It features darts and big-screen TV.

THE OARHOUSE LOUNGE
705 Yaupon Dr.
Yaupon Beach   278-5873

You will either love or hate this tiny place on Yaupon Fishing Pier, but it demands at least a viewing, which is why you'll also find it in the chapter on Attractions. The low ceiling and walls are hidden beneath strata of business cards, hats, trinkets, undergarments, nautical paraphernalia, photos, signs and gimmicks. Toilet seats hang beside the seven crude tables (some would say "crude" aptly describes the entire place). Pull the rope hanging above the table and the toilet seat opens to reveal the food menu — mainly raw bar and grill fare. The place can get fairly crowded, and the only air conditioning is the ocean breeze. Live music is often featured on summer weekends. The Oarhouse opens at 11 AM (noon on Sundays) and stays open until "whenever," but never later than 2 AM.

RAMPAGE
5712 E. Oak Island Dr.
Long Beach   278-1565

A watering hole that is among very few such places in a large island community attracts a wide variety of people. In Rampage's case, that translates into a reputation as a rough place which, de-

Insiders' Tips

servedly or not, has stuck with the establishment over the years. In any case, Rampage certainly is lively and popular. Aside from boasting about its margaritas, the club also boasts live bands that play until 1 AM about three weekends each month. A DJ spins the disks from Thursday through Saturday. Two pool tables and pin ball machines stand behind small tables and banquettes in a room striving for Caribbean atmosphere. Rampage is a private club with all ABC permits.

SHUCKERS

6220 E. Oak Island Dr.
Long Beach   *278-4944*

Home of the Oak Island Shag Club, Shuckers is a pleasant place for dancing into the wee hours to beach music. DJs spin the old hits, and free shag lessons are available in the evenings. Shuckers also serves a full menu, possesses all ABC permits and is open to the public.

South Brunswick

BOOT SCOOTERS

1601 Seaside Rd. (Rt. 904)   *579-4007*

This is the newest private club in South Brunswick, featuring live and recorded country music, line dance, two-step and a vast 5,000-square-foot dance floor. "Proper attire" is required. A shop on the premises, Tee Beaus #2 Western Wear, offers a wide selection of Western-style clothing and accessories for sale. Boot Scooters also features four pool tables and a full bar and is located just north of Highway 179 near the Food Lion.

HIGHTIDE CLUB

Hwys. 179 & 904 (Seaside Dr.)   *579-3272*

Featuring live rock, R & B and country bands from both Carolinas on Fridays and Saturdays, this small private club also serves a short menu of food, which is free on Mondays and Thursdays. There is also a pool table and no cover charge. Hightide is located in the corner of the shopping strip behind the Shell station.

STEAMERS

8 2nd St.
Ocean Isle Beach   *579-0535*

Recently reopened under new management, Steamers offers live music, which leans mostly toward beach, R & B and classic rock with a little country thrown in. It has an up scale appearance (despite the large-screen TV) and serves a light bar menu of appetizers. Steamers is a private club open from 4 PM to 2 AM Monday through Friday and 1 PM to 2 AM Saturday and Sunday.

Southport

HARBOR LITE BAR & GRILL

1109 N. Howe St.   457-9541

This small neighborhood bar has little to offer in terms of nightlife unless you're one of the local bar flies who likes to witness harmless practical jokes played on tourists who wander in. The folks are friendly, however, and after you've had a beer or two, they'll probably invite you back on Sunday nights when live bluegrass bands visit.

SHAMROCK PUB

309 N. Howe St.   457-0401

In the tradition of old-world pubs, the Shamrock is a place to socialize even after the adjoining restaurant stops serving. Its patrons range widely in age, and the place is generally very laid-back, even on Saturday nights when karaoke enlivens the room (9 PM). The bar has all ABC permits.

Welcome to "Wilmywood"

Believe it or not, are more movies are being made each year in Wilmington than in any other single American city except Los Angeles and New York. TV's "Matlock" series, starring Andy Griffith, is also made in Wilmington, as well as many TV commercials and industrial films. At the heart of this phenomenon is Carolco Studios, a 32-acre complex located a short distance from New Hanover International Airport on 23rd Street. Some of Carolco's sound stages — totalling more than 100,000 square feet — are among the largest in the East. And you've probably already seen Carolco's backlot several times on TV and on movie screens — although you probably thought you were looking at the streets of New York City, New Orleans, Beirut, Hong Kong, Cape Cod, Detroit or Bucharest.

Carolco Studios traces its beginnings to 1983 when founder and original owner Dino DeLaurentis produced Steven King's "Firestarter," the spark that ignited Wilmington's steadily-burning film industry. Wilmington's ideal weather, huge variety of interior and exterior locations, accessibility to airlines and shipping routes, and low labor costs offer the film industry a remarkably effective formula for success.

So, it's not surprising that so many Wilmingtonians have film experience. Local musicians performed in "The Radioland Murders". Local dancers went "Stomping at the Savoy." Hundreds of residents earn their livings as "techies" behind the cameras. Hundreds more work as onscreen extras. The Cape Fear Filmmakers Accord is a consortium of crews, staff and screenwriters that publishes its own directory. State-of-the-art recording studios serving the film industry have also sprung up around town. It's not unusual to see major Hollywood celebrities frequenting local restaurants and clubs while they're in town shooting a film. Just a glance at the following sample of movies and TV shows made in and around Wilmington (the list is always growing) makes it clear why Wilmington has earned its local nickname "Wilmywood."

Firestarter
The Exorcist III
Windmills of the Gods
Blue Velvet
Crimes of the Heart
Matlock (TV series)
Tune In Tomorrow
The Lost Capone
Alan and Naomi
Manhunter
Year of the Dragon
Everybody Wins
Little Monsters
Loose Cannons
Weekend at Bernie's
Cyborg
A Stoning in Fulham County
Track 29
Weeds
Too Young the Hero
Noble House
Betsy's Wedding
Dream a Little Dream
Golden Years
29th Street
No Mercy
Sleeping With the Enemy
Super Mario Bros.
Teenage Mutant Ninja Turtles
Teenage Mutant Ninja Turtles
    II: The Secret of the Ooze
King Kong Lives
The Squeeze
Billy Bathgate
Amos & Andrew
Summer Heat
From the Hip
The Fix

Collision Course
The Bedroom Window
Date with an Angel
Hiding Out
Raw Deal
Dracula's Widow
Trick or Treat
No Mercy
Traxx
Simple Justice
Mayberry Reunion
Burning Vengeance
Rambling Rose
Marie: A True Story
Cat's Eye
Silver Bullet
Maximum Overdrive
The Young Indiana Jones
    Chronicles (TV series)
Stomping at the Savoy
Chasers
T-Bone 'n' Weasel
In A Child's Name
The Hudsucker Proxy
The Crow
Household Saints
Bitter Blood
The Radioland Murders
The Road to Wellville
The Birds II: Lands End
Mafia Marriages
Down Home (TV series)
Linda
The Inkwell
The Twilight Zone
Labor of Love: The Arlette
    Schweitzer Story
Lovejoy (TV episode)

Inside
Water Sports and Rentals

Water, water everywhere and not a drop goes to waste on Cape Fear! Insiders say, "Once you get that salt water in your veins, you'll never leave." And no wonder. The waters of this part of the Atlantic are warmed by the Gulf Stream, which not only makes for long seasons of ideal bathing and water-sporting, but also brings a surprising array of tropical sea life — a bonus to the angler and diver. North Carolina's beaches are arguably the finest on the eastern seaboard given the combination of average weather and water temperatures, water quality, unpeopled clean beaches and availability of services.

Sports enthusiasts can splurge. Surfing, water skiing and windsurfing have recently been joined by the newest twist in inshore sport: ocean kayaking. An increasing number of beach-rental shops are adding kayaks to their inventories. The opportunities in this region for top-notch water sports are only limited by your desire and stamina. But, you should be aware of local ordinances.

For example, swimming and surfing within 100 feet of most fishing piers are forbidden, and walking on protected dunes carries a minimum $50 fine. Some beaches do not allow any dogs on the beach during the summer season, while others are more accommodating if the animals are leashed. The appropriate sections below and the chapter on Fishing will tell you more about local variations.

While not technically a Cape Fear water sport, even whitewater rafting is available to people on the Cape Fear Coast. Rafting trips are organized by Wilmington Parks & Recreation, 343-3685. Excursions on the highly-rated Chatanooga River in the North Carolina mountains afford adrenaline-pumping whitewater action and are available beginning in spring at reasonable prices.

We've listed information on boating in the Sports and Fitness chapter. That chapter includes details on safety and boat rentals. Sailing opportunities are listed here in this chapter. Basic information on maps and charts for boaters and boat ramps will be found in the chapter on Fishing. The point is, reading every section relating to water activities can provide invaluable information to complement your primary sporting interest.

Jet Skis/Waverunners

If you've got your own water

buggy, there are plenty of beach access points on Wrightsville Beach suitable for beach trailers. One of the easiest is the paved access to the left of the Oceanic Restaurant on South Lumina Avenue, provided there are no volleyball tournaments that day. On Topsail Island, large access points are fewer, largely due to dune erosion. Your best bet would be the crossover near the Surf City Fishing Pier. All the rental craft available on Cape Fear launch into protected waters, most often the Intracoastal Waterway and its channels. Access to open waters is usually available, but be sure to respect the limitations set by the individual rental services. They must operate within the parameters of their permits.

Watercraft Works, Inc., 675-2783, is located at 6118 Castle Hayne Road in Castle Hayne and rents jet-skis for use on the northeast Cape Fear River, an excellent course if you like a smooth ride. Customers must be 16 or older.

Topsail Water Sports, 102 North Anderson Boulevard, Topsail Island, 328-1141, has been popular for 8 seasons. They rent late-model waverunners and jet skis starting around $25 per 1/2 hour and wave skis at $10 per hour. Reservations are suggested, and most major credit cards are accepted. They're open 7 days a week, 9 AM to 6 PM during the high season.

S & S Water Sports, Inc., Topsail Beach, 328-7751, is located at the Breezeway Motel. S & S rents waverunners at $25 per 1/2 hour and $40 per hour. They are open from 9 AM to 6 PM daily. Grab one of their card brochures at visitors centers and restaurants and receive a $5 discount on the hourly rates.

Ocean Isle Marina, 579-0858, on Causeway Drive at Ocean Isle Beach rents waverunners and jet skis from the marina office/tackle shop.

On Holden Beach, check out **Sun-Daze Jet Ski Rentals**, 520-6111, located at the Intracoastal Marina on Cedar Landing Road (under the bridge on the mainland side). Hourly and daily rates are competitive, and they feature Yamaha waverunners and water bikes. Reservations are recommended. They also rent hot tubs for soothing those post jet-ski muscle aches.

Sunset Watersports, 301 Sunset Boulevard, Sunset Beach, 579-7365, has a limited supply of waverunners which demands early reservations.

Rowing

A favorite pastime on the Cape Fear River, but eclipsed by motorboating during the early 19th century, rowing went out of favor in the 20th century. The sport was revived in 1989 with the formation of the Cape Fear River Rowing Club whose members cruise past busy docks, old shipwrecks, historic downtown Wilmington and wild abandoned rice fields upriver — all the while enjoying plenty of exercise and friendly company.

By becoming a CFRRC member you are entitled to use the boats stored at the boat house in downtown Wilmington, share in activities such as group rows and annual "tip drill" exercises and compete at regattas along the east coast. Members are required to join the U.S. Rowing

Photo: Scott Taylor

Windsurfing is a popular sport at North Carolina beaches.

Association ($40 annually for individuals, $75 families, $25 students). This ensures that club insurance will be in force during rowing activities. This is the only nonrefundable fee involved in membership. After an initial "dry" lesson you must sign a waiver of liability, and pay the dues ($150 annually for singles, $225 families, $100 students). If you change your mind, your undeposited dues will be refunded. A series of free lessons will get the uninitiated started. The club maintains for members' use a variety of craft. Additional instruction is readily provided by advanced members, and a quarterly newsletter contains the latest news on club events, regional regattas and related items. To inquire about membership, contact Terri Krueger, 762-2878.

The UNCW rowing team, the Crew Club, is a non-varsity club sport open to attending students. They specialize in sweep rowing and compete regionally.

Kayaks and their wilder young cousins, ocean kayaks, are popular on both sides of Cape Fear's barrier islands. **Ship's Store Windsurfing and Sailing Center**, 256-4445/9463, rents kayaks starting at $15 per hour from their dock on Banks Channel at Wrightsville Beach. They also provide a kayak scenic tour ($40) and a two-hour course on Wednesdays and Saturdays in summer. It's a great way to explore the tidal marsh and canal habitats along Banks Channel and the Intracoastal.

Caribbean Trading Company, 256-2112, on Causeway Drive at Wrightsville Beach, rents and sells the sit-on-top kayaks from Ocean Kayak and Aquaterra as well as a full line of touring and whitewater kayaks from Aquaterra/Perception.

• **197**

Rentals start at $12 per hour.

Also check into **Topsail Water Sports**, 102 North Anderson Boulevard, Topsail Island, 328-1141.

Cape Fear Boat Rentals & Charters, 278-1880/9933, rents canoes and rowboats from Bluewater Point near the west end of Oak Island (Long Beach). Rates are reasonable ($6 first hour, $30 per day, $90 Monday through Friday,) and reservations are a wise idea.

Sailing

Whether you race a J-30 in regional events or sail a Sunfish in quiet channels, the Cape Fear coast has something to offer you. Consensus says "Cape Fear Country" offers sailing experiences seldom equaled with combination of windy weather, ample dockside services and challenging waterways.

An event eagerly awaited by salts throughout the region is the Holiday Flotilla, a Christmastime festivity held just after Thanksgiving in which boaters adorn their craft in the most flamboyant seasonal lighting and decoration possible and participate in an evening cruise through the channels of Wrightsville Sound. Prizes are awarded for the best decorated craft, and the fireworks are said to be the best in the area. Information about the regatta

can be obtained through most area marinas and the Seapath Yacht Club, 256-3747/6681, 328 Causeway Drive, Wrightsville Beach.

It would be useful to note that at Wrightsville Beach there is free anchorage in Banks Channel. Thirty days seems to be the average stay before the authorities pay a visit or post a nastygram, but many boaters have been known to stay longer. Complete information on anchorage and marina services will be found in the chapter on Marinas and Intracoastal Waterway.

For serious sailors, and those who just love to cruise, the **Wrightsville Beach Ocean Racing Association** (its initials, as spoken by locals, are "WoBora") is the organization of note. Founded in 1967, it is a very active nonprofit corporation that promotes and sponsors sailboat cruising and racing in the Cape Fear region and elsewhere along the North Carolina coast, and its members are a decidedly fun-loving bunch. WBORA provides race and cruise schedule management and development, hosts sailing seminars, participates in community programs, assists in youth sailing and organizes social activities around sailing events. Sailing events for both cruising and racing groups span the season from spring to fall, and social events are sprinkled throughout the year. Among the highlights of the racing season are the Coca-Cola Regatta (three races in one day), the Governor's Cup, The Bald Head Island Cruise and Race, which is followed by the year's landmark party, and the Mid-Summer Cruise from Masonboro Island to Cape Lookout Bight. Boats of various types may compete in races, and a performance handicap racing factor (PHRF) is figured into the standings. There is one specialty-class race in which only J-24s compete.

WBORA is a member organization of the U.S. Sailing Association, the South Atlantic Yacht Racing Union and a charter member of the North Carolina Yacht Racing Association. Membership is open to all, and dues depend on the extent to which you wish to participate. An annual handbook is published for members. WBORA does not maintain any permanent offices. Information on membership can be obtained from the association's officers. For 1994 they are: Sanford Doxey (Commodore), 256-6827, P.O. Box 1216, Wrightsville Beach, NC 28480; Paul Parker (Secretary), 395-6911; and Sam Barfield (Race Committee), 762-0803. Also, the Seapath Yacht Club, 256-3747/6681, 328 Causeway Drive, Wrightsville Beach, is a handy resource for keeping up with WBORA events. Ask for Manager George Bond or for information on posted messages.

Hobie Fleet 101, 256-6468 or 256-6624, is a local sailing club open to anyone interested in sailing Hobie Cats. It is part of Division 9 (NC, SC, VA, GA) of the North American Hobie Cat Association. Ownership of a Hobie is not required since qualified members can obtain use of the fleet boat for the summer for a mere $40. Family membership costs $25 annually, and meetings are held the first Wednesday of the month at the Holiday Inn Wrightsville Beach. Among their events are the Mid-Summer Offshore Regatta in July, open to Hobies of all classes, and the Frostbite Series which runs from October through Christmas. Other events and parties take place throughout the year.

Among the newer additions to Wrightsville Beach is Jerry Outlaw's **Water Ways, Inc.**, 256-4282 or (800)562-SAIL (7245), the only sailing school in the Carolinas certified by the American Sailing Association (ASA). Water Ways offers a battery of sailing courses taught entirely by USCG-licensed captains, including Outlaw himself. Seven courses are offered in all: Basic Sailing (2 days), Basic Coastal Cruising, Intermediate Coastal Cruising (Bareboat Charter), Coastal Navigation, Advanced Coastal Cruising, Celestial Navigation and Offshore Passagemaking. The Water Ways fleet boasts a variety of craft ranging from 13-foot rigs to a Hunter 33.5. The 13- and 20-foot boats are available for rent. Captained and bareboat charters are also available for local excursions.

Other charters that allow varying degrees of involvement in the actual sailing of the vessel are available on the **Downeast Rover** and **Pyewacket**. See the Attractions chapter for complete information.

Wrightsville Beach Parks & Recreation, 256-7925, offers weekly lessons in rigging and sailing a Sunfish for beginners ages 9 to adult June through August for an extremely reasonable fee.

The **Carolina Yacht Club**, 256-3396, 401 S. Lumina Avenue, Wrightsville Beach, is the oldest private sailing club on Cape Fear. The club sponsors regional competitions and events and offers training to members.

Ship's Store Windsurfing & Sailing Center, 256-WIND (9463), located at 275 Waynick Boulevard at Wrightsville Beach, rents Hobie Cats, 14' Day Sailors, Sunfish and more. Prices range from $15 per hour to $100 for four hours. They also provide lessons and offer group discounts. The center provides sailing packages for guests at the Blockade Runner Resort Hotel. The minimum age to rent is 18; the minimum age to ride is six. They operate a retail store in the Atlantic View Retail Center, 7220 Wrightsville Avenue.

John and Gay Maxwell's **Topsail Water Sports**, 328-1141, 102 North Anderson Boulevard (NC 50), Topsail Island, has been a local favorite for eight years. They offer Hobie Cats (14' and 16') and other small craft ranging from $30 per hour to $90 per day, plus tax. Half-day and full-day sail boat charters with a certified captain and lessons are also available. Reservations are necessary,

and most major credit cards are accepted. They're open seven days a week, 9 AM to 6 PM.

Surf Unlimited at The Winds Clarion Inn, 310 East First St., Ocean Isle Beach, 579-7575, rents sailboat and beach items such as umbrellas and chairs. Catamarans cost $25 to $75 with a $25 deposit. Surf Unlimited is open weekends, weekdays by appointment, between Easter and Memorial Day, and seven days a week Memorial through Labor Days (see also Water Sports).

SCUBA Diving and Snorkeling

Diving the Cape Fear waters offers rewarding experiences to collectors, nature-watchers and wreck-divers, despite there being no true coral reefs in these latitudes. A surprising variety of tropical fish species inhabit these waters, including blue angel fish, damsel fish and moray eels, as well as several varieties of sea fans, some as much as three feet in height. Spiny oysters, deer cowries, helmet shells, trumpet tritons and queen conchs can be found here.

Among the places where it is easiest to find tropical aquatic life is 23 Mile Rock, a 12-mile-long ledge running roughly perpendicular to the coast. Another 15 miles out, the

Lobster Ledge, a low-lying formation 120 feet deep, is a collector's target. There are several smaller ledges close to shore in shallower water better suited for less experienced divers. Visibility at offshore sites averages 40 feet, but inshore, visibility is seldom better than 20 feet. The Cape Fear coastal waters can be dived all year long, having temperatures ranging between the upper 50s in winter and low 80s in summer. However, many charters typically end their local diving season in early fall. Some charters organize destination trips thereafter.

Good snorkeling in the Cape Fear region is a matter of knowing when and where to go. Near-shore bottoms are mostly packed sand devoid of the rugged features that make for good viewing and collecting, but a good guide can lead you to rewarding areas. When the wind is right and the tide is rising, places like the Wrightsville Beach jetty offer excellent viewing with good visibility. The many creeks and estuaries support an abundance of life, and the shorter visibility that averages 15 to 20 feet is no obstacle in water so shallow. The waters around piers in Banks Channel at Wrightsville Beach are fairly good, but currents are strong and often murky. Only experienced snorkelers should attempt these waters or local inlets, which are treach-

erous, and then only at stopped tides. It is neither safe nor legal to swim beneath oceanside fishing piers. When in doubt, contact a local dive shop for information.

The Graveyard of the Atlantic, one of the most exciting diving spots in the East, offers unparalleled opportunities to wreck divers. From Tubbs Inlet (near Sunset Beach) to New River Inlet (North Topsail Beach) 20 of the dozens of known shipwrecks resting here are accessible and safe. Most are Confederate blockade runners, one is a tanker torpedoed by the Nazi sub U-158, and three were sunk as part of North Carolina's Artificial Reef program. (See the chapter on Fishing for more information on artificial reefs.) These wrecks and higher-risk wrecks can be located through local dive shops.

Wreck diving is an advanced skill. Research prior to a dive is essential in terms of the target, the techniques and the potential dangers, which in this region include live ammunition and explosives that may be found on World War II wrecks. Contact the proper authorities if you observe anything suspicious, and LEAVE IT ALONE! Under state law, all wrecks and underwater artifacts that have remained unclaimed for more than ten years are declared state property. Anyone interested in search-

Swimming and fishing don't mix. Don't cast your line into swimmers; and don't swim near fishermen.

Insiders' Tips

A young girl slides backwards into bliss.

ing for artifacts should file for a permit with the NC Department of Cultural Resources, 109 E. Jones St., Raleigh, NC 27611.

Divers Emergency Cards are identification cards that record one's name, address, blood type, drug sensitivity, an explanation that the cardholder may be suffering from decompression sickness and other pertinent medical and emergency information. They are wisely carried by all serious divers and are available free from UNC Sea Grant, 105 1911 Building, NC State University, Raleigh, NC 27650.

Charter boats can be arranged through all the dive shops listed here, but there are others. Also check the marinas for fishing charters that accommodate dive trips. The Bridge Tender Marina and the adjacent Hanover Fishing Center at Wrightsville Beach, 256-3636, are good resources for charters run by experienced crew. Boats booked by the Fishing Center often serve double duty as fishing charters, so if you need custom diving craft, check into the Bridge Tender Marina. Refer also to the chapter on Fishing.

Most dive shops can lead you to certification classes if they don't offer some themselves. Proof of diver's certification is usually required by shops or dive masters when renting equipment, booking charters or purchasing air-fills. The following are the better local dive shops and services.

Wilmington

AQUATIC SAFARIS & DIVERS EMPORIUM

5751 Oleander Dr.   *392-4386*

Aquatic Safaris is among Wilmington's largest full-service

charter services and dive shops for the recreational diver and snorkeler. Six specialized boats are available for charter at the Bridge Tender Marina on Airlie Road in Wrightsville Beach. They carry a full range of equipment for sale and rent. Snorkeling equipment is for sale only. They are certified by major manufacturers to perform repairs on all life-support equipment and most other equipment as well. They are open seven days a week during the summer and on weekends and by appointment off-season.

ENTROPY DIVE CHARTERS
Towles Rd.   *350-0039*

PADI-certified Captain Chris Klingenberger guides wreck and reef diving trips for up to six persons at a time. His Sea Mark vessels, equipped with full electronics, are docked on the Intracoastal Waterway at the foot of Towles Road (off Greenville Loop Road).

OFFSHORE ADVENTURES
301 Wood Dale Dr.   *799-2895*

Offshore Adventures is a service offering dive charters aboard its custom 31' Bertram, as well as SCUBA instruction during the warm season. In winter, destination dives are organized for those willing to travel.

WILMINGTON SCUBA AND WATER SPORTS
6014 Wrightsville Ave.   *799-0868*

Master SCUBA instructor Bob McIver operates one of the largest sport diving and snorkeling facilities in southeast North Carolina. Services include rentals, repair, sales, air and instruction in diving and snor-

keling. Aboard his customized 31' Bertram, he arranges dive trips to many of the better sites within 30 miles of the Cape Fear shore and books trips to Florida during the winter. His staff is entirely PADI- and SSI-certified, and the business is a National Association of Underwater Instructors (NAUI) facility. During the summer, Wilmington Scuba is open 9 AM to 6 PM Monday through Saturday and only for about an hour from 6 AM on Sundays. Their Cape Fear season closes by early November.

OCEAN RAY
1315 S. College Rd.   *392-9989*
(800) 645-5554

Not a dive shop, Ocean Ray is a 12-year-old manufacturer of quality custom-fit wet and dry suits that recently relocated to Wilmington. Wet suits are made in 3 mm and 6 mm thicknesses. Dry suits are 6 mm-thick G231 nitrogen-blown Rubatex. All suits carry a three-year warranty. Ocean Ray ships throughout North America and Europe and does alterations and repairs on all name-brand suits. Direct sales to the public are available at their retail outlet at the address above.

Topsail Island

EAST COAST DISCOUNT DIVE CENTER
Causeway Dr., Surf City   *328-1887*

Doug Medlin's East Coast Discount Dive Center was recently added to his **East Coast Discount Bait & Tackle Shop**. The Center provides complete dive services including sales, rentals, certification classes and air. The shop is staffed by certified divers and is open seven days a week from 7 AM to 11 PM during the high season. Charter excursions include dives on various World War II wrecks, 23 Mile Rock, 18 Mile Rock and many other sites on request. Trips to common dive sites begin as low as $35. East Coast Discount is open seven days, 7 AM to 9 PM.

South Brunswick

HOLDEN BEACH SURF & SCUBA
3172-4 Holden Beach Rd. SW   842-6899

Bob Huey's establishment is an almost brand-new full-service dive and surf shop that carries practically everything needed for diving including air-fills and computers. Bob is a USCG-certified boat captain and a diver, and his wife is a PADI-certified dive master. Together they can lead dive trips aboard their 30-foot custom dive boat, complete with platform. They conduct lessons at a nearby pool during the warm season. Their shop is open 10 AM to 9 PM, seven days a week in the summer and on weekends during the off-season. They are located on the mainland side of the waterway.

Southport

SCUBA SOUTH DIVING COMPANY
222 S. River Dr.   457-5201

Among the most respected diving experts in the Southport area is Wayne Strickland who specializes in dive charters to some of the less-frequented targets off the cape, plus such well-known sites as the *City of Houston* (a passenger freighter that sunk in 1878), Frying Pan Reef and 10 Mile Rock. He will arrange dives to any site along the Cape Fear coast. Prices generally range from $75 to $100, and price breaks apply to large groups. Trips are aboard 2 custom dive boats, the 42', 11-diver *Scuba South I* and the recently improved 52', 13-diver *Scuba South II*. Strickland has led museum-sponsored salvage expeditions, some of which he has documented on video. Artifacts he recovered are on display at the Southport Maritime Museum. Scuba South sells and rents a full store of equipment, provides air fills and carries both wet and dry suits.

SOUTHPORT SCUBA AND WATER SPORT
610 W. West St.   457-1944

Southport Scuba specializes in sales and rentals of equipment, instruction, charters and commercial diving. They also avail themselves to divers seeking local dive information. They share retail space with Ocean Outfitters, a purveyor of nautical apparel and accessories located near the Southport Yacht Basin.

Water Skiing

The protected waters of the lower Cape Fear River (from Carolina Beach south) are the most popular for water skiing in the greater Wilmington area. The area is convenient to public boat ramps in Carolina Beach, including the marina at Carolina Beach State Park and at Federal Point. Throughout most of the region, the Intracoastal Waterway's wider channels offer skiing opportunities, boat traffic allowing. The wide mouths of the Shallotte River and Lockwood Folly near Varnumtown are just adequate. The relatively-hushed surf along the South Brunswick Islands is well-suited to skiing, yielding about 22 miles of shoreline from Ocean Isle Beach to Sunset Beach.

Big Lake, in the community of Boiling Springs Lakes located 8 miles northwest of Southport on NC 87, is a long, narrow body of water that's excellent for water skiing. There is a free public boat ramp off Alton Lennon Drive.

Entropy Rentals, 350-0039, is one end of a business run by Pete Klingenberger who also designs and builds his own fiberglass Sea Mark power boats. Located on the sound side of Wrightsville Beach, Entropy rents Sea Mark boats of various sizes starting at around $120 for a 1/2 day. Skis are rented for a nominal extra fee, and the nearby protected waterways afford hours of skiing pleasure.

Surfing

California surfers who come to the Cape Fear coast agree: the surf may be less spectacular than on the west coast, but the water is warmer, the season longer and the surfers are less competitive. You don't need to jockey or fight for a spot in the zone when surf is glassy. The beaches running north and south (Topsail Island down to Fort Fisher) experience consistently better surf, especially when a northeaster blows, than the South Brunswick beaches with their east-west orientation. The South Brunswick beaches are better for body-boarding. With a northeast wind, the best surfing from Topsail down to Kure is on the south side of a pier or jetty. One of the most guarded secret spots is the area immediately south of the jetty at Masonboro Island's north end. Fortunately for protective locals, this is one of the most difficult places to reach since crossing Masonboro Inlet is a treacherous and difficult paddle, not recommended since the inlet is a boat channel with dangerous currents. It's better to cross over from the sound side (the Intracoastal Waterway) and hike to the beach.

Wrightsville Beach has the best overall conditions and the most stringent rules governing surfing. During the summer, surf zones (also called sounds) are limited to two-block segments of the beach, and they move south two streets at a time daily beginning at the north end on the 1st of the month. Any lifeguard can tell you where the zone is. Leash laws are also in effect year round; boards must be securely leashed to surfers' limbs. This prevents stray boards from denting another surfer's board — or another surfer's

There are many opportunities to cruise the waters on a paddlewheeler, sailboats, powerboats and party boats for small fees.

Insiders' Tips

Photo: Scott Taylor

A Peter Pan re-enactment on the Cape Fear dunescape.

head. Surfing within 150 feet of the fishing piers, indicated by yellow markers, is prohibited. On northern Topsail Island, surfing is prohibited near Onslow County's Public Beach Access pavilions.

Surfers on the South Brunswick Islands say the surfing near the piers is best, but on Ocean Isle Beach (where there are no rotating zones), ordinances require surfers to remain a full 1000 feet away from the pier (this is not well enforced). Staying clear just makes good sense, given the amount of lost fishing tackle, shattered poles and barnacle-encrusted pilings that lie in wait for reckless surfers. The occasional feat of shooting the pier is like a trainwreck: fascinating to watch and utterly terrifying.

Weekly beginner surfing lessons for advanced ocean swimmers ages 10 and up are offered by Wrightsville Beach Parks & Recreation, 256-7925, June through August. The course covers surfing etiquette, paddling, wave-catching, maneuvers and basic surfing principles.

Daily surf reports are broadcast by the radio station Surf 107-FM at 7:25 AM and 3:30 PM. Aussie Island Surf Shop maintains a 24-hour surf report phone line, 256-5454, for conditions at Wrightsville Beach. Reports by phone are also provided by Surf City Surf Shop, 256-4353. Surf shops everywhere can provide information on contests. Most shops also rent surfboards and boogie boards.

For information on upcoming or unannounced competitions, write the Eastern Surfing Association/SNC, P.O. Box 542, Wrightsville Beach, NC 28480.

Wilmington

Surf City, 530 Causeway Drive, 256-2265, has a reputation for a great selection of gear and apparel, surfing expertise and accessories including videos and skateboards.

Aussie Island Surf Shop, 1319 Military Cutoff Road (Landfall Shopping Center), 256-5454, is a hardcore shop carrying new, used and custom sticks, rentals and rollerblades.

Bert's Surf Shop, 5740 Oleander Drive, 392-4501 carries a wide selection of apparel, beach items and skateboards.

Hot Wax Surf Shop, 415 S. College Rd., 791-9283.

Wrightsville Beach

Bert's Surf Shop, 6 North Lumina Avenue, 256-9110.

Sweetwater Surf Shop, 10 North Lumina Avenue, 256-3821, keeps an excellent stock of jewelry and women's apparel.

Carolina Beach

Bert's Surf Shop, U.S. Highway 421, 458-9047.

The Cove Surf Shop, 107 Cape Fear Boulevard, 458-4671

Hot Wax Surf Shop, 725 North Lake Park Boulevard, 458-3244.

Topsail Island

Bert's Surf Shop, Highway 210 (North New River Drive) near Goldsboro Avenue, Surf City, 328-1010.

South Brunswick

Bert's Surf Shop, corner of Norton Street and Yaupon Beach Drive, Yaupon Beach, 278-6679.

Local Call Surf Shop, 609 Yaupon Beach Drive, Yaupon Beach, 278-3306, customizes boards and carries skateboards.

Holden Beach Surf & Scuba, 842-6899, 3172-4 Holden Beach Road SW, on the mainland side of the waterway, carries boards, accessories, wet suits and more.

Salty's Surf Shop, First Street (on the beach near the foot of Causeway Drive), 579-6223.

Surf Unlimited, 18 Causeway Drive, Ocean Isle Beach, 579-1525.

There is no shortage of places to rent a stick if you don't have one of your own. Check with the surf shops above or these specialty water sports shops:

Caribbean Trading Company, 256-2112, 602 Causeway Drive, Wrightsville Beach, rents boards for $15 per day. A $25 deposit (cash or credit) is required.

S & S Water Sports, Inc., North Anderson Boulevard, Topsail Beach, 328-7751 rents surfboards and boogie boards. They are located at the Breezeway Motel Restaurant and are open seven days a week, 9 AM to 6 PM.

Topsail Water Sports, 328-1141, also rents surfboards and boogie boards for $5 and $2 per hour, respectively. Day rates are discounted.

Beach Fun Rentals, 842-9600, on Holden Beach Road Southwest, on the mainland side of the bridge.

The Winds Clarion Inn, 310 E. First St., Ocean Isle Beach, 579-7575, rents floats ($5 per day), boogie boards ($8 per day), surfboards ($15 per day) and skim boards ($12 per day). They operate by appointment on weekends between Easter and Memorial Day and are open 7 days a week on the beach outside the hotel during the summer.

Swimming

The Cape Fear Coast is blessed with clean, relatively clear, refreshing waters and a long outdoor season. Water temperatures are comfortable usually no later than mid-spring, generally hovering in the 75-80 degree range. Only at the end of summer do temperatures approach those of waters further south. Most beaches consist of fine, clean sand. Together with the shores of the Outer Banks to the north, the Cape Fear coast gives evidence that North Carolina does indeed have the finest beaches in the east.

Except during storm surges, surf is generally moderate. Most beach communities employ lifeguards during the summer season, but the beaches are unstaffed otherwise. Swimming in a few areas is hazardous, such as at the extreme east end of Ocean Isle Beach and along the Fort Fisher Historic Site because of underwater debris and strong currents. All hazardous areas are well-marked. See the chapter on Sun, Sand and Sea for other tips on beach-going.

Those who enjoy pool-swimming can indulge themselves at the public pools maintained by local Parks & Recreation departments. There are 3 in Wilmington, at Legion Stadium, Northside Park and Robert Strange Park. Admission to them carries a nominal fee. Other pools are available to members of local fitness centers, particularly the YMCA, 251-9622, 2710 Market Street, and the YWCA, 799-6820, 2815 South College Road in Wilmington, both of which have excellent facilities and offer swimming instruction. The pool at Camelot Campground, 686-7705, 7415 Market Street, just a few minutes north of downtown Wilmington, is open to non-campers. In Long Beach, The Deck Entertainment Center, 278-4111, on Southeast 58th Street, operates a pool that is open to the public.

The varsity swimming teams at UNCW are strong Conference contenders and have hosted many Conference championships at the university's beautiful new facilities. The men's team finished 2nd in last year's championships, and the women had their 2nd straight winning season. Teams are open to attending students.

Wrightsville Beach Parks & Recreation, 256-7925, offers beginner and advanced beginner swimming lessons for youth ages 4-11. Lessons are conducted June through August in two-week sessions.

The MWR Recreation Division's Athletics Branch of Marine Corps Base Camp Lejeune sponsors stiff swimming competitions as part of their annual Grand Prix Series of sporting events. These include the Masters Swim I held in January, the Masters Swim II in June and the Davy Jones Open Ocean Swim in July. These events (and others listed in the Sports and Fitness chapter) take place within the confines of Camp Lejeune in Jacksonville, about 20 minutes from North Topsail Beach. All events are open to military personnel, civilian employees and the general public of all ages, and they typically attract a nationwide draw of competitors. Entry forms and information can be obtained by contacting Dr. Ron Gerughty, Fitness Director, 451-5430, between 8 AM and 4 PM, Monday through Friday.

Windsurfing/ Sailboarding

Depending on the wind, you can choose between long stretches of protected waters and great expanses of open sea to indulge in this remarkable sport. Experienced windsurfers go wave-hopping. Windsurfers of all levels go island-hopping, and beginners will find plenty of resources for learning from Topsail to Sunset.

One of the best and most popular windsurfing areas is The Basin, the semi-protected body of water off Federal Point at the southern end of Pleasure Island. Accessible from a public boat ramp down the road from the ferry terminal, the Basin is enclosed by The Rocks, a 3 1/3-mile breakwater that extends to Zeke's Island and beyond (see the chapters on Attractions and Fishing). Mott's Channel and Banks Channel on the soundside of Wrightsville Beach are popular spots, but you'll have to contend with the currents. Advanced windsurfers prefer the oceanside of the jetty at the south end of Wrightsville Beach where action is fairly guaranteed. Around Topsail Island, the choices are the Intracoastal and the ocean. The inlets north and south of the island are not well-suited to uninterrupted runs. Along Oak Island and the South Brunswick Islands, the ocean is your best bet, although limited stretches of the Intracoastal are OK for beginners despite the currents. Shallotte Inlet and River are narrow, but worth a shot. Up-to-date information on windsurfing competitions, usually held in the fall, are available at many of the outlets listed below.

Caribbean Trading Company, 256-2112, 602 Causeway Drive at Wrightsville Beach, rents sailboards at competitive rates and provides lessons. An eight-hour course starts at $100, and there are four-hour and private lessons ($20 per hour) also available. CTC is the bright coral-colored building before the fixed bridge at Banks Channel. They rent and sell a wide variety of other beach sports items.

Ship's Store Windsurfing and Sailing Center, 256-4445/9463, rents sailboards at reasonable rates by the hour ($15 1st hour) and in blocks of hours. Surfers put in at Banks Channel opposite the Blockade Runner Hotel. Instructors are available on Thursdays and Fridays during the summer to teach four-hour windsurfing classes ($60), and the store in the Atlantic View Retail Center on Wrightsville Avenue is open for sales all year.

Topsail Water Sports in Topsail Beach, 328-1141, rents wind boards for $15 per 1/2 hour, $40 per hour, and offers lessons. Reservations are recommended.

Cape Fear Boat Rental & Charters, 278-1880/9933, rents sailboards at excellent rates starting at $12 for the 1st hour. All-day rentals run $52, and for $150 you can windsurf from Monday to Friday. They are located at Bluewater Point near the west end of Oak Island (Long Beach).

Beach Access

Public beach access is a system of pedestrian right-of-ways, dune crossovers, parking lots and, at certain locations, rest room and shower facilities. A few have food concessions. Except in public lots on Wrightsville Beach, where parking meters must be fed during the summer only, parking everywhere is free. Signs indicating beach access paths are readily visible, marked with a large orange sun over blue water. Most communities prohibit glass containers and vehicles on the strand. Kure Beach also prohibits dogs and alcohol. Keep in mind that crossing dunes in most beach communities can earn you a $50 fine or more, except at approved crossovers.

On Wrightsville Beach, public access with rest rooms, metered parking and a shower are located across South Lumina Avenue from the Oceanic Restaurant and Crystal Pier. Rest rooms and a shower are located at the foot of Salisbury Street near Johnny Mercer's Pier. Parking is also available adjacent to the Holiday Inn to the north. Parking is available on either side of the Duneridge Resort, about one mile north of Salisbury Street. One lot has a rest room. At the north end of Wrightsville Beach, there is parking on both sides of Shell Island Resort.

At Carolina and Kure Beaches, public beach access points and parking generally are situated two blocks apart, at the foot of every second street. Public rest rooms and showers are also available, mostly along the boardwalk, the most popular being at the foot of Cape Fear Boulevard.

In North Topsail Beach, in addition to various access points without services, Onslow County maintains a large Public Beach Access (#2) about 2 miles north of Tilghman's Square in Surf City. This facility has ample parking, a handicap ramp to the building only, showers, rest rooms and phones. Snack vendors are usually on hand nearby. This facility is open April 1 to September 30 from 9 AM to 8 PM daily. Off-season it closes at 5 PM. A little more than 4 miles north, Onslow County Public Beach Access #1 is a bigger facility with similar amenities. It features handicap access to the beach and a concession on the premises.

In Surf City, access with parking and rest rooms is at the foot of New Bern Avenue. Handicap access is only to the dune-top deck. Along Topsail Beach, access with limited parking is available at the foot of nearly every cross street. South of Florida Avenue, a series of stairways provides crossovers with street parking along Ocean Boulevard.

Always bring light footwear to the beaches where the sand can be hot enough to scorch your bare soles.

On Caswell Beach Road about 1/2 mile east of the Fort Caswell Lighthouse the public beach access consists of a large gravel parking lot with no facilities. The area is open from 5 AM to 11 PM and prohibitions include camping, the use of alcohol, firearms, fires and cars on the strand.

In Yaupon Beach, there are nine beach access points with parking. The less crowded ones are, naturally, the ones farther from the pier, especially to the west.

There are 52 public beach accesses along the eight miles of Long Beach oceanfront on Oak Island. The Cabana at the foot of 40th Street East is one of the liveliest access points, being the site of Brunswick County Parks & Recreation's Summer Fun Beach Days (see the chapter on Attractions). There's plenty of parking, a concession stand and showers. Most other access points have no services except the one at the foot of S. Middletown Avenue

where retail and food stores are an easy walk from the beach. Most of the public accesses in Long Beach have limited parking, especially close to S. Middletown Avenue

The majority of beach accesses on 11 mile-long Holden Beach are private, but public access points abound at the east end (Avenues A-E), near Jordan Boulevard and at Ferry Road Several others are west of the bridge. Parking is generally prohibited along Ocean Boulevard A Regional Beach Access facility with showers, rest rooms and parking, open 6 AM to 11 PM, is located nearly under the bridge off Jordan Boulevard. On Ocean Isle, access is concentrated around the center of town, near the foot of the causeway. Beach access on Sunset Beach is indicated by small white posts about 100 yards apart. There are no sidewalks and little parking. The paved parking lot adjacent to Sunset Fishing Pier is convenient to the beach and pier facilities.

Old Baldy Stands Tall

Rising more than 100 feet above the sea surrounding Bald Head Island, the old octagonal tower known as Old Baldy is more than North Carolina's oldest standing lighthouse. Since coming into service in 1817, it has become a symbol of the courage and determination of those who sail the treacherous waters that gave Cape Fear its name and of the uniqueness of the very island over which it stands.

What is known as Bald Head Island today has been known at various times in the past as Cedar Island, Cape Island, Smith Island and Palmetto Island. This headland at the entrance to the state's only deep-water port may have always been devoid of vegetation. But legend has it that vigilant river pilots either trampled all the vegetation on the crest, or denuded the site of firewood. More likely, they may have cleared the vegetation to improve their view of incoming ships. Whatever the case, the headland became bald.

Old Baldy was not the first lighthouse erected on Bald Head, but it is certainly the longest lived, thanks as much to sound construction as to good luck. When the 1784 Colonial Assembly levied duties upon all vessels entering the Port of

"Old Baldy" is North Carolina's oldest standing lighthouse.

Brunswick to provide for beacons and buoys at the mouth of the Cape Fear River, additional duties were collected toward building a badly-needed lighthouse to guide ships into the difficult river channel. The authorization had specified that the light be situated "at the extreme point of Bald-head or some other convenient place near the bar of said river." After much delay, the lighthouse was completed and went into operation in 1795. Unfortunately, the builders took the wording of the authorization too literally. The lighthouse stood so close to the banks of the river that within two decades it succumbed to erosion and was taken down.

The new tower, 36 feet in diameter and 72 feet high, was built of hard brick masonry walls, 5 feet thick to a height of 20 feet and tapering in thickness above. It is capped by a thick stone platform supporting the light mechanism. The arched roof was built upon eight corner pieces sunk 10 feet into the brickwork and secured by anchors. Large windows admitted plenty of daylight for wickies to haul whale oil up the strong wooden stairs that spiraled upward to heavily planked floors made of local heart pine.

Along with the lantern, much of the brick had been salvaged from the original lighthouse. At first, this seemed to be a boon to Daniel S. Way, the builder of the new lighthouse. But Way made the unparalleled blunder of not visiting the island until long after being awarded the contract. He found that the bricks were not as numerous as he had expected. Even more vexing, it was necessary to move the mountain of bricks down a steep shore, ship them a mile over a shoal of 5 feet of water and up a shallow creek, then haul them up a high bluff and overland to the new building site, located 1/2 mile north of the old site. David Stick, author of the book Bald Head, stated, "That he did the job well is attested by the fact that Old Baldy still stands, having weathered three wars, numerous storms, and years of neglect."

Way's ordeal, and the confusion about whether Old Baldy became operable in 1817 or 1818 (records vary), seems somehow connected to the fact that its proposed completion date was April Fool's Day, 1817.

Old Baldy was relegated to secondary status when the lighthouse at Federal Point was built near New Inlet, north of Bald Head Island. (A hurricane had opened the inlet in 1761.) But as nature would have it, New Inlet became increasingly constricted and with the construction of the long breakwater known as "The Rocks," it was closed entirely in 1881. The river's increased flow past Bald Head Island threatened to bring down Old Baldy just like its predecessor, but luck was on Old Baldy's side. In August 1883, a 150-foot jetty was completed to prevent erosion, barely a month before a destructive hurricane slammed the island.

Old Baldy's small light was never adequate for guiding vessels around hazardous Frying Pan Shoals. So the old tower was again eclipsed, this time by the Cape Fear Light Station erected near the point of the cape and lit in 1903. This was where Cape Fear's most famous "wickie," "Cap'n Charlie" Swan, worked for 30 years. The three cottages where he, his two assistants and their families lived still stand today. It was during Cap'n Charlie's tenure that Bald Head Island's population peaked with 40 inhabitants, including that other famous wickie, Captain Sonny Dosher, keeper of Old Baldy for many years. During this time, Old Baldy performed its humble duty as a fixed harbor light until it was retired in 1935.

Old Baldy became a radio beacon station during World War II. In 1958, the new Oak Island light, the nation's brightest, was built, and the Cape Fear Light Station was demolished. Once again, Old Baldy stood alone on the island. Over nearly 200 years, Old Baldy has outlasted many changes yet remains a constant and enduring symbol of the Cape Fear heritage.

Old Baldy is a living museum and historic landmark open to the public. See the Attractions chapter for information.

Inside
Sun, Sand and Sea Tips

There's nothing like lazing around on a sunny beach under a Carolina blue sky, taking an occasional dip in the beautiful, clean waters off North Carolina's southeastern coast or cruising down the Intracoastal Waterway.

Vacationing by the water is the most popular way for people to relax, which probably explains why many visitors end up being residents on the coast by retirement age, if not before. It's the lure of island living; it's the simplicity of bare feet and casual clothing; it's the worry-free life of paradise. But everyone, including insiders, needs to be reminded that even in such a paradise, there are some good tips to follow for a safe, enjoyable vacation.

The Sun

No matter what your age or complexion, it's very important to wear sunscreen on the beach. In recent years, the sun has had more of a searing effect on even relatively insensitive skin. A sunburn, sad to say, is just going to fall off and make you look like you're molting in a week or so.

You can burn even on a cloudy day because up to 90 percent of the sun's rays penetrate clouds and can still damage your skin. Surfaces such as sand, concrete and water can reflect up to 85 percent of the sun's rays.

Sunscreen with appropriate SPF (sun protection factor) should be a daily habit. Especially on the beach, no matter how immune you have always seemed to be to sunburn, you should slather yourself in the best protection you can find. After swimming, put more on. Children need special skin protection. More than half of the skin damage done by the sun happens in the first 18 years of life. Waterproof sunblock will save you from having to constantly apply it as kids dart back and forth between the sand and the water many times during an hour.

Dermatologists recommend a sun protection factor of at least 15 for children. Infants need sunblock, a hat, lightweight clothing and a beach umbrella. Even under the umbrella, the reflective rays are still present.

Wide-brimmed straw hats are very popular in the Cape Fear area, and you can enjoy protection and look cool at the same time. In the heat of summer, wear light-colored clothing for maximum comfort. Look for linen and cotton clothing because these fabrics breathe better than synthetics. Synthetics feel much like

Photo: Curtis Krueger

The Wilmington port plays host to many beautiful "tall ships" each year.

Saranwrap after only a few minutes in the summer sun. Stay cool in the hottest part of the day, generally between 11 AM and 3 PM, by enjoying your air-conditioned accommodations. You can have a long morning on the beach and hours in the afternoon without exposing yourself to the depleting effects of excessive summer heat. It is generally 90 degrees and up in the summer.

Alcohol, which isn't allowed on area beaches anyway, is debilitating in the heat. Take a cooler of Gatorade or lemonade, and you'll enjoy yourself much more on the beach. Beer will just make you thirstier under the hot sun.

The Sand

Wilmington area beaches vary in width and shell diversity, but they all have one thing in common: beautiful expanses of sand. Sand though, slips inside your swimsuit when you swim, makes your hair sticky, cakes between your toes and is unpleasant if it blows into your sandwich. Take a nice blanket or old quilt along with you to put under your lawn chair. The sand will eventually creep over the edges, especially on a windy day, but this gives you a relatively clean base of operations for your beach visit.

Insiders take a gallon container of fresh water to the beach because it's wonderful for rinsing sand and salt out of your hair after a swim in the ocean. You can rinse your whole body if you're frugal with the stream. Many area beaches also offer shower facilities. And, especially if you have a drive after being at the beach, you'll want to shower and change clothing. Few things feel more wretched than a sandy, chafing swimsuit when you slip onto hot seats of your car.

Sand is also one of the greatest natural pumices available. City feet calloused by work shoes can actually get sanded down to smoothness in a vacation week of walking on the beach in bare feet. So, kick your shoes off and go for a walk. It's fun, healthy and interesting You can see all kinds of amazing things on a long stroll along the beach. The sand gives up wonderful gifts. Topsail Beach offers shark's teeth. Ebony in color and varied in shape, these teeth are available to the keen observer who looks for a characteristic glint in the sand or at the water's edge.

The Brunswick beaches yield other interesting treasures. Whole sand dollars are frequent finds. Look for skeletal ones that are all white, and discard the brown, furry ones. Arrowheads can also be found on these beaches if you are observant. Wrightsville Beach is poor shelling ground. Once upon a time, Shell Island at the north end of Wrightsville was prime shelling territory. It was also an actual island. Now, it is a developed beach area with very few shell treasures to be found in the sand.

The sand dunes bear some mention: please stay off of them. The dunes are a vital part of the beach environment and provide homes for a variety of beach animals. They retard erosion and protect the homes on the islands. Also, on the purely practical side, there is a stiff fine if you climb in the dunes or take any of the vegetation. Fines are as high as $500, and it could put a dent in your vacation allowance if you went on a wild romp through the dunes. So, be forewarned. There are some laws worth noting. Don't take glass containers on the beach; don't let your dog run loose until you check local ordinances; don't let your parking meter expire (bring plenty of quarters to Wrightsville Beach); don't take alcohol to the beach; and don't litter.

Area beaches welcome visitors, but there are marked beach access points for travel from your car to the sand. Without exception, beaches in this part of North Carolina are primarily residential neighborhoods with fairly limited commercial development. Most of the homes are private property, and residents don't take kindly to people tramping through their yards. Getting from the asphalt to the beach also requires footwear. The road can get

---

Prevent swimmer's ear by placing a few drops of 91 percent rubbing alcohol in each ear for a few seconds after each swim. Treat an existing infection with a 50-50 solution of rubbing alcohol and distilled white vinegar four to six times daily.

Insiders' Tips

Photo: Scott Taylor

A surfer calls it a day.

painfully hot, and there are some vicious sandspurs waiting for your delicate feet. The sand on the beach above the high water mark can sizzle in the summer, so protect your feet.

There is an interesting phenomenon that occurs on the beaches in the fall. At times, on a night walk, you can kick up a phosphorescent light show with bare feet in the sand. It sort of makes you feel like you're walking through stars. Night on the sand is a special time. Many a person has been inspired to take a night stroll and a dip in the ocean in the dark. A word of warning about taking a swim, however: if you leave your clothing and other possessions on the sand, pick out an easily recognizable landmark. The currents move curiously, and you can end up at another spot on the beach in the dark without so much as a clue to your whereabouts (and with little more than the night to clothe you).

The Sea

Ah, the beautiful sea. You can look serenely at it, splash around in it, boat on it, surf on it and use it in many other fun and relaxing ways. Since Wilmington is a major port, it is often easy to spot incoming or outgoing international freighters, so a pair of binoculars is a valuable asset for watching boats and ships. There are also many ways you can actually be on the water with readily available rental of windsurfers, sailboats and ocean-going kayaks. Swimming is tremendously popular on area beaches because the water is comfortable and clean. While floating around on an air mattress just beyond the breakers, one can often see 10 feet to the sandy bottom.

Many of the beaches in the area have lifeguards posted during the summer vacation season, and there is a good reason for this: there are some dangers in the sea that insiders respect. Riptides and undertows are the unseen dangers that lurk beneath the waves. If you are swimming and you are suddenly pulled in a frightening way by the currents, the most important thing to remember is to stay calm. Panic leads to exertion, which leads to fatigue. If you find yourself in a riptide, relax, and let it carry you on its natural course toward the sea. Within a few minutes, it will dissipate. Then, you can swim parallel to the shoreline to get out of the riptide area and back to shore. Do not try to swim straight back into shore against the riptide; you'll only tire yourself out.

Swim in areas with lifeguards and, if there aren't any, keep yourself close to shore. Pay attention to your location, and understand that it's important to be close enough to shore to get yourself in if there's a problem. Something many people don't realize is that inlets are not places to swim. They look incredibly inviting and seem safe, yet they are the most dangerous places for swimming. Any boater knows that inlets are daunting places for navigation in almost all cases because the currents are swift. If the prospect of being swept out to sea isn't scary enough for you, then consider this: sharks love to lie in the bottoms of inlets to aerate their gills.

The Cape Fear River isn't really suitable for swimming. It is 38 feet deep on average and known for deep, racing currents, as well as alligators. The Battleship *North Carolina*, moored permanently on the west bank of the river across from downtown Wilmington, is the regular hangout of Charlie the Alligator. He's the chief toothy beast beside the ship. While alligators aren't generally known for their aggression toward people, they have been known to snatch domestic animals, as well as waterfowl and other small creatures. So, don't send your dog for a splash in the Cape Fear.

Wrightsville Beach is a popular place for surfing, but there are some regulations regarding it, and you should ask the lifeguard about designated surfing zones. The zones shift each day. You must wear a bungee cord and will be immediately warned if you are not attached to your board. The tides are such an important factor in coastal communities that they're a part of the daily weather forecast. Be aware of them if you splash out to sandbars or islands at low tide. Changing tides could make the trip back to shore a daunting swim.

Regarding weather, take thunderstorms seriously, and get out of the water and off the beach when these often spectacular weather events take place. Lightning on the beach means business, and you

When combing the beaches for shark's teeth, scrutinize the course sand most carefully. The teeth show up best when they are wet.

Insiders' Tips

Photo: Curtis Krueger

Insiders know it is illegal to pick sea oats in North Carolina.

should seek immediate shelter inside a building or your car. Also, a hurricane watch is a good reason to leave an area and the worst reason to arrive to watch nature in upheaval. Area beaches are often evacuated when hurricanes threaten. Some of the area's worst storms involve tidal surges and high winds on sunny days. If you're going boating, pay attention to weather warnings because you may not be able to predict a storm if you look at the sky.

There are many opportunities for boating in the Cape Fear region. If you trailer your own boat, there are ample public boat ramps throughout the entire area. If you choose to leave your boat at the water, there are more than 70 marinas that offer a variety of services, including dry-docking, wetslips and storage. Boating possibilities include the Cape Fear River and its adjacent branches, the Atlan-

tic Ocean, the Intracoastal Waterway, and lakes. Fuel and other amenities are regularly available on the Cape Fear coastline, generally on the Intracoastal Waterway. For people without their own boats, there are charter services for sailing craft and, of course, tour and deep sea fishing boats that cater to all cruising needs. Boaters should understand the rules of the road when operating their own boats or when chartering someone else's. Boat traffic can border on congestion in some areas, such as Banks Channel in Wrightsville Beach, and it's important to have some understanding of the basics.

Perhaps the most important thing about boating is your preparation. Supplies are a good place to start. File a float plan. This can be as official or informal as your circumstances require. The point is that you should tell someone where

you're going and when you expect to return. Motors don't always work, and tides never stop. Don't make your loved ones on shore worry about your whereabouts if you're late returning. You are required to have one life jacket for each person on your boat, and the Coast Guard is within its rights to stop you and see that you have proper equipment. Adults may use their own judgement about wearing one; children should automatically be strapped into one. It isn't comfortable, but these things save people's lives.

Carry sufficient liquids, not only for the humans aboard, but for your dog if you choose to take Rover along. Discourage your pet from drinking sea water, and have fresh water available. And, obviously, don't drive drunk on the water. It's dangerous, and it's against the law. Carry an emergency kit that contains flares and various repair items. If you're going to be out after dark, attend to your running lights. The Intracoastal Waterway is also a highway for commerce, and you want to be sure that barges know you're out there in the dark. Educate yourself on basic navigation. Especially in congested areas, which abound on the Intracoastal Waterway at Wrightsville Beach and Carolina Beach, understand markers and their meanings. A Power Squadron course, probably available in your city or town, is an invaluable experience before boating.

Boats under sail always have the right of way over powercraft. If power is your chosen method of boating, be considerate of the instability your wake can create for slower boats. Remember that Wilmington is a major port, and some whopping vessels travel the shipping lanes into the Cape Fear River. Even if you're on a sailboat under sail, give these vessels wide berth. Large ships have a sucking action on the water around them, and barges require several miles in which to stop. If you sail in the way of commercial vessels, you should know that your right-of-way won't amount to much if impact occurs.

Emergencies happen on the water. The Coast Guard is particular about what constitutes an emergency, and they will not immediately come to your rescue in all situations. Generally, only life or environment-threatening situations will receive the attention of the Coast Guard. Running aground in the waterway is rarely considered an emergency. Commercial towing companies will arrive if you get stuck on a sandbar and call for help on your radio; and, believe this insider who has been stuck hard aground a few times, their service is worthwhile. For a yearly fee, you can arrange unlimited towing. A sailboat with a fixed keel is virtually guaranteed to go aground at some point, and it isn't always possible to get loose without a sturdy towboat.

The Cape Fear area's waters are full of shoals, so keep an eye on your depth-sounder. If you don't have one, and charts suggest shallow waters, steer clear of questionable ar-

eas. The Intracoastal Waterway is susceptible to shoaling near inlets, and you can't rely on charts for accuracy since changes occur frequently. Being out on a boat often inspires hunger, and it seems very romantic to poke about the channels in search of fresh oysters. This isn't recommended. Leave the oysters to the professionals who know the uncontaminated areas.

The Cape Fear region is rich in seafood, and visitors, especially those who rent beach houses where they can cook, will find wonderful variety in fresh fish and shellfish in area seafood stores. You can certainly catch your own fish and guarantee its freshness; but you don't have to do that if you aren't inclined to do so. The most important tips in purchasing the fruits of the sea involve your most basic senses. Start with your nose. Seafood shouldn't smell overly fishy. Continue with your eyes. A fresh fish with its head intact will have clear eyes that guarantee it just came from the water. A filet will look moist and will not be discolored or faded. Feel the fish. It should be firm. Insiders know that the Cape Fear area is abundant in delicious shrimp. For especially tasty steamed or boiled shrimp, buy shrimp with the heads on. A traditional shrimperoo includes sheets of newspaper spread on a big table heaped with steamed shrimp. Guests peel their own. It's a messy bit of heaven.

The Cape Fear region boasts the best that sun, sand and sea have to offer. Come prepared to enjoy a safe and fun visit. For more information, contact the Cape Fear Coast Visitor Information Bureau at 341-4030.

Inside
Fishing

For anglers, the Cape Fear Coast is nothing short of paradise. Blue-green waters tempered and cleansed by the Gulf Stream, rivers where many saltwater species breed and dozens of winding creeks teem with marine wildlife. Whether you're interested in lazing alongside a shady creek in slow pursuit of catfish, surf-casting for blues or pitting yourself against mighty deep-sea game fish, it's all here, usually within a 20-minute drive.

Since the early '70s, the Division of Marine Fisheries (an agency of the state's Department of Environmental Health and Natural Resources) has been involved in the creation of artificial reefs, which provide habitats for a variety of undersea life. These "reefs" consist of old ships, railroad cars, bridge rubble, concrete, or FADS (Fish Attracting Devices, whatever they are). Using the motto "We sink 'em — you fish 'em," the reef-builders have created 20 such reefs along the Cape Fear coast to date. Judging by the numbers of sheepshead, mackerel and billfish landed on an average day, the program seems to be paying off. (Surely, the men who landed the 937-pound tiger shark in the Poor Boy Shark Tournament in August of 93 think so.) A grease

chart will lead you to these sites, as well as to the scores of fish-filled wrecks littering this Graveyard of the Atlantic.

Small boat owners have unique fishing opportunities — around the pilings of Pfizer Pharmaceutical Company's long pier in the Cape Fear River north of Price's Creek, for example. The mouths of most creeks and some inlets are good spots, especially during incoming tides when you and your bait can drift in with the bait fish. Use caution at ocean inlets during strong outgoing tides.

Fishing licenses are issued by the NC Wildlife Resources Commission. They range greatly in price and privileges and may be combined with a hunting license. Licenses can be purchased at many sporting goods retailers and hardware stores.

In Wilmington, inquire at: Tackle Mart, 4100 Oleander Drive, 392-3472; Sears, Independence Mall, 3500 Oleander Drive, 452-6206; and Wal-Mart, 352 South College Road, 392-4034.

In Pender County, north of the Holly Shelter Game Land, Holland's Shelter Creek Fish Camp, Highway 53, 259-5743, sells hunting and fishing licenses and supplies and rents canoes ($10 flat fee). The restaurant is a local landmark specializing in catfish, atmosphere and conversation.

On Topsail Island, check Surf City Hardware, on the Causeway in Surf City, 328-3251.

In South Brunswick stop by Stewart Hardware, 1635 Howe Street, Southport, 457-5544; Island Tackle and Gifts, Highway 179, Ocean Isle Beach, 579-6116; or Holden Beach True Value, 3008 Holden Beach Road, 842-5440.

Call the Law Enforcement Division of the NC Wildlife Resources Commission at 662-4370 for more information on licensing. Also, familiarize yourself with regulations regarding bag limits and minimum sizes. Note that fishing from most bridges in the area is prohibited since most bridges transverse boat channels. For further information, call the Division of Marine Fisheries, toll-free: (800)682-2632.

So much for knowing what to do. What follows is information on where and when to do it: annual fishing tournaments, where to get up-to-date fishing reports, descriptions of the many fishing piers and boat ramps, a cross-section of head boats and charters, and surf fishing. Of course, we've included recommendations for some special places to cast your lure or net.

Cape Fear Coast Salt Water Fishing Tournaments

Lately, tournament fishing has been luring larger schools of anglers with tens of thousands of dollars in prize bait. Many contests recognize tag and release as requirements for entry as part of the Governor's Cup Billfishing Conservation Series. Check current listings at tackle shops, marinas and visitors centers.

May

CAPE FEAR OPEN MARLIN TOURNAMENT
Bridge Tender Marina   256-6550.
Wrightsville Beach

June

SHALLOTTE POINT FLOUNDER TOURNAMENT
Tripps Fishing Center   754-6080
Shallotte

SCOTTS HILL KING MACKEREL TOURNAMENT
Scotts Hill Marina   686-0896/0527
Scotts Hill

BALD HEAD ISLAND FISHING RODEO
Bald Head Island Marina   (800)234-1666

July

EAST COAST GOT-EM-ON KING MACKEREL CLASSIC
Carolina Beach Yacht Basin   458-9576
Carolina Beach

HAMPSTEAD KING MACKEREL TOURNAMENT
Harbor Village Marina   270-4017
Hampstead

August

POOR BOY SHARK TOURNAMENT
Hugh's Marina   754-6233
Shallotte Point

Photo: Scott Taylor

Do you think he sees us?

Photo: Scott Taylor

A fresh catch doesn't hang around long.

LONG BAY LADY ANGLERS
KING MACKEREL TOURNAMENT
Sure Catch Tackle Shop   278-5327
Southport

SNEADS FERRY
KING MACKEREL TOURNAMENT
New River Marina   327-9691
Sneads Ferry

TOPSAIL OFFSHORE FISHING CLUB
KING MACKEREL TOURNAMENT
Anna Marina   328-5681
Topsail Beach

September

SOUTH BRUNSWICK ISLES
KING MACKEREL TOURNAMENT
location to be announced   754-6644

**WRIGHTSVILLE BEACH
KING MACKEREL TOURNAMENT**
Atlantic Marine 256-3581
Wrightsville Beach

**U.S. OPEN
KING MACKEREL TOURNAMENT**
Small Boat Harbor 457-6964
Southport

October

**PLEASURE ISLAND
SURF FISHING TOURNAMENT**
Carolina Beach 458-8434
Regulations governing size and bag limits are posted at most piers and marinas. For more information, contact the Wilmington office of the Division of Marine Fisheries: (800) 248-4536 or (919) 395-3900.

Fishing Reports

The most up-to-date sources of fishing information are charter captains, fishing piers and tackle shops. The radio station Beach 106.3-FM (WCCA) airs fishing reports twice a day on weekdays at 7 AM and 5 PM. Star-Line, a telephone service of the *Wilmington Star-News*, provides daily fishing and weather reports for the price of a local call, 762-1996, ext. 2212.

Fishing Piers

Each of the piers on the Cape Fear coast has its own personality. Some have been made crooked by years of brutal ocean gales. Some are festooned with odd novelties and memorabilia. Most of them proudly display photographs of trophies reeled up from the sea. Almost all charge a fee

for fishing permits, good for a 24-hour period beginning at 6 AM. Bottom fishing generally costs $3 to 5 and king fishing about twice as much. Most piers offer season fishing permits, tackle shops, snack bars, wet cleaning tables and rest rooms.

Wilmington

RIVER ROAD PARK
6300 River Rd. opposite Sugar Pine Dr.
This county park, located south of the State Port about 8 miles from downtown Wilmington, features a new 240-foot fishing pier into the Cape Fear River. The park is handicap accessible and is open from 8 AM to dusk.

Wrightsville Beach

CRYSTAL PIER
703 S. Lumina Ave. 256-5551
Crystal Pier is located at the Oceanic Restaurant (it's often called Oceanic Pier). It has no tackle shop and prohibits vulgarity. Permits are sold at the snack counter at the rear of the building or at the restaurant's front desk.

JOHNNIE MERCER'S PIER
Foot of E. Salisbury St. 256-2743
This popular pier has a tackle shop that sells bait and an arcade that is a favorite hangout for teens.

Pleasure Island

CAROLINA BEACH PIER
Salt Marsh Lane and Canal St. 458-5518
This is the northernmost pier on Carolina Beach.

CENTER PIER

South of Tennessee Ave.   458-5739

Center Pier shares its parking lot with the fine Center Pier Restaurant. The tackle shop sells bait (not live) and is open 6 AM until 1, 2 . . . 3 AM, depending, apparently, on how good the fishing is.

KURE BEACH PIER

Avenue K   458-5524

Permits here are good only until midnight on the day they are purchased.

Topsail Island

BARNACLE BILL'S FISHING PIER

Shore Dr.   328-3661
Surf City

Barnacle Bill's and its adjoining restaurant, Dine Ashore (get it?), comprise a colorful attraction. It's a busy, cluttered place with a pool room, a salty clientele and loud country music.

JOLLY ROGER PIER

Foot of Flake Ave.   328-4616

This is the only ocean pier on the southern half of the island. It's about 6 miles south of Surf City. Its patio is what remains of a launch pad built for Project Bumblebee, the Navy's historic missile-development program.

OCEAN CITY FISHING PIER

New River Dr. (Rt. 210)   328-5701
          (800)358-2318

The white observation tower at the foot of the pier is another remnant of Project Bumblebee. The pier is located about three miles north of Surf City, opposite Herring's Bait & Tackle Shop.

SALTY'S PIER

1798 New River Inlet Rd.   328-0221
North Topsail Beach

The building at the foot of Salty's was once a recording studio. Now it houses a good selection of rods, reels and accessories for sale and rent, as well as fresh bait and a small variety of beverages and microwavable foods. Anglers can kick back and relax on bench seats with backs. Salty's is located just north of the Villa Capriani Resort.

SCOTCH BONNET FISHING PIER

New River Dr. (Rt. 210)   328-4261

There is something of an amusement park atmosphere here, due mainly to the huge game room opposite the tackle shop. The pier is 2.5 miles north of the Causeway, across from Tilghman's Square.

SURF CITY PIER

N. Shore Dr.   328-3521

Located one block south of Roland Avenue in the heart of Surf City, this is a busy, family-oriented establishment that prohibits alcohol and drunks. The busy snack bar rents chairs, umbrellas, rafts and body boards. Indoors, a large game room will keep the kids twitching their joy sticks. Special bottom-fishing rates apply to children: $2 daily; $15 season (April 1 to Nov. 30).

TOPSAIL SOUND FISHING PIER

Carolina Ave. at the foot of
Florida Ave.   328-3641

This is the only pier on Topsail Island's sound side. Among its most appealing aspects are its friendly proprietor, Kip Oppegaard, and Midori, his wolf-whistling parrot.

Behind them hangs a sign that reads, "Thank you for holding your breath while I smoke." This is also the place to book an Osprey Charter (see Charters, this chapter).

Southport

CITY PIER
Waterfront Park, Bay St.   No phone
This small pier near the mouth of the Cape Fear River is a municipal facility, and usage is free.

Oak Island

YAUPON PIER
Foot of Womblie Ave.   278-9400
This is the highest pier in the state. The owners were convinced by the persuasive March storm of 93 that some remodeling was in order, and they added 130 feet of pier. The Pirate's Cove Restaurant adjoins the pier, as does the unique Oar House Lounge, a must-see that won't appeal to everyone.

OCEAN CREST PIER
1411 E. Beach Dr. (near 14th Pl. E.)
278-3333/6674
The owners do not allow shark fishing, but do provide a shelter of sorts at the far end that is reserved for king fishers. The Windjammer restaurant adjoins the pier.

LONG BEACH PIER
2729 W. Beach Dr.   278-5962
Located near the far west end of Oak Island, Long Beach Pier is the longest pier in the state, measuring 1,012 feet. Some folks use shopping carts to move their gear the dis-

tance. Three things are not welcomed here: shark fishing, net casting, and profanity. The owners perform rod and reel repairs on the premises.

Holden Beach

HOLDEN BEACH PIER
441 Ocean Blvd. W.   842-6483
Holden Beach Pier prohibits the use of nets and the consumption of alcoholic beverages. They sell three- and seven-day fishing permits and live bait. A grill and snack counter adjoin a game room that's fairly busy in summer. The rest rooms are poorly kept. This is one of only three area piers (including Ocean Isle and Sunset Beach, below) that charge spectators a fee (25 cents) for walking the pier.

Ocean Isle

OCEAN ISLE PIER
Foot of Causeway Dr.   579-6873
The steep ramp to the pier gets slippery when wet. The large game room and small grill are popular in summer.

Sunset Beach

SUNSET PIER
Foot of Sunset Blvd.   579-6630
There is no running water at the cleaning table, but amenities include a snack bar, game room and bait for sale.

Boat Ramps

The NC Wildlife Resources Commission maintains free ramps for

Anglers try their luck in the surf.

pleasure boaters and anglers. Parking is generally scarce in the summer months in the busier locations (Wrightsville Beach, for instance). The ramps are identified by black and white, diamond-shaped "Wildlife" signs. For information on Public Boat Access, call 733-3633. Included here are some private ramps as well.

Wilmington

Dram Tree Park, at the corner of Castle and Surry Streets (off Front Street, downtown Wilmington) is located almost beneath the Cape Fear Memorial Bridge.

In **Pender County**, the Northeast Cape Fear River and its tributary creeks are accessible by three public ramps:

The west bank of the river can be reached from I-40 by taking NC 53 east about 1 7/10 mile, then County Road 1512 to its end.

A public ramp on the east bank is located on County Road 1520 about 7 7/10 miles north of NC 210. The intersection of NC 210 and secondary road 1520 lies about three miles east of I-40 (Exit 408).

Holland's Shelter Creek Campground and Restaurant, 259-5743, is located 7 1/2 miles down NC 53 from I-40. Canoes are for rent ($10 flat fee), and the restaurant offers a memorable glimpse of local style. Their private ramp gives access to Holly Shelter Creek. (See also the chapters on Camping and Restaurants.)

The Beaches

On **Wrightsville Beach** next to the Route 74/76 drawbridge is a public ramp accessible from either side of the main road. This access to the Intracoastal is very busy in summer months, especially on weekends.

On **Pleasure Island**, there are four ramps east of U.S. 421 at Snow's Cut near Carolina Beach. Coming south, make a hairpin right turn at the south end of Snow's Cut bridge, onto Bridge Barrier Road. Turn right at Spencer Farlow Road and follow 1/6 mile to the Wildlife sign. The lot is on your left. If you're coming north from Carolina Beach, exit Highway 421 at Lewis Road, immediately before the bridge. Spencer Farlow Road is ahead. Another ramp is at the end of Highway 421, south of the Fort Fisher ferry terminal.

Carolina Beach State Park, 458-8206, Dow Road, on Pleasure Island, has four ramps ($3 per day), a marina and ample parking. Access is to the Cape Fear River.

The ramp directly beneath the Route 210 high-span in **North Topsail Beach** is generally uncrowded. It is accessible from the last turnout from the northbound side of 210 before the bridge. Access is to New River Inlet.

Across the Intracoastal from North Topsail Beach is a ramp at the foot of County Road 1529. From U.S. 17, drive east from Folkstone on Old Folkstone Road (County Road 1518), which intersects 1529 about 2 miles on.

The privately owned ramp at Top-sail Marina, on North Anderson Boulevard in Topsail Beach (at the foot of the water tower) is available for a daily fee.

For freshwater fishing in north Brunswick, a public ramp gives access to historic Towne Creek and its tributaries at the eastern end of County Road 1521, about 1 1/2 miles east of Winnabow.

South Brunswick

At the foot of County Route 1101, accessible from Rt. 133 on the mainland side of **Oak Island**, the public ramp gives direct access to the Intracoastal Waterway.

In **Sunset Harbor**, at the end of County Route 1112 (about six miles south of Route 211; turn right at Lockwood Folly Road), east of Lockwood Folly River, a public boat ramp gives access to Lockwood Folly River and Inlet and the Intracoastal Waterway.

On **Holden Beach**, public boat ramps are located under the NC 130 bridge.

Freshwater anglers can launch into the east bank of the Waccamaw River at the Route 904 bridge at **Pineway**, about 5 miles north of the South Carolina border.

Head Boats and Charters

There are fishing charters a-plenty from Topsail's Treasure Coast to Sunset Beach. Choose among head boats accommodating dozens of people and charters that handle six or less. Head boats average $40 to $60 per person for full-day excursions; charters range from $420 to $600 per day. Certain considerations are common to all: first mate, rods, reels, bait, tackle, onboard coolers and ice are generally provided. Food and beverages usually are not, but can often be arranged aboard charters. Electric reels are optional, usually costing about 10 bucks. Reservations for charters are generally required. A few charters offer inshore and offshore trips, inshore being great for kids and first-timers. And, if you can't find enough friends to chip in for a charter, inquire about split charters. Remember that no one can guarantee sea conditions. If your captain decides to turn back before you've landed a smoker, rest assured he knows what he's doing. Captains reserve the right to cancel trips if conditions are unsafe for the vessel or passengers.

From Wilmington, charters running from Wrightsville and Carolina Beaches are the most accessible; there are none running directly out of Wilmington.

Wrightsville Beach

Hanover Fishing Center at the Bridge Tender Marina, 1410 Airlie Road, 256-3636 is like one-stop shopping for charters located less than 100 yards south of the drawbridge on Airlie Road. Reservations are taken here for a number of charters that are available for tournaments and diving trips (see also Diving in Water Sports chapter). All the charters offer half- and full-day trips. The charters running out of Wrightsville Beach generally tend to be slightly more expensive than elsewhere.

Tropico Charters, 256-2060, features two sportfishing boats for up to six passengers each. Specialty food packages can be arranged, and they'll even videotape your trip. Docking here also are The Green Machine, 256-8240, Defiance, (800)854-0824, and Sea Lady Charters (800)242-2493 or 452-9955. Tooth Doctor and Time Out may be booked at the marina's phone number.

Carolina Beach

Carolina Beach is the Gulf Stream fishing hub between Bald Head Island and Topsail. Look for all the following boats at the Municipal Marina.

CLASS ACTION
458-3348

Class Action books tarpon hunts July through September. All-day trips average 10 hours, but longer trips to Frying Pan Tower and the Gulf Stream are offered, too. The mailing address is P.O. Box 1133, Carolina Beach, NC 28428.

THE FISH WITCH II
458-5844

The Fish Witch II is a 48-foot Sport Fisherman. Tournaments, diving and company trips can be arranged,

Photo: Scott Taylor

"Oooooo, they're slimy!"

as well as six-hour shark trips, July through September. They prepare food packages, clean and pack fish and accept split charters. The mailing address is 1328 St. Joseph Street, Carolina Beach, NC 28428.

FLO-JO
458-5454

Capt. Ray Rothrock skippers the *Flo-Jo*. He also shares the helm of the *Adventuress*, one of the more frequently-recommended ships for diving trips, with Capt. Joe Nemeth. Their mailing address is 506 Augusta Avenue, Carolina Beach, NC 28428.

Topsail Island

OSPREY CHARTERS
Topsail Sound Fishing Pier   328-3641
Carolina Ave., foot of Florida Ave.

The *Osprey* specializes in medium and light tackle trolling for game fish, including dolphin, king mack, cobia and barracuda. The twin-engine *C-Hawk* accommodates four passengers for offshore trips and up to six inshore. Cellular phone allows ship-to-shore communication.

TOPSAIL MARINA
North Anderson   328-5681
Topsail Beach

Located in the heart of Topsail Beach, this is home to the E-Z-Go Charters. There are two 35 foot vessels and smaller craft available.

South Brunswick

With four locations to begin your sea hunt, Holden Beach is the charter/head boat capital of the South

Brunswick Islands. Two are located on the mainland side of the Intracoastal, beneath the Route 130 bridge (Holden Beach Road): Holden Beach Marina and Intracoastal Marina.

At least four charters run out of Holden Beach Marina, 842-5447, which is the number to call to book reservations for *Super Salty I*, the first Holden Beach boat to catch and release a 300-pound blue marlin (1991). *Super Salty I* provides narrated cruises and a wide variety of fishing trips for up to 12 anglers, including: all-day and all-night trips, 22-hour Sea-faris and 34-hour Super Sea-fari (60-80 miles out). If you're unable to reserve through the marina, call 842-4760 or 842-8138.

Alice-E, 842-9492, has electric reels available, and the crew works well with novices. *Sea Wolfe*, 842-8212, has overnight charters available.

Intracoastal Marina is next to Holden Beach Marina, on the south side of the bridge. There you can book the *Swag*, 842-9299, a 35 foot Somerset with a six-passenger capacity. Half-day and full-day trips and fishing packages of up to three days (including lodging) are available.

Directly across the waterway beneath the bridge is Pete's Seafood, with two charters docking there:

The *Stillsearching*, 842-8372, is a 36-foot twin diesel geared for full-day and full-night trips. They are willing to negotiate for extended trips up to 24 hours.

Mega-Flite, 842-9055, a 50-foot head boat, is the largest certified fishing vessel on Holden Beach. Half-days, three-quarter days, Gulf Stream trips, waterway and dinner cruises, private charters and shark fishing are available. For more information, call Captain Mike, 842-8119.

Independent Seafood is located on the waterway side of Ferry Road, three streets north of the bridge. Two charters dock here:

El Toro, 842-9299 (winter phone: 704-922-0433), accommodates up to six passengers.

Swag II, 842-4930, is a 42-foot vessel that offers Gulf Stream and tournament charters in addition to its regular half-day and full-day trips.

Southport

The Southport Marina and Yacht Basin are located near the foot of West Street.

OCEAN OUTFITTERS
610 W. West St.   *457-0433*
This multi-service shop provides full- and half-day inshore fishing charters and full-day offshore charters aboard the 38' Bertram *Rascal Fair* (six passengers). Overnight trips, snacks and meals are available. Captain "Ski" Sherfinski's *Trophy Hunter*, 457-5392, is a 30-foot craft for up to six passengers. *Lady Frances*, 457-0654, located at Yacht Basin and Bay next to the Shell Shop, is a 42-foot sport fisherman that hosts Gulf Stream trips. Catering is available. *Jobsite*, 579-3599 or 579-5515, a 33-foot Tiara Sportsfisherman, boards at Ocean Isle Marina, just over the bridge on Ocean Isle Beach.

Ocean Atlantic

CAPT. JIM'S MARINA
Calabash   *579-3660*
The Ocean Atlantic fleet features full galleys and welcomes the physically-challenged and shark fishing. Private charters for up to 80 passengers are available. Charters include a 16-hour marlin hunt. Breakfast sandwiches are available on all fishing trips.

Surf Fishing

The entire length of the Cape Fear coast beckons surf-casters. Even on the most developed beaches, there are few people to disturb you at times when surf fishing is best, early mornings and dusk. On Wrightsville Beach, exceptional surf fishing will be found behind the jetty at **Masonboro Inlet**, on the south end of the island. (Do not fish from the jetty itself.) If you have a power boat available, fishing the jetty on the south side of the inlet, off Masonboro Island, is something special.

The **Fort Fisher State Recreation Area** is an undeveloped four-mile stretch of pristine beach and tidal marsh, approximately 6 miles south of Carolina Beach, accessible by four-wheel-drive vehicle. At the entrance to the area, off Highway 421 before the NC Aquarium (bear left at the fork), there is a public beach access with rest rooms, a shower and snack bar. Otherwise, there are no services, so bring everything you'll need. (See also "Off-Roading" in the Sports and Fitness chapter.)

Inlets also accessible by four-

Photo: Scott Taylor

Cape Fear Coast rivers and sounds provide a variety of fishing opportunities.

wheel-drive vehicle are **New River Inlet**, at the north end of Topsail Island, and **Carolina Beach Inlet**.

A less-known and secluded fishing spot is on Pleasure Island off Dow Road. For 3 miles extending south of Spartanburg Avenue, foot paths enter the woods from the road. (You may notice cars and pickups parked here.) Foot traffic only is permitted since this is an environmentally sensitive area. The trails lead to the Cape Fear River, but the northernmost trails open upon a secluded inlet where bait fish are often stirred into a frenzy by the unseen feeders. It's also a good place to picnic and relax.

Fishing "The Rocks" is a special outing. The Rocks are a 3 1/3-mile breakwater extending from Federal Point (south of the Fort Fisher Ferry terminal). The water enclosed above Zeke's Island is called the Basin, and fishing on both sides of the barrier is excellent. Walking The Rocks can be a bit hazardous. Enter upon them only at low tide.

When fishing the beaches, observe local dune ordinances. Basically, keep off the dunes, except at established crossovers. In North Topsail Beach you may be tagged with a hefty $500 fine for ignoring the warning signs, which apply equally to private property.

Photo: Scott Taylor

This T-shirted piling was of no interest to a seagull seeking a perch.

Inside
Marinas and the
Intracoastal Waterway

The Middle Atlantic Intracoastal Waterway is a boating channel that was developed in the Roosevelt years following the Great Depression. Intended as a project to put people back to work and as a commercial waterway to encourage commerce, it was destined to become one of the great ways to experience the coast through travel and pleasure boating.

The Middle Atlantic Intracoastal Waterway runs from Norfolk, Virginia, to Miami, Florida and is maintained by the U. S. Army Corps of Engineers. It links sounds and rivers into the most extensive system of inland waters in the country and provides carefully charted and maintained cruising waters for every kind of boater. North Carolina's Intracoastal Waterway is a boating channel that generally lies between the mainland and barrier islands, stretching across sounds, down rivers and through man-made "ditches." It is largely undeveloped. Egrets abound in this virtual wilderness; dolphins speed alongside boats; and people from many points of origin convene to travel together and share stories.

There are many areas where a boater can drop the hook and spend a peaceful night in the safety of rec-

ommended anchorages. For shallow-draft boats, there are many possibilities for exploring inlets that have shoaled too much to allow commercial craft to disturb their magical solitude. The Intracoastal Waterway from Topsail Island south to Sunset Beach at the South Carolina line offers many exciting opportunities for both the cruising and the casual boater.

As the primary route for waterborne "Snowbirds" (cruisers who regularly travel north or south on the water to escape the heat of summer or the cold of winter), the Intracoastal Waterway is an interesting place to wave at people from faraway places. Most boats carry the point of origination on the stern and, if the kids get tired of the tranquility of the waterway, they can count states. Commercial craft also uses these waters, and an assortment of shrimp boats, commercial fishing boats, dredges and barges share the sometimes narrow channel with pleasure craft. Locals use the waterway regularly for recreation, and it's common to see waterskiers on the peaceful waters tucked behind islands, although this insider doesn't recommend waterskiing on the ICW because of the frequent commercial traffic.

Piers are great spots to capture your own "aerial" view.

Pleasure boating on the Intracoastal Waterway runs from the middle of March until the latter part of December, so there is a very long season to enjoy this special part of the Cape Fear area. Before embarking on the waterway, boaters should have a basic understanding of navigation. Learning to read a chart can prevent aggravation; knowing which markers to keep to the right and which to keep to the left can save a deep draft vessel from a sudden grounding.

The channel is generally well marked and is maintained by the Coast Guard and the U.S. Army Corps of Engineers, but it doesn't hurt to rely on more than the markers and charts. Especially for sailing craft, Claiborne Young's *Cruising Guide to Coastal North Carolina* is an indispensable book to have aboard because charts aren't updated on a fast schedule. Inlets and weather conditions can shift the bottom sands very quickly and, especially for boats without depth sounders, the bottom can meet the keel in a hurry.

Marinas

Visitors or insiders who choose to spend their vacation on the waterway can look forward to a delightful experience if they keep an eye on the weather, make adequate preparations in terms of supplies and know the amenities available along the route. Marinas provide the basic amenities for boat travelers. Fuel, overnight berths, ship's stores, repairs and nearby services can mean the difference between pleasure and misery on the water. The undeveloped areas are lovely; but, sometimes, there is no sight more beautiful than a friendly place that stocks what you need.

Topsail Island

Topsail Island is at the northern point of this guide's area. Surf City offers **Surf City Sport Center Marina**. This marina offers some overnight berths with power and water; fuel is readily available. Boats drawing more than 3 feet should be very careful because low-tide depths are less than four feet and there are some bumps in the channel, especially to port, that can bend a prop or grab a keel.

Farther south, Topsail Beach offers a more reliable route for deepdraft vessels. A seven-foot channel puts sailors more at ease, although serious attention must be given to the red entry marker to the south of **Topsail Marina**, 328-5681, 904 S. Anderson Blvd., Topsail Beach. No matter how great the temptation, do not spot this marina and head directly for it, or you will definitely find yourself aground. Topsail Marina, the former Annamarina, is a friendly and welcoming place. The people who run it are very accommodating and laid back. The marina offers overnight dockage, power, water, a ship's store and fuel. A repair facility, restaurant, grocery store and motel are a short walk away.

As you travel down the waterway, look to the mainland for the next facility. **Harbour Village Marina**, located at flashing daybeacon 96, 270-4017, 101 Harbour Marina Drive, Hampstead, is located beside Belvedere Plantation. There's a golf course, a large country club and tennis courts. The marina portion of the development has all of the amenities a boater could want, including transportation to restaurants. Boating guests can also enjoy swimming, tennis and golf opportunities.

Below Harbour Village, the Intracoastal Waterway is a straight shot to Wrightsville Beach. Page's Creek, just south of Figure Eight Island, is home to quite a cluster of marinas and marine services. The marina at Figure Eight Island is private, reserved for residents of the island. Continue down the waterway for hospitable marina accommodations.

The marinas at Page's Creek, including Mason's Marina, Canady's Marina, Johnson Marina, Scott's Hill Marina, Oak Winds Marina and Carolina Yacht Yard mostly cater to locals whose boats are permanently berthed there. You can find extensive repair services at Carolina Yacht Yard and Johnson Marina, as well as fuel. The others mostly provide slips or drydockage to regulars. Johnson Marina also has a ramp.

At Page's Creek, north of flashing daybeacon #122, keep to port upon entering the channel. As with most of the marinas along this stretch of the ICW, shoaling at the mouth of each channel is a chronic problem. Sounding the depths generally reveals shallow entry, followed by much deeper waters beyond the mouth. The folks at Oak Winds Marina cite the cause as the large pleasure craft that charge up and down the waterway.

MASON'S MARINA
7421 Mt. Pleasant Dr.   686-7661
Wilmington, 28405

CANADY'S MARINA
7624 Mason's Landing Rd   686-9116
Wilmington, 28405

JOHNSON MARINA

2029 Turner Nursery Rd.	686-7565
Wilmington,	28405

SCOTT'S HILL MARINA

Rt. 1, Box 541 A.C.	686-0986
Wilmington, 28405	

OAK WINDS MARINA

Middle Sound Loop Rd.	686-2127
Wilmington, 28405	

CAROLINA YACHT YARD

2107 Middle Sound Rd.	686-0004
Wilmington, 28405	

Wrightsville Beach

The next area south on the route is Wrightsville Beach. This is one of the best places along the coastline not only for services but also a tremendous amount of fun. The area is rich in marinas that welcome, in most cases, transient boaters.

Wrightsville Marina Yacht Club, 256-5745, P. O. Box 1215, Wrightsville Beach, 28480, is on the eastern shore just past the bridge. This is a luxurious place to dock for the night since the marina offers power, water, telephone, cable TV connections, fuel and mechanical repairs. There is even a swimming pool available for transients. Wally's Restaurant, one of the beach's nicest dining establishments, looms over the scene with its cheerful, peach-colored stucco exterior. Exceptional seafood and prime rib await the hungry boater who can enjoy dinner and walk leisurely back down the dock to fall pleasantly asleep in the V-berth.

On the western shore, directly across from Wrightsville Marina, is the **Bridge Tender Marina and Restaurant**, 256-6550, P. O. Box 1037, Airlie Road, Wrightsville Beach, 28480. The marina offers all amenities and presents an exceptional dining opportunity. The Bridge Tender is a Cape Fear area dining institution that prides itself on preparation of seafood and prime rib.

Next up are the fixed piers of **Carolina Yacht Harbor**, 256-3979, 1322 Airlie Road, Wrightsville Beach, 28480, on the western bank. Overnight berths, power, water and repairs are all available. Also, it's a really short walk to the Dockside Restaurant, a favorite spot for insiders as well as stars working on films at the local studio. A boater can also find overnight space at the **Dockside Marina**, 256-3579, 1306 Airlie Road, Wrightsville Beach, 28480, as well as all amenities.

Theses marinas are jammed together, creating many options for the cruising boater in need of provisions, services and night life.

Just past this cluster, Motts Channel opens to port. **Atlantic Marine**, 256-9911, 130 Short Street, Wrightsville Beach, 28480, offers repair services and is oriented to serving locals with its dry-docked small craft facilities. Gasoline is the only service for transients. There are no overnight berths available to transients.

Seapath Yacht Club, 256-6681, 328 Causeway Drive, Wrightsville Beach, *28480*, next up on Motts Channel, offers some transient dockage with power, water and fuel. A store provides many essential supplies, and George, the dockmaster, is a heck of a nice guy. Seapath is very close to Banks Channel, and the nearest approach to the Atlantic Ocean, although Bradley Creek Marina is just about as close to Masonboro Inlet.

As you travel south on the Intracoastal Waterway, you will pass Masonboro Inlet, one of only a few regularly open inlets in the state of North Carolina. Just below it, marinas come up.

Bradley Creek Boatominium, 350-0029, P. O. Box 4867, Wilmington, 28406, on the western shore, is a large, modern facility that, sadly for the transient, is not a place to stop for the night. This is a large dry dockage and wetslip facility that serves a regular community. No fuel is available. Roughly 2 percent of the slips are available for longer term rental.

Boathouse Marina, 350-0023, 6334 Oleander Drive, Wilmington, 28405, is a drydockage facility with haul-outs and repair service. It offers gasoline and has a ship's store.

Masonboro Boatyard and Marina, 791-1893, 609 Trails End Road, Wilmington, 28409, is a delightful place to spend the night. The scenery is absolutely lovely from the front row of floating docks. This facility specializes in repairs and has haul-out services, as well as below-the-water repairs and other maintenance services. If you want to do your own out-of-the-water repairs, this facility allows it. There is a ship's store and a friendly staff. There is a year-round community in this unusual place, and you are guaranteed to find some interesting conversation among the residents. Masonboro Boatyard Marina has been operated by the same people for 25 years. It is a particularly welcoming port of call for cruising boaters. As a bonus, the venerable Trails End Steakhouse is an easy walk for a charbroiled steak dinner.

A reminder about the channel depth here that applies to most of the coastline: Deep-draft vessels would do well to keep an eye on the tide tables and avoid low tide, even though regular dredging maintains the low tide depth around five feet at Masonboro.

Below Masonboro Sound, there is a stretch without marinas. The shoreline becomes residential in character, and you will not find another port until you get close to Carolina Beach. Just north of Snow's Cut, **Carolina Inlet Marina**, 392-0580, 801 Paoli Court, Wilmington, 28409, occupies the western bank. There is limited transient dockage at this marina, but one suspects a space can always be obtained. There is fuel, a ship's store, and a full assortment of repairs. Low tide depth is consistent

A ghost crab prowls the beach.

at 4 1/2 feet. The marina primarily serves boaters with longer term drydockage and wetslips.

Carolina Beach

Carolina Beach, a community that is squeezed between the Atlantic Ocean and the Cape Fear River, is very much a boating town. Yet, the beach only has one full-service marina. **Snow's Cut Landing Marina**, 458-7400, 100 Spencer Farlow Drive, Carolina Beach, 28428, lines the channel's western shore just south of Snow's Cut.

The newest marina on Carolina Beach is **Coquina Harbour**, 458-5053, 401 Virginia Avenue, Carolina Beach, 28428, and it is located on the eastern shore in this vicinity. Fresh water and power connections are available, and this marina may accept transients.

Carolina Beach Municipal Marina, 458-2985, Canal Drive, Carolina Beach, 28428, is found at the southern end of the channel in Carolina Beach. Fuel is available, but mooring is tight. The marina seems mostly dedicated to fishing charter boats and the southern side of it is packed with ticket booths. Don't expect to spend a night here.

Back on Snow's Cut, the **Carolina Beach State Park Marina**, 458-7770, P. O. Box 475, Carolina Beach, N.C. 28428, comes into view. There is a ramp, and the marina offers fuel, as well as ample overnight dockage. If you're weary of being on a boat, you can pitch a tent and roast marshmallows over a fire in the park, too.

It can be a very bumpy 15-mile ride from Snow's Cut across the Cape Fear River into Southport and the more protected Intracoastal Waterway (what we sometimes refer to as "yee-haa" boating). This is a major shipping lane to the State Port at Wilmington, as well as the route for the Southport-Fort Fisher ferry. If you take a northerly route up the Cape Fear River rather than crossing to Southport, you will find limited facilities, although the City of Wilmington is looking into greater opportunities to accommodate boaters in the near future.

Wilmington

Several miles up the Cape Fear River from Snow's Cut, **Wilmington Marine Center**, 395-5055, 3410 River Road, Wilmington, 28412, comes into view to starboard. This facility has recently changed ownership and direction, specializing in service and storage of larger yachts. Once the saddest-looking marina in the area, the new one is aiming to be the best facility around. This sole marina on the Cape Fear offers repairs and lift-out services, as well as fuel. Dockage, power, water, showers and fuel are available to transients and regulars.

On the Wilmington waterfront, there is limited overnight dockage available. **The Hilton Hotel**, 763-5900, 301 N. Water Street, Wilmington, N.C. 28401, offers water and power to overnight boating guests on docks in front of the hotel. At 50 cents a foot, it's a wonderful bargain to be in immediate proximity to historic downtown Wilmington. If you're docked here, please look through the dining, shopping and entertainment sections in this guide.

A word of warning: prepare for extremes at high and low tide. It's a long climb from your boat to the fixed pier at low tide.

The municipal docks are available for brief visits but are not set up for extended stays. The general rule seems to be a limit of 72 hours of free dockage all along the downtown waterfront. Longer stays may be arranged through the City of Wilmington by special permit. The situation on the downtown Wilmington waterfront is subject to change as the city ponders ways to better welcome boating guests to the community. Boaters may continue up the Cape Fear River's two branches for a view of natural surroundings, but larger craft, especially sailboats, may want to end their exploration of the river at downtown Wilmington.

Heading south from Wilmington, the N.C. State Port is visible with its huge orange cranes. As you approach Southport, you'll see to starboard the yellow cranes of the Military Supply Terminal at Sunny Point. At this point, you're square in the middle of the international shipping lanes, also the path of the almost hourly Southport-Fort Fisher automobile ferry.

Southport, Bald Head Island and Oak Island

Southport Marina, Inc., 457-5261, W. West Place, Southport, 28461, comes into view as you enter the quaint village. An immaculate place, its extensive docks welcome the cruising boater to the spot where the

Cape Fear River, Atlantic Ocean and Intracoastal Waterway converge. This is an attractive place covered in live oaks and steeped in history. The town deserves a leisurely look. Southport Marina, Inc. offers fuel, power, slips, restaurants, repairs, a clubhouse and supplies. It is also one of only about a dozen North Carolina marinas with pumpouts.

Bald Head Island Marina, 457-7380, easy to spot from Southport because of its wide-based lighthouse, Old Baldy, primarily serves a private, residential community where many of the homes are also vacation rentals. You can find a slip, fuel, restaurants and lift-out service, as well as a gracious welcome. Situated on a pristine island of apparent wealth, a visit to Bald Head Island Marina can be a highly enjoyable experience. Electric carts and bikes are available for rental since no gasoline-powered vehicles are allowed on this island.

Slipping back on a southward bearing into the Intracoastal Waterway at Southport, you'll see Oak Island on the port side. Three beach communities occupy this island: Caswell Beach, Yaupon Beach and Long Beach.

Oak Beach Inn and Marina, 278-9977, 57th Place West, Long Beach, 28461, located just before Lockwood Folly Inlet on Long Beach, offers transient dockage, a ramp, repairs, supplies and a restaurant. It does not offer fuel.

Sportsman's Marina, 278-5267, just west of unlighted daybeacon #32 at the approach to the Intracoastal Waterway's intersection with Lockwood Folly River, offers occasional shelter for the cruising boater. It offers limited transient dockage, supplies and fuel. There are several restaurants nearby.

Several marinas are in the Holden Beach area just to the south. **Taylor's Landing**, 842-7295, Route 1, Box 565, Supply, 28462, has a ramp, offers repairs, supplies, fuel and has a limited number of slips. **Holden Beach Marina**, 842-5447, on the waterway's northern banks, Route 1, Box 565A, Supply, 28462, offers slips and a full range of services. Cruising boaters regard it as one of the friendliest marinas on the North Carolina coast. **Captain Pete's Seafood**, 842-6675, 101 S. Shore Drive, Holden Beach, 28462, offers supplies, a restaurant and fuel. **Intracoastal Marina**, 842-9333, at the bridge, 1305 Cedar Landing Road, S.W., Holden Beach, 28459, has a boat ramp, wetslips, dry storage and supplies.

Tripp's Fishing Center, 754-6985, Route 6, Box 708, Shallotte, 28459, and **Hughes Marina**, 754-6233, Route 6, Box 716, Shallotte, 28459, are up

A baby loggerhead makes fast tracks for the water.

next on your southerly cruise. Both offer the full range of services, but Tripp's is not in the boatslip business at all. Look to Hughes Marina for overnight accommodations, although the current is unusually swift here, and you'll need to pay attention when docking.

Island Marina, 579-6019, Ocean Isle Plaza Suite 1, Ocean Isle Beach, 28469, has limited dock space but does sell fuel and supplies. There are nearby dining facilities. Ocean Isle Marina, 579-0848, #43 Causeway Drive, Ocean Isle Beach, 28469, offers boat, surfboard and jetski rentals and marine supplies.

Pelican Point Marina, 579-6440, Route 6, Box 48, Seaside, 28459,

comes into view on the starboard side near Seaside at Sunset Beach. This facility, located at marker 98 on the ICW, is a full service marina with repairs, dry storage, a ship's store, boat rentals and a nine-ton boat forklift. There is also a courtesy car available.

Marsh Harbor Marina, 579-3500, P. O. Box 4100, Calabash, 28459, has 221 slips, fuel, repairs, supplies and even a pump out station. This newly revitalized marina welcomes transients. Several Calabash restaurants are within easy walking distance. The marina's location up Calabash Creek makes it good shelter in all but a hard, southerly blow.

Inside
Sports, Fitness and Parks

Sports

Except for snow skiing, rappelling and rock climbing, just about every kind of sport you could ask for is offered in the Cape Fear region. (Actually, there is a ski club, based at the Holiday Inn at Wrightsville Beach, that organizes snow ski trips.) Local and county Parks and Recreation Departments organize a staggering selection of activities, including team sports for all ages. Be sure to check with them when looking into your sport. They offer seniors a plethora of activities including archery, croquet, Tae-Kwon-Do and water aerobics. Here are their main office numbers:

PARKS AND RECREATION DEPARTMENTS

Wilmington	341-7855
Athletic Office	343-3680
Wrightsville Beach	256-7925
Carolina Beach	458-7416
Long Beach	278-5518
Southport	457-7922
Brunswick County	253-4357
	(800) 222-4790
Onslow County	347-5332

We've included listings of where to find, or join, the sport of your choice. Useful businesses and ser-

vices are also listed. The daily Lifestyles pages of the *Wilmington Star-News* also provide a handy guide to recreation throughout New Hanover County.

Parents should note that registration fees for youth league sports are often discounted when registering more than one child in the same league. Be sure to inquire.

Two Wilmington sports shops bear special mention because they sell "recycled" goods (so much more attractive than "used"). The merchandise is in fine condition, but inventories change unpredictably.

PLAY IT AGAIN SPORTS
351 S. College Rd.   791-1572

SPORTS SOURCE
1414 S. College Rd.   799-9505

Baseball and Little League

There are several leagues in the Cape Fear region for youth baseball, but there are no public leagues for adults. Among the youth leagues are those sponsored by the area's several Optimist Clubs, organizations committed to service to youth. The youth leagues offer a wide variety of divisions, from tee-ball for toddlers to baseball for teens up to age 18, and some offer softball too. Registration generally takes place from late February through mid-March and carries a modest fee ($25-$30). Registrants will need to produce their birth certificates. Season games begin in April.

NEW HANOVER YOUTH BASEBALL
Wilmington   *791-5578*

BRUNSWICK COUNTY
PARKS & RECREATION
(800) 222-4790 , 253-4357

ONSLOW COUNTY
PARKS & RECREATION
347-5332

CAPE FEAR OPTIMIST CLUB
Wilmington   *762-8957*

WINTER PARK OPTIMIST CLUB
Wilmington   *256-9994*
256-4759

SOUTHEASTERN
ATHLETIC ASSOCIATION
Wilmington   *in season 313-0466*
off-season 763-5643

SUPPER OPTIMIST CLUB
Wilmington   *799-2063*

Basketball

The **YMCA**, 2710 Market Street, 251-9622, hosts leagues for boys and girls ages 6 to 12 during the winter and offers inexpensive court passes to teenagers who wish to join informal games. It also offers men's leagues throughout the year.

For adults and seniors, weekly and Saturday games are organized from December through March by **Wilmington Parks & Recreation**, 343-3680 or 341-7855.

Wrightsville Beach Parks & Recreation, 256-7925, offers four-on-four league games for adults on week nights from June through August.

Brunswick County Parks & Recreation, (800) 222-4790, offers one-week youth basketball camps in summer for ages 6 to 15. Referee clinics are also offered to persons of any age. An adult men's basketball league is also offered, with separate spring and fall divisions. Registration is open to teams only. There is a youth basketball league for children ages 5 to 13, running from December through March.

For those located on the northern Cape Fear coast, **Onslow County Parks & Recreation**, 347-5332, offers youth basketball for children ages 7 to 18.

Bicycling

Level landscape, predominantly well-maintained roads and generally light traffic make cycling the coastal plain nearly ideal. (One caveat: avoid Market Street in Wilmington.) State-funded touring routes are marked by rectangular road signs bearing a green ellipse, a bicycle icon and the route number. One of these routes is the River-to-Sea Bike Route (Route 1), stretching from Riverfront Park at the foot of Market Street in Wilmington to Wrightsville Beach, a ride just under 9 miles. You'll have to walk your bike across one unpaved railroad crossing. Exercise caution on the Bradley Creek bridge: the shoulder is ridged by uneven road seams.

The state-funded Bicycling Highways are worth trying. The Ports of Call (Route 3) is a 319-mile seaside excursion from the South Carolina border to the Virginia state line. Approximately 110 miles of it lie within the Cape Fear region, giving access to miles of beaches and historic downtown Wilmington. The Cape Fear Run (Route 5) links Raleigh to the mouth of the Cape Fear River at Southport. This 166-mile route crosses the Cape Fear River twice and intersects the Ports of Call.

Free maps and information can be obtained from the NC Department of Transportation Bicycle Program, P.O. Box 25201, Raleigh, NC 27611, (919) 733-2804. Although they are updated regularly, be ready to improvise when it comes to information on private campgrounds and detours.

The Wilmington Bike Map is a must-have for local cycling. Free copies can be obtained by contacting the City Transportation Planning Department, P.O. Box 1810, Wilmington, NC 28402, (919) 341-7888.

THE CAPE FEAR CYCLISTS CLUB
Wrightsville Beach   *392-5437*

The CFC is a good social and information network. They provide opportunities to join the U.S. Cycling Federation and discounts on equipment at local shops.

BIKE SHOPS

There are several excellent specialty shops in Wilmington. These listed sell new and used bikes.

TWO WHEELER DEALER
4406 Wrightsville Ave.   *799-6444*
Wilmington

YOW'S BICYCLE & REPAIR
5324 Wrightsville Ave.   *791-6280*
Wilmington

Bike Rentals

THE CARIBBEAN TRADING COMPANY
602 Causeway Dr.   *256-2112*
Wrightsville Beach

CTC offers earth cruisers and mountain bikes ranging from $4 per hour to $48 per week, plus many other types of beach recreation equipment.

THE PATIO PLAYGROUND
807 S. Anderson Blvd./NC 50   *328-6491*
Topsail Beach

You can rent bicycles for the measly price of $2 per hour and up to $45 per week, tax included. There is no deposit; identification is required.

OCEAN RENTALS
4014 E. Beach Dr.   *278-4460*
Long Beach

More than just a place to rent bikes on Oak Island, the shop rents practically anything you could possibly need for the beach.

Boating

Boating the lower Cape Fear involves competing at times with oceangoing vessels, "thin" water, or the treacherous shoals that won the Carolina coast the moniker "Graveyard of the Atlantic." A mile-by-mile handbook is Claiborne S. Young's *Cruising Guide to Coastal North Carolina* (John F. Blair, Publisher, 1406 Plaza Drive, Winston-Salem, NC 27103).

The upper Cape Fear River, its Northeast branch, and the winding creeks of the coastal plain offer a genuine taste of the old southeast to those with small boats or canoes. Tannins leached from the cypresses keep these waters the color of dark tea. Many creeks are overhung by trees, moss and occasionally snakes in summer. Winter is a particularly good time to go. For information on boat ramps, see the chapter on Fishing.

BOATING SAFETY, SERVICES AND INFORMATION

The U.S. Coast Guard Auxiliary conducts free Courtesy Motorboat Examinations (CME). The exams are not required for boat registration. For information, call 359-1867. For Boating Safety Course information, call toll-free (800) 336-BOAT (2628).

For Ship to Shore calling along the Cape Fear coast, contact the Wilmington Marine Operator on Channel 26. For Shore to Ship calls: 726-1070.

To report emergencies to the Coast Guard, all initial radio calls should be made on channel 16/ 158.8 mhz. The Wrightsville Beach Coast Guard station's telephone number is 256-3469.

North Carolina requires that motorized craft of any size be registered. Marine suppliers and shops supply the necessary forms and information. The cost is $5.50 per year, $13 for three years. Those eager to learn about boating and sailing can inquire at many places along the coast.

WRIGHTSVILLE BEACH PARKS & RECREATION
341-7855

ATLANTIC MARINE SALES & SERVICE, INC.
Wrightsville Beach   256-9911

TOPSAIL WATER SPORTS
Topsail Beach   328-1141

CAPE FEAR BOAT RENTAL & CHARTERS
Oak Island   278-1880/9933

BOAT RENTALS

Advance reservations for boat rentals are essential on weekends. Most proprietors require a deposit, a valid drivers license or major credit card, plus a signed waiver of liability.

Caribbean Trading Company, 256-2112, 602 Causeway Drive, Wrightsville Beach, that bright coral-colored building before the fixed

Greenfield Lake near downtown Wilmington is good for jogging and canoeing.

Insiders' Tips

bridge at Banks Channel, rents Phantoms (similar to Sunfish) for $15 per hour, $36 per 1/2-day and $60 per full-day.

The **Windsurfing & Sailing Center**, 256-WIND (9463), 275 Waynick Boulevard, Wrightsville Beach, rents Hobie Cats, Day Sailors, Sunfish and more. Prices range from $15 per hour to $100 per four hours. They also provide lessons.

Topsail Water Sports, 328-1141, 102 North Anderson Boulevard, (NC 50), Topsail Island, has been a local favorite for eight years. Located across from the Topsail Motel, they offer Jon boats and Hobie Cats (14 feet and 16 feet). Half-day and full-day sail boat charters are also available. They're open seven days in the summer, 9 AM to 6 PM.

Cape Fear Boat Rental & Charters, 278-1880/9933, Bluewater Point (Oak Island, off West Dolphin Drive), Oak Island, has a variety of water craft, including canoes, Hobie 16s and motorized inflatables. Prices range from $6 per hour to $300 for five days. They also offer four-hour sailing classes ($25 to $40).

The **Ocean Isle Marina**, 579-0848, 43 Causeway Drive, Ocean Isle Beach, rents fishing boats, pontoon boats, ski boats and sail boats.

Camping

(see Camping chapter)

Canoeing

Touring the lower Cape Fear River in a canoe isn't recommended for beginners because it's a commercial shipping channel.

A unique area to explore by canoe or small boat is Bald Head Creek and salt marsh, the state's largest single expanse of salt marsh, on Bald Head Island. Canoe safaris lasting one and two hours can be arranged through Island Passage 457-4944, located on the island.

Wilmington Parks & Recreation invites you to explore some of the region's most scenic rivers beginning each April, including the Black River (noted for its virgin stands of bald cypress), the Cape Fear, Moores Creek, and Long Creek. Call the Parks & Recreation Department at 341-7855 for information.

HOLLAND'S SHELTER CREEK FISH CAMP
Hwy. NC 53 east of I-40 and Burgaw
259-5743

Canoes can be rented at reasonable rates and you can put into Holly Shelter Creek right behind the restaurant.

Fitness Centers

The many fine fitness centers along the coast generally offer state-of-the-art apparatus and certified instructors. Aerobics classes have become standard, as have the use of Lifecycles, treadmills, free weights, and Stairmasters. Membership costs usually include a onetime registration fee plus a monthly fee for a required term.

Wilmington

BODYWORKS II
Long Leaf Mall, Shipyard
and S. College Rd.   791-8848
This center bills itself as "a woman's facility," and offers a monthly membership without contracts. Although small, it has a child-care area.

PRO-FIT
23 N. Front St.   763-7224
Wilmington's downtown professional crowd enjoys Pro-Fit (especially when it's spelled without the hyphen) as much for its chic location as for its excellent facilities.

WILMINGTON ATHLETIC CLUB
2026 S. 16th St.   763-9655
"The Wac" is a family-oriented establishment hosting sports, including basketball, racquetball and coed volleyball. It offers a steam room, sauna, an outdoor pool, a nursery with CPR-trained staff and swimming lessons. Fitness consultations and nutritional lectures are frequently offered. Short-term contracts are available.

WILMINGTON FAMILY YMCA
2710 Market St.   251-9622
Offering a wide variety of fitness and educational activities, the Family Y features ample facilities, such as a large gym, two indoor pools, Jacuzzi, racquetball courts, nautilus, and even sunbathing decks. Athletic fields with a track and playground are also available. Aerobics, Tai Chi Chuan, arthritis aquatics classes, a massage therapist and many other features are standard. League sports for adults and youth are organized seasonally, and youth are eligible for limited, reduced-rate gym passes in summer.

YWCA OF WILMINGTON
2815 S. College Rd.   799-6820
Its elaborate swimming programs are directed by Ken Winfrey, one of five teachers in the country certified to teach full-scale ocean lifesaving, and the facility trains and certifies more lifeguards than anywhere else in eastern North Carolina. Indoor activities occasionally include such less-common offerings as Tai Chi Chuan.

WILMINGTON PARKS & RECREATION
Wilmington Parks & Recreation, 341-7855 offers special exercise classes for youth who are overweight, physically impaired, and inner city-bound. Seniors will find fitness classes tailored to their needs, plus low-impact aerobics, water aerobics and floor "Slimnastics" for adults 55 and over.

The Beaches

AEROBICS PLUS
North U.S. Hwy. 17   270-9010
Hampstead
This is a small facility convenient to those located north of Wilmington.

COASTAL FITNESS

5140 Sellers Rd.   754-2772
Shallotte

Coastal Fitness, not far from the South Brunswick Islands, has a massage therapist on the premises. Daily and weekly memberships are available (great for visitors!). A staffed nursery, tanning beds and sauna are offered, as are CPR classes, martial arts and health supplies.

THE CREST FITNESS CENTER

38 N. Lumina Ave.   256-5758
Wrightsville Beach

The Crest has a nursery and is the only membership fitness center on Wrightsville Beach.

Flying

The dearth of sizeable hills and, therefore, reliable updrafts, limits aviators to powered flight. Among the surprises of a bird's-eye view is sighting the so-called Carolina bays, the enormous elliptical depressions in the earth first discovered from the air (see Lake Waccamaw State Park in the chapter on Camping).

BLUE YONDER FLYING MACHINES

Brunswick County Airport   278-8277
                                  520-8277

Some say that unless you feel the wind in your face, you're not really flying. Among that faction you might find Adam Parsons, who promotes the flying of Quicksilver ultralights. They look like a cross between a hang-glider and a Wright brothers' original. The Quicksilver aircraft meet all aviation requirements, even though the pilot (and passenger, in some models) is suspended in an open "cockpit." Adam offers introductory flights and training with a certified USUA instructor and sells a variety of Quicksilver aircraft.

Flyers can rent conventional aircraft at New Hanover International and Brunswick County airports. Most companies offer 24-hour charter service and flight training.

AERONAUTICS

                                 763-4691

AIR WILMINGTON

New Hanover International Airport 763-0146

Aeronautics and its affiliate, Air Wilmington, offer flight instruction, aircraft rentals and sightseeing tours.

ISO AERO SERVICE, INC.
OF WILMINGTON

1410 N. Kerr Ave.   763-8898
                               or 762-1024

At the Brunswick County Airport, Larry Ryan and John Martin offer flight instruction and other flight services through their company, **Ocean Aire Aviation, Inc.**, 457-0710. They can also arrange aircraft rental.

Football

League football beyond the scholastic realm is focused upon two organizing bodies, the Pop Warner league and Brunswick County Parks & Recreation. Look into registration during July; most teams commence practicing in August.

POP WARNER FOOTBALL

Wilmington   799-7950

Pop Warner organizes tackle football teams for boys and girls, age 7 to 14, in "Pee Wee," "Midget" and "Mighty Mights" divisions.

BRUNSWICK COUNTY PARKS & RECREATION
(800)222-4790, 253-4357

Brunswick County's league is open to kids ages 10 to 13. If you're interested in becoming a referee, inquire about Brunswick County's referee clinics.

Golf
(see Golf Courses chapter)

Horseback Riding

Although English (hunt seat) style is favored in this region, Western is available. Most stables and riding academies offer boarding, instruction, rentals and trail rides. Some stables do their own shoeing. Tack shops are scarce. Most stables and academies will assist you in locating the equipment you need.

Wilmington

CAMELOT STABLES, INC.
1806 Middle Sound Loop Rd.   686-0425

Camelot is located 6 miles south of Wrightsville Beach and 2 1/2 miles from Highway 17 and specializes in English riding. A field and ring with jumps are located on premises.

CASTLE STABLES
5513 Sidbury Rd.   686-1113

English-style instruction is offered on a plush 120-acre spread that includes a lighted training ring and a jumping ring.

FOX FIRE FARM
7724 Sidbury Rd.   686-4495

The folks at Fox Fire train riders

and their horses in English riding and help find horses for purchase and lease.

THE CASTLE HAYNE SADDLE SHOP
4331 Castle Hayne Rd. (Rt. 117)   675-1805
Castle Hayne

This friendly full-service shop is located minutes north of Wilmington. They carry everything necessary for riding (English and Western), including instructional videos. Expert leather repair can be arranged.

The Beaches

LO-DI FARMS
610 Old Folkstone Rd.   327-2040
Sneads Ferry

Convenient to Topsail Island, Lo-Di boards, leases and rents horses and ponies. Horses for special occasions can be reserved, and the owners will haul if needed.

COTTONPATCH FARMS
Cottonpatch Rd.   754-9288
Shallotte

Judy Hilburn's farm is a high-quality training facility that sells horses and teaches owners to ride and show. Judy occasionally breeds horses. Youth riders are welcome.

SEA HORSE RIDING STABLES
Boonesneck Rd.   842-8002
Holden Beach

Sea Horse provides English and Western lessons, shoeing and training. Their 18 acres, located three miles off Holden Beach Road, are laced with shady trails, and the kiddies will love the pony rides.

Photo: Scott Taylor

Coastal flatlands make great cycling.

Hunting

The 48,795-acre **Holly Shelter Game Land** in Pender County is the focus of local hunters' attention. It is a varied wetland of pocosins (swampy areas) and pine savannas, threaded by winding creeks. Small and large game abound, including, dove, deer, rabbit and black bear. Hunting wild turkey is limited to toms in spring. Be aware that snakes, including some poisonous species, inhabit the area.

The Game Land is north of Wilmington, roughly between Highway 17 west to the northeast Cape Fear River, and between NC 210 and NC 53. It is managed by the NC Wildlife Resources Commission (412 North Salisbury Street, Raleigh, NC 27604-1188, 919-733-7291), but much of it lies within private property, so obtain the necessary permission to enter.

Hunting, mainly for fowl, is allowed on **Zeke's Island Coastal Preserve**, which lies across The Basin from Fort Fisher. Access to it is only by boat or by foot across The Rocks, a tricky three-mile breakwater that is awash at high tide.

HUNTING LICENSES

Hunting licenses are issued by the NC Wildlife Resources Commission. They can be combined with fishing licenses and can be purchased at many locations such as sports shops and hardware stores. Inquire about licenses at the places listed below.

Wilmington

SEARS, INDEPENDENCE MALL
3500 Oleander Dr.   452-6206

WAL-MART
352 S. College Rd.
Wal-Mart shopping center   392-4034

North of Wilmington

HAMPSTEAD VILLAGE PHARMACY
Hwy. 17   270-3411, 270-3414
Hampstead

HOLLAND'S SHELTER
CREEK FISH CAMP
Hwy. 53   259-5743
East of Burgaw

SOUTH BRUNSWICK
STEWART HARDWARE
1635 Howe St.   457-5544
Southport

HOLDEN BEACH TRUE VALUE
3008 Holden Beach Rd.   842-5440
Holden Beach

Call the Law Enforcement Division of the NC Wildlife Resources Commission at 662-4370 for more information.

Jogging, Running and Walking

Among the most beautiful places in Wilmington to jog or walk is the 4 1/2-mile loop around Greenfield Lake, south of downtown. The scenic paved path bears mile markers and follows the undulating lakeshore across two wooden foot bridges. (Be careful, they're slippery when wet.)

On Wrightsville Beach, the approximately 2 1/2-mile Sidewalk Loop around Wrightsville Beach Park is also ideal. A popular longer circuit encompasses Causeway Drive, Lumina Avenue and Route 74. Wrightsville Beach Park also features an Outdoor Fitness Trail in the field off Causeway Drive.

Wilmington Parks & Recreation invites youth 6 to 14 years old to join the National Track Program. Call 341-7855 to register.

The Wilmington Road Runner Club, based at the YMCA at 2710 Market Street, 251-9622, provides information on technique, races and safety, and welcomes entire families. The Road Runner Club sponsors the Wilmington Tri-Span & City Circuit Run each July, a run that's sure to test your mettle.

The Lejeune Grand Prix Series, hosted by the Marine Corps Base at Camp Lejeune (near Jacksonville), 451-5430, offers several foot races and other challenges. These highly-competitive events draw nationally-ranked challengers. The Oktoberfest Family 5K Fun Run, in late-September, is not part of the Grand Prix Series, but is one of three runs designed to promote family wellness. It is open to anyone who can walk, run, jog, stroll or be carried 5K. The course is suitable for strollers and carriages.

The American Lung Association sponsors the Reindeer Romp, a one-mile and 5K walk or run held each December along Greenfield Lake. Prizes are awarded for performance as well as for costumes. Registration fees begin at $8 (children) and $12 (adults). For information, call the ALA: 395-5864 or (800)821-6205.

The Island Walking Club, sponsored by Carolina Beach Parks & Recreation, organizes daily invigorating beach strolls. Meet at 7 AM weekdays at the Carolina Beach Community Building, Third & Raleigh Streets.

Kite Flying

Steady beach winds are ideal for kite-flying. Of course, it pays to use common sense. Beware of power lines, piers and boat masts. Stunt kites, which can fly close to the ground, might annoy other beachgoers. Fort Fisher, the north ends of Topsail Island and Carolina Beach, and both ends of Wrightsville Beach are fitting places to tie your hopes and dreams to a colorful swath and send them aloft. Also check into the Onslow County Museum Kite Festival, 324-5008, held in Topsail Beach each April.

CAROLINA KITE CLUB
Wrightsville Beach   *No phone*

This informal club meets Sunday mornings, 9 AM-noon, at the south end of Wrightsville Beach. In summer, get there early: the small, metered parking area fills quickly.

KITES UNLIMITED
6766 Wrightsville Ave.   *256-8996*
Wrightsville Beach

Here's an excellent source for kites and supplies. Kites Unlimited is located in the Galleria shopping center and is open 10 AM to 9 PM Monday through Saturday; 1 to 6 PM Sunday.

Martial Arts

Whether it's the sword technique of Iaido, the open-hand style of Karate, or the throws and take-downs of Ju-jitsu that interest you; whether it's self-defense, physical fitness, mental focus or competition you desire; all that, and more, is available in the Cape Fear region. Martial arts schools generally offer classes on a term basis, usually monthly or yearly.

Wilmington

BUSHIN-KAI KARATE
2875 Carolina Beach Rd.   *385-2170*

Del C. Russ, an instructor for 31 years, teaches Japanese sword art (Iaido), plus Aiki-kai Aikido and Kodachi.

CHAMPION KARATE CENTER
4231 Princess Place Dr.
(behind Burger King)   *343-9398*

Owner/instructor John Maynard welcomes physically-challenged students, including the sightless. Maynard was personally trained by Chuck Norris, and his studio is part of Norris's United Fighting Arts Organization. Champion offers a weight room and guidance for those interested in competition. Maynard also operates a location in Hampstead.

MARTIAL ARTS CENTER
2595 S. 17th St.   *799-1188*

Jim Irwin, a sixth degree Black Belt, includes study in Okinawa, Kempo and Kobudo at his studio. He also offers private instruction, schedules permitting.

JUNG'S TAE KWON DO ACADEMY
4623 Market St.   *392-6980*

Jung's teaches traditional Karate, Kung fu, and Hapkido. Instructor Yong Jung is a ninth dan degree Black Belt with 41 years of experience. He is assisted by a fifth dan Black Belt instructor. The Academy also sells equipment.

STOVER'S MARTIAL ARTS
4302 Holly Tree Rd.
at Shipyard Blvd.   *791-3656*

Stover's is Wilmington's oldest school of martial arts. Mr. Stover, a seventh degree Black Belt, stresses fundamentals in a variety of styles, including Karate, Kempo, Ju-jitsu, Kung-fu and traditional weapons. Classes meet evenings, Monday through Thursday.

For Karate, also check into the Wilmington Family YMCA, 2710 Market Street, 251-9622, and the YWCA of Wilmington, 2815 South College Road, 799-6820.

The Beaches

COASTAL FITNESS
5140 Sellers Rd.   *754-2772*
Shallotte

In south Brunswick, Coastal Fitness offers Karate and Kung-fu. Participation involves membership, available in short terms.

Off-Roading

For the most part, off-roading on Cape Fear means driving on the beaches; practically everything inland is private. While most popular beaches prohibit vehicles, there are a few relatively unspoiled areas where off-road enthusiasts (especially those who fish) can indulge themselves. Driving off-road is a two-edged sword: the vehicles that make these beautiful areas accessible also erode them. Observe regulations and use common sense when off-roading. This is your living room.

The best off-roading around is at the Fort Fisher State Recreation Area, an undeveloped four-mile reach of strand and tidal marsh located five miles south of Carolina Beach, off Highway 421. The earth within the marsh area is firm, and fiddler crabs, egrets, ibis and herons are common. The deeper tidal pools are suitable for bathing, especially for toddlers. Passage onto the beach is through marked crossovers only. The sand here is loose and very deep. At high tide, the strand becomes very narrow and may prevent you from turning around. Also, the marsh floods at high tide. Plan accordingly.

On Topsail Island, off-roading is permitted along New River Inlet, at the northern end of the island. The approach to it is by River Road, from the north end of Marine Drive. A permit is required between Oct. 15 and April 15.

The north end of Carolina Beach, at the end of Canal Drive, is also open to off-roading. This area becomes busy in the warmer months.

Racquetball

Check listings for Fitness Centers to locate those that have racquetball courts. Each year a racquetball and a handball tournament are sponsored by the Wilmington Family YMCA (251-9622), which has four courts available to members by reservation.

Rugby

CAPE FEAR RUGBY CLUB

395-2331

The 100-member club produces the Cape Fear Sevens Rugby Tournament each July. Considered one of the finest showcases of Sevens rugby in the East, the event attracts 70-odd teams from Europe, Canada, Japan, and South Africa — well more than 700 players. Games are held at UNCW (College Road) and are free. Ranked second in the state in 1993, the club is always interested in recruiting new members. Other numbers to call are 762-8324 and 763-0902.

Skateboarding

As much a statement of identity as it is a sport, skateboarding has its fair share of adherents in the region and divides broadly into indoor and outdoor factions. The indoor facility of note is **Middle School Indoor Skate Park**, 270-3497, located in Hampstead. It features a six-foot ramp, a three-foot-deep bowl and a full street course. Take Highway 17 to Hampstead, turn west onto Peanut Road and right onto unpaved Pansy Road.

Outdoor skating is concentrated in downtown Wilmington where hills keep skaters zipping through their tailslides and flips. Businesses and police don't look kindly upon them, despite the likelihood that skaters' presence on deserted streets after hours may deter crime. There is no apparent organization among skaters in terms of teams or competitions. Surf shops are the best resource for equipment and repairs.

Soccer

Soccer fever is sweeping Cape Fear. Youth leagues are extremely popular. The fields are constantly busy on weekends, and adult leagues are springing up. The investment necessary to play is generally limited to a onetime registration fee (averaging $25) and shin guards (approximately $12).

You can find soccer supplies at **Corner Kick Soccer Shop**, 1537 South College Road, 791-8010. Specializing in soccer accessories and clothing, Corner Kick also sponsors a league team.

The following organizations support Cape Fear soccer.

CAPE FEAR
YOUTH SOCCER ASSOCIATION

P.O. Box 5454, Station 1   675-9693
Wilmington, 28403

The Association's program recently expanded to include adults. Licensed coaches lead the teams. Games are held at the Hoggard High School athletic fields on weekends during fall and spring. Register in July and in January.

WILMINGTON PARKS & RECREATION
Athletic Office 343-3680

An adult soccer league plays from May through July. The league's growing popularity often makes it difficult for new teams to enter, especially late in the preseason. Games are held at Legion Stadium on Carolina Beach Road, 2 1/2 miles south of downtown Wilmington.

YMCA
251-9622

The Y also sponsors league games for boys and girls, ages 3 to 11 during the spring and fall.

BRUNSWICK COUNTY PARKS & RECREATION
(800)222-4790 or 253-4357

From September through November, Brunswick County Parks & Rec organizes youth soccer for players ages 5 to 14 (the oldest players must still be in middle school). From June through August the soccer camps are popular. Early registration is recommended.

ONSLOW COUNTY PARKS & RECREATION
347-5332

Onslow Parks & Rec hosts a coed league for adults 30 years and older. Teams (up to 20 players) can register for $170. Play starts in February and continues through mid-May. Games are played at Hubert Bypass

Park in the town of Hubert, convenient to the northern Cape Fear coast.

Softball

Wilmington Parks & Recreation, 341-7855, hosts adult men's, women's and coed leagues and a league for seniors during spring and fall. The adult leagues run in two seasons. Team registration for the fall season is in August. Registration for the spring season is in March. Fees range from $200 to $400 per team.

Wilmington's **Cape Fear Optimist Club**, 762-8957, has softball for girls, the "Cape Fear Belles," in two age groups, 13 to 15 and under 12. The Belles' 13 to 15 year-old All Star Team won the 1993 state championship.

Also check into Wilmington's **Winter Park Optimist Club**, 256-9994 or 256-4759, and **Wrightsville Beach Parks & Recreation**, 256-7925.

Carolina Beach hosts a two-day, open softball tournament in August. If you can scrape up a team, your own softballs and the $100 entry fee, you're in. Call **Carolina Beach Parks & Recreation** for information.

Brunswick County Parks & Recreation, (800)222-4790, sponsors separate softball leagues for adult men and for girls in the spring and an adult coed league in the fall. People of all ages are welcomed to participate in their umpire clinics. Call for schedules and fees.

Refer also to the section on "Baseball" in this chapter for information on the Optimist Clubs, Onslow County Parks & Recreation and the

Southeastern Athletic Association, other sponsors of softball leagues.

Summer Camps

Day camps and sports camps, rather than overnight camps, are the norm in the Cape Fear region. For sports camps, children must own basic personal equipment, including protective gear. Team items such as bats and balls are provided. Day campers only need swim suits, towels and sneakers to get the most out of their camp experiences.

ASHTON FARM SUMMER DAY CAMP
5645 U.S. Hwy. 117 S.   259-2431
Burgaw

Ashton Farm is 72 acres of an historic plantation, located about 18 miles north of Wilmington. Owners Sally and Jim Martin provide children ages 5 to 13 with down-to-earth fun. Kids participate in farm life, sports with minimized competition and nature. Among the activities are swimming, canoeing, riding, softball, hiking, crafts, animal care, rodeos, archery and ice cream-making. One-week sessions ($75 per week) from June to August are available (daily with permission). Discounts apply for additional weeks and/or additional children registered. A special "Mini Camp" ($40) is available for three days in June for preschoolers. The camp provides round-trip transportation to Wilmington, camper health insurance and drinks. Single-day camps have been added to coincide with school holidays and weekends.

UNIVERSITY OF NORTH CAROLINA AT WILMINGTON
601 S. College Rd.   Athletic Dept.: 395-3232

UNCW sponsors one-week summer sports camps in baseball, basketball, tennis, swimming, volleyball and soccer. Attendees may be as young as 3 years old or as old as seniors in high school. Camps are also available for men's and women's basketball. Camps can be arranged for full- or 1/2 days and for team or individual instruction. Registration opens in June, and prices range from about $60 for a 1/2-day junior session to $250 for full-week adult camps.

BRUNSWICK COUNTY PARKS & RECREATION
(800)222-4790 , 253-4357

Summer sports camps in baseball, soccer and wrestling are offered at various parks in Brunswick County from June through August. Register early.

WILMINGTON FAMILY YMCA
251-9622

Camp Tuscarora is a day camp offering daily trips to nearby Poplar Grove Plantation. Archery, swimming, music and overnight trips are among the many offerings. Inquire about their "Campership" scholarships. Five two-week sessions begin in mid-June. Cost is $55 per week for members, $65 for nonmembers, plus a onetime registration fee of $25.

Kiddy Korner Kinder Kamp is a 1/2-day preschool day camp offering age-appropriate activities to a maximum of 25 participants. Fees are $15 for members, $20 for non-members. Weekly and three-day sessions are offered. Scholarships are available.

YWCA OF WILMINGTON
799-6820

Summer day camps for tots and juniors are open weekdays from June through August. Fees begin at $15 per day, plus a parent membership of $15 and a nonrefundable annual registration fee.

WRIGHTSVILLE BEACH PARKS & RECREATION
256-7925

Summer Day Camp orchestrates a variety of activities for children ages 6 to 11, including organized games, arts and crafts, field trips and beach fun. Two-week sessions run June through August.

Tennis

Practically every larger public park in the Cape Fear region has at least two courts (see Parks, below). The University of North Carolina at Wilmington also hosts summer tennis camps for youth (see Summer Camps, above).

Wilmington Parks & Recreation

offers tennis for youth and seniors from March through November. Mr. PeeWee tennis for ages 4 to 7 takes place September through November and March through May.

THE GREATER WILMINGTON TENNIS ASSOCIATION
392-5807

The GWTA organizes tournaments for serious players. The tournaments are open to all in singles, doubles and mixed doubles divisions. Registration fees vary, beginning around $10. Call Wilmington Parks & Recreation for information (343-3680).

THE USTA TEAM TENNIS ASSOCIATION
Wilmington   392-5807

The Association organizes adult league team tennis from March through May. Match-winners may go on to compete at the district, sectional, and national levels.

THE WILMINGTON TENNIS LADDER
Wilmington   395-6674

The Wilmington Tennis Ladder is a monthly newsletter and a service that matches players in open challenges in every category. The season (August 1st through late January) is designed to prepare players for the USTA Team Tennis tournaments that begin in March. The newsletter lists category captains and current standings. The cost is $15 for six months.

The Beaches

Wrightsville Beach Parks & Recreation, 256-7925, sponsors all levels of group instruction for adults and children age 5 and up, from March through October, and a Women's Tennis Day every Thursday, 9 AM to noon, year round (weather permitting).

There are several places in south Brunswick County where courts are available:

BRIARWOOD GOLF CLUB
off Ocean Isle Rd.   754-4660
East of Shallotte

Ocean Isle Beach has public courts on Third Street across from the Museum of Coastal Carolina.

SEA TRAIL PLANTATION
211 Clubhouse Rd.   579-7663.
Sunset Beach

All six of the **Brunswick County District Parks** maintain tennis courts for public use. For information, call Brunswick County Parks & Recreation: 254-4357.

If you break your strings or need a new pair of shorts, stop by **Tennis With Love, Ltd.** at 4303 Oleander Drive, 791-3128. This shop specializes in restringing tennis and racquetball frames and carries clothing, shoes and accessories. A shop that lives up to its name.

Track and Field

Track and field is school-related in this region, but **Brunswick County Parks & Recreation** recently launched a small pilot program for youth in the Leland area (northern Brunswick County). The program operates in summer and emphasizes fun and technique more than winning.

Triathlon

Superheroes can tackle the annual **Wilmington Triathlon** in mid-September. The combination 2K salt water swim, 45K bike race and 10K run can be entered by individuals and three-member teams, ages 14 and up. Entry forms are available from the YMCA (2710 Market Street, Wilmington, 28403). For information call 762-3357 or 251-9622.

The Marine Corps Base, Camp Lejeune, hosts the annual **Lejeune Grand Prix Series** from January through October. The series consists of 11, each one more grueling than the next. Among them are the Tour d'Pain (February), the European Cross Country (March), the Armed Forces Day 5K (May), the Mud, Sweat & Gears Duathlon (June), the Wet & Wild Biathlon (August), and the Lejeune Triathlon (September). Events take place within the confines of Camp Lejeune (near Jacksonville). Events are open to civilians of all ages. Entry forms and information can be obtained by contacting Dr. Ron Gerughty, Fitness Director, 451-5430, 8 AM to 4 PM Monday through Friday.

Ultimate

Like any beach community worth its salt, those on Cape Fear take their frisbee seriously. Wilmington was the only town represented by two teams in the 1993 World Championships: UNCW men's team (1993 national champs) and the Port City Slickers, 791-8623, an unaffiliated men's team, half of which is made up of UNCW grads. UNCW women's team was also 1991-92 national collegiate champs. All three of these power-houses participate in a sport that is undergoing a surge in popularity, even to the point that talk is focusing on whether to introduce referees.

Volleyball

If you're not accustomed to playing in sand, you're in for a workout. Some say it will either whip you into shape or kill you. But not all volleyball in the area is outdoors. If you survive the summer playing in sand, your improved agility and jumping may manifest themselves dramatically on a hardwood court in winter.

YMCA

2710 Market St.   251-9622
Wilmington

In conjunction with the Federal Outdoor Volleyball Association (FOVA), the Y sponsors one tournament each month from March to October at Wrightsville Beach. There are three doubles divisions — novice, intermediate and advanced, and sign-up is at 8:30 AM on weekends. Games begin at 9 AM.

CAPT'N BILL'S BACKYARD GRILL

4240 Market St.   762-0111
Wilmington

These are the only sand courts within city limits. They are located behind the North 17 shopping center. Join a pickup game for a buck per player, or register your team in one of Capt'n Bill's leagues.

WILMINGTON PARKS & RECREATION
343-3680

Wilmington Parks & Recreation has fall and spring coed volleyball for adults. Teams must register early to participate in this crowded league, usually by the end of July for the fall season and by early January for the spring.

WRIGHTSVILLE BEACH
PARKS & RECREATION
256-7925

Wrightsville Beach Parks & Recreation sponsors doubles tournaments with round-robin play in men's, women's, and mixed categories. Games are held March through October on the beach strand.

If you'd like to put up your own net on Wrightsville Beach, you'll have to get permission from the folks at Parks & Recreation. It's easy. On Carolina Beach, check with the lifeguard on duty in the zone where you'd like to play before staking your net.

BRUNSWICK COUNTY
PARKS & RECREATION
(800)222-4790

Adult team volleyball in Brunswick County is sponsored by

Of the two bridges leading into Wilmington, cyclists prefer the Route 421 North bridge, which is wider and safer than the Cape Fear Memorial Bridge.

Insiders' Tips

Brunswick County Parks & Recreation. Players must be 18 or older and out of high school. The season runs from late-October through March. Inquire about registration early.

ONSLOW COUNTY
PARKS & RECREATION
347-5332

Folks 16 and older from Onslow and northern Pender counties may enter teams in Onslow County Parks & Recreation's volleyball league . Contact them in July for registration information. The indoor matches commence during the third week of September.

SHARKY'S PIZZA & DELI
Ocean Isle Beach Causeway   579-9177

The owners have added a sand court and offer docking facilities (come by boat!). Food and refreshments are within "serving" distance.

Water Sports

(see Water Sports chapter)

Wrestling

Brunswick County Parks & Recreation, 253-4357 or (800) 222-4790, is about the only agency sponsoring wrestling teams outside the schools. Coached and organized by county Athletic Coordinator Joe Rosselli, the league boasts two national champs among its alumni. The county has a Scholastic league (ages 5-14) and a Freestyle league (any age). Mr. Rosselli also conducts a summer wrestling camp.

Yoga

In addition to the listings below, fitness centers occasionally offer classes. For individual instructors, information and contacts, check the bulletin boards at the Tidal Creek Food Co-op (4406 Wrightsville Avenue in Wilmington, 799-2667) and Doxey's Market & Cafe (Landfall Shopping Center, 256-9952).

WILMINGTON FAMILY YMCA
2710 Market St.   251-9622

The Y offers regular classes for members and is a good resource for locating private instructors.

SUN & MOON
BOOKSHOP AND BOUTIQUE
7110 Wrightsville Ave.   256-9131
near Wrightsville Beach

Sun & Moon is a clearinghouse for information on New Age, holistic and natural health and healing traditions. The shop sponsors yoga classes as well as lectures and seminars.

HAREN (ED PICKETT)
c/o Unitarian Universalist Fellowship
4313 Lake Ave.   395-4431
Wilmington, 28403

A proponent of Kripalu Yoga, or "posture-flow" yoga, Ed instructs informal weekly classes in Wilmington. Kripalu Yoga emphasizes spontaneous movement rather than static form and is thought to be a rediscovery of yoga's most ancient traditions. Classes are open to anyone for a voluntary donation.

WRIGHTSVILLE BEACH
PARKS & RECREATION
256-7925

Wrightsville Beach Parks & Recreation offers year-round morning and evening classes emphasizing flexibility, alignment, conditioning and stress-reduction techniques.

Parks

We've grouped state, county and city parks by location since all three types can be found within Wilmington or Carolina Beach city limits. Refer to the Index if you're unsure of a park's location.

Wilmington

The 32 public parks maintained by the City of Wilmington differ widely. From the historic Riverwalk of downtown's Riverfront Park to the athletic fields of Empie Park to the sunken cypress stands of Greenfield Lake, there is always a park nearby with the kind of recreation or quiet you desire. Here is a cross-section of the larger city parks and their facilities. A complete listing can be obtained from the Parks & Recreation Department, 302 Willard Street (near Greenfield Park), 341-7855. Inquiries about particular facilities can be directed to the Parks & Recreation Department's Athletic office, 343-3680.

EMPIE PARK
Park Ave. at Independence Blvd.

Empie has lighted baseball fields, picnic shelters, a playground, bike racks and a concession stand. Due to popular demand, tennis courts here must be reserved in advance ($3 for city residents; $4 nonresidents) by calling the Parks & Recreation Athletics office at 343-3860.

GREENFIELD PARK
Rt. 421 (Carolina Beach Rd.)

Greenfield Lake and its surrounding gardens are the centerpiece of Wilmington's park system and a scenic wonder that changes character from season to season. Among the city's oldest parks, it was a working plantation and, later, a carnival grounds. The lake attracts a wide variety of birds and is rumored to contain alligators. When the azaleas bloom in early spring, the area explodes into a dazzling profusion of color. Stands of flowering magnolia, dogwood, long leaf pine, and live oak — many hung with Spanish moss — line the shady five-mile lake shore drive.

On the north side of the 158-acre park are lighted tennis courts, playgrounds, picnic areas, a concession stand and docks where canoes and

Surfers catch the best waves during storm surges.

Insiders' Tips

paddle boats are available for rent. A free public boat ramp is located on West Lake Shore Drive immediately east of Route 421. The benches at mid-span on Lions Bridge are a wonderful spot to relax on a breezy day. Open-air performances are presented in summer at the amphitheater off West Lake Shore Drive, adjacent to the Municipal Rose Garden. An excellent place to observe wildlife is from the Rupert Bryan Memorial Nature Trail, an easy 1/3-mile looped boardwalk through dense cypress swamp. The trail head is through the parking lot off East Lake Shore Drive between Yaupon and Cypress Drives.

LEGION STADIUM
Carolina Beach Rd. (Rt. 421)

Located beside Greenfield Lake, approximately 1 3/5 miles south of the Cape Fear Memorial Bridge, Legion Stadium is the home of several local high school sports teams. Lighted athletic fields, tennis courts and a swimming pool are also available, with plenty of parking. The pool fee is $1 for adults and 50 cents for children.

HUGH MACRAE PARK
Oleander Dr. east of S. College Rd.

This county park of tall pines is, appropriately, the site of the Piney Woods Festival each August. Play-

grounds, lighted tennis courts, athletic fields, sheltered picnic areas and a concession stand explain this park's popularity.

NORTHSIDE PARK
Between 6th & MacRae Sts., north of Taylor St.

The pool is the main attraction here, and sheltered picnic areas are available, too. The pool fee is $1 for adults and 50 cents for children.

RIVERFRONT PARK
Water St.

This, for many locals, epitomizes Wilmington life. Once congested with the wharves of the state's busiest port, the Riverwalk is now a place for quiet strolls, sightseeing, shopping, live outdoor music and dining. The stern-wheeler *Henrietta II* and the tour boat *Capt. Maffitt* dock here. You'll also find a visitors' information booth. Visiting historic sailing ships often dock here and usually offer tours.

ROBERT STRANGE PARK
8th and Nun Sts.

The heart of this park is its swimming pool (fee: $1 adults, 50 cents children). Other facilities include a recreation center, rest rooms, playground, picnic shelters, softball fields, and lighted tennis and basketball courts.

SNOW'S CUT PARK

River Rd., near Snow's Cut bridge

Divided into two sections along River Road, one directly beneath the bridge and the other 100 yards west, this county park offers shaded picnic grounds, sheltered tables, a gazebo and pedestrian access to Snow's Cut. It is located very near Carolina Beach Family Campground. For shelter reservations call 341-7198.

Pleasure Island

CAROLINA BEACH STATE PARK

Dow Rd.   458-8206
Carolina Beach

This is one of the most biologically diverse parks in North Carolina and a contender for Most Beautiful on Cape Fear. Maritime forest, sandhill terrain, waterfront and sand ridges support carnivorous plants and centuries-old live oaks. Five miles of easy trails wind throughout the park. The marina offers boat ramps and 42 boat slips off the Cape Fear River. Excellent overnight camping facilities are available. The park is located on Pleasure Island, 1 mile north of Carolina Beach and 1/5 mile from Highway 421, off Dow Road. Day-use is free.

THE COVE AT FORT FISHER STATE HISTORIC SITE

Hwy. 421 S.   458-5538

This is a beautiful getaway, about six miles south of Carolina Beach. Bordering the beach and a rocky sea wall, a grove of windswept live oaks provides shade, with picnic tables and grills. Come to fish and sunbathe — but don't swim: dangerous currents and underwater hazards make it risky. Parking is available south of the museum, near the Ft. Fisher Memorial and at the museum itself, across the road. The nearest rest rooms are at the Fort Fisher Recreation Area Public Access, 1 mile south. Otherwise, there are no facilities.

Brunswick County

There are six District Parks maintained by the **Brunswick County Parks & Recreation Department**, all with excellent facilities. Listed here are the parks closest to coastal residences. For information, call 253-4357.

NORTHWEST DISTRICT PARK

Hwy. 74/76, 2 miles west of the Leland overpass.

SMITHVILLE DISTRICT PARK

Hwy. 133 near Southport

SHALLOTTE DISTRICT PARK

Old Hwy. 17, 1 mile south of Shallotte

Photo: N.C. Travel and Tourism Division

The Governor Dudley mansion in Wilmington was built about 1825 as the home of
Edward Bishop Dudley, the first popularly elected governor of North Carolina.

Inside
Golf

The Cape Fear coast currently is developing new golf courses faster than anywhere else in North Carolina. South Brunswick already boasts more than 25 excellent facilities, many as part of golf real estate developments and resorts. Courses throughout the Cape Fear region receive more accolades, nominations and citations from the national golf press than you can shake a nine iron at. The area features several world-class courses bearing the signature designs of Tom Fazio, Pete Dye, his son P.B. Dye, Jack Nicklaus, Dan Maples and Willard Byrd. Wind is frequently a factor on Cape Fear, particularly on Bald Head Island. Players familiar with the Myrtle Beach area are discovering that Cape Fear courses offer far less crowded, less hurried playing than that southern neighborhood at prices that encourage multiple rounds per day, all year long. PGA and fund-raising tournaments are increasingly finding host clubs in this region, giving added credence to the belief that the Cape Fear coast is a duffer's dream come true.

Green fees vary according to season and location. At semiprivate courses, they range widely from $19 to $100 and up but average between $30 and $40. Fees are highest during the peak months (late-March to early-May and mid-September to early-November) and at the more exclusive clubs. Courses farther from Wilmington offer an excellent balance between price and playing conditions. Summer rates and discounts for seniors, corporations and groups are common at practically every course. Many pro shops at the courses rent clubs to travellers unable to pack their own.

Most travel agencies and local hotels arrange golf packages directly. Some people prefer central reservations services for the convenience and attractive discount rates.

Tee-Times, Inc., (800) 447-0450 or 256-8043, is a Wilmington-based service that can arrange everything for your golf vacation — tee times, accommodations, airline tickets and rental cars.

Coastal Golfaway, 791-8494 or (800) 368-0045, books packages from Wilmington to Hilton Head, SC, which often include breakfasts.

The Wilmington Golf Association, (800) 545-5494, disseminates information on packages provided by the area's leading courses and hotels.

The American Lung Association Golf Privilege Card offers discounts on more than 270 rounds of golf played at 150 courses throughout North Carolina. Most courses are located on the coast, and five are in South Carolina. The card costs $40, and out-of-state residents are welcomed. Inquire about the buy-three-get-one-free opportunity. Some restrictions apply. Contact the American Lung Association of North Carolina, (800)821-6205 or 395-5864, P.O. Box 3577, Wilmington, 28406.

The Cape Fear Golf Card For Seniors offers substantial savings for players ages 50 and up. Fourteen participating courses, most located between Hampstead and Calabash, offer card-holders a complimentary green fee. All you do is reserve tee times in advance and pay a cart fee. Some courses even allow more than one round per card. The privilege costs $19 each, $32 per couple and is good for one year. For information contact: Cape Fear Golf Card For Seniors, 295-3045, P.O. Box 4144, Pinehurst, NC 28374.

Brunswick County Parks & Recreation, (800)222-4790 or 253-4357, sponsors a youth golf program affiliated with the national "Hook a Kid On Golf" program. Registration is limited, so inquire in April about the upcoming season that runs from June through August.

Courses

Described below are some of the better courses on Cape Fear, judged according to overall beauty, location and variety of challenges. With one exception, all courses are semiprivate or public. An increasing number of courses offer practice facilities and pro shops that do repairs, but we've also included a few independent driving ranges throughout the area and pro shops that come highly recommended by insiders.

Wilmington

THE CAPE GOLF & RACQUET CLUB
535 The Cape Blvd.   *799-3110*

Located one-mile north of Carolina Beach, this semiprivate par-72 championship course is meticulously landscaped amid 24 lakes, ponds and marshland. The eight-year-old Bermuda fairways make up a championship yardage of 6,800 yards with a 73.5 rating from the blue tees and a slope of 135. Signature double greens grace the 15th and 17th holes. The grounds include a fully-stocked pro shop, driving range, putting and chipping greens, as well as locker rooms with showers, a cocktail lounge, the full-service Mulligan's Pub, banquet facilities and a snack bar. Club members also have access to the Cape's swimming pool and tennis courts. Green fees vary from inexpensive to moderate.

ECHO FARMS
GOLF & COUNTRY CLUB
4114 Echo Farms Blvd.   *791-9313*

This semiprivate course is distinguished by lakes that come into play on nine of the 18 holes, stands of moss-draped hardwood and some of the finest bent greens in Wilmington. Designed by Gene Hamm, this former dairy farm (the original farmhouse near the 17th hole is still occupied) is now a par-72 challenge rated between 69.6 and 72.7 with slopes from 121 to 131.

Echo Farms recently completed improvements totalling more than $1 million, fully returning the course to its initial glory (it was built in 1974). A driving range, practice greens, full restaurant, bar and snack lounge are open to all. The pro shop does regripping. Under the direction of Banks Guyton, who once coached Curtis Strange, Echo Farms has developed a fine teaching facility offering clinics and private lessons. The course is located five miles south of downtown Wilmington on Carolina Beach Road (U.S. 421).

INLAND GREENS
Inland Greens Dr.   *452-9900*

This little-known par-3 course is a good place to sharpen your short game. Holes average just over a 100 yards, and the greens are in good condition. Located almost midway between Wrightsville Beach and downtown Wilmington, it is hidden off Cardinal Drive between Eastwood Road and Market Street.

LANDFALL
1550 Landfall Dr.   *256-8411*

Play on Landfall's two superlative courses, designed by Jack Nicklaus and Pete Dye, is restricted to members of the exclusive Landfall Club. Memberships are available to Landfall property owners and non owners, and the rewards for golfing members include chal-

Photo: N.C. Travel and Tourism Division

A golfer tees off at Baldhead Island.

lenges unparalleled in the majority of area courses. Both courses are tastefully situated along the Intracoastal Waterway in a perfectly manicured setting.

The par-72 Nicklaus course is perhaps the more forgiving of the two, playing just under 7,000 yards from the back. With a rating of 72.6 and slopes ranging from 120 to 137, it looks easier on paper than it really is, thanks largely to the many carries over marshes and water. The sixth hole, for instance, is a tough par 3 playing 190 yards from the back (85 from the front), with little more than marsh all the way to the green. Hole 17's island green is backed with a bunker that's a poor bailout given its five-foot forward lip.

Another island green is the signature hole on the Dye course. Completely water-bound, the kidney-shaped 11th green (135 yard par 3)

slopes away from the sand trap that collars half its perimeter. The Dye course is probably the tougher of the two. It is a par-72 rated at 73.9 from the back (slope: 116-135). Plenty of uneven lies, marshes and pot bunkers demand that players push the envelope of their games to the utmost. Both courses feature bent greens. Fairways and roughs stay green all year. Members also have access to Landfall's elaborate sports center featuring 14 tennis courts (hard, composition and grass), croquet, NCAA short-course pool and many indoor facilities.

PORTERS NECK PLANTATION

1202 Porters Neck Rd. 686-1177
(800)423-5695

Porters Neck is an aficionado's course, a combination of picture-perfect aesthetics and strategic challenges that could only have been designed by Tom Fazio, *Golf Digest's* top-ranked golf architect in America. This is a championship course (par 72, slope 130) that emphasizes careful club selection and pin placement. Impeccably maintained fairways undulate in sometimes deceptive fashion. Enormous waste bunkers and lakes abound, some of which span the entire distance from tee to green (Holes 11, 13, 14). Distinctive waste mounds, planted with native grasses, add to the course's unique look. Each hole presents conditions to make the most accurate golfer uncomfortable, yet leave no player unfulfilled. Located about six miles from Wilmington, this course winds through a private residential development on the Intracoastal Waterway. Green fees are at the high end of the local scale. Public play is invited; however, the club is expected to turn private in the near future. The pro shop offers limited services such as regripping. The entrance gate is 1 1/3 miles in from the property limit on Porters Neck Road.

WILMINGTON GOLF COURSE
311 Wallace Ave.   *791-0558*

Relatively flat and among the more populated courses, the "Muni" is Wilmington's only municipal course. It features a practice fairway left of the ninth hole. Entrance to the par-71 facility is either from Oleander Drive or from Pine Grove Drive, a seven-minute drive from downtown. Compared to other local courses, the Muni has a relative dearth of water hazards, but the stream crossing the fairways of holes (495 yard par 5) and 12 (519 yard par

5) is in just the wrong place for many golfers. There is only one serious dogleg. The clubhouse and pro shop are open everyday from 7 AM until sundown. It houses showers and lockers in the men's room only. Green fees are $6 weekdays for city residents, higher on weekends, and nine-hole rounds are available. Groups are limited to fours, and no one-somes or two-somes are permitted before 1:30 PM.

Carolina Beach

BEAU RIVAGE PLANTATION GOLF & COUNTRY CLUB
6230 Carolina Beach Rd.   *392-9022*
                                 (800) 628-7080

Elevations as much as 72 feet and scads of bunkers (including two waste bunkers) place this five-year-old course among the more dramatically landscaped courses in New Hanover County. It is a semiprivate par-72 course (slope: 114-136) in which water hazards come into play on eight holes. Hole 4 (206 yard par 3) is notable for its island tee-box for the ladies and a carry that is entirely over water. Its well-watered bent-grass green is protected on three sides. The pro shop performs some repairs, and its inventory emphasizes soft goods. Lessons are available. A bar and grill and restaurant provide attractive settings for post-round analysis. Beau Rivage is a residential development, and club memberships are available to nonresidents. A 32-suite hotel adjoins the clubhouse.

Topsail Island

OLDE POINT

Hwy. 17 N.   270-2403
Hampstead

The 11th hole is called Jezebel for its wickedly frustrating ways. Considered one of the two toughest holes on all the Cape Fear coast by many area pros and amateurs (the other being the 17th at Marsh Harbor in Calabash), this long, narrow 589-yard par-5 is a gradual dogleg right that slopes laterally downward to the right (into the woods) and consistently defies players' depth perception. The course is buffeted by winds almost all year round, especially the second hole (372 yard par 3) where the wind is usually in your face and the well-bunkered green is surrounded on three sides by water. With four tee positions and slopes of 115-136, Olde Point is among the finer challenges along the northern Cape Fear coast.

BELVEDERE PLANTATION GOLF & COUNTRY CLUB

2368 Country Club Dr.   270-2703
Hampstead

Developed in 1975, Belvedere Plantation's course continues to undergo improvements begun last year and now enjoys a larger clubhouse complete with dining room. It is a narrow par-71 course with plenty of water and small Bermuda greens. Hole 3 (180 yard par 3) stands out for its carry over water to an elevated green. The blue tees are rated slightly higher than the course's overall par 71 and have a slope of 131. Belvedere is a busy course with affordable green fees and discounts for residents of local counties. The clubhouse has a limited pro shop and snack bar. Although part of a residential community, Belvedere offers club memberships to nonresidents as well, which include use of the pool and tennis courts. Golf schools lasting three to four days are available with overnight accommodations on the course. Belvedere is located less than a mile from Topsail Greens Country Club, about 17 miles north of Wilmington off Highway 17 North.

TOPSAIL GREENS COUNTRY CLUB

Hwy. 17 N.   270-2883
Hampstead

This semiprivate par-71 course has a slope range of 113-121. While its overall length is not particularly daunting, it presents respectable challenges and several birdie opportunities to blue-tee players and a sense of satisfaction to those playing the shorter tees. Five holes require sizable carries over water, and two others have water beside the fairways. Greens of Bermuda grass are mostly elevated. The eighth is the signature hole, a 159-yard par 3 played to an island green protected on both forward flanks by sand traps. The course is laid out on a roughly east-west axis, and hole 14 is about 200 yards from the Intracoastal Waterway. Winds are capricious. Green fees are on the low end of the average, making Topsail Greens popular yet not overrun. This 20 year-old course is located near two other excellent courses (Belvedere Plantation and Olde Point), about 17 miles outside Wilmington. Lessons, practice facilities and a restaurant are among the extras. Topsail Greens hosts the annual American Cancer Society Tournament, played in August, in which four men or women per team play a scramble. Winners are eligible to compete in the state championship tournament in early autumn.

NORTH SHORE COUNTRY CLUB

Hwy. 210	327-2410
Sneads Ferry	(800)828-5035

Notorious for its long carries over water, North shore is among the best-conditioned courses in the Topsail Island area. With a championship slope of 137 (seniors 115), it is also among the most challenging. In fact, not very long ago it was rated among the top-20 new courses of the decade by *Golf Reporter Magazine* and called "one of the best new courses in 1989" by *Golf Digest*. Its Bermuda fairways are fraught with extensive mounding, tall pines and menacing blue waters to keep you from the bent-grass greens. Occasional strong sea breezes may greet you as you step up

to the elevated tee boxes. The ninth hole (412 yard par 4) is memorable for its necessary 250-yard tee shot; anything less is in the drink. Designed by Bob Moore, North Shore is located on the mainland side of the North Topsail Beach high span, a crossing that rewards you with a spectacular view of the course, the surrounding waterways and the ocean. Extras at North Shore include a pro shop, bar and grill, driving range, putting green and lockers. Special summer rates and late-day discounts are available.

Caswell Beach

OAK ISLAND GOLF & COUNTRY CLUB

928 Caswell Beach Rd.	278-5275
Caswell Beach	

One of Brunswick County's older courses, this George Cobb creation is home to the Southport-Oak Island Masters Putting Tournament. It is a forgiving course, par 72, that will be enjoyed by players of varying skills. Its wide Bermuda fairways are relatively short, lined with live oaks and tall pines and not too fortified with water hazards. But that ocean wind! The clubhouse is less than 200 yards from the Atlantic, and sea breezes can frustrate the best players. Hole #9 (handicap 18) may send you to the Duffer's Restaurant & Lounge early. This course, with its Bermuda greens, driving range, putting green and swimming pool, underwent improvements recently and remains quite popular.

Photo: N.C. Travel and Tourism Division

Golf in the South Brunswick Islands can be magnificent.

Holden Beach

LOCKWOOD GOLF LINKS

100 Clubhouse Dr.	842-5666
Holden Beach	(800)443-7891

This classic Willard Byrd-designed par-72 course was nominated by *Golf Digest* as the Best New Course in 1988. Beautifully set at the confluence of Lockwood Folly River and the Intracoastal Waterway, it has no parallel fairways. Tricky, sloping bentgrass greens are protected by ample clear ponds, particularly at the eleventh hole (which is best approached from below, putting uphill). The unique touch of lining some water hazards with "beaches" of oyster shells makes for handsome landscaping but difficult sighting of white balls and potentially frustrating wedge work. Lockwood's amenities include a restaurant and lounge, driving range, putting green and pro shop.

BRIERWOOD GOLF CLUB

Off Hwy. 179 (Village Rd.)	754-4660
Shallotte	

Brierwood was the first course built along the South Brunswick Islands. Located about seven miles north of Ocean Isle Beach, it is a par 72 semiprivate championship course distinguished by plenty of freshwater obstacles surrounded by residential properties. The new clubhouse includes a pro shop and the Blue Heron Bar & Grill. Calls for tee times can be received 24 hours a day.

Ocean Isle Beach

BRICK LANDING PLANTATION

Hwy. 179	754-5545
Ocean Isle Beach	(800)438-3006

With 41 sand traps and 12 water holes, this handsome waterfront course was rated by *Florida Golf Week* magazine as among the top-50 distinctive golf courses in the southeast. Its Bermuda fairways wind among fresh water lakes and through salt marshes, offering duffers striking visual contrasts and championship challenges. The 17th hole finishes dramatically along the Intracoastal Waterway. Total course length is 6,943 yards, a par-72 rated at 72.1. Amenities include a snack bar, a lunch and cocktail lounge and practice facilities. Golf schools, clinics and full-time instructors are available, as well as tennis and family vacation packages.

Sunset Beach

SEA TRAIL PLANTATION
211 Clubhouse Rd.   579-8949
Sunset Beach

With its three par-72 courses and overnight accommodations, Sea Trail is an all-out golf resort known locally for its attractive balance of price, friendliness and outstanding playing conditions. About a mile from the beach, Sea Trail has its share of wind and water. Three sets of tees on each course — the Dan Maples (slope: 121), Rees Jones (132) and Willard Byrd (128) — present a variety of challenges that make these Bermuda fairways and bent-grass greens memorable. Maples' 17th hole (190 yard par 3) is the signature hole with its scenic appeal, a large oak tree blocking the right-hand approach and deep bunkers. A restaurant (Tavern on the Tee at the Maples clubhouse), two lounges and many meeting facilities add to Sea Trail's appeal. The pro shop accentuates "soft" merchandise rather than equipment. Two clubs, one for members and one for resort guests, offer tennis and swimming. Golf packages, including bookings at neighboring courses, are arranged on-site.

MARSH HARBOR GOLF LINKS
Hwy. 179   579-3161
Calabash   (800) 552-2660

It wouldn't be enough to describe Marsh Harbor as the course with the toughest hole on the Cape Fear coast (according to a formal survey of area pros and amateurs). While the par-5 17th certainly is redoubtable, this championship par-71 Dan Maples creation is better known as one of the most lavishly beautiful courses on the Brunswick coast. Don't be misled by the blue-tee yardage (6,690). The design emphasizes shotmaking and trickiness, yielding a blue-tee rating of 73.3 (slope: 134). Holes tend to be short, tight off the tees, with generally small Bermuda greens. All are well-bunkered, perhaps to compensate for the relative lack of water hazards, and there are plenty of doglegs. Five fairways are marsh-bound. There are some excellent par-3s, and players with single-digit handicaps will be formidably challenged. The much-touted 17th hole (570 yards from the blue tee) demands two virtuoso carries over marshes before reaching the very well-protected green.

Marsh Harbor is a public course with green fees at the medium-to-high end of the coastal average. Its upscale, elegant character is also evident in the handsome, well-stocked pro shop. There are six pros on staff to provide instruction. A restaurant-styled snack bar, driving range and putting greens are available and the use of carts is required (included in green fee).

THE PEARL GOLF LINKS

Hwy. 179   579-8132
Calabash

These two par-72 courses, east and west, will have you wanting to play 36 straight, so start early. Architect Dan Maples endowed these links with theatrical bent-grass island greens, washboard fairways and solid challenges that yield ratings of 73.1 (east) and 73.2 (west). Course lengths are on the long side (7,011 west; 6,895 east), so break out the lumber and let 'er rip. *Golf Digest* nominated the Pearl for Best New Public Resort Course in 1988. A snack bar, cocktail lounge and driving range are open year round.

Southport

THE GAUNTLET GOLF CLUB

Hwy. 211 at St. James   253-3008
Plantation   (800) 247-4806

With a championship slope of 142, it's no wonder that designer P.B. Dye called this "My most challenging course yet," or that it was named by *Golf Digest* one of the Top New Public Golf Courses in 1992. Its carries over many water hazards have been described as heroic, while its multilevel fairways, bulkheads and variety of grasses are stamped with the Dye hallmark. Each hole bears a name indicative of its character, such as The Moats, Loch Ness, Quest and The Moor. The final three holes, which include the #1 handicap (a 152 yard par 4), play

into and over a series of marshes and lakes offering a spectacular finish. Five sets of tees present a variety of plays. Most tee boxes are elevated. The Gauntlet and St. James Plantation are located 4 miles outside Southport and offer wonderful views of the Intracoastal waterway. Caddies, a complete practice facility and lessons are available. The Round Table Restaurant and Lounge are attractive. The Gauntlet is a semiprivate establishment and plans are in the offing to construct overnight resort accommodations on the premises.

Bald Head Island

BALD HEAD ISLAND CLUB

457-7310/7311

Extremely demanding due as much to the ocean wind as to George Cobb's brilliant design, this par-72 course is among the most unique scenic gems on the east coast. Exposed greens on its ocean side contrast sharply with interior holes lined with palms and pines. Four sets of tees yield course lengths of 5,150 to 7,040 yards. The links-style finishing holes run alongside the ocean. The Club has hosted the Carolinas Pro-Pro Tournament. Bald Head Island is accessible only by ferry, and tee times are required. A driving range and snack bar are available with other elegant amenities nearby.

"Golf Getaway" packages can be arranged year round through Bald Head Island's Property Management Office, 457-5002 or (800) 234-1666. Two-tiered pricing (weekday and weekend) includes parking, round-trip ferry ticket, cart and green fee for one round.

Equipment & Repairs

TEE SMITH CUSTOM GOLF CLUBS
1047 S. Kerr Ave.   395-4008
Wilmington

Tee Smith has been customizing and repairing clubs commercially since 1975 and carries the approval of pro shops throughout the Wilmington area. Simple repairs such as regripping often have a one-day turnaround. They carry a full line of top-name brands and are open all year Monday through Friday 9:30 AM to 6 PM and 9:30 AM to 1 PM on Saturdays.

THE GOLF BAG
12525 Hwy. 17 S.   270-2980
Hampstead

Few pro shops boast the breadth of services and supplies offered by Tom Tirey at The Golf Bag. As affable as he is knowledgeable about the game, Tom customizes and repairs clubs and maintains a full line of golf equipment, accessories and "all the little things," including gift items and instructional videos. He emphasizes his stock of ladies' golf apparel and equipment for lefties. The Golf Bag is located 1/2 mile from Olde Point golf course (about 14 miles from Wilmington).

Driving Ranges

COASTAL GOLF CENTER AND CAROLINA CUSTOM DISCOUNT GOLF
6987 Market St.   791-9010

Located four miles outside Wilmington on Highway 17 near the intersection of Military Cutoff Road, this is an excellent one-stop facility for practicing, instruction, equipment and repairs. Stations on the well-lit 257-yard driving range feature well-kept grass mats and tees. Three PGA instructors are on staff and the pro shop offers all repair services including regripping, reshafting and other customizing. The pro shop carries a varied inventory of apparel, accessories and books. Coastal Golf Center is one of five affiliated stores based in Raleigh. Hours are 9 AM to 10 PM Monday through Saturday during the summer and are somewhat curtailed throughout the rest of the year.

PERFECT GOLF PRACTICE FACILITY
5026 Oleander Dr.   791-7155

Newly opened last summer, this facility offers an undulating grassy field with raised greens complete with flags to imitate course conditions. Stations are grass only (no fixed tees) and include club stands. The facility is lighted and open year round. Summer hours are 10 AM to 10 PM seven days a week.

VALLEY GOLF CENTER & DRIVING RANGE
4416 S. College Rd.   395-2750

Convenient to Carolina Beach and Wilmington, this large, lighted facility has 40 tee stations plus mats and grass, as well as sand trap areas. A covered hitting area allows practicing during inclement weather. The fully-stocked, air-conditioned pro shop offers repairs and instruction with PGA staff professionals. Valley Golf Center is open everyday 9 AM to 10 PM year round.

South Brunswick

HOLDEN BEACH DRIVING RANGE
Hwy. 130 (Holden Beach Rd.)   *842-3717*

This lighted practice facility offers lessons by Class-A PGA professionals and, as any good resort-area attraction should, it has batting cages next door.

PRO TEE PRACTICE RANGE
Hwy. 179   *754-4700*
Ocean Isle Beach

This attractive, lighted facility is designed for more serious practitioners of the game who appreciate quality. Two 18-station Bermuda grass tee-boxes flank a mat area with rubber tees. The air-conditioned pro shop offers basic accessories, refreshments and snacks, and the management performs minor equipment repairs. Pro Tee is 1/2 mile west of the Brick Landing Plantation Golf Course and is open from 8 AM to 11 PM during the summer.

Inside
Ferry Services

A ferry can be viewed in two ways. First, it's a mode of transportation that saves miles of driving in search of a bridge. Second, it can be one of the cheapest ways to take a tour.

The **Southport-Fort Fisher ferry** turns what would be about two hours of driving time into approximately 30 minutes of leisurely shore-watching that becomes, thanks to onboard tour guides, a special attraction for the tourist or resident in search of an outing. On the Fort Fisher side are the remains of a fort, one of the last strongholds of the Confederacy. This earthen fort was instrumental in keeping the port of Wilmington open to blockade runners, which provided vital supplies to Southern troops.

The Fort Fisher Civil War Museum, a visitors' center, is open on a seasonal schedule (see the Attractions section) and provides an interesting opportunity for ferry riders who find themselves with time to spare before boarding. Likewise, the North Carolina Aquarium at Fort Fisher, home of a shark exhibit and the largest aquarium tank in North Carolina, is very near the ferry landing.

The ferry ride provides a fascinating view of the mouth of the Cape Fear River just above Southport. The climate-controlled passenger lounges of the *Gov. Daniel Russell* or the *Sandy Graham* are comfortable spots from which to note both natural and man-made wonders. Even on hot summer days, the breeze caused by the ferry's movement makes standing on the upper deck a pleasant experience. The route takes riders directly across commercial shipping lanes leading to the North Carolina State Port Authority, and it is likely that you'll catch sight of a freighter coming in from Asia, Africa or Europe on your brief voyage.

The ferry passes dredge spoil islands that are nesting sites for the brown pelican, and dolphins are often spotted on their migratory paths. The ferry is also pursued by the beggars of birds: sea gulls. Send the kids down to throw up bread crumbs or anything edible, and watch the excitement on their faces as the birds compete for a snack. The ferry passes the intake canal screens that lead to Carolina Power & Light's Brunswick Nuclear Power Plant. Huge yellow cranes mark the spot of the Military Ocean Terminal at Sunny Point, the largest distribution center in the country for military supplies. Fort Caswell comes into view, marked by the Oak Island

Lighthouse. This fort changed hands four times during the Civil War. The fort is now owned by the North Carolina Baptist Assembly and is used as a conference center.

To the south, Old Baldy, a familiar lighthouse landmark, stands on Bald Head Island. The lighthouse is undergoing extensive renovations and will eventually be open to the public for touring. Another lighthouse to the north is the Price's Creek Lighthouse, built in 1849. This lighthouse figured prominently in guiding Confederate blockade runners through New Inlet during the Civil War.

You will arrive at Southport, a quaint fishing village positioned at the mouth of the Cape Fear River where this body of water meets the Intracoastal Waterway. Southport is home to a cluster of interesting shops, galleries and restaurants. It was the film location of "Crimes of the Heart," and anyone there can point you toward the house that was used in the movie. The Southport-Fort Fisher Ferry can be included in the River Circle Tour that includes Orton Plantation Gardens, Brunswick Town, the Carolina Power & Light Visitors' Center, Historic Wilmington, Battleship *North Carolina*, the North Carolina Aquarium at Fort Fisher, the Fort Fisher Civil War Museum, Carolina and Kure Beaches and Southport and the Oak Island Beaches.

The Southport-Fort Fisher Ferry departs about every 50 minutes from each side of the river in the spring, summer and fall. There's a longer wait in the winter. A pedestrian crossing is 50 cents; ride a bike and it's $1. Generally, a one-way crossing is $3.00 per vehicle that measures 20 feet or less. A vehicle or combination measuring up to 32 feet is $6. Call in advance for information on larger vehicles.

The rates and schedules are subject to change. For ferry schedule information, call Southport at 457-6942 or Fort Fisher at 458-3329, or write: P. O. Box 10028, Southport, NC, 28461.

Southport - Fort Fisher

SUMMER SCHEDULE
(APRIL 1 TO OCTOBER 31):

Departs Southport	Departs Fort Fisher
8:00 AM	8:50 AM
8:50 AM	9:40 AM
9:40 AM	10:30 AM
10:30 AM	11:20 AM
11:20 AM	12:10 PM
12:10 PM	1:00 PM
1:00 PM	1:50 PM
1:50 PM	2:40 PM
2:40 PM	3:30 PM
3:30 PM	4:20 PM
4:20 PM	5:10 PM
5:10 PM	6:00 PM
6:00 PM	6:50 PM

Insiders' Tips

The Southport-Fort Fisher ferry is an inexpensive way to take a wonderful 30-minute cruise on the mouth of the Cape Fear River.

Bottlenose dolphin are a frequent sight in the waters off the Cape Fear coast.

8:00 AM	8:50 AM
9:40 AM	10:30 AM
11:20 AM	12:10 PM
1:00 PM	1:50 PM
2:40 PM	3:30 PM
4:20 PM	5:10 PM
6:00 PM	6:50 PM

Passenger Ferry to Bald Head Island

The Bald Head Island Ferry is purely for passengers. The island offers special opportunities to experience an interesting bit of North Carolina history. The island is home to Old Baldy, North Carolina's oldest lighthouse. Although the island is mostly residential in terms of development, it possesses exceptional natural beauty with quiet, unspoiled beaches and maritime forests. The most notable feature of Bald Head Island is that cars are not allowed on the island. Travel is by foot, bicycle or electric cart.

To reach the ferry, go to Indigo Plantation in Southport and leave your car in the parking lot. A round-trip ferry ticket is $15.

The ferry departs every hour on the hour from 8 AM to 10 PM seven days a week. There is no ferry at noon or 8 PM. Parking costs $4 per day.

Special summer ferry packages are being made available to visitors and include passage, parking, lunch or dinner and an historic tour. Prices range from $20 to $30 per person, Monday through Thursday. For reservations, call 457-7390 or (800) 234-1666.

JEWELLE
ON PRINCESS

A GALLERY OF FINE CONTEMPORARY ART

Featuring originals and
Limited Editions by

PETER MAX

JOHN LENNON

MICHAEL FINSTER

JOHN CUTRONE

CRAIG GURGANUS

MILES DAVIS

NEMO

GAR

Exhibiting sculpture, paintings,
photography, lithographs, textiles,
jewelry, stained glass, furniture,
vintage posters, and Poupet dolls.

president and owner
PAULA JEWELLE BRYAN

910: 343-5997
910: 343-1170 fax

located at 112 Princess Street
historical downtown Wilmington

Inside
The Arts

Through the centuries, the relative isolation of Wilmington and surrounding areas has placed the region off the beaten path of the arts. An outsider may not think of Wilmington at all when it comes to the arts; after all, it's a mighty long way from New York City. Wilmington is not an arts mecca in the traditional sense; nevertheless, there is a long-standing tradition of valuing the arts across the spectrum of artistic disciplines. Since the 1700s, Wilmington has had a special affection for the arts that has woven itself into the local social fabric.

Wilmington loves its artists. Since the small city is really just a large town, locals take keen personal interest in the achievements of their resident artists. Whether theatre, painting, sculpture, music or dance, Wilmington encourages the activities of its artists. In the finest tradition of a Southern city, some unorthodox ways of artists are tolerated with affection. Different expressions are viewed with interest; different artistic attitudes are perfectly acceptable. Artists also seem to love Wilmington. Although it is an uphill climb for artists to make a comfortable living working here, there seem to be other factors — call them inspirational — that satisfy and nurture the creative drive.

The **Arts Council of the Lower Cape Fear**, 20 Market Street, Wilmington, 763-2787, strives to be the central facilitator and coordinator for the arts in the area. It has direct and indirect impact on the growth of the arts. It stands as an advocate for regional creativity, searches for ways to locate funding through grants for exceptional artists and seeks to focus community attention on this resource. It sponsors the A+ Program in the public schools.

The Arts Council of the Lower Cape Fear administers the Emerging Artists Program annually, a project grant program that provides financial support to developing professionals. The North Carolina Arts Council, as well as interested organizations and individuals, sponsors the program. The program began in 1987 and has offered grants of approximately $1,000 each to more than 60 local artists in a full range of disciplines.

St. John's Museum of Art and **Thalian Hall Center for the Performing Arts** are two major strongholds of the arts in Wilmington that have been primary showcases for the visual and performing arts in the region for many years.

St. John's Museum of Art, 114 Orange Street, Wilmington, 763-0281,

Photo: N.C. Travel and Tourism Division

A box seat in Thalian Hall — a classic 19th-century American community theater.

was established in three buildings. A showcase for 19th and 20th century visual art, the museum owns an extensive collection of the works of such artists as Mary Cassatt, Minnie Evans, Claude Howell, Elisabeth Augusta Chant and others. The museum presents touring exhibitions and is also actively supportive of local artists through exhibitions, lectures and walk-through tours. A tremendously popular exhibition is the annual juried Wilmington Artists Exhibition the winter.

Thalian Hall Center for the Performing Arts, 310 Chestnut Street, Wilmington, 343-3664, is a treasure for the Cape Fear area. Since its construction in 1855-1858, Thalian Hall has been the center of the region's theatrical activity. From 1860 until 1932, Thalian Hall was leased by private entrepreneurs who booked the big names in entertainment. Lillian Russell, Buffalo Bill Cody, Maurice Barrymore and John Phillip Sousa were some of the performers who graced the hall. The hall has gone through several restorations and, at this time, offers three performance spaces. There is a 752-seat main stage, a 250-seat Council Chamber and a 136-seat studio theatre. With a lively performing local arts community and the addition of touring companies, at least one of the spaces is in use each evening or afternoon. More than 35 area arts and civic organizations use the facility and more than 250 performances in music, theatre and dance are presented each year.

The **Community Arts Center**, 120 South Second Street, Wilmington, 341-7860, is another special facility that focuses on the arts. This center, operated by the City of Wilmington, is primarily a learning center where anyone may come to take lessons in a full range of disciplines. Music, pottery, ceramics, dance, painting, drawing and more are offered at the center. For nominal fees, students of all ages can experience hands-on work under the direction of highly-skilled local artists and craftspeople. There is something for every age and level of ability.

The Arts Council publishes a Cultural Directory which provides an overview of arts organizations in the area and is the source of the following information.

Visual Arts

ACME ART
711 North 5th Ave.
Wilmington   *458-8259 or 763-2789*
This is an artists' cooperative of working studios. The organization offers membership, rehearsal space and rental studios. It hosts the recurring Full Moon Art shows and performances. Look for some interesting expansion in this onetime renegade arts organization.

ST. JOHN'S MUSEUM OF ART
114 Orange St.
Wilmington   *763-0281*
This exceptional museum houses a collection of 19th- and 20th-century North Carolina and American art and presents temporary exhibitions. It represents North Carolina artists and nationally known artists of all eras. The Sales Gallery represents more than 80 artists in the

Southeast. The nonprofit museum offers ongoing classes for children and adults in its Cowan House studio, as well as lectures, concerts, symposia, etc. on the visual arts and related cultural topics. A docent program provides guided tours and art appreciation talks to school and civic groups.

WILMINGTON ART ASSOCIATION

P. O. Box 3033, Azalea Station
Wilmington   791-2855

This association is composed of local visual artists. It holds juried exhibitions in the spring and fall; it also holds meetings on topics of interest and sponsors frequent workshops and critiques.

COMMERCIAL GALLERIES

FIDLER'S GALLERY AND FRAMING

The Cotton Exchange
Wilmington   762-2001

Fidler's specializes in limited edition reproductions by Bob Timberlake, Sallie Middleton, Bev Doolittle, Neil Watson, Robert Bateman, James Gurney, John Stobart and others. This gallery also carries some original work.

JEWELLE ON PRINCESS

112 Princess St., Wilmington 343-5977

A new gallery in downtown Wilmington, Jewelle on Princess offer contemporary paintings, photography, art glass, ceramics, sculpture, folk art, jewelry, and poupeé dolls from France. The collection includes prints and originals from Peter Max, John Lennon, Miles Davis, Michael Finster (grandson of Howard Finster), Craig Gurganus (whimsical art from surfboards, and John Cutrone.

GOLDEN GALLERY

The Cotton Exchange
Wilmington   762-4651

Mary Ellen Golden's original watercolors of the area scenery, son John W. Golden's exceptional photography and husband John C. Golden, Jr.'s music cassettes are in this distinctly "family business."

NEW ELEMENTS GALLERY

216 N. Front St.
Wilmington   343-8997

New Elements offers changing exhibitions of fine art by local and regional artists. Works in oil, watercolor, collage, mixed media and original arts are displayed. Decorative and functional pieces in glass, ceramics, jewelry, fiber, and wood are also offered. Exhibiting artists include Dorothy Gillespie, Claude Howell, Kyle Highsmith, Nancy Tuttle May, Hiroshi Sueyoshi, Michael Van Hout, Dina Wilde-Ramsing, Gladys Faris, Betty Brown and Mary Shreves Crow.

Music

AZALEA COAST
CHORUS OF SWEET ADELINES

240 Mare Pond Pl.
Hampstead   270-3313

This organization exists to promote and preserve the art of singing four-part harmony for women.

BLUES SOCIETY
OF THE LOWER CAPE FEAR

415 S. 2nd St.
Wilmington   343-9643

Amateur and professional musicians devoted to the preservation and encouragement of the blues

Photo: N.C. Travel and Tourism Division

*Formally opened in 1858, Thalian Hall has been a center
of community life ever since.*

make up this lively group. There are free jam sessions locally, and the organization sponsors an annual blues contest for amateurs.

HARMONY BELLES
1341 John's Creek Rd.
Wilmington   *799-5850*
A local women's group formed in 1986, this group sings four-part harmony a capella.

LARRY THOMAS & ASSOCIATES, INC.
P. O. Box 20
Wrightsville Beach   *791-7410*
Founded in 1985 as a volunteer organization dedicated to jazz and Caribbean music, this group's major goals are to promote, present and propagate these genres. The group also seeks to expose youth to the positive values of this music in order to bring about a wholesome

cultural exchange within the community.

WILMINGTON BOYS CHOIR
P. O. Box 3578   *799-7253*
Wilmington   *343-0669*
This is a choral group for boys ages 8 to 15 with a repertoire of classical and traditional music. Annual tours have taken the group to Washington D.C. in performance at the Kennedy Center.

WILMINGTON CHORAL SOCIETY
P. O. Box 4642
Wilmington   *458-5164*
A large chorus for mostly classical vocal works, the society presents up to four major concerts each season. Members rehearse weekly. This organization was founded in 1929.

WILMINGTON POPS WIND ENSEMBLE
408 N. 3rd St.   *No phone*
Wilmington

This woodwind band rehearses weekly during the summer and presents up to 10 local concerts in the spring and summer.

WILMINGTON SYMPHONY ORCHESTRA
4701 Wrightsville Ave., Bldg. #3
Suite 208   *791-9262*
Wilmington

University of North Carolina at Wilmington students and faculty members, as well as musicians from the community, comprise this symphony orchestra. There are five classical concerts per season.

WOMEN OF WILMINGTON CHORALE
814 Darwin Dr.
Wilmington   *799-5073*

Classical and folk repertoire are the focus of this group, which is most active in the summer. No auditions are required.

Theater

Wilmington has a rich theatrical tradition that is continually expanding. Wilmington's Thalian Hall, the oldest continuous community theater in the country, hosts professional and amateur productions on an almost nightly basis. There are several local theatrical companies that present original and popular productions in various locations around the area, including Kenan Auditorium at the University of North Carolina at Wilmington, the Scottish Rite Temple on 17th Street,

schools, and churches. Additionally, Wilmington continues to be on the circuit for touring dance companies, symphonies and musicals.

AD HOC THEATRE COMPANY
403 1/2 Dock St.   *763-2603*
Wilmington

This company offers experimental theater with plays by local writers.

CELEBRATION THEATRE
P. O. Box 5774   *763-9655*
Hanover Center
Wilmington

Celebration Theatre has a commitment to plays that celebrate life and the potential for good in all people. Productions include religious theater, children's plays and original scripts.

FIVE & DIME CULTURAL PRODUCTIONS
1916 Wolcott Ave.
Wilmington   *251-7817*

This company is dedicated to producing plays from the modern and classical theater that are illustrative of timeless human foibles and the potential and absurdity inherent in life in the 20th century.

OPERA HOUSE THEATRE
306 Nun St.
Wilmington   *762-4234*

A professional theater company presided over by artistic director Lou Criscuolo, this group stages seven major productions and two to three experimental works each season in Thalian Hall. Guest artists and directors are frequent.

PLAYWRIGHTS PRODUCING COMPANY
4018 Crofton Pl.
Wilmington   395-0861

A nonprofit company supporting emerging North Carolina playwrights, this organization looks for
scripts-in-progress that are read by
actors and critiqued by the audience. Selected productions or original plays are presented.

TAPESTRY THEATRE COMPANY
228 N. Front St., #308
Wilmington   763-8830

A nonprofit professional theater
company, this group is dedicated to
producing small, important works
of contemporary and classical theater.

THALIAN ASSOCIATION
P. O. Box 1111
Wilmington   251-1788

The oldest theatrical group in the
area, the Thalian Association stages
five productions annually, including
three musicals. The Second Stage Series of small plays in Thalian Hall's
Studio Theatre are performed during
summer. An allied group, the Thalian
Association Children's Theatre, stages
performances by young casts and holds
workshops for children.

UNIVERSITY THEATRE, UNIVERSITY OF NORTH CAROLINA AT WILMINGTON
601 S. College Rd.
Wilmington   395-3446

The University Theatre, produced by the school's Department of Fine Arts, is an educational theatre devoted to the creative advancement of theatre arts. Four major plays are produced during the academic year with experimental work produced on demand. University Theatre provides an environment for students to participate in and learn about all aspects of theater.

WILLIS RICHARDSON PLAYERS
508 Barclay Hills Dr.
Wilmington   791-1584, ext. 209

A community theater specializing in dramas by minority playwrights, the Willis Richardson Players perform works of particular interest to minority audiences.

Dance

CAPE FEAR THEATRE BALLET
P. O. Box 3612
Wilmington   799-0900 or 395-0093

Founded in 1991, this company's mission is to bring dance theater to southeastern North Carolina. It offers public performances, educational workshops, master dance classes and community outreach special events.

Writers

NORTH CAROLINA WRITERS' NETWORK
P. O. Box 954
Carrboro   (919) 967-9540

This state organization helps writers sharpen their skills in poetry, fiction, nonfiction, play writing and technical writing. Writer workshops and conferences are often held in the Wilmington area. This organization is an important resource for local writers.

NORTH CAROLINA POETRY SOCIETY
838 Everetts Creek Dr.
Wilmington   371-4333

The objectives of the society are to foster the writing of poetry; to bring together in meetings of mutual interest and fellowship the poets of North Carolina; to encourage the study, writing and publication of poetry; and to develop a public taste for the reading and appreciation of poetry.

Crafts

QUILTERS BY THE SEA
10076 S. Oldetown Wynd
Leland   371-9555

This group encourages the highest standards of design and technique in all forms of quilting. Activities include quilt shows and exhibits, as well as seminars and workshops on all levels of quilting.

SEASHORE WEAVERS AND SPINNERS
418 Windemere Rd.
Wilmington   799-2193

This organization exists for those interested in weaving, spinning, natural dyeing and other fiber-related crafts.

AZALEA COAST SMOCKERS GUILD
228 Forest Rd.
Wilmington   395-5201

This group teaches smocking and heirloom sewing and publishes a newsletter for its members.

"Christmas 1989"

Curtis Krueger
PHOTOGRAPHIC ARTIST

Fine Art Photographs for Home
or Office

2145 Wrightsville Avenue • Wilmington, NC 28403

(910) 763-0401 or (910) 762-2188
"Inside New Hanover Printing"

Film

CAPE FEAR FILMMAKERS ACCORD
21 Market St.
Wilmington 763-3456

A nonprofit organization of film industry professionals, this group promotes TV and film production in southeastern North Carolina. It publishes a directory of locations and contacts, serves as a liaison with business and government and can provide initial scouting locations.

CAPE FEAR CAMERA CLUB
637 Robert E. Lee Dr.
Wilmington 791-2827

Founded in 1987, this organization is a forum for photographic interests within the community. More than 50 members participate in education, travel, outings, workshops and friendly competition.

Wilmington's Artistic Journey

Claude Howell sits in his fourth-story apartment in downtown Wilmington overlooking the city that has been his home since his birth in 1915.

Founder of the Art Department at the University of North Carolina at Wilmington and recipient of numerous accolades for a superior career as an artist, Howell also is regarded widely for his scholarly writings and journalistic musings. His personal journal is currently being bound into 140 volumes and soon will be available at the New Hanover County Public Library.

Howell is a keen observer of the life around him and graciously has shared his observations of the development of the arts in Wilmington:

❝I've lived in Wilmington all my life. I've always been interested in one thing, which was being a painter; except, right in the beginning, painting was third on the list. I wanted to be, first, a ballet dancer; second, an architect; and third, a painter. Well, I don't like mathematics, so architecture was out. I didn't have the physique to be a ballet dancer, so that was out. So, I chose painting.

When I was growing up, when I went to high school, there was very little culture in Wilmington. It was sort of a dead period. There had been culture in Wilmington in the 1700s and also around the time of the Civil War, but when I was growing up there were no galleries; there was no museum; there was no theatre. Thalian Hall, which was an opera house then, had been closed. So there was absolutely nothing.

I was 21 years old before I saw my first exhibition of original oil paintings. That was not in Wilmington; that was in Washington, D.C. I went on a trip. And that was the only way that you could see anything that was at all contemporary in those days.

Miss Elizabeth Chant arrived in Wilmington in 1922 and opened her studio and began to teach. A lot of people were interested in the arts like me: young and very naive and unknowledgeable. But she also organized, or got

Claude Howell relaxes in his studio.

the nice women in Wilmington to organize, around 1923, the Wilmington Artists' League. And they had meetings; and they put on exhibitions — not just of their work because women of Wilmington had frequently done that — they brought in exhibitions.

One of the first ones that I remember was in the parish house of St. James Church. It had just been built and that was in 1923. Well, this really sort of opened the eyes of a lot of people in Wilmington — mainly women — to the value of the arts.

There also was this to be considered — we pooh-pooh it today, but I think it's one of the greatest influences on culture in Wilmington — the women's clubs. The North Carolina Sorosis, which was organized in Wilmington, had an annual exhibition. And several times — it was always statewide — the state show was in Wilmington. Judges would come down. It was a juried show. And this was very exciting to local people who were studying art.

Finally, after many, many tries, several of us were able to get in the show. Sometimes, they were held at the beach in the summertime at the Ocean Terrace Hotel, but generally they were held in their Sorosis clubhouse, which was next door to the City Hall. It's now torn down, and it's the parking lot of Thalian Hall. It was a great big brick building with white columns in the front.

A lot of the shows were not too good, but at least it was original art and was an attempt. Sorosis also had monthly lectures, and they had an art department. They would have lectures on the old masters; they had lectures on every conceivable subject. Not so much Matisse and Picasso and

Cezanne, they were almost unknown names in those days.

Wilmington was terribly isolated, which, of course, was and still is its greatest virtue. Very few people knew about Wilmington in those days. The people of the state were doing their own thing. They paid no attention to Wilmington; Wilmington paid no attention to the state. So, we always felt that we lived in the state of New Hanover, rather than the state of North Carolina. When you crossed the river, you came into the then-known world, but Wilmington was an unknown place.

I wish that it could stay that way and still continue to grow and be a good place. It's being discovered now. We have lots of new people — very cultured people — who are used to big cities and big museums, and they are volunteering in St. John's, which is quite active nowadays.

For a long time, we had only isolated exhibitions. One of Miss Chant's students was Ethel Williams, whose father ran Belk-Williams, which is now Belk-Beery department store. Bill Beery began working there, and when Mr. Williams retired, he bought him out.

Ethel went to Harvard and studied museum management, and she came back to Wilmington imbued with the idea of having a museum in Wilmington. This was around 1938, and it was during the heyday of Miss Chant. And Miss Chant was probably responsible for instilling this little bee in her bonnet. Well, Ethel decided to get a whole group of us together, which she did, and she decided to run a membership campaign. Our goal was $500 to open the museum. We didn't raise it. We couldn't get quite enough interest; but we opened the museum anyway.

This was during the time of the WPA and the PWAP. The government agreed that they would pay the salaries of the workers to operate the museum if we could pay the utilities and the rent. The city paid for the utilities; it wasn't very much. We opened in the old Williams Mortuary on Princess Street between Second and Third. Because it was a mortuary, nobody would rent it, so we got it cheap. It was a wonderful building, a three-story building. That, too, has been torn down.

Well, we opened on Halloween night, and I think it was 1938 with a loaned exhibition of work from the Metropolitan Museum of Art. It was exciting. We also had loaned exhibitions from the Museum of Modern Art. We showed Picasso, we showed Matisse, we showed Cezanne, we showed all the modern American painters. It was highly successful from the standpoint of attendance. We never had any money, but we had changing exhibitions once a month. Also, during this time, it was so successful we had an extension gallery at Wrightsville Beach in the Ocean Terrace Hotel, and in the summer, when tourists were here, we had the annual Wilmington Artists Association exhibition. This, too, was a juried show. This went on from 1938 to, I think, 1941.

You know what happened in 1941: Pearl Harbor. Well, immediately we had Camp Davis — we had Camp Davis even before Pearl Harbor — but we had soldiers everywhere. The money that the city gave to us was taken away and given to the USO.

The WPA folded. It was over. That was all of Roosevelt's rehabilitation program. So, that meant we didn't have any staff, and we didn't have any utilities. We couldn't raise enough money and, in 1941 we had to close. But, it didn't die because, if you've ever read Crockett Williams *Art in New Hanover County*, which is a very good book by the way, Crockett wrote that culture in Wilmington is like a phoenix. It dies down, and then, from the ashes, it springs up again. This has been going on since the 1700s. We've had innumerable organizations. This time, in the 1990s, we think we've beaten the phoenix because art seems to be here to stay. Certainly, St. John's is a thriving organization. We don't have very much money, but it has community support. And I don't think they would let it close.

Well, you have the museum closing in 1941. What happened then? Nothing. There was nothing in Wilmington for nearly 10 years. No concerts. Because of the war and the Depression, community concerts were nonexistent. There was no theatre. Thalian Hall was closed; the plays were put on by the Thalians in the high school auditorium, which wasn't very conducive to good theatre. We had a restoration of Thalian Hall toward the end of that period; it opened and has been open ever since, except during the more recent renovation. I have lived through, I think, four renovations of Thalian Hall. Of course, each time it is better, but always, it's a little different and historians sometimes quibble about that; but it is a more useable theatre.

It's strange that in the last several decades the arts — and I say the arts meaning music, theatre and art itself — have flourished. There seems to be an awakening everywhere.

During the late 1930s during the time of the Wilmington Museum of Art, the North Carolina Museum was putting on the Annual Exhibition of North Carolina Artists. Frequently, a Wilmington artist would win the prize, and there were more from Wilmington in that show than any other city in the state, including Chapel Hill, Raleigh, Winston-Salem and Durham. Well, during the period when the museum here closed and we sort of went into a deep sleep, Winston-Salem became the center of the arts in this state, and there was very little here.

I always would have to exhibit other places; I couldn't exhibit in Wilmington. There was a movement by people here, all this time, to try to get a gallery or museum started. The first step was when Hester Donnelly and Virginia McQueen opened the artists gallery on Post Office Alley. This lasted a number of years and had changing monthly exhibitions, primarily of local people. Occasionally they would import someone, and there were several historical shows that were very exciting. One was portraits before the Civil War from Wilmington homes. That was a good show.

Now, the gallery foundered at the end, and it was just at this time that Guy Faulkner and Jimmy McCoy were running the St. John's Tavern in the old St. John's Lodge on Orange Street. Well, Jimmy died. His brother, Henry, who didn't live in Wilmington, offered to give the building to an organization here with a 99-year lease if they would open a gallery. So, Hester Donnelly and a great many other people got together and formed an organization called St. John's Organization so that they could accept this gift. Later on, Henry gave the building outright to Wilmington in memory of his brother.

That's how St. John's got started, but it took a long time to get it going. It opened in 1953; it recently celebrated its fortieth birthday That, at last, gave Wilmington artists a place to exhibit. But it wasn't all sweetness and light because, in the beginning, they had only amateurs running the gallery, and that made a lot of professionals mad, including me. And then, they got a professional, and they decided that they needed to import shows. This made a lot of the would-be artists in Wilmington furious because they only wanted a place to exhibit their own work.

So, we had that fight to overcome; but it has weathered all these storms. And now the art of painting seems to be flourishing in this community."

Inside
Places of Worship

Stand on the corner of Market and Third Streets in downtown Wilmington and notice the surprising number of churches that dominate the immediate scene. These are only a few of the many churches and temples in Wilmington. New Hanover and adjacent counties are also full of houses of worship.

As these buildings signify, worship is woven inextricably into the historical and social fabric of life in the Cape Fear area. Since the middle of the 18th century, religion has been a constant factor in the spiritual and physical development of the region.

There are more than 200 churches in the Greater Wilmington area. Much to the delight of the visitor who appreciates fine architecture and interesting history, some of these houses of worship are among the most fascinating structures on the various historic tours. Their continued function as contemporary sites of worship makes visiting these places a special experience.

As would be expected in a Southern city, the dominant religious affiliation is Baptist, and nearly a quarter of Wilmington's churches house some form of Baptist faith. Since the Baptists are a multifaceted denomination unto themselves, there are ample representations of Southern Baptist, Free Will, Missionary, Grace, and Independent congregations.

The second largest denomination is Presbyterian with 14 churches in New Hanover County; the United Methodists follow closely with 13 churches.

Religions practiced in Wilmington include Jewish, AME, AME Zion, Mormon, Nation of Islam, Lutheran, Unitarian, Baha'i, Eckankar, Episcopal, Roman Catholic, Unity, Metropolitan, Wesleyan and others.

Wilmington's port city orientation allows for considerably more religious diversity than many Southern cities. You will find extremely conservative, middle-of-the-road, and very liberal doctrines practiced within the various Wilmington houses of worship. There is a noticeably high level of tolerance of one religion for the other, and nothing in the area's history suggests so much as a twinge of discomfort within one denomination for another. Actually, it has been common for very different denominations to be supportive of each other.

Something historically interesting about Wilmington churches is that they were racially integrated before the Civil War; now they are largely segregated along racial lines.

The integration that initially existed was within the context of mid-19th century mores. While Black people were relegated to the balconies or special sections of churches, it was understood for a very long time that worship was equally important for both races. Both slaves and free Blacks attended all area churches. At the end of the Civil War, Black congregations split from white-controlled churches and built their own separate church communities, often with the support of the white community.

The visitor can expect to be welcomed into churches throughout the area, and the would-be resident is virtually guaranteed a suitable spiritual home among the diverse choices.

Vacationers who choose to attend services can easily find listings in the Southern Bell Yellow Pages and call for directions and information. For the most part, church congregations "dress" for Sunday and you may feel more comfortable wearing traditional Sunday best at many mainstream churches, particularly those located in downtown Wilmington. God surely doesn't mind you in your flipflops and T-shirt, but you might feel a bit out of place in most churches and may want to pack a dress or suit if you plan to include worship in your vacation plans.

However, it has been mentioned to this insider that churches across the area may generally agree with remarks made by a parishioner from St. James Episcopal: "Oh, we don't mind how they're dressed as long as they come. In fact, when we see them in their vacation clothes, that lets us know they're from out of town and it gives us a chance to welcome them."

New residents with chosen denominations and affiliations must simply consult the phone book to select a church or temple. The larger churches list service times in the yellow pages, as well as regular programs.

Since it would be impossible to list every church in this guide, we've selected those that are large, architecturally or historically significant, and conveniently located. The history of churches in the Cape Fear area is more than enough to fill several books. If you want to know more, drop by the North Carolina Room at the New Hanover County Public Library in downtown Wilmington.

Baptist

FIRST BAPTIST CHURCH
529 N. 5th St.
Wilmington 28401   763-2647

The congregation of the tallest

church in Wilmington (with a spire of 197 feet) was organized in 1808. Construction began on the building, a Gothic Revival brick structure, in 1860 but was not completed until 1870 because of the Civil War. In 1890, this church installed the first power-driven pipe organ. Since this was the first Baptist church in the region, it was the mother church of many other Baptist churches in Wilmington.

GRACE BAPTIST CHURCH

1401 N. College Rd.
Wilmington 28405   *799-6442*

This is an Independent Southern Baptist Church established in 1953. Approximately 1,000 members attend this church, which is conveniently located for visitors on the I-40 entrance into Wilmington. The church has a Bus Ministry that provides transportation for people throughout the area. Grace Baptist Church is the home of the Wilmington Christian Academy, the largest private school (K-12) in the region.

PINE VALLEY BAPTIST CHURCH

3940 Shipyard Blvd.
Wilmington 28403   *791-1949*

Pine Valley Baptist was originally named Tabernacle Baptist, and it was located downtown. With the 1960s exodus to the suburbs, Pine Valley Baptist Church was established at the corner of Partridge and Shipyard Boulevard The initial building was completed in 1961 and has had several changes. A $500,000 renovation was just completed in 1993. There were 14 charter members in 1961; there are approximately 1,000 members today.

WINTER PARK BAPTIST CHURCH

4700 Wrightsville Ave.
Wilmington 28403   *792-4725*

This church was originally a mission Sunday school of First Baptist Church. It was far out in the suburbs in 1911, 4 miles from downtown, when it became a church in its own right. It opened along the north and south sides of the Wilmington-Wrightsville Beach railway line when Winter Park, a planned residential development created by developer Hugh McRae, had 124 residential lots. The initial church membership was 37; today's membership exceeds 1,600.

LONG LEAF BAPTIST

317 Shipyard Blvd.
Wilmington 28412   *763-2479*

Originally a mission of Sunset Park Baptist Church, this church had its beginnings in a neighborhood of shipbuilders during World War II. The church was established in 1944 on a then-sandy path in the woods: Shipyard Boulevard. Now serving approximately 500 members, the church also broadcasts its services on WWAY-TV 3 on Sunday mornings.

Presbyterian

FIRST PRESBYTERIAN CHURCH

125 S. Third St.
Wilmington 28401   *762-6688*

The congregation was organized as early as 1760. Rev. Joseph R. Wilson was pastor of this church from 1874 until 1885. His son, Thomas Woodrow Wilson, grew up to become President of the United States. The building, a blending of Gothic,

Renaissance and Tudor styles executed in stone, is the fourth home to the church. The previous three burned down. The last sanctuary burned on December 31, 1925.

CHESTNUT STREET
UNITED PRESBYTERIAN CHURCH
710 1/2 N. Sixth St.
Wilmington 28401   *762-1074*

This church was originally a mission chapel of First Presbyterian Church. Fourteen people withdrew to form a new congregation in 1858. The chapel was surrendered by the mother church to the new, Black congregation which purchased it from Second Presbyterian in 1867. It has served a Black congregation since that time.

LITTLE CHAPEL ON THE BOARDWALK
N. Lumina and W. Fayetteville St.
Wrightsville Beach 28415   *256-2819*

In 1905, Lumina, a beach pavilion and dance hall, was the home to a Sunday school for families that summered at the beach. St. James Episcopal and First Presbyterian donated funds to build a small church on Wrightsville Beach. A boardwalk ran behind the church before dredging took place in the 1930s. In 1952, this church had its first regular minister. Artist Claude Howell painted "The Miraculous Draft of Fishes" on the walls of the overflow room.

Methodist

FIFTH AVENUE
UNITED METHODIST CHURCH
409 S. Fifth Ave.
Wilmington 28401   *763-2621*

This Gothic cathedral, a brick structure, was built in 1889. Of congregational note, Charlie Jones Soong, whose daughter became the wife of Generalissimo Chaing Kai shek, converted to Christianity here in 1881.

GRACE UNITED METHODIST CHURCH
4th St. and Grace
Wilmington 28401   *762-5197*

A modified Gothic structure, this church has been through 5 sanctuaries since its organization in 1797. Four sanctuaries burned. The newest one was constructed in 1950. The remains of West Indies missionary William Meredith, the founder of Methodism in Wilmington, rest under the alter.

TRINITY METHODIST CHURCH
1403 Market St.
Wilmington 28401   *762-3316*

In 1889, some members of Grace and Fifth Avenue Methodist Churches met to organize a Sunday school in the remote eastern section of Wilmington near Eighth Street. At that time, there was little development beyond Thirteenth Street. In 1891, the mission was recognized as

Insiders' Tips

Speed limits are enforced strictly in most beach communities. So, don't hurry to get where you're going.

the Market Street Methodist Episcopal Church. In 1920, work began on a new building at Fourteenth and Market beside New Hanover High School. Both the school and the church were built in the Neoclassical Revival style, designed by the same architect and constructed simultaneously. The church was named Trinity Methodist and the opening ceremony was on Easter Day, 1922. Church membership is approximately 700; the average size of the Sunday congregation is 200.

Catholic

SAINT MARY'S ROMAN CATHOLIC CHURCH
412 Ann St.
Wilmington 28401   762-5491

Construction began on this Spanish Baroque style building in 1908 and was completed in 1911. The brick and tile building is built on the plan of a Greek cross with a high dome over the crossing. Numerous historical writers have referred to it as a major architectural creation. A coin given by Maria Anna Jones, the first black Catholic in North Carolina, is placed inside the cornerstone. Rosa Greenhow, a Confederate spy, was a member of the congregation.

ST. THERESE CATHOLIC CHURCH
209 S. Lumina Ave.
Wrightsville Beach 28415   256-2471

In 1895, two oceanfront lots were donated by John Michael Corbett, an Irish-American merchant from Wilmington, for a church that would become known as Saint Mary By The Sea. Because it was unheated, the few native Catholics attended winter masses in a private home on Harbor Island. In 1944, Bishop Eugene McGuinness dedicated a new church under the title of Saint Therese, as requested by the donor, Countess Kathleen Price of Greensboro. Hurricane Hazel destroyed most of the church, but it was rebuilt in 1955. This church by the sea serves 300 registered families in the parish.

Episcopal

ST. JAMES EPISCOPAL CHURCH
25 S. Third St.
Wilmington 28401   763-1628

Created by an Act of the General Assembly in 1729, this parish covered all of New Hanover County. The cornerstone was laid in 1751. In 1781 the church was stripped and used as a blockhouse, a hospital and a riding school for the cavalry. When the British evacuated Wilmington after the Revolutionary War, they took all of the church records, and efforts to retrieve them have all failed. During the Civil War, the church was made into a hospital by Union troops when its rector refused to offer prayers for President Lincoln. The church is the home to "Ecce Homo," a painting taken from a Spanish ship blown up during an attack on Brunswick Town across the river in 1747. The church was designed by Thomas U. Walter, a Philadelphia architect best known for his cast-iron dome on the U.S. Capitol.

ST. MARKS EPISCOPAL CHURCH
6th and Grace St.
Wilmington 28401   763-3210

This church was the first Episcopal church for Blacks. It was established in 1875. It was the first instance of a cornerstone being laid for a black Episcopal congregation in North Carolina. The church has enjoyed uninterrupted services since that time.

ST. ANDREWS ON-THE-SOUND EPISCOPAL CHURCH

101 Airlie Rd.
Wrightsville Beach 28415   256-3034

This church was built to serve summer residents of Greenville, Masonboro, and the Wrightsville Sound areas. It was placed at the junction of the Shell Road and rail line from Wilmington to Wrightsville Beach in 1924. The Spanish Colonial style church was an outgrowth of Mt. Lebanon Chapel, built in 1835. Incidentally, Mt. Lebanon Chapel is the oldest surviving church structure in New Hanover County. Built on the site of the former estate of Thomas H. Wright to provide seasonal services for the summer population, Mt. Lebanon Chapel was outgrown and fell into severe disrepair until 1974 when it was restored. At this date, it is a popular spot for weddings.

ST. PAUL'S EPISCOPAL CHURCH

16 N. 16th St.
Wilmington 28401   762-4578

Although the current building was finished in 1958, it follows the master plan established in 1925. Gothic forms dominate this church which is made of rough stucco, brick and stone exteriors. The congregation was formed in 1858; in 1914, it moved to its current site. This church is the home of the Wilmington Boy's

Choir, a group that has performed around the country, including performances at the Kennedy Performing Arts Center in Washington, D.C.

Jewish

TEMPLE OF ISRAEL

1 S. Fourth St.
Wilmington 28401   762-0000

Home to the first Jewish congregation in North Carolina, here Dr. Samuel Mendelsohn was rabbi for nearly half a century. The building, characterized by Moorish Revival architecture and small onion domes, was once shared for two years with neighboring Methodists when the Methodist church was destroyed in 1886. The Christian and Jewish communities in Wilmington have historically enjoyed pleasant relations. The Temple of Israel is a Reform congregation.

B'NAI ISRAEL SYNAGOGUE

2601 Chestnut St.
Wilmington 28405   762-1117

This onetime Orthodox congregation is now conservative. The B'nai Israel Synagogue was the second (and only other) Jewish temple established in Wilmington. It is 85 years old.

AME (African Methodist Episcopal)

ST. STEPHEN AME CHURCH

Fifth St. and Red Cross St.
Wilmington 28401   762-9829

This congregation was formed in 1865 by a group that broke away from First Baptist Church. The present structure was built between

1880 and 1885. Construction was interrupted by several problems, including the earthquake of 1886. This is one of seven black congregations created after the freeing of slaves at the close of the Civil War. An interesting feature is a large swimming pool in the basement which is used for community programs.

Lutheran

ST. PAUL'S
EVANGELICAL LUTHERAN CHURCH
6th and Market Sts.
Wilmington 28401   *762-4882*

Germans arrived in Wilmington in the early 1800s. North Carolina's Lutheran Synod took note of a growing German population and sent two pastors, Bernheim and Linn, to organize the church in 1858. The congregation began worship services in 1861, the same year as the advent of the Civil War. The Gothic style building was temporarily occupied by Union troops during the war after the fall of Fort Fisher in January of 1865. The Bellamy Mansion served as Union headquarters, and the enlisted troops camped in St. Paul's churchyard. Horses were stabled in the unfinished church, and wooden furnishings were used as firewood. The smoke from the campfires blackened the steeple and exterior of the church. Although the congregation was discouraged, they completed the building in 1869. The original building burned in 1894 but was promptly replaced. There have been several additions and renovations through the years.

Greek Orthodox

ST. NICHOLAS
GREEK ORTHODOX CHURCH
608 S. College Rd.
Wilmington 28403   *392-4484*

Originally housed in a portion of what is now St. John's Museum of Art in downtown Wilmington, this church relocated in the late 1970s to the building formerly occupied by Grace Baptist Church on South College Road in the suburbs. There are 130 families consisting of more than 300 individuals in the congregation. Most of the families trace their origins to the Greek Isle of Icarus, and there is speculation that so many Greeks found their way to Wilmington because the landscape is reminiscent of their homeland. People in Wilmington are very familiar with this church because of the congregation's incredible authentic Greek food! The church holds a festival the second weekend of September and serves up delicious foods (including pastries), Greek dancing, and crafts.

Inside
Service Directory

Whether you're a visitor or a new resident, you will find service information readily available. The area has the usual reliable information sources in several comprehensive phone books, two of which directly serve Wilmington. Much information is also available in a crush of printed matter lining brochure racks all around the area.

Vehicle Registration

New residents are required to have North Carolina tags on their vehicles within 30 days of establishing residency. The first step in this process is to procure car insurance through a company licensed in North Carolina. The next step is getting a North Carolina title, which costs $35. The minimum cost of registration, a onetime cost per vehicle, is $95, and a tag costs $20 each year. The registration cost is figured on 3 percent of the amount listed on the bill of sale or the assigned value of the car. In order to get a title and tag, newcomers must go in person to the appropriate office and take their previous out-of-state title, proof of insurance and policy number and be prepared to state vehicle mileage. No deviation from these requirements is acceptable. The folks

behind the counter do not tolerate excuses or explanations about why you may not have a necessary document. No documentation — no tag. For information call 763-6752.

Something important to know for North Carolinians who make an in-state move is that your annual tag renewal notice will not be forwarded to your new address. Perfectly law-abiding newcomers have had intimate experience with the oversight that can be caused when one doesn't pay attention to an expired sticker. Local law enforcement officials will bring it to your attention and tell you that it happens to a lot of people who move. Armed with title and tag, your car now qualifies for auto inspection. Within 10 days of being registered, your car has to be inspected at a service station or auto repair center that offers N.C. Inspection Station services. It is your responsibility to notice the four-inch high number that indicates the expiration date on your sticker, and make yearly arrangements to have this procedure done before this date.

Drivers Licenses

You are required to obtain a North Carolina license within 30 days of establishing residency. In-state newcomers must report a change of address within 60 days. Out-of-state newcomers must take their current license, a completed DL 123 form, proof of insurance and proof of residency. A written examination, as well as a vision test, must be passed. If your driving record is questionable, you may also need to take an on-the-road test. The fee for a four-year license is $10 CASH. (No checks, no credit cards; take real money because that's all they'll take.) The license must be renewed every four years in the month of your birthday, and you will receive notification by mail.

New Hanover County offices are located at 1 Station Road, 350-2005, and 2390 B-5 Carolina Beach Road at South Square Plaza, 251-5747. There are also convenient Express offices around Wilmington, such as Eckerd Drugs at Hanover Center on Oleander Drive. Check your local phone book for the addresses of offices in Pender and Brunswick counties.

Special Laws

Wear your seatbelt, or be prepared to pay a big fine. North Carolina has recently beefed up its efforts to get people to wear their seatbelts through a Click-It or Ticket program that has officers actively watching to be sure you and your passengers are properly restrained. Children under 3 must ride in crash-tested car seats. Children up to 6 must be in car seats or seatbelts, no matter where they sit in the car. No sitting on daddy's knee is allowed.

Random stop points are set up around the area.

If it's raining, the law requires that you turn on your full headlights. Motorcyclists are required to wear helmets and burn headlights at all times without exception.

School Registration

Students transferring into the New Hanover County School System must take a certified birth certificate, proof of address and immunization records to the Board of Education, 1802 S. 15th Street, Wilmington, N.C. 28401, 763-5431. The county and city have a merged system. For information about other systems consult the Schools and Education chapter in this guide.

Voter Registration

This is a community that takes the democratic process seriously, and you'll quickly discover that Cape Fear people are actively involved in local government. Register to vote by going to any branch of the County library or the Board of Elections Office, 24 North Third Street, Wilmington, 28401, 341-4060. You must be at least 18, be a permanent legal resident of the state and precinct for at least 30 days before an election. Take identification, such as a driver's license, Social Security card, passport, or birth certificate that bears your full legal name in order to register. You also have to take proof of your current address, something that shows you are a resident.

Community Information

The Greater Wilmington Chamber of Commerce, located beside the Coast Line Inn on Nutt Street, 762-2611, is a great resource for area information on housing, attractions, special events, retirement options, business and manufacturing and much more. Cheerful folks, the staff at the Chamber of Commerce is genuinely pleased to help you find whatever information you may need.

The Cape Fear Coast Convention and Visitors Bureau, 24 North Third Street, Room 101, 341-4060, also offers an abundance of helpful assistance and racks of written information. There is also a video to acquaint you with the area.

There is no better single resource for community information than the New Hanover County Public Library. The main branch, 201 Chestnut Street, 28401, 341-4390, has an extensive collection of information about the region and expert reference librarians to aid you in your search. The North Carolina Room is jammed with books and documents related to the history of Wilmington and the Cape Fear region. The extremely knowledgeable staff is eager to assist.

Emergency Phone Numbers

Just as in the rest of the country, dialing 911 is the way to reach law enforcement assistance or emergency medical care.

COAST GUARD

For search and rescue, boating accidents, or any life-threatening situation, call the Wrightsville Beach Station, 256-3469.

All initial radio calls to the Coast Guard for emergency assistance should be made on channel 16/158.8 mHz. To report an oil pollution incident, call (800) 424-8802.

COUNTY SHERIFF'S OFFICES

New Hanover County	341-4200
Onslow County (Northern Topsail Island)	
	455-9119
Pender County	259-1212
Brunswick County	253-4321

FIRE DEPARTMENTS OR RESCUE SQUADS

Consult the inside front cover of your local phone book to note emergency numbers. Most communities have the 911 number available for summoning help in all emergency situations.

Wilmington	341-7845
Wrightsville Beach	256-7912
Carolina Beach	458-8208
Burgaw	259-1212
Southport	457-7911
Shallotte	754-6262
Castle Hayne	911
Hampstead	270-3322
Acme - Delco - Riegelwood	655-2542

POLICE DEPARTMENTS

Wilmington	343-3600
Wrightsville Beach	256-7911
Carolina Beach	458-8208
Topsail Beach	328-4851
Surf City	328-7711
North Topsail Beach	328-0042
Caswell Beach	278-5595
Yaupon Beach	278-9242
Long Beach	278-5595
Holden Beach	842-6707

Ocean Isle Beach	579-2166
Sunset Beach	579-2151
Southport	457-7911

Bald Head Island: Consult information in your home rental packet for security services.

OTHER NUMBERS

Alcoholics Anonymous	762-1230
Crisis Line (teenagers)	(800)672-2903
Federal Bureau of Investigation (FBI)	
	762-9389
Health Department:	343-6500
Mental Heath Center	251-6640
Rape Crisis (Wilmington)	341-5799
Domestic Violence/Rape Crisis	
(Brunswick Co.)	754-5856
Social Services	341-4700

Animal Services

HOSPITALS
HANOVER
REGIONAL ANIMAL HOSPITAL

4711 Oleander Dr.	791-1446

A good avian vet is hard to find. Hanover Regional is probably the most trusted facility in the area for the treatment of birds. Doctors Huntsman, Thompson and Hohenwarter also provide across-the-board care for all other common domestic pets as well as reptiles and exotics. Formerly known as Treadwell Veterinary Hospital, Hanover is a member of the Animal Emergency Clinic of Wilmington and sees clients by appointment.

DINEEN ANIMAL HOSPITAL

1132 Floral Pkwy.	799-3400

Dineen maintains a 24-hour emergency service. Full medical and surgical services, as well as dentistry and grooming are offered in this animal hospital.

NEEDHAM ANIMAL HOSPITAL

1531 41st St.	799-2970

Needham maintains a 24-hour emergency service and is among the few hospitals that will care for injured wild animals.

BOARDING

If you need to board your pets over a holiday, be sure to reserve your place well in advance.

Meadowsweet Kennels, 791-6421, Greenville Loop Rd.

Eastwood Kennel, 452-2224, 218 Hillsdale Dr.

Nature of Things, 452-2225, 5746 Oleander Dr.

Sylvia's Pet Care Center, 799-2375, 26 New Bern Ave.

Automotive Service

DEALERS
BAUGHMAN TOYOTA

5640 Market St.	791-9735

BOB KING AUTO MALL

(Audi, GMC, Mercedes, Pontiac, Suzuki, Volkswagen)

515 New Centre Dr.	799-3520.

CAPE FEAR FORD

4222 Oleander Dr.	799-4060

D & E DODGE-AMC-JEEP/EAGLE

6220 Market St.	299-4210

EVERHART NISSAN

College Rd. & Market St.	392-4300

JERRY PORTER LINCOLN MERCURY-ISUZU

5501 Market St.	791-9634

NEUWIRTH HYUNDAI

219 S. College Rd.	452-1992

Rippy
CADILLAC-OLDSMOBILE-MITSUBISHI
1020 Market St.   763-2421

WES HOWELL VOLVO & SAAB
4010 Market St.   763-1711

WILMINGTON HONDA
3302 Market St.   762-8460

AUTO REPAIRS
HOSPITAL AUTOMOTIVE
46 Covil Ave.
Wilmington   762-7553
This Mom 'n Pop operation has prided itself on quality repair at reasonable cost for 15 years. While they do excellent work on both foreign and domestic cars, they really shine on work performed on truck-type cars such as Chevy Blazers and Ford Broncos. Count on this repair service for a very high level of competence and a fair price.

COASTAL REBUILDERS
48 Covil Ave.
Wilmington   762-4335
These folks concentrate on electrical repairs to alternators, starters and regulators for foreign and domestic cars. Fast, good service, apparent knowledge and fair prices are part of this long-established Wilmington operation. They share a building with Hospital Automotive and, although the businesses are not related, they make a great combination for moments when a specialist and generalist are needed in the form of "shade-tree" mechanics.

AAMCO TRANSMISSIONS
4213 Oleander Dr.
Wilmington   799-1033
If you've got transmission worries, these are good people to know. They service imports, light trucks, vans and RVs. This unassuming little business is part of the world's largest transmission service.

RV REPAIRS
When it comes to RV repairs, most sales-service-rental establishments are not fitted to perform repairs to the chassis, which, in this context, applies to power train (engine, transmission, axles), generators, cooling systems, and brakes. For chassis repairs, a reliable automotive mechanic is needed. Two shops in Wilmington used and recommended by Howard RV Center are Bobby's Garage and Jerry's Garage.

BOBBY'S GARAGE
5815 Market St.
Wilmington   392-0466
Bobby's has made a name for itself for skilled repairs and computerized diagnoses on practically every kind of road vehicle, foreign and domestic. It is among the shops recommended by insiders for chassis repairs on RVs. The garage is located on the south-bound side of Market Street (Highway 17) about four miles from midtown Wilmington.

JERRY'S GARAGE
118 Middle Sound Loop Rd.
Wilmington   686-1053
Jerry's is capable of chassis repairs on RVs and automotive repairs in general. The garage is located

down a long driveway on Middle Sound Loop Road a bit more than 1/10 of a mile off U.S. Highway 17 at Ogden, 3.5 miles outside Wilmington. Watch for the lighted sign on the right side of the road. They are closed on Saturdays.

HOWARD'S RV CENTER
6811 Market St.
Wilmington   *791-5371*

The folks at Howard's are skilled at performing all interior and most exterior repairs, including fiberglass, plumbing, electrical and air conditioning. They install hitches and wireups, supply LP gas, parts and accessories and excel in sales and rentals. They do not perform chassis repairs.

TOMMY'S RV STORAGE AND SERVICE
1747 Ashe Little River Rd.
Ash   *287-3384*

Located about 10 miles north of Shallotte off Rt. 130 and 4 miles from Little River, Tommy's performs basic interior and exterior repairs, installs hitches and wiring and provides long-distance towing and storage. They do not perform repairs on power train, generators or fiberglass.

Bus and Taxi Service

Greyhound Bus Lines, 762-6627, is the only long-distance overland carrier serving Wilmington. The station is located at 210 Harnett Street, between 2nd and 3rd Streets.

There are plenty of taxi and limousine services to choose from in Wilmington. Many of them also serve to unlock cars for car-owners who have locked themselves out. The usual charge is $15.

Coastal Yellow Cab	762-3322
	762-4464
Port City Taxi, Inc.	762-1165
Affordable Affluence, Inc.	251-8999
Cape Fear Limousine Service	763-2102
Formal Limousine Service	395-1191
Prestige Limousine Service	399-4484

Car Wash Facilities

DETAIL PLUS APPEARANCE CENTER
145 S. College Rd.
Wilmington, 28403   *452-2338*

Located at Market Place Auto Center, this company will make your car look absolutely beautiful. All the minute details of restoring the finish and interior work, including upholstery and carpet shampooing, are performed at this detail center.

AUTO SPA CAR WASH
3835 Oleander Dr. and 325 S. College Rd.
Wilmington   *799-6511, 799-0070*

You can get your car washed by a crack team of washing experts and choose from a long list of special services in addition to basic washing. It's open 7 days a week.

Car Rentals

There is no shortage of car-rental companies on Cape Fear. There are national chains and independents. Several new-car dealerships also lease cars long-term.

Avis Rent A Car, New Hanover International Airport, Wilmington, 763-3346 or (800) 831-2847.

Budget Rent-A-Car, New Hanover International Airport, 762-8910. Budget is under the same ownership as Sears Car & Truck Rental, 762-0497.

Triangle Rental, 3111 Market St.,

Wilmington, 251-9812

Thrifty Car Rental, 3621 Market St., Wilmington, 763-1178.

A & A Auto Rental, Inc., 119 Village Rd., Shallotte, 754-8200 (Sundays and nights, 754-6139).

Government Offices

NEW HANOVER COUNTY MANAGER'S OFFICE
320 Chestnut St.
Wilmington, 28401   341-7184

HEALTH DEPARTMENT
2029 S. 17th St.
Wilmington, 28403   343-6500

DEPARTMENT OF SOCIAL SERVICES
1650 Greenfield St.
Wilmington, 28403   341-4700

BRUNSWICK COUNTY COUNTY MANAGER, COUNTY OFFICE
Shallotte   253-4331

PENDER COUNTY MANAGER'S OFFICE
Administration Building
Burgaw   259-1200

Laundromats

Coin laundries are adequate in the area, and you can choose the one that is most conveniently located. For cleanliness and gorgeous scenery, the **Wrightsville Beach Laundromat**, 84 S. Lumina Avenue, Wrightsville Beach, 256-2842, is a nice place to do an odious task. **Carolina Coin Laundry**, 952 S. Kerr Avenue, Wilmington, 799-7627, is another clean center where one can

shop and dine nearby while awaiting the cleaning process.

Libraries

NEW HANOVER COUNTY
Main Branch
201 Chestnut St. (Reference)   341-4390
Carolina Beach Library   458-5016
Myrtle Grove Library   341-4475
Plaza East Library   256-2173

Liquor Laws & ABC Stores

Don't you dare be less than 21 if you expect to buy liquor in the Alcohol Beverage Control stores in North Carolina. While wine and beer are sold in the grocery stores and convenience marts, hard stuff is only sold under the very watchful eye of the government. Don't drink and drive, don't allow anyone in your car to have an open container of alcohol, and be sensible in your use of liquor. For more information call the Alcohol Beverage Control Board, 523 S. 17th Street, Wilmington, 28401, 762-7611.

Media Information

NEWSPAPERS
THE WILMINGTON STAR-NEWS
1003 S. 17th St.   343-2000

The *Star-News* is the only major daily paper in the region. It is a New York Times-owned periodical that concentrates on the local scene as well as national and international news. It is also the oldest daily newspaper in North Carolina. One edition is published everyday, covering New Hanover, Bladen, Brunswick,

Columbus, Duplin and Pender counties as well as Jacksonville and Camp Lejeune. It is distributed throughout the Cape Fear region, and home delivery is available. Out-of-town subscribers can receive all editions or the Sunday *Star-News* only. Circulation is 52,000 daily and 64,000 on Sundays.

THE CHALLENGER
514 Princess St.
Wilmington   762-1337, (800)462-0738
The *Challenger* is a state-wide, minority-focused publication based in Wilmington and Fayetteville. Published weekly on Wednesdays, it is a subscription-based periodical with limited newsstand distribution.

THE WILMINGTON JOURNAL
412 S. 7th St.   762-5502
This weekly is the voice and mirror of the area's African-American community. Each Thursday it is available at news racks throughout the city and by subscription.

THE ISLAND GAZETTE
Pleasure Island Plaza B-4
Carolina Beach   458-8156
If you're looking for real estate on Pleasure Island, the *Gazette* is probably your best first source. It is a weekly published on Wednesdays and is available at newsstands throughout Pleasure Island. Mail subscriptions are available. Its focus is on southern New Hanover County with emphasis on Pleasure Island and issues that affect it.

THE TOPSAIL VOICE
Hwy. 17
Hampstead   270-2944
This 2-year-old weekly, published on Wednesdays, is the largest news-

paper in the greater Topsail Island area. The *Voice* covers local politics, commerce and sports (often emphasizing fishing) throughout the region from Sneads Ferry south to Ogden. It includes classifieds and op-ed pages. With a circulation nearing 6,000, the *Voice* is a fast-growing periodical available by subscription and at racks and news boxes throughout its coverage area as well as at a few locations in Wilmington.

THE BRUNSWICK BEACON
4709 Main St.
Shallotte   754-6890
This weekly community newspaper, published on Thursdays, distinguishes itself by having won dozens of awards during the past decade for advertising and editorial content. It covers and distributes to all of Brunswick County, with particular emphasis on the southwestern portion of the coast. The *Beacon* is among the last of the small independents still produced and printed entirely at one location. About 13,000 copies are circulated each week to subscribers, retail outlets and news racks, and departments include real estate and classified listings.

THE STATE PORT PILOT
105 S. Howe St.
Southport   457-4568
Covering the six towns in the Southport-Oak Island sphere, this weekly newspaper concentrates on community perspectives, carrying news on government, society and sports. With a circulation averaging more than 7,000, the *Pilot* includes a classifieds section and is available by subscription and at news racks

throughout its coverage area every Wednesday.

ENTERTAINMENT MAGAZINES
THE BEAT
3175 Wrightsville Ave.
Wilmington   395-5622

The only magazine on the Cape Fear coast dedicated exclusively to music, *The Beat* is an eclectic mix of in-depth reviews, news and entertainment covering all styles from punk rock to classical art. Published monthly, it includes comprehensive listings of musical events, plus free classifieds for musicians. It is available free at clubs, restaurants, retail shops and visitors' information booths and by subscription.

ENCORE MAGAZINE
255 N. Front St., Wilmington   762-8899

Arts, entertainment, real estate, local sports (especially golf) and essays make up this free weekly published each Tuesday. Certainly the most widely distributed free entertainment periodical in the region, *Encore's* many highlights include festival and holiday roundups, recipes, attractions, personal ads, and Chuck Shepherd's syndicated "News of the Weird" column. *Encore* is available at news racks practically everywhere in Wilmington, at many retail outlets elsewhere and by subscription.

TRAVELHOST MAGAZINE
912 Twisted Oak Pl.
Wilmington   256-0067

This magazine is placed in hotels around the area and offers good information for places to shop, dine, and explore the many attractions of the Cape Fear area.

TELEVISION STATIONS
WECT-TV 6, NBC
322 Shipyard Blvd.
Wilmington, N.C. 28403   791-6681

WWAY-TV 3, ABC
615 N. Front St.
Wilmington, N.C. 28401   762-8581

WJKA-TV 26, CBS
1926 Oleander Dr.
Wilmington, N.C. 28403   343-8826

WUNC-TV 39 Center for Public Television
No local address or number is available since this station emanates from Chapel Hill.

RADIO STATIONS
WAAV 980 AM
211 N. 2nd St.   251-9228

This news/talk station features Rush Limbaugh and various talk shows throughout the day and evening.

WCCA 106.3 FM
3084 Frontage Rd., Shallotte   754-8948

Beach music and golden oldies comprise the music. Fishing reports are a part of the daily offerings of this small station.

WGNI 102.7 FM
1890 Dawson St.   763-6511

Top 40 dominates this popular Wilmington station that also dominates the radio market.

WHQR 93.1 FM
1026 Greenfield St.   343-1640

Owned by Friends of Public Radio, WHQR airs art music (classical, jazz), blues, New Age and folk music, plus a wide array of news and talk features syndicated by National Public Radio and American Public Radio.

WMNX 97.3 FM

1890 Dawson St.   763-6511

"Coast 97" is the major urban contemporary format in the Wilmington market.

WSFX 107 FM

N. Front St.   251-0001

"Surf 107" adheres to a mainstream rock format. If you came of age in the late '60s and early '70s, look to this station for a flash to the past.

WWQQ 101.3 FM

721 Market St.   763-9977

"Today's hot country favorites" is the tag line for this station, the older of Wilmington's two county music formats.

This is the most powerful station in the Cape Fear area. With country music's wide appeal, there are many closet country listeners who wouldn't change their dial from this setting.

Zip Codes

Bald Head Island:	28461
Boiling Spring Lakes:	28461
Calabash:	28467
Carolina Beach:	28428
Hampstead:	28443
Holden Beach:	28462
Holly Ridge:	28445
Kure Beach:	28449
Oak Island (Caswell,	
Yaupon, Long beaches):	28465
Ocean Isle Beach:	28469
Ogden:	28405
Shallotte:	28459
Southport:	28461
Sunset Beach:	28468
Surf City:	28445
Topsail Beach:	28445
Wilmington:	28401 - 28412
Winnabow:	28479
Wrightsville Beach:	28480

Rental Services

Beach Fun Rentals, 842-9600, is on Holden Beach Road Southwest, on the mainland side of the bridge.

General Rental, 6816 Gordon Road, Wilmington, 28405, 395-1620 rents lawn and garden, party and banquet and construction supplies, tents and more.

Holden Beach Rental Services, 842-6485, 108 Jordan Boulevard, is on the island.

Rent America, rent-to-own appliances, offers TVs, furniture and stereos, 4208 Oleander Dr., Wilmington, 28403, 799-7368.

Storm & Hurricane Information

Disaster Preparedness Information: 341-4123

American Red Cross: 762-2683

New Hanover County Department of Emergency Management (non-emergency): 341-4300

Brunswick County Department of Emergency Management (non-emergency): 253-4376

Hurricanes are notoriously capricious and infamously damaging. Since 1990, Wilmington has been spared direct hits at least twice when hurricanes were mere hours from landfall. But, they aren't the only storms to beware of on Cape Fear. The March storm of 1993 had a barometric pressure lower than Hurricane Hugo, which devastated

Charleston, SC, in 1989. Nonetheless, the havoc wreaked by Hazel in 1954, Diana in 1984, Cape Fear's worst recent storm, and Hugo, which damaged houses on the South Brunswick Islands, looms large in the minds of coastal Carolinians. Hurricane Hazel had slammed Oak Island head-on with 150-mph winds and a 17-foot storm surge (high seas) and essentially razed every building in Long Beach before killing 95 people along its swath through the mid-Atlantic states. Coastal inhabitants take the motto "Be prepared" extremely seriously.

The first element of preparedness is knowing what the weather forecasters are talking about. Unwelcome visitations by hurricanes are likely from June 1 through Nov. 30. The hurricane itself is a cyclone in which maximum sustained surface winds exceed 74 mph (63 knots) blowing counterclockwise around a calm center of low pressure called the "eye." Five categories have been devised to express the damaging force of a hurricane. This and other useful information about tracking hurricanes is available in most area telephone directories. All categories are damaging, and when winds exceed 100 mph, damage by wind and water is always severe.

The National Hurricane Center in Coral Gables, Florida, issues the following notices regarding a hurricane's strength and direction as required. Monitoring radio or TV coverage of a storm's progress is essential.

A **hurricane watch** is issued when hurricane conditions are likely within the next 36 hours at specified areas of high risk.

A **hurricane warning** is issued when hurricane-force winds, high water and rough seas are expected within 24 hours or less at a specified area. Residents in that area must be prepared to evacuate on notice.

Be prepared. Maintain a hurricane evacuation kit at all times within your household. Inspect it before each hurricane season. Make sure lamps, camp stoves, flashlights, etc., are in good working order. The kit should include enough nonperishable food to feed each family member for three days (don't forget the can-opener), personal medications and prescriptions, first aid kit, battery-operated radio and flashlight, extra batteries, drinking water (1 gallon per person per day), blankets (or sleeping bags) and pillows, road maps, sanitary supplies, change of clothing, entertainment (books, cards, toys), baby food and diapers, if applicable. These supplies will be invaluable if you need to use a public shelter until the danger has passed. Also consider preparing an

There are two drawbridges on the Cape Fear River from Highway 421 into Wilmington. The most southern one, the Cape Fear Memorial Bridge, has been known to get stuck on occasion.

Insiders' Tips

inventory of your property ahead of time to expedite insurance settlements.

From the moment a tropical storm has been upgraded to a hurricane, if not sooner, keep your car fueled in case of evacuation. Don't wait for a storm to shop for emergency supplies; they quickly disappear from store shelves immediately upon the issuance of a hurricane watch. Fill jugs and even bath tubs with water in advance of a storm in case water service is cut off or the water supply is contaminated. Secure all outdoor objects—yard tools, garbage cans, signs, patio and deck furniture, etc. — to prevent them from becoming deadly missiles in high wind. Owners of larger boats generally run their craft inland well in advance of a hurricane. Leave yourself plenty of time to navigate the crowded waterways. Fasten small craft securely.

Listen to radio and TV reports for announcements about **shelters** and their locations, unless you intend to use a safely located hotel. Emergency Management officials set up shelters in the larger public schools first, opening others as needed. Alcoholic beverages, pets and weapons are forbidden in shelters.

If time allows, arrange with your vet or kennel to board your **pets**. If evacuating, ask friends or relatives who live inland to care for them. No pets are allowed at shelters, but Animal Control officers there will receive pets on a first-come basis. As a last resort, leave your pets home with enough food and water to sustain them for at least three days.

If you are not evacuated, stay indoors if your home is sturdy and on high ground. Leave low-lying areas and mobile homes immediately. Motor homes should be securely anchored. Before evacuating, shut off water and electricity, and lock up. Give yourself plenty of time to evacuate to avoid being marooned at home or in a car. Most local beach communities are linked to the mainland by only one bridge.

During the storm, stay indoors and away from windows. Avoid using electrical appliances.

After a storm, each county sends in damage assessment teams to ascertain whether it is safe for residents to reenter. Reentry passes are required by residents to reenter their communities and homes. Sometimes reentry is restricted to daylight hours. Each municipality works a little differently in distributing passes to property owners. Some municipalities charge a fee. Don't wait for a storm warning to find out how to get a reentry pass. Call your local town hall or emergency management office well in advance of hurricane season, and find out what their procedure is. Avoid using candles for lighting; water may be unavailable for fire prevention. Do not drink piped-in water until authorities give clearance; supplies may be contaminated.

Tornadoes also have been known in the Carolinas (averaging 14 per year statewide). They may occur at any time of year and any time of day, but the peak season is March through June, and peak hours are 3 to 9 PM. They can travel extremely slowly or up to about 70 mph. Watches and warnings are also issued for tornadoes over radio and TV broadcasts. A tornado watch means tornadoes are possible. A warning means a tornado has been sighted. Tornadoes are generally associated with severe thunderstorm activity.

Many of the precautions used for hurricanes apply to tornadoes with some variations. In buildings, basements offer the best protection. Interior rooms or hallways are next safest places. Get under a sturdy piece of furniture. People in motor homes and automobiles are at greatest risk. If you're in a car, abandon it. Lie flat in the nearest ditch or depression. Flying debris causes most deaths and injuries during tornadoes.

1994 Tax Rates

Each town and county has its own property tax rate based on a $100 valuation.

Brunswick County	68.5 cents
Southport	72.5 cents
Sunset Beach	16.7 cents
Holden Beach	18.0 cents
Shallotte	47.0 cents
Pender County	89.6 cents
Topsail Island	34.0 cents
Surf City	45.0 cents
Burgaw	60.0 cents
New Hanover County	61.5 cents

Properties in Fire Districts outside of the city limits pay an additional tax of 25 cents.

Wilmington	58.0 cents
Wrightsville Beach	23.5 cents
Carolina Beach	44.0 cents
Kure Beach	39.0 cents

There is a 6 percent sales tax levied for purchases made in North Carolina.

Utility Services

ELECTRICITY

Wilmington, Boiling Spring Lakes and municipalities in New Hanover County are provided with electrical power by Carolina Power & Light (CP&L), (800)672-5911.

Topsail Island is provided electrical service by Jones-Onslow Electric Membership Corporation. They can be reached at all times and in emergencies at 353-1940 locally or (800)682-1515 when calling long distance.

On Oak Island (Caswell, Yaupon and Long beaches) and outside city limits in Brunswick County, service is provided by Brunswick Electric Membership Corporation, 457-9808.

In Southport, electrical power is served by the City of Southport, 457-7910 and by Brunswick Electric, listed above.

GAS

To arrange gas hookup throughout the Cape Fear region, contact North Carolina Natural Gas (NCNG), 763-3305. You will be asked to fill out an application in person at one of their offices (main office: 1321 S. 10th Street, Wilmington) and provide two forms of identification. If you are renting the property needing service, a deposit is required which will vary according to your location and the number and type of appliances to be used. No deposit is required of homeowners.

TELEPHONE

Southern Bell, a BellSouth company, is the largest provider of telephone service to residents of Wilmington, Pender County and portions of Brunswick County, including Southport and Oak Island. Residential service can be arranged by phone by calling 780-2355 locally or (800) 767-2355 when calling long distance. Costs that may or may not apply when establishing new service include an initial connection charge, installation work charge, a refundable deposit and advance payment. These costs depend on whether you have had service previously, whether there is existing equipment on the premises, whether you're a renter or homeowner and on your overall credit history.

Carolina Telephone, a Sprint company, 347-9011, provides telephone service to Onslow County, which includes the north half of Topsail Island.

Atlantic Telephone Membership Corp., 754-4211 or (800) 682-5309, provides telephone, voice mail and cable TV services to more than 22,000 resident members in Brunswick County.

The Cape Fear region is well-provided with voice mail, cellular and answering services with local offices based in Wilmington and Jacksonville, as well as telephone equipment dealers at several convenient locations. A wide array of vendors is listed in area yellow pages and directories.

WATER AND SEWER

In Wilmington, arrange water and sewer service directly through the city, 341-7884. Offices are open from 7 AM to 3:30 PM, and there is an emergency response capability, so you can call the same number at any time.

Surf City and North Topsail Beach are provided water and sewer by way of Surf City's municipal works. For service, call the Public Utilities office, 328-3921. The town of Topsail Beach is provided only water by the city. Service there can be arranged through the Town Hall, 328-5411. Residents in Topsail Beach rely on septic tanks for sewerage.

In South Brunswick, water and sewer services are provided by the respective towns: Caswell Beach, 278-5471; Yaupon Beach, 278-5024; Long Beach, 278-5011; Southport, 457-7910; Ocean Isle Beach, 579-2166; Holden Beach, 842-6488; Sunset Beach, 2579-2990.

TRASH/RECYCLING

In Wilmington, weekly trash and recycling pickup is provided by the city and can be arranged by calling 341-7875 during business hours. Carolina Beach residents can call 799-5256 for information. In Wilmington and Carolina Beach, residents place their recyclables (newspaper, aluminum and plastic containers, and glass) curbside. Where there is no pickup, residents are asked to take their recyclables to dropoffs, open 24-hours a day, at these locations:

Ogden Village Shopping Center Hwy. 17.

Monkey Junction and KMart, at the intersection of Hwy. 421 and Rt. 132.

Wrightsville Beach Recycling Center at the government complex, Causeway Dr.

Castle Hayne, near Hardees, Hwy. 117.

Trash pickup on Topsail Island is provided by the towns (see numbers for water and sewer above). There is a dropoff location for recyclables (newspaper, plastic and aluminum containers) in Surf City.

Trash pickup in Southport and Oak Island is provided by a private contractor. Check with the town or city hall in your community to arrange service (see the numbers listed above in Water and Sewer). The recycling program in Southport and Oak Island can arrange curbside pickup of newspaper, glass, plastic and aluminum containers. There are also dropoff locations:

Southport-Oak Island   457-9484
Hwy. 133.

Caswell Beach   278-5471
south side of Town Hall.

Long Beach   278-5011
48th St. SE, Monday-Friday.

Bald Head Island   457-9700
Bald Head Island Maintenance Dept. (This location is open 24 hours a day but only takes aluminum and glass.)

Western Union

Still the most practical way to send money anywhere, Western Union continues to provide telegram, mailgram, cablegram and opiniongram services. For information about these and for locations to pick up or send money transfers, call toll-free, (800)325-6000. Credit card transfers can be arranged by calling (800)225-5227. Spanish-speaking customers can call (800)325-4045. Offices are concentrated in the larger cities (six in Wilmington, eight in Jacksonville; also see the white pages for complete listings).

209 N. 2nd St.
Wilmington   762-1801

121 Moore St.
Southport   457-5494

Ford Enterprises
Hwy. 17 Bypass
Shallotte   754-6114

Calabash Insurance Agency
Hwy. 179
Calabash   579-5970

The nearest offices to Topsail Island are in Jacksonville: 101 Chaney Avenue   347-2217/3266.

LANDMARK
Real Estate, Inc.

Buyers and sellers have consistently chosen Landmark as their real estate company in Wilmington and Wrightsville Beach.

Landmark, in business over 30 years, has experienced phenomenal growth not only in listings and sales but we have expanded to our present staff of 52 sales agents, management and support personnel.

We have developed over 40 subdivisions and are currently working in 15 subdivisions with over 200 new homes in our inventory.

With two locations to serve you, one at Wrightsville Beach and one in Wilmington, we specialize in residential sales. As specialists in relocation, we offer a separate relocation department with 1-800 telephone numbers to assist our out of town buyers.

Come visit our new 8,600 square foot regional office building located at 803 South College Road.

527 Causeway Drive
Wrightsville Beach, NC 28480
(910) 256-3750
1-800-253-3630

803 South College Road
Wilmington, NC 28403
(910) 799-8855
1-800-554-8129

Inside
Real Estate

There's an insider joke that new-comers are required to get their real estate licenses when they move into the area. Real estate is one of the biggest businesses in the Cape Fear region. Although there are already more than 200 real estate offices and about 1,000 people with their licenses in the Greater Wilmington area (and this doesn't take into account Topsail Island to the north or the long string of Brunswick beaches to the south), people in this business can stay busy night and day.

There have been some important changes in the way real estate companies operate within North Carolina. Anyone contemplating a real estate transaction, whether buying or selling, needs to know this information. Previously, agents all represented the seller. Now agents may also represent the buyer. Since buyers have come to realize that agents can be wonderful resources for information, this allows buyers to be represented and protected to a much greater degree than was previously the case. A dual agency may also be created when buyer and seller are represented by the same broker-age firm. In any case, full disclosure is required so that all parties know who is working for whom. The best thing to do is ask your Realtor to explain how this works.

The Cape Fear area is limited to an approximately 180-degree radius of land. Unlike inland cities, where real estate sales are possible in all directions, one can't go very far east in this coastal community without landing in the Atlantic Ocean. This creates a scarcity of land. Conse-quently, land has a disproportion-ately high value in some areas. Local real estate company representatives report that as of 1993 it is very hard to find a 1/2-acre piece of land in any location that is less than $30,000. Prime lots can go for $150,000 and higher in some oceanfront locations.

These prices are likely to con-tinue to climb if the current trend holds. There has been a tremen-dous amount of positive publicity about the region in national and state publications during the past few years, so many people are be-coming acquainted with the area. Quite a few are deciding to make the move to Wilmington and the Cape Fear Coast. As demand continues to increase, prices continue to rise.

However, it is still remarkably af-fordable to buy a home in the Wilmington area compared to other regions of the country. Something particularly interesting about the real estate market for potential homebuyers is the extreme diversity in neighborhoods, housing and prices. There are new homes for as low as $70,000; there are truly vintage homes in need of repair for even less. At the top end, one may spend well into the millions for a fine home in an upscale, secluded neighborhood.

It would be impossible in this guide to write about every neighborhood because, even as this goes to press, new neighborhoods are sprouting all over the area. What follows is information about established neighborhoods, average prices and other general facts.

Neighborhoods

Downtown

If a personal, even intimate, neighborhood of homes that date from as early as the 1700s appeals to you, then downtown Wilmington is for you. This National Historic Registry neighborhood, as well as adjacent areas with the same architecture but without the designation at this point, create an intensely personal living environment.

Many of the homes date from the mid to late 1800s, as well as into the first quarter of the 20th century. There are stunning examples of Victorian, Italianate, Renaissance, Neo-Classical and Revivalist architecture. Homes in the area feature high ceilings, hardwood floors, fascinating detailing, front porches and all of the interesting characteristics one would expect in both the mansions and cottages of the district.

The neighborhood is home to upwardly mobile families, a host of artists (both struggling and successful), many singles, and, recently, quite a few children. Downtown is probably the melting pot of the area, home to the most diverse group of Wilmingtonians in the entire city.

While quite a few retired people live downtown, maintenance of the homes may not be appealing to older people. The homes were not built for energy-efficiency, and it takes a pile of money to convert one. Storm windows are subject to district approval. One will not find vinyl siding within the Historic District; in fact, it is not allowed as an improvement. This means the wood-sided homes require regular painting, so low maintenance is not a feature of downtown living.

If you are looking for history and charm, downtown is definitely the place to locate. Since relatively few homes come on the market in the more established center of the neighborhood, this suggests that the folks who live in the vintage homes are pleased with the environment and not put off by the maintenance procedures associated with century-old homes.

There are quite a few rules that apply to homes within the district. The exterior paint color comes under the auspices of the Historic District Commission. Changing the existing color of a home requires obtaining a Certificate of Appropriateness. People who have failed to follow this relatively simple (yet time consuming) procedure have found themselves in unhappy circumstances. One man who painted his home with a San Francisco palette

Photo: Scott Taylor

Bodysurfing at Wrightsville Beach.

(without seeking approval from the commission) had to stop painting in the middle of the job, and the house has stood partially painted for many years.

Within the district proper, most homes have been restored, but there are still handyman bargains to be had in the areas outside of the district. It takes a person with vision and guts to redo some of the architectural gems in these neighborhoods. The level of downtown neighborhood restoration is the most stable at the river and diminishes as you head east toward the ocean toward about Eighth Street.

The residential neighborhoods to the north of Market Street are generating high interest at this time and are seeing quality restoration efforts. The North Fourth Street Business District Project, a renewal effort supported in part by the City of Wilmington (as well as business owners and residents along this corridor) promises to open new options to people who want to live downtown. To the south, the natural boundary of the neighborhood is the Cape Fear Memorial Bridge. Quality restorative development is happening on South Second and Queen Streets, as well as Castle Street.

Downtown houses are hot in this market. Unless a house is outrageously overpriced, it moves relatively quickly because the downtown lifestyle appeals to a specific segment of the market that seems to watch and wait for opportunity. Houses average $150,000 in the district, but one may spend considerably more or much less. The general market is single family homes. There are also a few condominium developments and some opportunities to have a rental apartment within one's own home.

Two rediscovered neighborhoods are the Mansion District and nearby Carolina Heights. Both flank Market Street beyond 15th Street. These neighborhoods date from the 1920s. Architectural style varies. In

Photo: Scott Taylor

Weatherworn oaks dot the coastal landscape.

the Mansion District, one may certainly purchase a mansion-style home. In Carolina Heights, there are bungalows. This neighborhood, which begins roughly at 17th Street and continues to 23rd Street, has a lot of interesting housing opportunities. There are fixer-uppers; there are also fixed-up homes that are very reasonable in price.

Wilmington and New Hanover County Suburbs

Some of the venerable old neighborhoods are among the best places to live in Wilmington. Forest Hills is, without dispute, a fine address. This large and very stable neighborhood

was once a suburb of downtown. Today, it is a conveniently located older neighborhood of homes that date from as early as the 1920s. Well-maintained lawns, large setbacks, quietness and gorgeous live oaks are the hallmarks of this neighborhood. Lots of different kinds of folks live in Forest Hills, and it may well be one of the more diverse neighborhoods in the area in terms of the ages and family configurations of the homeowners.

As would be expected, there are relatively few resales in this neighborhood. There is diversity in square footage and architectural style, so there is diversity in price. One may find a home for as low as the $70s, and one may also spend several hun-

dred thousand here. The very attractive feature of this neighborhood is its proximity to shopping, services and the way the folks there keep their yards in manicured shape.

Perhaps the most active — or hot — part of the Greater Wilmington area right now is a neighborhood called Woodbury Forest. Averaging $179,000 to $240,000, homes in this spot for traditional nuclear families boast good construction, good schools, energy efficiency and interesting architecture. It is located just to the north of the intersection of 17th Street Extension on South College Road. The spot places the neighborhood within easy access to both downtown and the beaches.

Pine Valley, located near South College Road near Longleaf Mall, is about 30 years old as a development. It has attracted many Wilmingtonians to its quiet, pine tree-dotted blocks. A nearby golf course and clubhouse are easily accessible to people who want to live in a stable neighborhood that isn't necessarily exclusive in terms of price. Homes, largely brick ranches, range from $80,000 to more than $200,000.

Northchase, 2832 Northchase Parkway West, Wilmington, NC 28405, 799-5723, is a relatively new neighborhood located near Interstate 40 to the northeast of Wilmington. It is a convenient location for folks employed at nearby Corning and has the advantage for the corporate traveler of being only 3 miles from the airport. Homes range from about $70,000 to $235,000, and lots are available beginning at $20,000.

There are many patio home communities in the area. A dominant developer of these communities is Dallas Harris Real Estate. Local agents appreciate the good floor plans, quality construction and thoughtfulness of these developments. Inland Greens & Cedar Ridge, between Eastwood Road and Market Street, have patio homes located around a regulation par-3 golf course. These homes have three

Photo: Clay Nolen, N.C. Travel and Tourism Division

The Zebulon Latimer House in Wilmington is an ornate four-story residence that indicates the opulent lifestyle of affluent Wilmingtonians in the mid-19th century.

bedrooms, cathedral ceilings and a double garage. Prices begin at $122,500. Eastport, a similar community located less than 2 miles from Wrightsville Beach on Eastwood Road at Military Cutoff, offers homes with private backyards starting at $142,000.

New Hanover County Mainland Waterway Communities

Across the Intracoastal Waterway from Wrightsville Beach is the planned community of Landfall. This neighborhood, walled and protected by guards at security gates, offers a pristine environment of immaculate lawns, beautiful homes, golf courses designed by the likes of

Jack Nicklaus and Pete Dye, a tennis facility overseen in person by Landfall resident Cliff Drysdale, an eight-lane Olympic-size swimming pool, and more. More than 500 families call this neighborhood home. An estimated 700 additional lots are waiting to be built upon. Homesites begin at $60,000; homes begin at $225,000. There are single family homes, villas and low-maintenance patio homes from which to choose. Home prices can reach $1.5 million.

Greenville and Masonboro Sounds are the areas located to the south of the road to Wrightsville Beach. This land along the sound is home to many attractive neighborhoods. These neighborhoods often have direct access to the water and, in some cases, neighborhoods have their own boatslips for the use of community residents. These county neighborhoods have the economic advantage at this writing of being outside of the city of Wilmington, which means there are no city property taxes. The other side of the coin is that they also have alternative systems, or combinations of systems, for services such as water, sewer and waste disposal that come as a package for city residents. One may have county sewer or a septic tank; one may have a community water supply or a well.

Shandy Lane's brochure says, "If the road didn't end at Shandy Lane, those traveling on it would end up in the Intracoastal Waterway." This is a secluded estate with gently rolling topography and an abundance of waterway views. It is within five minutes of Wrightsville Beach and 20 minutes of downtown Wilmington, so services are all within easy access. These homes average $300,000. Shandy Lane is located just off Greenville Loop Road where it curves toward the ICW.

In the same vicinity is Turtle Hall, a beautiful neighborhood with what are admittedly exclusive homes. Expect to pay $500,000 and up for homes close to the water. This neighborhood has a charming harbor for the use of residents. There is also an attractive gazebo at the harbor where one can spend many peaceful hours watching the boats go by.

Whispering Pines is a very active neighborhood located near the ICW to the south. Homes start at $100,000 with living space something more than 2,000 square feet. This location is described by local agents as a good place for people who are moving up. Located off Masonboro Loop Road, this neighborhood is close to Masonboro Sound and the Intracoastal Waterway, although it is not close enough to qualify as waterfront property.

Waterway Communities North of Wilmington

Porters Neck Plantation, 1202 Porters Neck Road, Wilmington, NC 28405, 686-7400 or (800) 423-5695, is north of Wilmington and Wrightsville Beach just off Ocean Highway 17. The Tom Fazio-designed golf course is a key feature of this very attractive neighborhood of homes that will appeal to active people. There is a sports complex, complete with heated lap pool, clay tennis courts and a fitness center. Traditional single-family homes are available in sizes ranging from 1,600 to 2,000 square feet with prices beginning at $162,900. The newest section of this development is Bishop's Park, a neighborhood of single-family homes where lots begin at $43,000 and homes at $159,900.

Figure Eight Island is a private neighborhood of very expensive homes and homesites. Lots can range from $125,000 to $300,000; homes can run from close to $500,000 and up. There is a yacht club and private harbor for residents of this lovely island where there is no commercial development. Shopping is available in nearby Ogden and Hampstead.

South of Wilmington

Travel south of Wilmington down Highway 421 toward Carolina Beach and notice all of the different neighborhoods along the way. Notice, too, that two themes dominate this area: golf and water. Where the Cape Fear River rushes to meet the Atlantic Ocean, this increasingly narrow strip of land is home to heavy residential use with recreation a constant consideration.

Echo Farms is a quiet residential area of new homes and golfing opportunities that offers the convenience of a 10-minute or less drive into downtown Wilmington. The neighborhood has a mix of families and retired persons living in it. Homes may begin in the $70s but can go for $150,000.

Beau Rivage has patio homes that range from a low in the $70s. It is another neighborhood centered around golfing that also has an on-site restaurant and country club. The Cape, nearly at Carolina Beach, has homes that are particularly appealing to retired persons and those interested in golf. Capeside Village has retirement homes beginning in the high $60s.

Wrightsville Beach

Wrightsville Beach is highly residentially developed. For the most part, houses are close together, and a person who craves the mythical remote island life is not going to find it here. Happily, development has been largely controlled, thanks to vigilance on the part of the locals,

and the relative density of development is quite palatable.

This is a pretty beach town. It's clean; there is little in the way of garishness; and the local constable does a fine job keeping order in the face of masses of visitors. A person who appreciates small town living in a beach atmosphere with the convenience of a nearby city will love this place. There are 8 miles of clean beach on which the resident will enjoy a variety of activities such as jogging or simply strolling. On just about any day of the year, one can observe surfers waiting for "the big one," although this is not Hawaii, and big waves are usually reserved for the hours preceding big storms.

There is very little for sale on this popular, beautiful beach these days as far as single family homes are concerned. Many of the existing homes stay in families generation after generation. Quite a few of them are only used as summer homes since many of them are not heated. When homes do go on the market, the price tag is large. A local Realtor recently sold a 1,500 square foot cottage — an older house that survived Hurricane Hazel — and the cost was nearly $200,000.

One may spend dizzying amounts for housing on this island and Harbour Island (the connecting island to the mainland) and the mainland itself. Homes can fetch half a million dollars for 2,500 square feet. Naturally, the higher prices are on homes on the oceanfront, waterway and channels.

Since the available land is all but exhausted in terms of development on the island — and since locals are

Photo: N.C. Travel and Tourism Division

Uniformed demonstrations and re-enactments make Fort Fisher a worthy excursion.

not appreciative of highrises — most of the opportunities for purchase are in condominiums. One may easily spend $200,000 to $300,000 for a two-bedroom condominium on Wrightsville Beach. Something to note is that the northern end of the beach, an area called Shell Island, is in danger from erosion unless continual expenditures are made to keep the ocean at bay. Since there has been considerable development at this point, presumably the erosion problems will continue to be addressed by dredging and renourishment.

Dune Ridge Resort, Cordgrass Bay, and the Sterling Edition of Wrightsville Dunes are condominium developments on Wrightsville Beach that may cost from $250,000 to $500,000 for oceanfront to $200,000 to $400,000 for soundside.

Carolina Beach, Kure Beach, and Fort Fisher

Cross over the bridge on Highway 421 at Snow's Cut, a U.S. Army Corps of Engineers project that connects the ICW with the Cape Fear River and waters to the south, and fall right into Carolina Beach.

This island represents some very interesting prospects for home ownership in the Cape Fear region. Prices are considerably lower than the rest of New Hanover County because the area is somewhat outside of the immediate Wilmington area. The beaches have suffered an undeserved reputation as rowdy places — not entirely undeserved but very much changed for the better in recent years. Folks in Wilmington proper have held onto a tradition of thinking that no beach is as good as Wrightsville.

The truth is that Carolina Beach is a very nice beach town with clean beaches, an abundance of fishing opportunities, several nice restaurants, shopping opportunities and a growing sense of community unity that makes living here a charming prospect. Carolina Beach is the new-growth area for New Hanover County's coastal dwellers. There is an assortment of ownership opportunities on Carolina Beach that range from condominiums to cottages. There are several highrises, many multistory buildings on the northern end, an abundance of small homes, and, particularly toward the south end at Fort Fisher, quite a few larger homes.

Homes may be purchased for prices as low as the $70s and can rise to hundreds of thousands of dollars along Carolina Beach, Wilmington Beach, Kure Beach and Fort Fisher. The farther south you go on this island, the more fascinating the scenery. Down at Fort Fisher, there is beautiful live oak foliage. At the most southerly tip of this strip of land, a resident can enjoy the watery panorama of the river converging with the Atlantic Ocean near Bald Head Island.

Topsail Island

Topsail Island is rumored to have some of the best opportunities for beach real estate. Located 45 minutes north up Ocean Highway 17 from Wilmington (take Highway 210 past Hampstead, then a right on Highway 50 into Surf City), this community has surprising diversity in housing. There is everything from large contemporary beach homes to mobile homes, and the prices, of course, reflect the difference. Unlike the decidedly pricier beaches to

the south, Topsail Island offers homes for $100,000 or less in some cases. Newer, 2,000 square-foot homes can run as high as $200,000, although there are not yet many homes this large on the island. The norm is more 1,500 to 1,800 square feet, and prices can range from $175,000 to $200,000. Lots across the waterway can still be purchased for as low as $8,000 for a 1/2 acre site.

The few condominium developments range in price from as low as $40,000 for a one-bedroom unit with a view of the water at Topsail Reef to a high of $200,000 to $300,000 for a unit at St. Moritz. The average for a two-bedroom condominium on the island is between $80,000 and $100,000. A three-bedroom unit may average $120,000.

Topsail is mostly a second-home market. There are only about 2,000 year-round residents on this still quiet island. Recent development has put all of the necessities of life close to residents with ample grocery stores, convenience marts and other services either available on the island or the mainland. There are quite a few restaurants, but the aspiring resident or the winter visitor should be aware that many of them close from the end of Thanksgiving until April.

Brunswick Beaches

Oak Island
Across the water from Southport is a very different island: Oak Island. This island has three beaches: Caswell, Yaupon, and Long Beach.

All of these communities have resort rentals, but they are overwhelmingly occupied by permanent residents. There is very little in the way of commercial development, and activity on the island is generally families getting together at the church or the firehouse for social occasions. Prices for single-family homes range from $50,000 to $600,000. At the center of the island, one can expect to pay from $70,000 to $90,000 for a small home. Long Beach, the biggest geographical area on Oak Island, has oceanside properties for under $100,000.

HOLDEN BEACH

The next island down (or to the right since this part of North Carolina's coastline shifts to an east-west configuration) is Holden Beach. There is a remarkable bridge connecting the mainland with Holden, and some say it's a surprise attraction in itself. There is a breathtaking view of the whole island, the marshes, the Intracoastal Waterway and the Atlantic Ocean from the top of this fixed bridge as it lifts 65 feet above the mainland (at high water) and careens dizzily to the island. This is another family beach. In fact, every beach we'll tell you about in the rest of the chapter, which will geographically take us to the South Carolina line, fits into the family beach category.

Prices for real estate are climbing rapidly. An oceanfront cottage of 1,800 square feet may cost $180,000 and up. An oceanfront lot with wide beach strand ranges from $135,000 to $250,000. Second row lots, depending upon view and water access by way of a canal, begin at $37,000 and may be as high as $60,000. Duplexes, condominiums and other multifamily dwellings on the oceanfront begin at $130,000.

OCEAN ISLE

Ocean Isle Beach is about 6 miles long and 1/4 mile wide. It is very much like the surrounding beaches except that it has a high-rise that is visible from quite a distance. Most of the property is single-family homes that may range from several hundred thousand on the ocean to $100,000 or so.

SUNSET BEACH

This beach may have thousands of visitors in the summer, but it is home to only about 80 year-round residents. It is overwhelmingly occupied by single-family dwellings, but there is a trend toward large duplexes on the oceanfront. This is because the island homes are on septic systems, and the oceanfront lots are the only ones that can accommodate two systems on one lot. Lots may range from $50,000 to $300,000 depending upon location. Four finger canals, regularly dredged, escalate the cost of interior lots. Duplexes of 2,000 square feet can cost $300,000. Single homes may range as high as $400,000. In general, homes average between $135,000 and $150,000.

CALABASH

Carolina Shores is a golf-oriented neighborhood that attracts a high proportion of retired folks to its appealing setting. Homes, mostly one-story plans, cost between $100,000 and $250,000. Calabash and Carolina Shores have had some disputes in the recent past that essentially amounted to the development trying to secede from the town. Things have settled down considerably. The Town of Calabash is a quaint fishing village with its share of famous restaurants that specialize in Calabash-style seafood. Calabash homes range from $80,000 to $150,000 and attract a wide range of families and individuals who appreciate the easy pace of the area.

Southport

This charming fishing village attracts not only retirees but also families and folks who have decided to get out of the rat race. Southport's geographical location on the Cape Fear River near the Atlantic Ocean provides some lovely coastal scenery. Bald Head Island lies between Southport and the ocean. Oak Island serves as a barrier to the ocean on the south side.

Southport's quaint historic neighborhood of homes that date from the later 1800s offers mostly restored, single-family residences. The handyperson can still find a smaller dwelling for around $50,000 but, as a local Realtor says, you can also expect to put another $50,000 into it before you move in. Houses on the waterfront are larger, and a

Cape Fear Memorial Hospital

THE CAPE FEAR AREA'S...

- Only private, not-for-profit healthcare system

- Leader in personalized care for more than 36 years

- Preferred hospital for members of Physicians Health Plan

Main Campus and Doctors Park
5301 Wrightsville Avenue
Wilmington NC (910) 452-8100

Outpatient Rehabilitation Center
5220 Oleander Drive
Wilmington NC (910) 452-8308

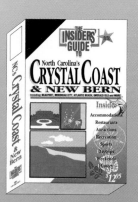

2,500 square foot home may run from $250,000 to $300,000. Newer homes may cost more. Along River Drive, one can spend up to $500,000. Naturally, the farther back from the water, the lower the price. A nice finished house in Southport will average around $150,000 for 1,500 square feet.

There are no condominium developments in Southport itself. Subdivision areas are growing rapidly just outside of Southport, such as Indigo Plantation and Marsh Creek. These neighborhoods have some big, beautiful new houses that can cost as much as $490,000 for 2,500 square feet. Part of the attraction is found in the gorgeous views of the

marshes. Indigo Plantation is also the neighborhood where the Bald Head Island passenger ferry departs and arrives.

Bald Head Island

It takes 20 minutes to cross from Indigo Plantation to Bald Head Island on this beautiful bit of land where there are no highrises, no shopping malls, and no crowds. There are also no cars. Everyone travels by electric golf cart or bicycle. You'll find a clubhouse with a pool, a George Cobb-designed golf course, tennis courts, a marina, limited shopping and opportunities for fine and casual dining. This is a resort atmosphere and, to be sure, the year-round residential population count is quite low. It is largely a vacation spot where most of the homes are available for weekly rental. Homesites range from $40,000 to several hundred thousand dollars. New cottages start as low as $140,000 but can rapidly rise toward the $500,000-range. Single-family homes, townhouses and villas dot the island and are connected by a meandering golf cart path.

Inquiries about real estate sales should be directed only to Bald Head Island, (800) 234-1666.

Real Estate Companies

There are, as previously mentioned, an abundance of real estate companies that will be happy to assist you in your search for a new home. The companies included here represent a fraction of the reputable companies working along the Cape Fear Coast.

Wilmington

Adam and Hilliard Realty, 3912 Shipyard Boulevard, 28403, 799-7500, (800) 628-7089, specializes in single-family and multifamily residential sales in Wilmington and New Hanover County. Properties from the river to the sea in both new and existing neighborhoods are offered by this Realtor. This company has been in business since 1979. It is the exclusive agent for the Birch Creek development on Wrightsville Avenue and Valleygate Villas off Shipyard adjoining Pine Valley. Adam and Hilliard Realty is a member of the Genesis Realty Network.

Bland and Associates Realtors, 4106 Shipyard Boulevard, Wilmington, 28412, 799-1194, and 107 West Salisbury Street, Wrightsville Beach, 256-5200, also (800) 768-1194, is a member of the Homequity Relocation Center. This medium-sized company sells homes throughout New Hanover County.

Century 21 Gardner and Associates, 1041 S. 39th Street, 28403, (800) 277-0021, offers residential and commercial properties throughout New Hanover and Brunswick counties. Established in 1977, this company sells more than 400 properties a year. New developments handled by this company include Brunswick Cove in Brunswick County and Cavalier Woods in Wilmington. This is an Inrelco company that specializes in relocation.

Intracoastal Realty Corporation, P.O. Box 505, Wrightsville Beach, 256-4503 or (800) 533-1849, is a huge company that is an exclusive affiliate of Southeby's International Realty. This company literally covers the waterfront from the river to the sea in New Hanover County and has listings virtually anywhere within the region. It is a member of All Points Relocation Service, Inc.

Landfall Associates, 1801 Eastwood Road, 28405, 256-6111, (800) 227-8208, deals exclusively with the fine properties in Landfall, a private neighborhood of single homes, villas, patio homes, condominiums and homesites. The community boasts numerous amenities including Jack Nicklaus and Pete Dye golf courses and the Cliff Drysdale tennis/sports center. The neighborhood has 24-hour security, high elevation and meticulously maintained landscaping. Landfall Associates has handled Landfall properties for approximately eight years.

Landmark Real Estate, Inc., 803 S. College Road, 28403, 799-8855 or (800) 554-8129, offers residential properties in New Hanover, Brunswick and Pender counties. Landmark Homes, 5022 Wrightsville Avenue, 28403, 392-7201, is the builder division of this company that specializes in residential developments that include Meadowbrook, Gorman Plantation, the Cedars, Summerfield, Parsley Woods, South of Woodberry, Oxford Place, Middleborough, Laurel Ridge, Cabriolet, The Chaise, South Crossing, and Carolina Beach and Liberty Landing in Brunswick County.

Pellegrino Properties, 112 Market Street, Wilmington, 251-2550 or (800) 849-5796, is a relatively young company that specializes in property (both residential and commercial) in Wilmington's historic district. It also has properties on Wrightsville Beach and Carolina Beach, as well as other areas within New Hanover County.

Coldwell Banker SeaCoast Realty, 222 Causeway Drive, Wrightsville Beach, 256-2714, and 5710 Oleander Drive, Wilmington, (800) 522-9624, is a medium-sized company that offers real estate services for Wrightsville Beach and the surrounding areas of Wilmington. This company specializes in waterfront properties.

The Prudential Carolinas Realty, 530 Causeway Drive, Wrightsville Beach, 28480, 256-9299, or 4130 Oleander Drive, Wilmington, 395-2000 or (800) 336-5654, is a large company that covers the Greater Wilmington area.

RDG Real Estate, Highwood Park Plaza, 3137 Wrightsville Avenue, 762-3347, (800) 829-3270, (800) 829-3270, has been handling residential and commercial property sales in the Cape Fear region for more than 25 years. One of the oldest locally-owned firms in Wilmington, RDG also handles property sales in New Hanover, Brunswick, Pender and Onslow counties. Historic district, waterfront and lots and land sales are all specialties of this diverse company.

Re/Max, 1948 B Eastwood Road, 28403, 256-4627, (800) 299-9909, specializes in extraordinary properties at Landfall, Wrightsville Beach and Figure Eight Island. This relatively new company created by the merging of two has 16 years of combined experience between the two partners. Re/Max has its own international relocation network and is a full-service residential agency.

Carolina Beach, Wilmington Beach, Kure Beach and Fort Fisher

CAROLINA BEACH REALTY

307 N. Lake Park Blvd.   458-4444
Carolina Beach   (800)222-9752

This real estate company has been in business for 25 years, selling most of the island and specializing in beachfront properties. It enjoys brisk business in condominium sales along Carolina Beach. It sells single-family homes in Kure Beach since condominiums aren't allowed there.

GARDNER REALTY

C-4 Pleasure Island Plaza   458-9997
Carolina Beach
458-8503

Gardner Realty has been in business selling homes and condominiums from Federal Point, just south of Monkey Junction below Wilmington, to Fort Fisher at the southern end of the island.

WALKER REALTY

501 N. Lake Park Blvd.   458-3388
Carolina Beach

This company sells houses and condominiums on the seven-mile-long island. Many vacation renters who contract with tis company for

rentals eventually return as home purchasers. Self-described as "one of the new kids on the block," this company has established a reputation for quality service since it began eight years ago.

TUCKER BROS. REALTY

201 Harper Ave.   458-8211
Carolina Beach

Tucker Bros. Realty has worked on the island, selling homes from Federal Point just south of Monkey Junction to Fort Fisher, since 1973. The owners are Carolina Beach natives.

UNITED RESORTS

201 Harper Ave.   458-4401
Carolina Beach

Although this company does a robust business in vacation rentals, as do all of the other real estate companies listed here, it specialized in not only sales on the island, but in Wilmington and surrounding areas. It is in the Multiple Listing Service for much of the Cape Fear area.

Topsail Island

TOPSAIL REALTY

712 S. Anderson Blvd.
Surf City   (800)526-6432

This large company sells properties on Topsail Island and the surrounding mainland.

PELLEGRINO PROPERTIES

Louie Pellegrino

Lou started his real estate career in Manhattan. Having a successful career in neighboring Connecticut, Lou specialized in upscale and waterfront properties, as well as relocation for Yale University. He is a graduate of UNC Wilmington with a B.S. in Business Administration. Having been salesman of the year for three consecutive years, Lou opened his own real estate firm in 1992.

452-6928

A FULL-SERVICE REAL ESTATE COMPANY SPECIALIZING IN . . .

Waterfront Properties • Beach Properties
Historic Homes • Residential Homes
Golf Communities • Commercial Properties

OPEN 7 DAYS A WEEK
"Because Your Home Is Your Castle"

Andi Hall

Originally from the Midwest, Andi has a background in management and over 5 years of real estate experience. She has been in the area for 9 years, is a member of the Board of REALTORS, a past volunteer and supporter of Easter Seals, Young Life, and Public Radio. Andi enjoys singing and writing music in her spare time. FOR ALL YOUR REAL ESTATE NEEDS . . . ANDI HALL IS THE ONE TO CALL!!!

350-8555

112 MARKET STREET ❖ HISTORIC WILMINGTON, NC 28401
(910) 251-2550 ❖ 1 (800) 849-5796

PELLEGRINO PROPERTIES

JEAN BROWN REAL ESTATE
P.O. Box 2367
Surf City (800)745-4480
This company sells properties on Topsail Island as well as on the mainland side of Pender County.

CENTURY 21 ISLAND REALTY
200 North Shore Village
Sneads Ferry (800)334-4848
This company serves Topsail Island, as well as Pender and Onslow counties.

Figure Eight Island

FIGURE EIGHT REALTY
15 Bridge Rd.
Wilmington 686-4400
While other companies may sell Figure Eight houses, this is the only real estate company located on the island.

Southport and Oak Island

COLDWELL BANKER SOUTHPORT-OAK ISLAND REALTY
1030 N. Howe St.
Southport (800)243-8132
This company covers Southport and Oak Island.

MARGARET RUDD & ASSOCIATES, INC., REALTORS
210 Country Club Dr.
Yaupon Beach (800)733-5213
Southport, Long Beach, and Brunswick County are the territory covered by this large real estate company.

SCRUGGS & MORRISON REALTY
4324 E. Beach Dr.
Long Beach 278-5405
This company serves Southport,

Oak Island, and Brunswick County.

South Brunswick Islands: Holden, Ocean Isle, and Sunset Beach, including Calabash

ALAN HOLDEN REALTY
128 Ocean Blvd., W.
Holden Beach (800)720-2200
This is the largest and oldest real estate company handling sales and rentals on Holden Beach.

SLOANE REALTY
16 Causeway Rd.
Ocean Isle Beach (800)843-6044
This company is owned by the first permanent family located on Ocean Isle Beach.

SUNSET PROPERTIES
419 Sunset Blvd.
Sunset Beach In state (800)446-0218
Out of state (800)525-0182
On the island for six years, this company regularly handles 200 properties only on Sunset Beach.

NATIONSREALTY
9960 Beach Dr.
Calabash (800)225-2559
This company specializes in properties in Calabash and Carolina Shores.

Services

The following includes some of the companies that offer products and services for home building and improvements.

McKenzie Supply Co., 212 S. Kerr Avenue, Wilmington, 791-4994, is Wilmington's Kohler kitchen and bath showroom. It has a special section for the physically challenged.

Drapery World Interiors, 5908 Oleander Drive, Wilmington, 791-8732, specializes in custom draperies, upholstery, miniblinds and verticals and has more than 1,000 fabric selections.

Becker Builder's Supply Co., 4614 Market Street, Wilmington, 791-7761, has been supplying building materials for new construction and maintenance since 1918.

Showroom Lighting, 5022 Wrightsville Avenue, Wilmington, 799-8141, sells residential and commercial lighting fixtures, table and floor lamps, ceiling fans and indoor/outdoor lighting systems.

Deborah Jamieson and Associates, Inc., A.S.I.D, 6317 Oleander Drive, Wilmington, 395-1818, offers commercial and residential interior design services including space planning and furnishings.

The Williams House

Jean and Woodrow "Corky" Fountain moved into one of the oldest houses in Wilmington's Historic District ten years ago after inheriting it from Jean's mother. This 8,000-square-foot home at 10 S. Fifth Avenue, has been converted to apartments. The Fountains occupy two of the spacious downstairs sections of this house that is a living museum. Mr. and Mrs. Fountain share some of their considerable knowledge about the home.

"Welcome to the Williams House. This was built in 1868 by George Washington Williams, his wife Martha, and their twelve children. That's why the house is so big. You have to have a big house when you have a big family.

He was a cotton broker but he and his partners sold out to Alexander Sprunt, and that made Sprunt the largest cotton broker in the South. But he had these ships and he would send the cotton over and the ships would come back empty, so they put ballast stones in the hold so the ships could come back safely. This house is built on the ballast rocks, some as big as automobiles — huge stones.

There's also a tiny little fern in this historic district that grows nowhere else, and that came over as spores in these rocks and you'll find it only in the historic district in Wilmington.

As you came in our little entry — which isn't too little after all -- this came over in boxes from Philadelphia and was assembled here as this beautiful foyer with the tiles in the floor, all very colorful. The wood is walnut here, and, as you'll notice, all the doors and all the woodwork are handcarved. This was done by a freed slave named Frederick Sadgwar. He did all the handcarved work on the woodwork in this house which is all Indian mahogany. There is no more Indian mahogany. They used it up. So, the house could never be duplicated as it is now.

As you walk out of the vestibule, you come into the stairhall. The floor here is heart cypress and the stair rail is walnut. It's called a running staircase because it goes three flights without pause. The bend in the wood was accomplished by steam under pressure. The wallpaper is sort of gaudy and that's because it's authentically duplicated Victorian wallpaper by Schumacher. The little hall tree is older than the house itself. It's an antique I picked up from Ginny Jennewein. The original people who lived in the house said, "Where is the hall tree?" and I said when mama bought the house there was no hall tree and they said there was always a halltree. So, Ginny helped me find one.

This is our study and library. The floor is the original parquet floor with each little piece put in separately to make the design. You can see the nails. The windows, which come down to the floor, are hand-blown glass. There are sixty-seven windows in this house. The fixtures for the lights came from England. They are duplications for lights at the turn of the century.

The dining room is the original dining room of the Williams family. It has the pocket doors which are cut crystal and, fortunately, the original panels.

When the daughter was married in 1886, a Queen Anne Eastlake parlor was added to the house for the party after the wedding. So, for the reception, they added a humongous room. The dimensions are about thirty by twenty. It has a bay window with big windows in it. On the opposite side there's a bay cabinet which duplicates the window. The drawers come out on the diagonal because the concave marble accommodates that. It has French beveled mirrors and beautiful handcarved tiers for displaying wedding gifts. There's also a fourteen-foot tall cabinet that is like a breakfront to display wedding gifts.

The chandelier is an original, sort of a basket fashion with great big crystal at the bottom and hanging crystal from the top. The mantle has vaseline glass tiles and I call this a rainbow room because when the sun shines in you can almost always find a rainbow reflected somewhere.

We had a picture of the party that was held in this room — the wedding reception — and they had draped the vaulted ceiling with so much smilax that you could almost see Tarzan and Jane in the jungle. You've never seen so much smilax in your life.

I took a magnifying glass and looked at the refreshments and they had coconut-covered snowballs and they were so big. You know today we have little finger foods and tiny canapes -- they had such mammoth refreshments in great big cut bowls. It was all really big.

This daughter lived on South Fourth Street where her daddy built a house for her. When she was expecting her first child, she died in childbirth. To this day people say the nursery is haunted.

The house is approximately 8,000 square feet of heated floor space.

Originally, it was 26 rooms until it was converted to apartments. It took almost two years to renovate the home before we moved in.

This house had a house on the lot when the Williams built here. They added this house to the one that was here so there are three architectural times to this house. There's the original house, built in 1843, that is Colonial; the main part of the house is Italianate Victorian; and the Queen Anne Victorian wing was built in 1886."

Photo: Scott Taylor

Even when it's raining kids have fun on the Cape Fear Coast.

Inside
Schools and Child Care

The quality of life in a community is often reflected in that community's attitude toward its children. In the Cape Fear region, there is widespread interest among the adult population—people both with and without children — in the well-being of children. The community is concerned with the quality of education and care provided to its youngest members. In recent years, there has been accelerated community effort to bring educational opportunities to a much higher standard than was previously offered. As a result, area schools that once lagged behind both the state of North Carolina and the nation in test scores and other tangible measures of achievement have experienced encouraging advances.

Public Schools

New Hanover County Schools

The New Hanover County School System serves the city of Wilmington as well as the county. In 1993-1994, the system served 20,269 students from kindergarten through grade 12. The system's mission is to provide a total educational environment for its students on the basis of each individual's abilities and interests. The tenth largest public school system in the state, New Hanover County Schools strive to provide all students with the opportunity to develop as creative individuals able to function competently in society.

The system faces all the familiar challenges encountered by every American school system. No matter where you may currently live, odds are that the issues of education are pretty much the same there as here. There is a constant need for more funding, better facilities and a continual quest for educational excellence that will serve the needs of all children from diverse socioeconomic circumstances. The system addresses these concerns with a tangible program called the Effective Schools Program, a long-term plan implemented four years ago. The system's stated goal is to be "one of the best school systems in the southeastern United States by the turn of the century." The system earned an exceptional rating on the accreditation standards applied by the Southern Association of Colleges and Schools.

The school system is known for thorough examination of both its successes and failures in a determined effort to continually improve the education of its students. Suffering nearly an 11 percent dropout rate in 1988, the system called upon the business community, as well as other volunteers, to help professionals and parents reverse this situation. According to 1991 figures, the dropout rate declined to 7.7 percent. Figures for 1992-1993 show that the dropout rate has been reduced to 3.5 percent.

In test scores, success is measured in several different academic ways. The North Carolina Test scores for 1993 placed the New Hanover County Schools well ahead of state averages in writing for grades 4, 6 and 8. On the Iowa Achievement Test, students scored above the national average in all grades tested. Combined SAT scores rose 11 points in 1991-1992 over the previous year, although there was a slight drop in 1992-1993. Against a national average of 902, the North Carolina average was 859, and the New Hanover County average was 853. People from regions outside the South should understand that a much higher percentage of students takes the SAT in this region than in much of the country, so that factor should be taken into account.

In 1993, nearly 80 percent of the system's graduates planned to continue their education beyond high school. More than $4.5 million was awarded to graduates that year in scholarships and financial aid. The system produced three National Merit Scholars in 1993, as well as seven National Merit Finalists, one semifinalist and 12 Commended students. Fourteen students were selected for enrollment in the North

Carolina Governor's School, and six were selected to attend the North Carolina School of Science and Math.

The system has had the benefit of tremendous support from the business community as well as from community volunteers. Volunteers in 1993 numbered more than 2,500. These individuals contributed in many different ways, including tutoring, working to lower the dropout rate, and offering opportunities for students to gain exposure to the corporate realm beyond the classroom. Volunteers contributed almost 100,000 hours to the system.

Much of the assistance from business comes through the Chamber of Commerce Education Foundation, a community education support organization that provides $120,000 for 69 mini-grants to supplement system-funded education. Other programs under the auspices of this foundation include Project Business, Cape Fear Careers, Community Resource File, ROCAME (Region O Council for the Advancement of Minorities in Engineering), a Scholars Reception and a yearly showcase of school talent, "Best Foot Forward," a variety show held at Thalian Hall.

The 1993 budget for New Hanover County Schools was $89,600,000, with 70 percent coming from the state, 26 percent from local monies, and 4 percent from the Federal government. Per pupil expenditure was $4,106, placing the system 58th out of 132 public school systems in North Carolina. Of the total budget, 70 percent was used for direct instructional costs. There

Quality
live-in child care...

with a special European *flair*.

- carefully screened European au pairs
- about $170/week for any size family
- AuPairCare counselors in your area

800-4-AUPAIR

AuPairCare

are approximately 1,388 certified staff members and 2,956 school employees in the system.

The system is organized as K-5, 6-8, and 9-12, using the middle school concept instead of junior high schools. The school year runs from the end of August until the first part of June, although year-round schooling is now available at several elementary and middle schools as part of a pilot program. The program is voluntary for students and teachers. After considerable investigation, the Board of Education perceives the advantages of year-round schooling to include increased learning, a reduction in stress levels in both students and teachers, greater time and opportunity for effective enrichment and remediation and higher motivation. At this writing, the North Carolina General Assembly is giving consideration to lengthening the school year from 180 days to 200, and year-round schools may well be the forerunners of how the system will operate in the near future.

While still in high school, students in the New Hanover County Schools may engage in advanced studies at the University of North Carolina at Wilmington, as well as enroll in courses at Cape Fear Community College for part of the instructional day. In 1993, the Gregory School of Science, Mathematics and Technology opened its doors to allow students to experience a high-tech program of study that integrates science and mathematics throughout the elementary curriculum. This is the first magnet school in the system, and it has been enthusiastically received within the community.

The system offers the Lakeside Alternative School to students with special needs, primarily those identified as at-risk. This school operates an extended day program for students who must also work in jobs.

More than 250 courses are available to senior high school students at four high schools. Aside from major content areas, including social studies, mathematics, computer science, English, foreign language, and the full range of sciences, students are able to participate in Army, Navy, and Air Force JROTC Honor units as well as a broad range of extracurricular activities and programs. There are many programs in vocational education, including marine sciences and oceanography. A cultural arts curriculum includes band, strings, chorus, drama, art and dance.

Middle schools offer a similar, though more limited, curriculum upon which the senior high program is based. In the elementary schools, there is emphasis on hands-on experience in all of the disciplines. Elementary school students participate in a curriculum based on the use of manipulatives to build a foundation that will support the learning of concepts in the middle grades and high school. A comprehensive program has been designed for exceptional children at all grade levels.

Basketball and football are big parts of the interscholastic athletic program. What else would you expect from the sports-minded city that produced such athletes as Michael Jordan, Meadowlark Lemon and Roman Gabriel on its public school courts and fields? Volleyball, baseball, soccer, wrestling, golf, tennis, and track are also offered.

Students who are new in New Hanover County should immediately enroll in school. The parent or guardian of a kindergartner must bring a birth certificate along with the child's social security card and immunization record to the system office at 1802 South 15th Street in Wilmington. Children entering kindergarten must be 5 years old on or before October 16th of that year. Parents of students who have been previously enrolled in school should bring the student's last report card to the appropriate school. For information on schools and everything you need to know about how the public schools can serve your child, call the director of School-Community Relations at 763-5431, ext. 221.

ELEMENTARY SCHOOLS

Edwin A. Alderman
2025 Independence Blvd.   799-3350

Heyward C. Bellamy
70 Sanders Rd.   799-6988

John J. Blair
6510 Market St.   791-7553

William H. Blount
3702 Princess Place Dr.   763-4259

Bradley Creek
6211 Greenville Loop Rd.   791-7073

Carolina Beach
4th & Atlantic Sts.   458-9472

College Park
5001 Oriole Dr.   791-5444

Forest Hills
602 Colonial Dr.   251-6190

Gregory School of Science and Mathematics
319 S. 10th St.   251-6185

Mary W. Howe
1020 Meares St.   251-6195

Dorothy B. Johnson
110 McRae St.   251-6155

Ogden
421 Middle Sound Rd.   686-9506

Pine Valley
440 John S. Mosby Dr.   791-9005

J. C. Roe
2875 Worth Dr.   791-7020

Annie H. Snipes
2150 Chestnut St.   251-6180

Sunset Park
613 Alabama Ave.   762-8130

Mary C. Williams
801 Silver Lake Rd.   799-7749

Winter Park
204 S. McMillan Ave.   791-5453

Wrightsboro
640 Castle Hayne Rd.   762-3715

Wrightsville Beach
220 Coral Dr.   256-3171

MIDDLE SCHOOLS
Myrtle Grove
902 Piner Rd.   791-2223

Noble M. C. S.
6520 Market St.   791-8724

Roland-Grise
4412 Lake Ave.   791-2363

Emma B. Trask
2900 N. College Rd.   799-2826

D. C. Virgo
813 Nixon St.   251-6150

Williston
401 S. 10th St.   763-7684

SENIOR HIGH SCHOOLS
John T. Hoggard
4305 Shipyard Blvd.   791-0230

Lakeside
1805 S. 13th St.   251-6161

Emsley A. Laney
2700 N. College Rd.   799-8400

New Hanover High
1307 Market St.   251-6110

Brunswick County School System

The Brunswick County School System serves approximately 8,400 students in six elementary schools, three middle schools and three comprehensive high schools. You may contact the Brunswick County School System at 754-9282, Board of Education, 8360 River Road Southeast, Southport, 28461.

Columbus County School System

The Columbus County School System, 642-5168, P.O. Box 729, Whiteville, 28472, serves 7,700 students in 18 accredited schools, including the Boys Home at Lake Waccamaw. There are 19 schools, including three high schools, two middle schools and 14 combinations of middle and elementary schools.

Pender County School System

The Pender County School System, 259-2187, has 11 accredited schools with an enrollment of nearly 5,000 students. There are six elementary schools, three middle schools and two high schools.

Private Schools

New Hanover County offers several private schools for all grade levels. There is a broad assortment of focus and curricula among the private schools, and the phone book is a great place to look for your particular interest. All private schools can't be listed within this guide, but this list suggests the available alternatives.

CAPE FEAR ACADEMY
3900 S. College Rd.
Wilmington   791-0287

Cape Fear Academy is the dominant secular private school in the region. Established in 1967, this coeducational day school is open to

CAPE FEAR ACADEMY

3900 South College Road
Wilmington, NC 28412

Contact: Mrs. Susan Harrell
Director of Admissions
(910) 791-0287
FAX (910) 791-0290

COMPELLING REASONS TO CONSIDER
CAPE FEAR ACADEMY:

· Personal attention from faculty
· Small classes
· Solid college preparation
· High levels of accountability expected
· Opportunities for leadership and
  community service
· Parental involvement
· Highly qualified faculty
· Challenging academic classes
· Environment that fosters self-reliance
· Emphasis on personal responsibility

Member of NAIS, NCAIS, SAIS · Accredited by Southern Association of Colleges and Schools
Cape Fear Academy accepts students without regard to race, religion or ethnic origin.

students interested in a traditional, college preparatory education. There are approximately 350 students in Pre-kindergarten through Grade 12. Pre-kindergarten and kindergarten students participate in half-day programs with after-school care available. The Lower School is comprised of Pre-kindergarten through grade 6. Weekly instruction by a professional faculty includes art, music, science, foreign language (Spanish), computer science and physical education.

The Upper School concentrates on college preparation in the classroom coupled with individual development through extracurricular activities. Students in Grades 7 and 8 must satisfactorily complete courses in English, science, social studies, math, physical education, art, music and foreign language. At grade 9, students begin to fulfill graduation requirements. As far as success ratings for the school, 100 percent of the graduates attend four-year college programs; approxi-

mately 85 percent of these students are accepted into their first-choice college or university. The composite SAT score with 100 percent of the students being tested is 1052, well above North Carolina's average of 859. Students in the seventh grade are considered annually for the Duke University Talent Identification Program. Half of the class meets the criteria for this prestigious program.

Tuition and fees vary with grade level and activity. The basic regular tuition is $3,107 per year for pre-kindergarten and kindergarten and $5,261 for Grades 1-12. Finance programs are available.

WILMINGTON CHRISTIAN ACADEMY
1401 N. College Rd.
Wilmington   791-4248

This is the largest private school on the Cape Fear coast. More than 500 students are in this school, which serves K-12 students as well as preschool students and offers daycare facilities. Located on the campus of Grace Baptist Church, Wilmington

Christian Academy's focus is on fundamental Christian education. The handbook presents the Doctrinal Statement and purpose of the school that states: "The teachers are born again, academically qualified Christians who are prepared to lead and help you in the most important areas of your life." The curriculum, which includes a college preparatory program, includes English, Bible, physical science, biology, chemistry, mathematics (advanced and elective), history, government, health, physical education, computer science, foreign language, music, art and sociology.

Tuition is on a sliding scale based on the number of children attending from each household. In grades 1 to 6, tuition is $1,990, payable over 10 months each year. In grades 7 to 12, tuition is $2,100.

ST. MARY CATHOLIC SCHOOL
217 S. Fourth St.
Wilmington   762-6517

St. Mary employs eight full-time teachers and eight part-time teachers to teach approximately 185 students in Grades 1-8. Its mission is to "ensure learning for all our students within the framework of Catholic Christian values, to help our students grow in a manner consistent with their needs, interests, and abilities, and to prepare them to live in a changing world as self-directing, caring, responsible citizens."

Grades 1 to 4 are structured, self-contained classes. Curriculum includes science, social studies, computers, Spanish, music, art, physical education, religion, reading, phonics, creative writing and math. Grades 5 to 8 have departmental teachers who rotate to different classrooms. Classes include science, social studies, math, language arts, literature, writing, computers, Spanish, music, art, physical education and religion. Tuition is based on a sliding scale depending upon how many children from a family attend the school. Rates are also lower for families of the Catholic faith. Tuition for one Catholic child is $1,900; for a child of another faith, tuition is $2,442. There are payment plans available.

Special Education

CHILD DEVELOPMENT CENTER, SCHOOL FOR DEVELOPMENTALLY DISABLED
4702 S. College Rd.
Wilmington   392-6417

A United Way agency, the Child Development Center serves children with developmental disabilities who are ages 3 years through 8. Open weekdays from 7:30 AM until 3:30 PM, the center serves 52 children in a full-time educational setting. There are no fees because this center operates under the auspices of the public school system.

UNITED CEREBRAL PALSY DEVELOPMENTAL CENTER
500 Military Cutoff Rd.
Wilmington   392-0080

Children from New Hanover and surrounding counties who have physical impairments can be referred by a parent, physician or community agency to this special education center. Known as "The Exceptional Preschool," the center serves children who have cerebral palsy or

Photo: Scott Taylor

Recess is always great.

other physical developmental delays. The center also accepts children without disabilities because the school believes that it is beneficial to bring students with and without physical disabilities together in a quality preschool program. Educators and therapists facilitate learning through play and promote development in areas such as gross and fine motor, speech and language, social-emotional, cognitive and independence skills.

Home Schooling

The State of North Carolina allows for schooling outside both public and private schools for children whose parents who prefer to administer their child's education. Supervised under the auspices of the Division of Nonpublic Education, home schooling requires participation in standardized testing, immunization and the administration of the educational program by a person with a high school diploma (or the equivalent of one) for nine months a year.

There is a group, Wilmington Homeschool Organization, that provides information for parents interested in educating their children at home. For information, call 799-8344. If, by the time of publication of this guide, that number changes, a few questions around the community can produce a contact person reasonably quickly. The group appears to be relatively informal at the moment since only approximately 100 students were being home- schooled in New Hanover County in 1993.

Child Care

Child care is an increasing concern and business in the Cape Fear area. Since the phone book is flooded with child care possibilities, including church-affiliated day care centers to preschool development centers to after-school care, the choices can be somewhat bewildering for parents.

The **Child Advocacy Commission**, 401 Chestnut Street, Suite H, 763-7430, maintains a detailed data bank of child care resources in the Cape Fear area. This organization does not make recommendations, but it offers information and referrals that allow parents to make informed choices. There is no charge for this service. The Resource and Referral number is 763-6911. The Child Advocacy Commission also works to develop cooperative efforts with governmental and other community service agencies to promote an awareness of children's issues. It sponsors community services activities, educational information and assistance to community agencies, civic groups and individuals. The commission offers on-site child care training for providers and businesses.

There are approximately 50 day care centers and services in the area. The North Carolina Department of Human Resources regulates these businesses and establishes guidelines for enrollment capacity. A Small Day Care Home serves a maximum of five preschool children or up to eight children if at least three are school age. A Large Day Care Center may serve 80 or more children.

The Child Advocacy Commission provides helpful guidelines for deciding which center or service is right for you and your children. They offer detailed lists of things to look for when you go to investigate the suitability of a center, such as staff qualifications, offered programs, space, health concerns, safety, meals and fees. Parents can take great comfort in knowing that this kind of organization exists because, if their information packets are an indication, this organization takes a fierce interest in the well-being of children. Ask for their general information packet that contains important tips to help a parent accurately assess the quality of care offered in any center.

The following list of daycare centers is partial, and no recommendations are made. However, these centers have demonstrated consistent efforts. The yellow pages of the phone books (there are two in Wilmington) will provide an entire listing of centers.

A LITTLE CLASS
106 Pine Grove Dr.
Wilmington   452-3433
This center, located in Winter

Park, has programs for children from ages 2 1/2 to 12. The program is Academic and Independent. Tuition is $65 per week for full time or $3 per hour for part time. Capacity is 36.

ADVENTURE WORLD
4604 Longleaf Hills Dr.
Wilmington 392-0868

Located in Winter Park and Long Leaf, this center has programs for children as young as 1 month and as old as 5 years. Focus is on child development and independent learning. Tuition is $82 per week for full time or up to $4 per hour for part time. Capacity is 173.

CAROLINA PRESCHOOL
6501 Carolina Beach Rd.
Wilmington 392-1560

Located at Monkey Junction south of Wilmington, this center accepts children ranging in age from 1 month to 12 years. Child development and independent learning are the programs. Tuition is $60 per week for full time or $2.50 per hour part time.

CLASSY BEARS PRESCHOOL
6620 Windmill Way
Wilmington 791-7872

Located near Blair School on Market Street north of Wilmington, this center accepts children from 1 month to 11 years old. This center also concentrates on child development and independent learning. Tuition is $30 to $80 per week. Part time is $15 per day. Capacity is 104. No part timers may be under age 2.

CREATIVE WORLD
4202 Wilshire Blvd.
Wilmington 791-2080

This center is located in New Hanover County near Wrightsboro east of Wilmington. It accepts children from 2 months to 12 years of age. In addition to child development and independent learning, it also has an academic program. Tuition is $33 to $70 per week for full-time or $3 per hour for part-time. Capacity is 148.

DISCOVERY PLACE OF WILMINGTON
3806 Cherry Ave.
Wilmington 799-0560

Located in Lincoln Forest, this center accepts children from 6 months to 5 years of age in a child development and independent learning environment. Full-time tuition is $65 to $80 per week. Capacity is 75.

EARLY CHILDHOOD LEARNING CENTER
4102 Peachtree Ave.
Wilmington 392-4637

Located in the Winter Park area, this center accepts children from 2 to 5 years of age in child development, independent learning and academic programs. Full-time tuition is $81 per week. Part-time is two days per week and costs $160 per month. Capacity is 99.

GRANNY'S DAY CARE CENTER
7010 Market St.
Wilmington 686-4405

Serving New Hanover County to the north and east of Wilmington, this center accepts children from 6 months to 5 years of age in a child development program. Tuition is $85 per week. Capacity is 45.

HEADSTART PROGRAM
OF NEW HANOVER COUNTY
507 N. 6th St.
Wilmington   762-1177
Located in downtown Wilmington, this center serves children who are 4 years old. This nonprofit child development and academic program also has an extensive food program. Call to inquire about fees. Capacity is 216.

TOTAL CHILD CARE
4304 Henson Dr.
Wilmington   799-3556
This center is located near Northchase at Wilmington's northeast corner close to incoming Interstate 40. It accepts children from 1 month to 12 years of age. Child development and independent learning are the focus of the program. Full-time tuition is $40 to $80 per week or $2 per hour for part-time. Capacity is 127.

PARK AVENUE SCHOOL
1306 Floral Pkwy.
Wilmington   791-6217
Located near Independence Mall off Oleander Drive, this center accepts children from 1 month to 12 years of age. The program is based on child development, independent learning and academic development. Full-time tuition is $34 to $69 per week. Capacity is 200.

SHAW SPEAKES DAY CARE CENTER
718 S. 3rd St.
Wilmington   343-1441
This center is located in downtown Wilmington right beside the

Cape Fear Memorial Bridge. It accepts children from two months to 12 years of age. The nonprofit program is based on child development and independent learning. Full-time tuition is $35 to $55 per week. The part-time rate is $3.50 per hour. Capacity is 78.

Home Child Care

There is a robust cottage industry in child care as is evidenced by browsing through offers for child care in local newspapers and tabloids. According to the Child Advocacy Commission, the care providers list changes on an almost weekly basis, and a parent must be especially cautious in selecting home child care.

In-home care has some obvious advantages. If you have an infant, it's very nice to have a person come into your home. Live-in help or an in-home caregiver are the alternatives in this case. Word of mouth is an important way to learn about good nannies. Ask people with in-home child care about their experiences.

Since Wilmington is a vacation area, there are companies that specialize in resort child sitting services as well as regular sitting services for locals. The **Sitter Network, Inc.**, 256-9444, has bonded sitters trained in child CPR, and it offers qualified child care for vacationers and locals who need a break for short or extended times. It also offers nanny placement services.

TLC Unlimited, 799-5132, is another sitter service that also has bonded sitters who are trained in child CPR and bonded. As far as qualifications and recommendations, both the Sitter Network and TLC Unlimited services are very similar. Nanny placement is also a specialty of TLC Unlimited. As with the Sitter Network, TLC Unlimited goes to pains to screen its employees in order to ensure that a child's sitter is qualified, enthusiastic, and productive.

The **Aupair** system is just becoming available locally. Although local child care referral systems have mixed information regarding the availability of this service, there does appear to be a way to make arrangements for care by calling 1-800-4-AUPAIR. The rate averages $170 per week for all families. Persons who wish to find long-term child care through this international program may also call the Raleigh office of the Child Advocacy Commission at (919) 571-1520 for information.

Inside
Retirement and Senior Services

Retirement has come to entail complex decisions at the end of the 20th century in America. Changing lifestyles have made it necessary for more options for retirement to be made available to retirees and their families. Fortunately, there are increasing opportunities in both the public and private sectors for establishing a retirement plan based on the needs and preferences of individuals and couples.

Within the context of budgetary considerations, the first choice in a retirement plan is location. Where do you want to live and why? The Cape Fear Coast is a tremendously attractive retirement destination to retirees across the nation, particularly from the northeast, because of scenery, services, and, perhaps most importantly, the weather.

Throughout most of this century, particularly the latter half, many a winter-weary Northerner has gone to latitudinal extremes in search of respite from the winter land of snow and ice. They have gone in droves to Florida, land of sunshine. Recently, some of these retirees have taken a more conservative approach and decided that they don't really want a retirement location that is largely without discernible seasons. Wilmington is very appealing to retirees

who want four distinct seasons that are within reasonable temperature ranges. Wilmington's daily range in temperatures is moderate due in large part to its maritime location. Afternoon sea breezes make the summer heat more comfortable. Although there can be some beastly hot days with high humidity, there is nothing to match Florida's excessively oppressive heat. The afternoon temperatures in the Cape Fear area may reach 90 degrees or more a third of the days in midsummer, but several years may pass without reaching the 100-degree mark. The average temperature in July is 79.8 degrees.

In the winter, the numerous polar air masses that reach the Atlantic Ocean must pass over the Appalachian Mountains and are moderated into relatively short periods of cold weather. Most winters are short and mild. According to records kept since 1870, there is only one entire day each winter when the temperature fails to rise above freezing. The mean temperature in January, for example, is 47 degrees. Rainfall in the area is usually ample and well-distributed throughout the year, concentrated mostly in summer thunderstorms between June and August. Retirees who enjoy gardening will appreciate the fact that the growing season may be as long as 302 days for some flowers and vegetables.

For northern retirees who get sentimental over the winter holidays spent in their point of origin, there is the occasional snow to delight the senses, but there is no real inconvenience with which to contend. Snow is usually a matter of flurries, although there have been occasions upon which more than a foot of snow has managed to accumulate. Snow on the sand is an odd sight that causes locals to flock there to see it. An important insider tip to heed is that Southerners are very dangerous on roads when it snows because they are unaccustomed to driving in wintry conditions. (Retirees who suddenly find themselves delighted at a Christmas snow would do well to stay at home and enjoy the sight without venturing onto roads.)

Apart from agreeable weather patterns, the Cape Fear coast has much to offer its retired population. There is ample shopping, first rate medical care, some diversity in housing opportunities, a full range of cultural activities, and an increasing awareness on the part of local government and business that the seniors are coming.

Census figures for 1992 indicate that nearly 50,000 citizens age 60 and over reside in the Cape Fear region. At this writing, New Hanover County is experiencing an increase of 10 percent per year in the population of citizens who are age 60 and up. In the year 2,010, it is projected that 13.6 percent of the population in New Hanover County will be 65 and older. In Brunswick County to the south, seniors will account for nearly 15 percent of the population. Pender County to the north will have a population of which 16.4 percent is seniors.

Retirees, in fact, are being increasingly attracted to North Carolina on the whole. Between 1980 and 1990, the number of people 65 and older increased by a third in the state. North Carolina ranks fifth in the nation for migratory retirees, according to the North Carolina Division of Aging. Given the special attributes of coastal North Carolina, it would not be surprising to see population projections surpassed in the next decade.

Where To Live

People from all walks of life and all socioeconomic circumstances will discover several options for living situations in the Cape Fear area. If you are fortunate enough to have good health and a comfortable financial situation, there are many

Picnic among the windswept live oaks at Fort Fisher.

Insiders' Tips

neighborhoods from which to choose. You may not wish or need to move into a retirement community at this point in your life. Retirees relocating from areas with a higher cost of living will discover bargains in the overall real estate market. If independent living is in your forecast for some time, there are many reasonably priced homes on the market.

It is altogether possible to find a new house at the beach for $100,000 on some islands, with the definite exception of Wrightsville Beach, Bald Head Island and Figure Eight Island. There are exclusive, walled, suburban neighborhoods with security guards and golf courses; there is an artsy, urban neighborhood in Wilmington's downtown historic district for seniors who favor evening walks to the cafe after the theater. There are apartment and condominium communities of every possible description in every kind of neighborhood. Whether you're buying or renting, visit with a local Realtor for information. (See the Real Estate section in this guide.)

Senior Adult Retirement Communities

Senior Adult Retirement Communities, neighborhoods with congregate housing intended specifically for older occupants, offer a variety of social and recreational amenities. These communities feature single homes or apartments that center around several services. They may include meals in a central location, pools, transportation and activities. They may or may not feature health care services. You are advised to contact the Chamber of Commerce in the area you choose for relocation and to contact the **Cape Fear Council of Governments, Department of Aging**, for information at 1480 Harbour Drive, Wilmington 395-4553. The Cape Fear Council of Governments is a rich resource for information through its Area Agency on Aging Administrator. The agency oversees senior services in New Hanover, Pender, Brunswick and Columbus counties. A free Community Resource Guide, published by the agency, is readily available.

Lake Shore Commons, 1402 Hospital Plaza Drive, Wilmington, 251-0067, is a neighborhood in a park setting on picturesque Greenfield Lake near downtown Wilmington. The lake is a tremendously interesting ecosystem of cypress trees, Spanish moss, and assorted amphibians, birds and reptiles. It is also a spot where sidewalks surrounding the lake allow for interesting walks or jogs. Three meals a day in an elegant dining area, housekeeping, all utilities and no-charge personal laundry are some of the features of this community. There are no leases or buy-in fees; there is only a monthly charge that averages $900 a month and includes three meals a day. There is no health care service.

Plantation Village, 1200 Porter's Neck Road, Wilmington, 686-7181 or in state (800) 334-0240 or out of state (800) 334-0035, is a life care retirement community located on 50 acres within Porter's Neck Plantation. The campus has a library, bank facilities, auditorium, swimming pool, woodworking shop, a crafts room, and many more amenities. Boaters will appreciate its access to the Intracoastal Waterway. There are 136 private apartments and villas in place with more development on the drawing board. While the entry fee starts at $88,770 there is a 90 percent return of capital plan. Monthly service starts at $1,060 for an individual. Add an additional $566 for a second person. Utilities, cable TV, and lawn maintenance are included.

This is a unique retirement community in that it receives people in good health age 62 and older and is able to offer professional, long-term nursing care services from nearby **Cornelia Nixon Davis Center**. Before nursing care is needed, there is a wellness center on the campus, a 24-hour nurse on call, and the visit of a doctor each week. For the monthly service rate, it also offers 240 hours of assisted living services. Plantation Village has yard maintenance included, but it provides garden plots for people inclined to poke about in the dirt. Gardeners will appreciate the fact that this was once a working plantation where peanuts, rice and cotton were grown in abundance.

Capeside Village, 1111 Cape Boulevard, Wilmington, 392-4107, at The Cape Resort and Golf Club is a community of manufactured homes in a landscaped, golf course setting. Three bedroom and two bath homes begin at $64,900 including homesite. Close to shopping, entertainment and the beach, this convenient location south of Wilmington is pleasantly secluded. The ability to drive is important in this location.

Jensen's Coastal Plantation, just north of Wilmington at 5 Loblolly Trail, Hampstead, 270-3520, is a manufactured housing community, also beautifully landscaped, of individual homes. One buys the house and leases the land. These quality homes range in price from the low $60s to low $70s for a two-bedroom/two-bath plan. There are quite a few amenities included in this price. Each home has a 12 x 12 utility shed, peripheral plantings, cement driveway, all appliances, energy-efficient heating and cooling systems, a screened porch and more. This is a community for healthy individuals who are at least 55 years of age and appreciate independence within the context of a planned community. A clubhouse (membership is $10 per year), swimming pool, regular potluck suppers and various activity groups provide ample social opportunities.

There are many other retirement and life care communities in Greater Wilmington and the adjacent coastal counties. It would be impossible within the context of this guide to list all of them. This is a brief listing of some of the larger and longest established ones. Services vary widely among these homes, and the Cape Fear Council of Governments can be helpful in directing you to one that suits your particular needs.

CATHERINE KENNEDY HOME
207 S. 3rd St.
Wilmington   762-5322

This downtown Wilmington home is a nondenominational, non-profit private home operated by a self-perpetuating board of directors. It is the oldest home for the aged in the United States, having been organized in 1845 by Catherine deRosset Kennedy and known as The Ladies Benevolent Society. In 1963, space and facilities were included for men. Healthy residents enjoy three meals a day, stimulating activities and comfortable private rooms. While there is an infirmary, the Catherine Kennedy Home is not a nursing home. Residents who apply must be 62 years of age or older, ambulatory and in good health upon admission.

A very attractive feature of this home is its location on a beautiful campus in historic downtown Wilmington. It is a pleasant stroll away from shopping, dining and entertainment. Additionally, all of the city bus lines converge just a few blocks away. There is no admission or entrance fee. There is a nonrefundable fee of $2,500 upon moving into the home, and a schedule of the varying fees (based on accommodations and services required) is available by calling or writing.

CAPE FEAR HOTEL APARTMENTS
121 Chestnut St.
Wilmington　　　　　　　*762-0487*
This Housing and Urban Development program (HUD) is privately owned and operated. It is located in the heart of downtown Wilmington and allows residents access to shopping, dining and entertainment possibilities within only a few blocks. The fairly compact spaces are generally one bedroom units with a separate living room, individual kitchen and private bath. Utilities and cable TV are included in a monthly rental payment that is based entirely on income. Currently, payment is 30 percent of income. This income includes any interest one has in savings accounts. The income limit for admission is $21,050 for each individual.

CEDAR COVE
RETIREMENT AND REST HOME
27 Jasmine Cove Way
Wilmington　　　　　　　*395-5220*
Cedar Cove is a Rental Retirement Community and rest home. There is no buy-in fee or investment required. It offers private and semi-private rooms for independent individuals and couples who may require some assistance and supervision with daily living. Facility amenities include a formal parlor, library, TV lounge, craft, music, and activities rooms. A licensed beauty shop/barber shop is on the premises.

Nursing Homes

Retirement, once considered a late-in-life event, is falling closer toward the middle years now. In the Greater Wilmington area, there are more than 40 documented individuals who have seen their 100th birthdays come and go. While many people are able to situate themselves in later life in retirement communities, living basically independent lives, there are some people who require more extensive care.

As life lengthens in the population and retirees outgrow the services of their chosen retirement community, there is increasingly greater demand for all levels of nursing homes. Three types of homes in the region fall under the category of nursing home. They vary in the different levels of care offered to residents. A **Skilled Nursing Facility** (SNF) provides 24-hour nursing services for a person who has serious health care needs but does not require the intense and expensive level of care provided in a hospital. Many of the facilities are federally certified, so they may participate in Medicare or Medicaid programs.

An **Intermediate Care Facility** (ICF) provides less extensive care than an SNF; nursing and rehabilitation services are generally not provided on a 24-hour basis. This kind of facility specializes in providing housing and services for persons who can no longer live alone but need minimal medical supervision or help with personal or social care. Medicare or Medicaid programs are usually available.

Board and Care Facilities provide shelter, supervision, and care, but do not offer medical or skilled nursing services. This kind of facility is not licensed to participate in Medicare or Medicaid programs.

A partial listing of area nursing homes includes the following:

BRITTHAVEN OF WILMINGTON
5429 Oleander Dr.
Wilmington   *791-3451*
SNF

This is a 50-bed skilled nursing facility. It accepts Medicaid and Medicare patients.

CORNELIA NIXON DAVIS HEALTH CARE CENTER
1011 Porters Neck Rd.
Wilmington   *686-7195*
SNF, ICF

Located at Porter's Neck Plantation just north of Wilmington, this is a 194-bed center that accepts Medicaid and Medicare. This center, located on the site of a former plantation, is highly regarded for the quality of its care and attractiveness of its facility.

HILLHAVEN REHABILITATION AND CONVALESCENT CENTER
2006 S. 16th St.
Wilmington   *763-6271*
SNF, ICF

Located directly across from the New Hanover Regional Medical Center and in the midst of physician offices, this center provides occupational and physical therapy services in addition to being a skilled and intermediate care nursing facility. Medicaid and Medicare, VA, private insurance and private pay patients are the categories of acceptable payment.

PINNACLE CARE CENTER
820 Wellington Ave.
Wilmington   *343-0425*
SNF, ICF, Assisted Living

This 180-bed health care facility

Weekend parking on the downtown Wilmington deck is free.

Insiders' Tips

provides long term medical services with three levels of care: skilled, intermediate and retirement. They also provide outpatient rehabilitation services. This center accepts Medicaid, Medicare and private pay.

AUTUMN CARE OF SHALLOTTE
237 Mulberry St.
Shallotte   754-8858
SNF, Home for the Aged

This Brunswick County home is a 110-bed skilled and intermediate care facility.

OCEAN TRAIL CONVALESCENT CENTER
430 Fodale Ave.
Southport   457-9581
SNF, Home for the Aged

This Brunswick County home is a 106-bed facility that provides intermediate care. It accepts Medicaid patients.

GUARDIAN CARE OF BURGAW
P.O. Box 874
Burgaw   259-2129
ICF

This Pender County facility has 72 beds, offers intermediate care and accepts Medicaid.

If a person is able to reside in a private home setting with family or friends, but needs some assistance and supervision during the day, there is day care service available in the area. Day care for adults is provided by **Elderhaus, Inc.**, 1606 Princess Street or 1950 Amphitheater Drive, Wilmington, 343-8209.

This Intermediate Care facility is supervised by Registered Nurses and other health personnel. The program offers a stimulating environment for persons primarily 60 and over who need daily care. Field trips, arts and crafts programs, educational opportunities, lunch and snacks are provided for participants.

Activities, Organizations

There is an abundance of organizations, associations, support groups and activities specifically designed for the senior population. For detailed information, contact the **American Association of Retired People** in Wilmington at 762-2683. Opportunities for involvement in senior programs, including volunteer work, employment, education, health and enjoyment also may be found by contacting the following organizations.

KATIE B. HINES SENIOR CENTER
409 Cape Fear Blvd.
Carolina Beach   458-6609

This Carolina Beach center provides a full program of activities for senior citizens. Regular exercise programs, bingo, shuffleboard, blood pressure checks and regular covered dish suppers are just a few of the activities.

NEW HANOVER SENIOR CENTER
2222 S. College Rd.
Wilmington   452-6400

This larger center is incredibly busy, offering a long list of classes and programs for participants. On Wednesdays, there is a free ballroom dance for people over 50 years of age; tap dance classes, aerobics, jazzaerobics and line dancing are some of the other dance programs available. The center hosts a variety of support groups and computer classes and offers free haircuts to women the first Friday of each month. Lunch is served Monday through Friday on a sliding scale basis.

RSVP
2222 S. College Rd.
Wilmington   452-6400

The Retired Seniors Volunteer Program puts the talents of retired members of the community to work. Its motto is "Sharing the Experience of a Lifetime."

SCORE
Service Corps of Retired Executives
152 N. Front St.
Room 212, Main Post Office Bldg.
Wilmington   343-4576

Retired executives have an op-portunity to share their knowledge with new business owners in a mentoring relationship.

SENIOR AIDES PROGRAM
Job Counseling and Training for Senior Citizens
255 N. Front St.
Wilmington   251-5040

The Senior AIDES program places people 55 and older into employment situations in expectation that these placements will become permanent employment for these capable individuals.

SHIPP
Seniors Health Insurance Information Program
Wilmington   452-6400

Volunteers with this organization are trained by the North Carolina Department of Insurance to help people with Medicare problems, questions about Supplemental Insurance or long-term care issues.

REGION O SENIOR GAMES
2222 S. College Rd.
Wilmington   452-6400

The games are sports events in which senior citizens compete. They include archery, golf, running, swimming and more. The local group competes in national events and is known to bring home quite a few awards.

Inside
Volunteer Opportunities

Volunteer efforts are a big part of life in Wilmington and its surrounding beach communities. Although Wilmington is a rapidly growing city, there is still a keen sense of small town values. People take an active interest in helping their neighbors. There is genuine awareness that everyone who benefits from the community's resources has a social responsibility to give something back. Newcomers will quickly discover that involvement with good causes and organizations not only helps the community; it also helps strangers become members of the family. People are known by their works, and those who involve themselves in doing good works will be welcomed into many social and business circles. Newcomers looking for employment would do well to involve themselves in philanthropic efforts because the volunteer arena offers a good and fast lesson on how the community functions.

The demand for volunteer time and talent is extremely high. The spectrum of volunteer opportunities is also broad. No matter your particular interests, you are likely to find plenty of places where you can donate your time and talents. It is, in fact, very easy to become overrun with requests for your help once you donate your efforts. Although tens of thousands of people volunteer annually — and this may be a conservative estimate — Wilmington lacks a central coordinating agency to match volunteers with tasks and organizations. The local United Way publishes a partial directory of its own human services agencies and, while this is a good resource for getting involved with approximately two dozen United Way agencies, it isn't a volunteer coordination organization. The Community Services pages of the phone books contain a listing of all the human service agencies. Again, there are limitations because many organizations that utilize volunteers aren't listed.

So, the best advice on becoming involved is to select an interest and pick up the phone. The opportunities are overwhelming. The arts, the senior population, health services, nutrition, historic preservation, the environment, minority interests, business development, human relations, housing, schools and education, special festivals and more make up the volunteer possibilities in the Cape Fear region.

The following is a condensed listing of organizations that would appreciate your involvement.

Human Services

AMERICAN RED CROSS, CAPE FEAR CHAPTER
1102 S. 16th St.
Wilmington 762-2683

Volunteer positions include blood services aides, registered nurses, disaster team members, service to military case workers, health and safety class instructors and office aides. This very active organization has a high community profile and is extremely responsive to people in need.

BRUNSWICK COUNTY LITERACY COUNCIL
P. O. Box 6
Supply 754-7323

This organization helps adults in Brunswick County learn to read by pairing them with interested volunteers. Volunteers are carefully screened, trained, and matched with adult students. Volunteers are also needed in a variety of functions including publicity, office help, and newsletter publication.

CAPE FEAR AREA UNITED WAY
255 N. Front St.
Wilmington 251-5020

As with most United Way organizations, this is the funding body for a large number of community organizations. It has an information and referral service that may direct interested volunteers to various human service organizations.

CAPE FEAR LITERACY COUNCIL
608 Shipyard Blvd.
Wilmington 392-7323

As with the Brunswick County Literacy Council, this organization pairs volunteer reading tutors with adults.

CAPE FEAR MEMORIAL HOSPITAL
5301 Wrightsville Ave.
Wilmington 452-8380

Volunteers are needed to work in the gift shop, at the general information desk, the surgical information desk, central supply, purchasing, the pharmacy, imaging services, the patient representative program, the emergency center and the Lifeline program, and as needs arise.

CAPE FEAR SUBSTANCE ABUSE CENTER
721 Market St., 3rd Floor 343-0145
Wilmington Crisis line: (800)672-2903

Outpatient treatment for substance abuse, rape crisis counseling, a telephone crisis line and an emergency youth shelter are the functions of this agency.

DOMESTIC VIOLENCE SHELTER AND SERVICES
708 Market St.
Wilmington 343-0703

Women and children who have

You can purchase nonstudent borrower's cards for UNCW's Randall Library that are valid for six months for just $5.

Insiders' Tips

suffered domestic violence are sheltered by this agency. Volunteers are needed to help with direct services, office work, to serve as children's advocates, provide transportation, work in the recycled clothing shop, serve as court advocates and act as on-call workers in emergency situations.

GOOD SHEPHERD HOUSE
511 Queen St.
Wilmington 763-5902

This day shelter for homeless people needs volunteers to work at the front desk greeting guests, answering the phone and distributing toiletry items for the shower. Volunteers are also needed to sort clothing, distribute fresh clothing, do laundry and drive the van to take clients to work or on errands. People interested in working in the kitchen are needed to set up for lunch, serve meals and clean up.

HOPE HARBOR HOME (DOMESTIC VIOLENCE SHELTER)
P. O. Box 230
Supply 754-5856

At this domestic violence shelter in Brunswick County, volunteers are needed to serve as client advocates, work on the speakers bureau and help organize and implement fund raising activities.

HOSPICE OF THE LOWER CAPE FEAR
810 Princess St.
Wilmington 762-0200

This organization serves the needs of clients and their families when terminal illness occurs. Volunteers who will visit terminally ill clients, do office work and help with fund raising events are needed.

NEW HANOVER REGIONAL MEDICAL CENTER
2131 S. 17th St.
Wilmington 343-7704

While there are 70 "set" areas of volunteer involvement, opportunities are actually limitless. An average of 800 active volunteers work in the hospital each year in virtually every sector of hospital activity. Direct patient services, oncology volunteers, mailroom clerks, flowers, transportation for discharged patients, lobby receptionist positions, gift shop clerks, clerical assistance and courtesy van drivers are part of the varied volunteer opportunities available here. People with ideas for new volunteer activities are encouraged to call.

PARENTS SUPPORTING PARENTS
1501 Dock St.
Wilmington 762-1744

Support parents are needed to provide a listening ear to other parents dealing with the problems associated with parenting children with special needs.

SALVATION ARMY
820 N. 2nd St.
Wilmington 762-7354

This organization provides shelter for the homeless and assistance for people in difficult circumstances. It needs volunteers in fund raising activities and public relations efforts. Volunteers may serve on the Advisory Board, Ladies Auxiliary and in the shelter, which serves men, women and children. Volunteers may also work at the thrift store,

Loggerhead turtles are an endangered species.

Christmas fund raisers, the toy and food distribution center, the annual Coats for the Coatless drive, and on disaster relief teams. When Hurricane Andrew struck Florida in 1992, the Salvation Army from Wilmington was there with its mobile kitchen, and volunteers were part of the team.

SOUTHEASTERN SICKLE CELL ASSOCIATION
508 Castle St.
Wilmington 343-0422
Volunteers provide support services as well as fund raising activities and community education for this organization that concentrates its efforts on a disease that affects one in 400 African-Americans. Volunteers with public relations and promotions experience are needed to develop community awareness. Nurses are needed to do screenings.

STEPPING STONE MANOR (ALCOHOL REHABILITATION)
416 Walnut St.
Wilmington 762-1743
This is a rehabilitation center for problem drinkers and substance abusers. It needs volunteers to work in community education and fund raising as well as to cook in the center kitchen and drive residents to AA meetings at the YMCA.

VOLUNTEER AND INFORMATION CENTER, BRUNSWICK COUNTY
P. O. Box 333
Supply 754-4766
This agency provides emergency information and referral assistance for Brunswick County residents. Volunteers are needed to help the Brunswick County Council on the Status of Women in periodic food drives to replenish the food warehouse. Volunteers may also work to

prepare used clothing for distribution, provide office help and work in the Tree of Hope/Christmas Basket program.

Children

Public Schools offer a wide variety of volunteer opportunities that are essentially the same system to system. Help in the classroom. Tutor. Serve as a mentor for at-risk students. Work in dropout prevention programs. Help minority students achieve success in engineering/science careers. Get involved with the PTA/PTO. Basically, there are virtually limitless opportunities for volunteer help in our public schools. If you want to volunteer your time to the public schools, contact the Community Schools/Public Information Office in each system.

NEW HANOVER
COUNTY SCHOOL SYSTEM
1802 S. 15th St.
Wilmington 763-5431

BRUNSWICK COUNTY
SCHOOL SYSTEM
Central Office
Southport 457-5241

PENDER COUNTY SCHOOL SYSTEM
925 Penderlea Hwy.
Burgaw 259-2187

CHILD ADVOCACY COMMISSION
401 Chestnut St., Suite H
Wilmington 763-7430
This organization works as an advocate for children in three main areas: child care resource and referral, the juvenile restitution program, and Project First Stop, an educational/counseling program for first offenders under the age of 16 and their parents. Volunteer assistance in many areas is needed.

CROSSROADS, INC.
2414 Wrightsville Ave.
Wilmington 763-7440
This organization, founded and directed by Wilmingtonian Jack Dunn, is a volunteer-run program that helps disadvantaged children learn to succeed. Volunteer tutors and mentors work with children living in public housing and low-income neighborhoods.

CHILDREN'S HOME SOCIETY
3806 Park Ave.
Cedar Park Office Plaza
Wilmington 799-0655
Volunteers are needed for the Coastal Area Advisory Committee that educates the public about its services and provides feedback to the agency on its effectiveness in rendering adequate services to the Cape Fear area. Fund raisers are needed, as well as outreach volunteers and members of the Stork Bri-

gade, a group that provides transportation for infants released for adoption.

BOY SCOUTS OF AMERICA, CAPE FEAR COUNCIL
110 Long Street Dr.
Wilmington   *395-1100*

This organization requires a tremendous number of volunteers to serve Boy Scouts in the Cape Fear area. Board and committee members are needed as well as a host of leaders, coaches and advisors.

COMMUNITY BOYS' CLUB
901 Nixon St.
Wilmington   *762-1252*

The Community Boys' Club primarily serves minority youth. It relies upon volunteer involvement in fund raising, implementing special programs and working as adult role models for youth.

BRIGADE BOY'S CLUB
2759 Vance St.
Wilmington   *392-0747*

This venerable organization needs volunteers who will serve as photographers, class instructors, arts and crafts teachers, coaches, tutors, and group club leaders for both boys and girls.

GIRLS, INC.
1502 Castle St.
Wilmington   *763-6674*

Volunteers are needed in fund raising, as tutors, and group leaders and in many other capacities for this organization that primarily serves minority girls.

GIRL SCOUT COUNCIL OF COASTAL CAROLINA
108 E. Lockhaven Dr.
Goldsboro   *(800)558-9297*

The Girl Scouts need volunteers in many positions. Troop leaders, consultants, organizers, trainers, product sales coordinators (we're talking cookies here) and communicators are needed to aid this organization.

FAMILY SERVICES
2841 Carolina Beach Rd.
Wilmington   *392-7051*

This organization offers family counseling, consumer credit counseling, traveler's aid and the Big Buddy program for the lower Cape Fear. Volunteers are needed as office helpers, child sitters (while parents are in counseling sessions) and big buddies to be reliable, trusting friends to boys and girls in need of positive role models. The Big Buddy Program requires a minimum commitment of one year.

YMCA
2710 Market St.
Wilmington   *251-9622*

If you're a real hands-on volunteer, this is certainly the organization for you. Be a youth sports volunteer, a nursery attendant, a Special Olympics volunteer or a person who helps with maintenance of this facility.

YWCA
2815 S. College Rd.
Wilmington   *799-6820*

Youth programs, clerical help and maintenance are just a few of the areas where the YWCA needs your volunteer assistance. If you want to be a tutor at six locations throughout the Cape Fear area, this organization can use your help.

Seniors

NEW HANOVER COUNTY
DEPARTMENT OF AGING
2222 S. College Rd.
Wilmington   452-6400

This governmental organization can point you in many directions if you wish to become involved in volunteer efforts that both serve and involve senior citizens. This agency was formed in 1983 to serve older adults by promoting visibility and representation, providing support services that encourage independent living and operating as the focal point of aging services in the community.

ELDERHAUS, INC.
1606 Princess St.
Wilmington   343-8209

Program aides, activity assistants, meal servers and van assistants are needed for this agency that provides daycare for senior citizens. Volunteer board members oversee the operation of this organization that serves seniors in two locations through fund raising, public relations, education and more.

RETIRED SENIOR
VOLUNTEER PROGRAM
2011 Carolina Beach Rd.
Wilmington   452-6400

RSVP taps the talents of retired people in "Sharing the Experience of a Lifetime." Volunteers have special assignments matching their interests, skills, and abilities in schools, libraries, hospitals, nursing homes and other places. Volunteers in this program are age 60 and older.

SENIOR AIDES PROGRAM
255 N. Front St.
Wilmington   251-5040

This organization benefits from the assistance of volunteers in an advisory council capacity. People who volunteer to work for this program donate their time in public speaking, representing the agency at community fairs, preparing publicity materials, giving management and technical assistance and assisting in personnel placement of Senior AIDES through resume preparation, job interview skills, job search assistance and more.

The Arts

ARTS COUNCIL
OF THE LOWER CAPE FEAR
20 Market St.
Wilmington   763-2787

The Arts Council has a number of programs that need volunteer involvement. The annual Piney Woods Celebration of the Arts, a two-day cultural arts event held at Hugh McRae Park, needs a host of volunteers to help with parking, admission, preparation, publicity and more. The Arts Council has a volunteer Board of Directors with administrative committees in the areas of advocacy, finance, fund raising, membership and publications/information.

ST. JOHN'S MUSEUM OF ART
114 Orange St.
Wilmington   763-0281

This extraordinarily fine museum of visual arts needs volunteers to work in many interesting capacities. Things are always happening at this lively center, and volunteers are needed to serve as docents, and in membership, publicity, fund raising, the gift shop, and much more. The museum constantly has new projects underway such as a cookbook, art trips to other cities, a film series, artist sales, exhibitions, education programs and special events. If you love the visual arts, this is a wonderful place to offer your volunteer services.

(See Arts Chapter for additional arts organizations that use volunteers.)

Historic Preservation and Community Development

HISTORIC WILMINGTON FOUNDATION
209 Dock St.
Wilmington   762-2511

Volunteers interested in preserving the architectural heritage of the region are invited to work in public relations, membership, the deRosset Committee (named for the Foundation's home that is under continual renovation), education, preservation action, urban properties and gardens. There is a yearly Gala, the primary fund raiser, that relies on a host of volunteers for logistics, publicity, entertainment, food and everything else required to throw a major, glittering party and auction.

DOWNTOWN AREA REVITALIZATION EFFORT (DARE)
201 N. Front St.
Wilmington   763-7349

DARE concentrates on revital-

ization of the Central Business District in downtown Wilmington. There are 36 volunteers on the Board of Directors who represent a cross-section of the community. Thirteen are designated by other organizations; seven are elected based upon their profession; and sixteen serve as at-large members. This body expedites quality development of the commercial district by offering a wide range of services and detailed information to potential downtown businesses.

LOWER CAPE FEAR HISTORICAL SOCIETY
126 S. 3rd St.
Wilmington   762-0492

Volunteers are needed for publicity, fund raising, membership and planning at this venerable organization that seeks to accurately preserve the history of the area. Volunteers also work as docents and archivists in the society's home, the Latimer House. The society sponsors the yearly Olde Wilmington by Candlelight Tour of Homes.

WILMINGTON COMMUNITY DEVELOPMENT CORPORATION
511 Cornelius Harnett Blvd.
Wilmington   762-7555

This organization nurtures business development through the Small Business Incubator and other programs aimed at economic development. A relatively new endeavor, this organization looks for volunteers interested in broadening the area tax base by helping launch new businesses by offering low-cost office space, financial advice, marketing advice and more.

Inside
Hospitals and Medical Care

The Cape Fear area offers excellent medical facilities and care. For most of this century, residents generally went inland to more sophisticated medical facilities in search of state-of-the-art technology to treat serious illness. However, within the past decade, medical services in Greater Wilmington have taken a dramatic turn for the better, and there is an emerging sense of regional pride over local medical care services.

There are currently more than 230 licensed practicing physicians and 24 practicing chiropractic physicians serving the Greater Wilmington area. They have access to some of the most technologically progressive facilities and equipment in the state by way of the two larger hospitals that serve the area.

Several small hospitals dot the Cape Fear coast. Care beyond their services is immediately referred to Wilmington's larger hospitals, but these smaller facilities also offer excellent health care for a broad range of medical services. Vacationers along the Brunswick Beaches and Topsail Island may find these smaller hospitals convenient for medical service.

Hospitals

NEW HANOVER REGIONAL MEDICAL CENTER
2131 South 17th St.
Wilmington   343-7000

New Hanover Regional Medical Center is a 568-bed hospital operated by trustees appointed by the New Hanover County Board of Commissioners. It offers basic, high quality care, but it increasingly offers specialized care for the more critical illnesses and conditions.

New Hanover Regional's Coastal Heart Center, which has become a magnet for patients with heart disease from New Hanover and surrounding counties, provides some of the best physicians, surgeons and support staff in the state of North Carolina. Services in this center, particularly important for a community with a booming retirement population, include cardiac catheterization, angioplasty and open heart surgery. New Hanover Regional Medical Center provides a full range of services for patients with cancer. Services include chemotherapy, radiation and surgery. **CanSurvive**, a support group for those who have coped with cancer, was created to allow these individuals to share their experiences.

Designated by the state as one of eight regional Trauma Centers, this hospital provides a mobile intensive care unit, **VitaLink**, that can transport the most seriously ill and injured patients from the region's community hospitals at any hour of the day or night. Equipped with life-sustaining systems and trained staff, the vehicle is also in constant communication with the hospital until the patient arrives. A paramedic and registered nurse are always onboard.

New Hanover Regional BirthPlace specializes in obstetrical services, offering more than two dozen rooms that combine home-like decor with sophisticated facilities to allow a family-centered birthing experience. Round-the-clock care by highly trained nurses gives even the tiniest or sickest infant a fighting chance for life. The hospital also has a Geriatrics Nursing Unit, a 24-hour Poison Control Center, a host of wellness programs, and is literally surrounded by the offices of most of the physicians in the area.

A recently-opened **Medical Mall**, at the intersection of Seventeenth Street and Glen Meade Drive, makes outpatient services such as MRI, X-rays, mammography and lab tests convenient.

As emotional and mental problems have become increasingly viewed as treatable conditions, a free-standing psychiatric hospital on the hospital campus, **The Oaks**, 343-7787, 2131 S. 17th Street, attracts patients from the entire region. The Oaks provides specialized care for 62 adult, adolescent and acute inpatients. A staff of 100 responds to the needs of these patients in a comfortable setting that opens onto peaceful gardens. Evergreen is The Oaks' partial hospitalization program that provides day therapy for patients who go home each night. There are evening programs and services for patients coping with various addictions.

New Hanover Regional Medical Center is accredited by the Joint Commission on Accreditation of Healthcare Organizations.

CAPE FEAR MEMORIAL HOSPITAL
5301 Wrightsville Ave.
Wilmington   *452-8100*

Cape Fear Memorial is an acute care, not-for-profit community hospital of 142 beds. A recent $8.5 million dollar renovation was completed in 1992, providing additional space for the hospital's increasingly expanding services. The hospital offers a wide range of medical, surgical and ambulatory care, which includes emergency services. Outpatient surgery, radiology, ultrasound, magnetic

Insiders' Tips

Be patient about bridge openings. Remember, it's a whole lot harder to stop a boat in the water than a car on the road.

910-341-3300   **UЈ**   *fax 910-341-3419*

daniel gottovi, m.d.
internal medicine / pulmonary medicine
diplomate ABIM, FCCP

1202 medical center drive
wilmington, nc 28401

resonance imaging, laboratory facilities and a pharmacy are some of the services offered.

Women's Services offers a special environment for obstetric and gynecological needs, including a family-oriented birthing center and breast diagnostic program. An Outpatient Rehabilitation Center includes the Sports Medicine Clinic, which was opened in the summer of 1993. Also located in this center is Occupational Health Services, a comprehensive program for business and industry to promote employee wellness.

Cape Fear Memorial Hospital is tremendously committed to providing programs that promote wellness and healthy behaviors. The department offers programs on nutrition, CPR certification, exercise, smoking cessation and stress management. For persons ages 50 and older, this hospital offers free membership in the Healthy Horizons program. This program, with its membership at approximately 10,000, offers free education programs, free blood pressure testing, free assistance with insurance claims and a host of special events and benefits to its members.

The hospital's **Lifeline**, a personal emergency response system that links the user with Cape Fear Memorial Hospital's Emergency Center, is a vital connection for potential patients who may live alone and require sudden medical care. The **ASK-A-NURSE Program**, 452-8381 or (800) 832-8841, connects callers with registered nurses 24 hours a day. This free service offers callers health information, physician referrals and community resource suggestions. All requests for information are kept confidential.

Cape Fear Memorial Hospital is accredited by the Joint Commission on Accreditation of Healthcare Organizations and is a member of the Coastal Carolinas Health Alliance.

PENDER MEMORIAL HOSPITAL
507 Fremont St.
Burgaw   *259-5451*

Pender Memorial Hospital is a general acute medical and skilled nursing facility with a bed capacity of 66. It offers a wide range of inpatient and outpatient services that include ambulatory/same day surgery, laparoscopy, laboratory, radiology, respiratory and physical therapy.

THE BRUNSWICK HOSPITAL
U.S. Hwy. 17
Supply   *754-8121*

This hospital is licensed for 60 beds. A 24-hour physician-staffed emergency department, full medical and surgical services and an Inpatient Adolescent Psychiatric Care program are offered in this hospital that is close to the Brunswick Beaches.

J. ARTHUR DOSHER MEMORIAL HOSPITAL
924 S. Howe St.
Southport   *457-5271*

J. Arthur Dosher Memorial Hospital is a 40-bed, acute care hospital located in Southport. Established in 1930, this small, efficient hospital offers general medical services. It has an emergency room with 24-hour physician coverage, a radiology department, comprehensive surgical services and a cardiac stress test lab. It provides intensive/coronary care. There are more than 125 employees, more than 120 volunteers and 13 physicians representing six medical specialties.

Immediate Care

For nonsurgical medical services, the Cape Fear area has more than half a dozen immediate care businesses. Vacationers or residents with relatively minor injuries, illnesses or conditions may prefer the convenience of visiting these centers over making an appointment to see a personal doctor. Illnesses and injuries beyond their capabilities are referred to area hospitals.

These medical service facilities offer emergency care but are not open 24 hours a day. In most cases, they are not open seven days a week. If you need care and choose one of these centers, you're advised to phone ahead.

DOCTOR'S IN IMMEDIATE CARE
4606 Oleander Dr.
Wilmington   *452-0800*
East Side of Wilmington

This center has walk-in immediate care for any illness or minor injury for all ages. Complete laboratory and X-ray facilities are on the premises. It offers a full range of

Insiders' Tips

Don't let steamed crabs come in contact with anything that touched uncooked crabs — not pots, nets, counters, or containers. That's how you keep food bacteria-free.

Photo: Scott Taylor

A future captain surveys the sea.

women's physicals and Pap smears.

DOCTOR'S URGENT CARE CLINIC
1601 S. College Rd.
Wilmington   *395-1110*
East Side of Wilmington
Women's health services include Pap smears, breast exams, pregnancy testing and contraceptives. This clinic specializes in adult and pediatric care related to minor illnesses and injuries. Complete laboratory and X-ray facilities are on the premises.

MEDAC,
CONVENIENT MEDICAL CARE
3710 Shipyard Blvd.
Wilmington   *791-0075*
South Side of Wilmington
MEDAC has qualified emergency physicians from New Hanover Regional Medical Center, registered nurses and registered X-ray technologists. It treats accidental and minor illnesses,   and offers physicals and worker's compensation services.

NORTHSIDE MEDICAL CENTER
406 N. 4th St.
Wilmington   *251-7715*
Downtown Wilmington
This center's primary population is the minority community where it addresses the same needs as other walk-in medical centers. It also concentrates on nutrition and other wellness programs. The doctor specializes in internal medicine.

Express Care

Hwy. 17
Shallote   *579-0800*

Three miles south of Shallotte between Sunset Beach and Ocean Isle Beach, this facility specializes in minor illnesses and injuries.

Penslow Medical Center

Intersection of Hwy. 17 and Hwy. 50
Holly Ridge   *329-7591*

This is a family practice that welcomes walk-ins.

Visitors to **Topsail Island** are within a 45-minute drive to hospitals and clinics in Wilmington. For serious injuries and illnesses, the Cape Fear Coast has ample EMT services that can be reached by calling 911.

Physician Groups

Wilmington Health Associates, P.A., 1202 Medical Center Drive, 341-1031, is a large group of physicians who specialize in such areas as pulmonary medicine, cardiology, gastroenterology, neurology, hematology/oncology, infectious diseases, dermatology and endocrinology. General medical care is also offered.

Carolina OB-Gyn Centre, P.A., 343-1031, 1802 South 17th Street, Wilmington, specializes in obstetrical/gynecological services. It provides medical care in the areas of infertility evaluation, laser surgery, office ultrasound, antepartum testing, sterilization, sterilization reversal and menopause therapy. This group has been in practice continually since 1977.

Hanover Medical Specialists, P.A., 763-5182, 1515 Doctor's Circle, Wilmington, offers specialist services in cardiology, endocrinology/diabetes, gastroenterology, hermatology/oncology and pulmonary/allergy. This group began in approximately 1974. Each specialty is housed in its own building, there is a wide range of in-house testing for cardiology, and this group has the only certified diabetic teaching nurse in the area.

Hanover Urological Associates, P.A., 763-6251, Glen Meade Road, Wilmington, and 452-5254, 5305 Wrightsville Avenue, Wilmington, specializes in pediatric and adult urology, cancer care, male infertility and impotence, laparoscopic surgery, prostate ultrasound and vasectomy surgery.

EYEWITNESS NEWS 3

Coverage You Can Count On!

5:30, 6:00, and 11:00 p.m.

Inside
Higher Education and Research

Before Wilmington became the tourist mecca it is today, the Port City had always been a major commercial hub. Early centers for higher learning were accordingly of the vocational ilk, and it wasn't until the mid-20th century that institutions of broader education were established. The Cape Fear coast's present growing economy and desirable location are again attracting industry, creating the need for higher levels and greater specialization of learning as never before. Wilmington now qualifies as a college town, being home not only to the University of North Carolina at Wilmington, a senior four-year institution with a masters-level graduate program, but also to the excellent vocational/technical schools Cape Fear Community College and Miller-Motte Business College. Institutions of higher learning nearest to the greater Topsail Island area are Coastal Carolina Community College in Jacksonville and those in Wilmington, listed below.

THE UNIVERSITY OF NORTH CAROLINA AT WILMINGTON
601 S. College Rd.   *395-3000*

UNCW is successfully living up to its responsibilities as the only public university in southeastern North Carolina. *U.S. News & World Report's* 1992 guide, *America's Best Colleges*, named the university one of the top 25 universities in the south, based on the opinions of 2,500 college presidents, deans and admissions directors from around the nation. The university's marine biology program was recently ranked seventh best in the world by the *Gourman Report*. It has sites close to estuaries and the ocean. The primary site is its four-acre Center for Marine Science Research at Wrightsville Beach.

Forty-six undergraduate degree programs and 14 graduate degree programs are offered within the university's four schools: the College of Arts and Sciences, the Cameron School of Business Administration, the School of Education and the School of Nursing. Four-year undergraduate programs lead to the Bachelor of Arts and Bachelor of Science degrees. There is also a variety of pre-professional programs and special programs in several areas including marine science research and continuing education. Through the Contract Extension Program, students may study freshman and sophomore level courses at three regional community colleges, including Brunswick Community College in Supply, and be eligible to apply for admission to

UNCW as baccalaureate degree candidates.

The university originated as Wilmington College in 1946 and became a senior four-year college in 1963, two years after occupying the present 661-acre tract of land bordering South College Road. It became the fifth campus of the University of North Carolina in 1969. Today the fully-accredited university occupies 70 air-conditioned buildings predominantly of modified Georgian architecture.

Sixty-seven percent of the more than 400 instructional and research faculty hold doctoral degrees. Class size averages 30 students with a faculty-to- student ratio of 1:17. There are approximately 8,000 students currently enrolled.

The recently enlarged William Randall Library, 395-3760, contains more than 380,000 volumes and subscribes to 4,890 serial titles. A 73-seat auditorium is equipped for various types of audiovisual use. The library is a partial depository for U.S. Government publications and has a current inventory of 450,000 items in hardcopy and microtext. Randall Library is a full depository for North Carolina documents, which are readily available to all users, including nonstudents. (Nonstudent memberships are available for $5 semiannually. The fee includes a parking permit, if needed.)

The Center for Marine Science Research, 256-3721, is dedicated to fostering a multidisciplinary approach to basic marine research. Basic and applied research programs are available on undergraduate and graduate levels, making use of the Center's 15 laboratories, video equipment/editing facilities, machine tool shop, aquatic specimens holding room and USDA-licensed animal facility. Additional lab space is available for research requiring constant flow-through seawater.

The Center maintains eight research vessels ranging in size from 13 to 22 feet and highly specialized equipment that includes a robot data-gathering vehicle. The Center serves as host for the NOAA-sponsored National Undersea Research Center for the southeastern U.S. and houses headquarters for the NC National Estuarine Research Reserve (NCNERR) through a cooperative agreement with the NC Division of Coastal Management. The NCNERR program manages four estuarine reserve sites as natural laboratories and coordinates research and education activities.

Other instructional and research resources at UNCW include the 10-acre Herbert Bluenthal Memorial Wildflower Preserve, campus-wide computing services and the Division

Cape Fear Museum is a delightful experience full of regional history.

Insiders' Tips

for Public Service and Extended Education. Noncredit, continuing education programs and courses designed for personal and professional enrichment comprise the Division for Public Service and Extended Education. These include topics in art, languages, investing and estate planning, SCUBA diving, photography, professional development, adult scholar enrichment, music and more. Programs can be custom-designed to fit particular needs.

Student life on campus is enhanced by a full battery of services and entertainments, food service facilities, three student periodicals, a musical-format radio station and student activities. Kenan Auditorium hosts theatrical, symphonic and instructional events year round. The university sponsors 16 intercollegiate sports and as many varsity teams, both men's and women's, including golf, tennis, swimming and diving. Both UNCW Ultimate teams are top-ranked nationally. Sports facilities include several fields, tennis, volleyball, outdoor basketball courts and a physical education complex that includes Trask Coliseum, the Seahawks' home basketball court.

UNCW's school year is divided into four sessions consisting of the standard fall and spring semesters plus two summer sessions. For information on undergraduate admissions, the number to call is 395-3243; for graduate studies call 395-3135. For information on Public Service Programs and Extended Education call 395-3193.

CAPE FEAR COMMUNITY COLLEGE
411 N. Front St.   *343-0481*

Concentrating on 35 one-year and two-year technical and vocational programs, Cape Fear exerts a major educational presence in the area, despite (perhaps because of) recent overcrowding. There are two campuses, one in downtown Wilmington and one in Burgaw, about 21 miles north of Wilmington. Two-year programs, some leading to associate's degrees, include studies in the fields of business, chemical technology, microcomputing, criminal justice, education, electrical and nautical engineering, hotel and restaurant management and paralegal technology. Among the one-year programs are administrative office technology, a renowned boat-building curriculum, dental assistance, industrial electricity and mechanics, nursing, marine and diesel mechanics and welding. Studies in basic law enforcement training, phlebotomy and real estate lead to certificates. CFCC maintains a library that is open to the public at no charge and offers financial aid, courses in high school equivalency (G.E.D.),

Insiders' Tips

Enjoy many interesting films and lectures at little or no cost at St. John's Museum of Art and the Cape Fear Museum.

adult literacy and Human Resources Development. Many special programs and seminars are free or very reasonably priced.

MILLER-MOTTE BUSINESS COLLEGE

606 S. College Rd.   *392-4660*
(800)868-6622

Miller-Motte is a well-respected 78-year-old collegiate alternative for students desiring employment-targeted training. The school is an accredited institution that maintains a strongly monitored job-placement service to assist their graduates in becoming employed — Miller-Motte's primary mission. With the help of a board of advisors made up of faculty, employed former students and regional employers, Miller-Motte's curricula are constantly updated to keep pace with changes in the regional job market. The school is well-known and trusted among employers in southeastern North Carolina.

Miller-Motte offers 15- and 18-month diploma programs in business management, accounting, administrative assistance, medical assistance and microcomputer specialties. Nine-month and 12-month certificate programs are available in word processing, general office accounting, general office technology and medical unit clerk studies. Financial assistance, student services and internships in some programs are available.

THE CAPE CENTER FOR ALTERNATIVE PROGRAMS OF EDUCATION, SHAW UNIVERSITY

224 N. Front St.   *763-9091*

The Cape is one of ten accredited satellite programs of Shaw University in Raleigh and has been operating in Wilmington for eight years. The school offers only night classes that lead to bachelor's degrees in psychology, sociology, criminal justice, religion and philosophy, public administration, business management and liberal studies. Transfer credits from two-year and four-year institutions are accepted, and life experience can earn students up to 27 credit-hours. Classes tend to be small, and total enrollment is generally under 200.

BRUNSWICK COMMUNITY COLLEGE

U.S. Hwy. 17 N.   *754-6900*
Supply

With three locations — the main campus in Supply, a campus in Southport and the Industrial Education Center in Leland — BCC serves more than 1,300 curriculum students and more than 3,000 others in continuing education courses. The college offers one-year and two-year certificate, diploma and associate's degree programs in 15 disciplines. These include administrative office technology, air conditioning, heating and refrigeration, automotive mechanics, various business studies, cosmetology, dental assisting, real estate, recreational grounds, nursing and medical records and welding. The General Education program works in conjunction with the University of North Carolina at Wilmington to expedite transferals from Brunswick's two-year curricula to UNCW's four-year programs.

Through its New and Expanding Industry Program and its Small Business Center, Brunswick Community College works closely with area businesses and industry to tailor curricula to regional needs. The college also assists industry in seeking, evaluating, training and retraining employees according to changing standards. BCC will custom-design courses to fit various needs and typically conducts industrial courses at the job site to upgrade employees to associate degree levels. Brunswick Community College is fully accredited and is widely known as a substantial educational value for the tuition dollar.

Research Facilities

Not surprisingly, the major emphases of research performed on the Cape Fear Coast are in the fields of oceanography, wetland and estuarine studies, marine biomedical and environmental physiology, and marine biotechnology and aquaculture.

The University of North Carolina at Wilmington is the single most important sponsor of such research, and the **Center for Marine Science Research** is its primary research organ. Faculty members in the departments of biological sciences, chemistry, and earth sciences all participate in the Center's programs while performing marine science re-

search. Additional research equipment at the Center not mentioned earlier in the description of the University includes a low-temperature aquarium room, an atomic absorption spectrophotometer and an extensive microscopy capability. The Center also serves as host for the NOAA-sponsored National Undersea Research Center (NURC) for the southeastern United States. NURC annually supports fisheries management, ocean-floor processes and other research projects from the Gulf of Maine to the Gulf of Mexico. This support is based upon competitive proposals.

Although the **Division of Marine Fisheries**, an agency of the NC Department of Environmental Health and Natural Resources, maintains an office in Wilmington, all its research functions are conducted in Morehead City. This agency acts as steward for the protection of all coastal wetlands, waterways and the ocean within a three-mile limit. UNCW's Center for Marine Science Research assists with research needed by the Wilmington branch of Marine Fisheries.

Masonboro Island and Zeke's Island comprise two of the four components of the **North Carolina National Estuarine Research Reserve**, the others being Rachel Carson Island and Currituck Banks in north-eastern North Carolina. Masonboro Island is the last and largest undisturbed barrier island remaining on the southern North Carolina coast. It also happens to be among the newest. Its 8 miles of thin beach and expansive marshes were separated from Pleasure Island in 1952 when Carolina Beach Inlet was cut through to the Intracoastal Waterway. (Pleasure Island had been created in the 1930s by the digging of Snow's Cut.) A controversial move at that time, Masonboro's separation created one of the most productive estuarine systems along the coast. In plain English, that partly means that loggerhead turtles, endangered by relentless development of nearby nesting grounds (the beaches) have a place in which to nest undisturbed into the foreseeable future. This is also true for a multitude of bird species, mammals, lizards, shellfish and aquatic vertebrates.

The National Estuarine Research Reserve system was created by Congress to preserve undisturbed estuarine systems for research into and education about the human impact on coastal habitats. Masonboro and Zeke's Island are now living outdoor classrooms and laboratories for researchers, students, naturalists and hobbyists.

Masonboro is accessible only by boat. Fishing, picnicking, sunbathing, surfing, walking, shelling and (for the time being, at least) camping are permitted. The North Carolina National Estuarine Research Reserve has limited its presence on Masonboro and Zeke's Island by allowing traditional activities to continue, including hunting within regulations, pending future conclusions that may result from steady monitoring.

The Zeke's Island component of the reserve, located immediately south of Federal Point in the Cape Fear River, actually consists of three islands — Zeke's, North Island, No-Name Island — and The Basin, the body of water enclosed by the breakwater known locally as The Rocks. Because the Basin has been relatively isolated from the Cape Fear River so long, it exhibits a salinity level very near to that of the ocean, presenting researchers with something of a huge ocean aquarium. Zeke's Island is similar to Masonboro in every way minus the ocean surf. Activities pursued on Masonboro are generally common on Zeke's Island. Access to Zeke's Island is by boat and by walking across The Rocks, preferably at low tide (a potentially hazardous proposition). For further information about these islands, see the chapters on Attractions, Camping and Sports.

Another preserve that has received its fair share of scientific scrutiny is Permuda Island (the name is an obvious corruption). This string bean of a spit bears substantial archaeological significance in that large tracts consist essentially of huge shell middens created by prehistoric inhabitants over a vast span of time. Such sites are rare in the ever-shifting, acidic soils of the state's barrier islands. Despite decades of farming in the modern era, the archaeological resources survived intact. Saved from development by a combination of local conservation strategy and unlikely profitability, the island passed into state ownership several years ago. Of further interest is the theory that Permuda Island represents an original barrier island later eclipsed by the growth of what today is called Topsail Island. A similar theory has been posited for North Island near Ft. Fisher (mentioned above) and other privately-owned islands along the Pender County coast such as Hutaff and Lee Islands. (The only other islands behind the barriers are dredge spoil mounds created by the Army Corps of Engineers.) Permuda Island is located near the north end of Topsail Island and is not open to the public. The island remains in a natural state and is managed by the NC Dept. of Environment, Heath and Natural Resources/NCNERR and the Dept. of Marine Fisheries.

To inquire about the Cape Fear components of the NC National Estuarine Research Reserve and other coastal resource issues, call John Taggart, the Coastal Reserve Coordinator at UNCW's Center for Marine Science Research, 256-3721.

Within the realm of marine biotechnology, nutraceuticals — foods with therapeutic values such as beta carotene and fish oils — have burgeoned as a field of active developmental research. At the forefront of this research in the Lower Cape Fear is **Maricultura, Incorporated**, a small, private, development-stage company located in the former Babies Hospital (7225 Wrightsville Avenue, 256-5010) next to UNCW's Center for Marine Science Research. Founded in 1984 by CEO and Chairman Thomas Veach Long, II, Ph.D., Maricultura specializes in the development of high-value materials, especially for nutritional applications in humans and animals. These materials are derived by fermentation of marine microorganisms. In addition to performing contract developmental research for the government and private concerns, Maricultura depends upon internally generated funding for original research and development and markets its products to outside firms for practical application.

When driving along U.S. 421 through Kure Beach, you may wonder what that large array of strange-looking racks on the oceanside of the road is all about. Another array stands across the road. Curiously enough, these arrays are historical landmarks designated by the American Society of Materials Testing. The racks are used for atmospheric testing and have been in place since 1935. They are the property of the **LaQue Center for Corrosion Technology, Inc.**, headquartered at Wrightsville Beach. The Center, which pronounces its name "luh-

KWEE," conducts tests upon any material subject to corrosion, particularly alloys and coatings such as window fixtures and paints, under various corrosive conditions, whether atmospheric, marine or artificially induced. Testing makes up about 98 percent of their lab work, but they also perform related research into corrosion technology. The LaQue Center sponsors seminars such as the popular "Fundamentals of Corrosion and Its Control," which is offered four times each year at local hotels. Through an internship program affiliated with UNCW and Cape Fear Community College, the Center employs students as operating assistants for round-the-clock test monitoring. The annual Riverfest Marine Exposition in October also features the Center's own corrosion exposition on Front Street. Open-house tours of the Wrightsville Beach facility are conducted periodically and may be arranged for groups on request.

The Fort Fisher Hermit

During the turmoil of the 1960s, students, reporters and curious tourists often came to the old bearded man with leather-tanned skin who lived alone on the salt marsh south of Fort Fisher. They came to ask his opinions about those troubled times that the hermit said were like "a wave of mental illness sweeping the country." He told them wise things: "We need two presidents; the job is just too big for one man.... The biggest freeloaders are our 400 or 500 congressmen and senators.... I don't think mankind is headed for destruction. Man has been around 500 million years, and I am not ready to give up on him yet."

The hermit was Robert Edward Harrell who, for 17 years until his death in June, 1972, lived in a World War II-era concrete bunker not far from where the North Carolina Aquarium at Fort Fisher now stands. It's an inhospitable place,

Photo: George Harrill

Robert Harrel lived for more than 17 years in the salt marshes of Fort Fisher.

Photo: Fred Pickler

Harrell fishes with a seine net.

scorched by the summer sun, mosquito-ridden, frozen and wind-scoured in winter. It's also a beautiful place, serene, teeming with wildlife; and in the late 1950s it was totally desolate. The bunker, a small rectangle with no windows, was stuffed with the hermit's ragtag accumulations of driftwood, Styrofoam surfboards, sunglasses, newspapers and tin cans. Long planks of wood steepled over the open doorway sheltered the entrance outside of which crates, makeshift tables and collected debris lay scattered about. He had dug a few shallow, brackish wells nearby. The 1929 Chevy in which he slept, during his early years there, was Fort Fisher's first dune buggy.

Visitors were often treated to endless conversation and were asked to sign his guest register; the hermit could talk a blue streak. Harrell claimed to have 17,000 visitors a year. He was renowned for his fishing skills, and some folks asked to know his best fishing holes. The hermit's iron frying pan, seeded always with at least 91 cents, was in plain sight, and if people added to it or paid him for his photograph, he always gave something back. He generously shared his "millionaire's ration," made from any number of foods abundant on the tidal flats: crabs, oysters, fish, shrimp, turtles, raccoons, opossums .... One young visitor named Harry Warren was given a fragment of a Civil War cannonball, an event which probably led the boy to become a foremost hermit authority. The hermit's abode was everything to him, except when Hurricane Helene in 1958 drove him to hitchhike to Wilmington. "I like to be alone," he was heard to say, "but not that alone."

Harry Warren, now a researcher for the Cape Fear Museum, holds two photographs. Lifting one of a well-groomed young man in white shirt and tie he says, "For some reason, this man—" then he lifts a photo of the hermit, a grizzled, bearded old man wearing nothing but baggy shorts and a straw hat, "—became this man. It's a pretty stark transition."

Robert Harrell was born on Ground Hog Day in 1893 near Gaffney, SC. By his appearance and his membership in Boiling Springs (NC) High School's Athenean Literary Society in 1913, one might have expected him to successfully pursue the American dream. Instead, he eked out a living as a sidewalk tinker in Shelby, NC, and as a linotype operator. He married and had four sons and a daughter who died young. When one of his sons committed suicide in the 1930s, his family moved north. Harrell stayed behind.

His first sojourn at Fort Fisher ended sometime prior to 1955 when his brother retrieved him from a Wilmington jail. The trouble began because Harrell's pet jaybird wouldn't eat. Knowing the bird would be more likely to eat something alive and moving, he scurried about for live food. A local real estate woman happened to cross his path and when she inquired about his frantic behavior, he asked, "Have you got anything that will wiggle?"

The earliest confirmed date of Harrell's permanent residence on the salt marsh is 1955, but he was fond of claiming that he "rode out Hazel" — Hurricane Hazel that is — one year earlier. He subscribed to an unaccredited discipline called biopsychology and claims to have come to Fort Fisher to write a book, A Tyrant in Every Home. "He was a pretty good writer," Warren says. "I do think he was serious about [writing] it. He claimed to have finished a 500-page manuscript and sent it to his sister, but a manuscript has never been produced. . . . I think he mainly came to get away from some troubled times he was having. He had a history of being institutionalized. I think this was the final escape from that."

At an age when most people think about collecting Social Security, Harrell began a new life with little more than the clothes on his back. He quickly became something of an attraction in Kure and Carolina Beach, often supplementing his meals of seafood, wild greens and berries with food purchased or scavenged from the local A&P. Regular visitors practically adopted him and brought him food and fresh water. He took to his celebrity well and began recording his visitors' signatures. Several registers were known to exist. It's possible most were lost in the several fires that ravaged Harrell's extremely flammable abode. Only one register survives, a 1949 calender book containing about 2,500 signatures dated between November 1971 and June 1972, now part of the Cape Fear Museum's hermit collection.

Harrell wasn't the only loner to come to Fort Fisher. In the late 60s, there was the less-famous "Wild Man" of Fort Fisher, Empie Hewett, who, according to local legend, was "a little touched." Harrell was the only person Empie would have anything to do with. Then there was Preacher Vaughn.

Preacher Vaughn got it into his head one day that he, too, would live on the marsh. So he drove his old camper down there and proposed to the hermit that he would teach the "new-time" religion, and the hermit would teach the "old-time" religion. Sometimes they showed up on the Carolina Beach boardwalk doing just that, but it wasn't meant to last. Harry Warren explains, "The hermit kind of got the idea that Preacher Vaughn wasn't everything that he was supposed to be, and as the story goes, the hermit took all of [the preacher's] tires off his vehicle and left it sitting down there."

Before long, the state became interested in developing the Fort Fisher Historic Site, and it just didn't seem proper that a hermit should live there. The federal government got interested too. It seems Harrell was living in the "buffer zone" of the Sunny Point arsenal across the river. Early attempts to oust the hermit, locally referred to as the state's "Hermit Eradication Program," failed miserably because Harrell had an uncanny sense of the officials' arrivals and would vanish into the maze of trails and shrubs.

The archaeologist directing the development of the Historic Site, Stanley South, was called upon to make his own report to the government concerning the hermit. Of the many points made in his case for ignoring the hermit, South said, "The Fort Fisher hermit is almost a historic site in himself." Not only would it look bad for the government to bear down on one harmless individual, said South, but removing the hermit would be comparable to removing "all the rabbits and coons in Brunswick."

And so the life and legend of the Fort Fisher hermit flourished, and visitations by tourists and truth-seekers continued. "I've got a job to do here for God and humanity," he was quoted as saying, "And I've got to work as long as I can wiggle." He appealed to the hermit in everyone, that part of us that wants to be left alone, to live in harmony with nature, to escape our entanglements. But even Harrell couldn't escape it all. There is mystery surrounding his death and enough evidence of foul play to have allowed his son, George, to succeed in having the investigation reopened in the '70s. It remains open to this day. Some of the hermit's artifacts are on display at the North Carolina Marine Resources Center at Fort Fisher. His final resting place is in Shelby. Carved on his tombstone and painted on a cement post near his former homestead is his epitaph: He Made People Think.

Inside
Airports

There may be some Wilmingtonians who wax nostalgically about the tiny brick building that served as air terminal until the sleek new terminal opened in 1990. Gone is the little old hot dog/snack bar in favor of a comfortable coffee shop, separate lounge and gift shop. Now luggage is delivered to travelers on a carousel conveyor instead of being unloaded at their feet by baggage handlers. In fact, the airport, complete with baby-changing areas accessible to fathers, has fully entered the late-20th century. Even the tall palm trees in the atrium will remain forever green, thanks to the wonders of polyurethane, a many-splendored thing. However, as any visitor can tell you, New Hanover International Airport is, in every way that counts, still small-town friendly.

The increased number of air travelers — 410,000 in 1992 — is one clear indication of the quiet boom the Lower Cape Fear region is experiencing. The average number of daily flights connecting Wilmington to major hubs has risen to 22. Airlines serving the terminal are American, Delta, and USAir. The airport is convenient to travelers destined for the counties of New Hanover, Pender, northern Brunswick and southern Onslow (Topsail Island included).

Located north of town, just off 23rd Street, the New Hanover Airport is within 10 minutes of downtown Wilmington by car and about 17 minutes from Wrightsville Beach. Upon exiting the airport, a right turn leads you to Route 117 that brings you into downtown Wilmington (a left turn, heading south), or north into Castle Hayne (a right turn).

Visitors to the South Brunswick Islands (Holden Beach, Ocean Isle Beach and Sunset Beach) and Calabash can fly by commercial airlines into the Grand Strand Jetport in Myrtle Beach, SC, 35 miles south of Shallotte. (New Hanover International is 35 miles north of Shallotte.) Those traveling by commercial airlines whose destination is Oak Island, Southport or points north, would do well to use New Hanover. Others, who pilot or charter small aircraft and who are destined for Brunswick, may want to take note of the very accessible Brunswick County Airport, located just outside Southport.

Note: all phone numbers are preceded by area code 910 unless otherwise indicated.

Wilmington

New Hanover International Airport

1740 Airport Blvd. (off 23rd Street, 2 miles north of Market Street; 1 mile north of Carolco Studios)

Airport Information 341-4125 (Weekdays 10 AM-6 PM)

AIRLINES

American-American Eagle, (800) 433-7300, has three arriving and three departing flights daily that connect with domestic and international flights from their Raleigh, NC hub.

Delta Air Lines, (800) 221-1212, has connecting flights through Atlanta, GA via their commuter line, Atlantic Southeast Airlines, (800) 282-3424.

USAir-USAir Express, (800) 428-4322, has nine daily flights that connect with Charlotte, NC.

PARKING INFORMATION
762-3985

Short-term parking rates are 50 cents per 20 minutes. There is a maximum charge of $5 per day.

Long-term parking costs $1 per hour. The maximum charge is $4 per day.

CAR RENTALS

There are a few air travelers who don't require automobiles on the Cape Fear Coast: the die-hard urban trekker who plans to remain in town to the exclusion of all else the region has to offer; the cyclist who prefers to burn calories rather than fossil fuels; and the boater who es-chews terra firma. Otherwise, an automobile is a near-necessity. Four rental companies, offering cars compact to full-size, maintain agents at the airport. Reservations and a confirmation call in advance of your arrival are always recommended.

Avis	763-1993
	(800)331-1212
Budget	762-9247
	(800)527-0700
Hertz	762-1010, 763-5404
	(800)654-3131
National	762-8000
	(800)CAR-RENT (227-7368)

TAXI AND LIMOUSINE SERVICE

Boaters and urban trekkers may need to hire a ride to their destinations from one of four local companies. (See also the Service and Information Directory.)

Coastal Yellow Cab	762-3322 , 762 4464
Port City Taxi, Inc.	762-1165
Affordable Affluence, Inc.	251-8999
Cape Fear Limousine Service	763-2102
Formal Limousine Service:	395-1191
Prestige Limousine Service:	399-4484

South Brunswick

The Brunswick County Airport

380 Long Beach Rd. (Route 133)
Southport   457-6483

This full-service airport, complete

with small terminal, hangars, fuel service, and a 4,000-foot paved and lighted runway, can accommodate general aviation aircraft from the smallest ultralights to fairly sizable private jets. Tie-down fees for piston aircraft are $3 per day, $30 per month and $270 per year. The Brunswick County Airport is also the east coast home of Blue Yonder Flying Machines, purveyors of the Quicksilver ultralight aircraft (see "Flying" in Sport & Fitness chapter). The airport is located near the foot of the Oak Island bridge, on the mainland side.

The **Ocean Isle Airstrip**, 579-9559, is a small landing strip (4000 ft., paved) accommodating only small private piston aircraft and air tours. Usage is free; no fuel is available.

TAXI SERVICE

LC's Taxi Service	287-3197
Oak Island Cab	754-2515.
Sun & Sea Taxi Cab	249-6705

AIR CHARTERS, RENTALS, LEASING

Adventurous souls can charter small aircraft at New Hanover Airport for a bird's-eye view of the Cape Fear region. Most companies offer 24-hour charter service, sales, service and rentals, and all offer flight training. Unless otherwise noted, all are located at New Hanover International.

Aeronautics	763-4691
Air Wilmington	763-0146

ISO Aero Service, Inc. of Wilmington
1410 N. Kerr Ave.   763-8898, 762-1024
(Fax: 763-8820)

Ocean Aire Aviation, Inc.   457-0710

Helicopter services are available to the Cape Fear coast from outlying towns:

Greenwood Helicopters
  Washington, NC   (919)975-2194

Helicopters of Charleston, Inc.
Charleston Executive
Airport, SC   (800)264-8550

US Helicopter, Inc.
Wingate, NC   (704)233-4254

Inside
Commerce
and Industry

During most of the 20th century, the Greater Wilmington area has experienced what some business leaders describe as an "immunity" to national and State economic trends. There have been good and bad episodes, but the general Wilmington economy has neither performed as well in prosperous times nor as badly in recessionary times as regions with similar demographics. Economic immunity seems to create a kind of unspectacular (but sometimes appreciated) economic stability for the Cape Fear area.

This middle-of-the-road economic situation makes it hard to get rich in traditional, professional employment because there is not tremendous opportunity to work for large corporations. Locals view the relatively few corporate professional employees with a degree of awe and often speak of amazement at their high salaries and profuse benefits. By far, the people in the Cape Fear area work in smaller businesses for someone else or are engaged in some kind of enterprise of their own. The entrepreneurial spirit of the region can go a long way in allowing motivated people to create their own jobs in a geographic setting loaded with natural possibilities.

Geography seems to be the most important factor in setting Wilmington apart from the overall North Carolina economy. Its maritime environment creates opportunities for business based on what is naturally available — the sea, the river, the many beautiful views — instead of that which must be manufactured.

There have been, of course, significant times in history when Wilmington relied heavily on her natural resources in a manufacturing and agricultural way. Despite some successes, it has not always worked well over the long run. In the few cases when these businesses succeeded, there were struggles.

Early settlers took advantage of the area's natural resources in the creation of their economy. Lush pine forests gave rise to a lumber industry in the 18th century that continues, but to a lesser degree, today. Related products, such as tar, turpentine and pitch, were dominant businesses in the 19th century, but have since fallen away. Rice was an early source of profitable income for the area; cotton was a primary source of commerce, too, and the downtown wharves were once the site of the largest cotton exporting operation in the world. After the War Between

Photo: Curtis Krueger

Tugboats wait ready for duty at the North Carolina State Port.

the States, the economy shifted away from cotton and rice plantations because the labor supply was no longer available.

Technology, by way of the railroads, provided jobs for 4,000 families in the first part of the twentieth century and made Wilmington a major rail center. The Atlantic Coast Line, a technological marvel and the prize of the Wilmington economy, moved the area's products efficiently into the inland market. Then, in 1955, the railroad announced a closing that would send a considerable segment of the city population south to Jacksonville by 1960. This was a severe economic loss. Not only were good-paying jobs lost with the railroad, but service businesses all over the area lost steady customers.

The North Carolina State Port Authority, seeking to cash in on the area's natural location as an international shipping port, established a deep-water terminal at Wilmington about 45 years ago, a move that may represent the region's earliest foray into the realm of service. The loss of the railroad, however, was detrimental to the success of this facility for a long time. A lack of good roads was another problem that was not solved until 1991 when Interstate 40 connected Wilmington to the rest of the country's superhighway system. While the State Port endured land transportation obstacles, ships were getting bigger and, suddenly, the turning basin in the Cape Fear wasn't deep enough. Now, thanks to aggressive lobbying, the State has decided that the port can be good for all of North Carolina and funding

has been approved to deepen the basin by three feet in 1993 and 1994.

The Wilmington facility now receives 500 ships a year loaded with diverse cargoes such as salt, plywood and hardboard, textile chemicals and dyes, staple fiber, yarn and burlap, leaf tobacco, automobiles, retail items and food products. In combination with the port at Morehead City and two inland facilities at Greensboro and Charlotte, more than 26,000 North Carolinians make their living through this increasingly vital industry that handles approximately 2,000,000 tons of cargo a year.

Tourism is one of the most important industries to arise in the latter half of the 20th century in the Cape Fear area. Since the scenery is a constant and people are always drawn to the sea, this industry provides a highly stable base. Even in the midst of economic downturns in more prosperous Raleigh, Greensboro and Winston-Salem, people in those cities will still vacation at the beach. They may defer the mortgage, but they will not give up the opportunity to spend a week relaxing by the sea. The opening of Interstate 40, a fast, functional (though rather boring) corridor has also thrown wide the gate for all types of commerce and industry. No industry, perhaps, has witnessed such dramatic results from the laying of this precious asphalt as the tourism industry. In the last decade of the 20th century, we are in a steadily improving economic situation based on our greater overland accessibility.

At this writing, more than 60,000 visitors a year drop by the Cape Fear

Coast Convention and Visitors Bureau in downtown Wilmington. On a typical weekend at Wrightsville Beach, more than 70,000 cars cross the bridge to the eight-mile long island. It is safe to say that tourism has seized the local economy in a tremendously dramatic way in the past three years. There are more than 3,000 beds in hotels, motels and inns in the Greater Wilmington Area, and these establishments are experiencing nearly full occupancy on a year-round basis. In the summer, it is often difficult to find accommodations on short notice. The development of resort properties with recreational amenities is on the rise particularly in the waterway communities of Topsail Island to the north and the Brunswick Beaches to the south.

Tourism, of course, is much more than accommodations. Businesses that profit from the steady flow of visitors are also thriving. Convention facilities and all of the attendant services represent a growing segment of the economy. Visitors need a full range of services, and there are many entrepreneurs who are more than willing to provide them. Restaurants number in the hundreds and continue to proliferate at an astounding rate with many of them enjoying capacity dining on weekends. Retail stores that serve tourist needs in beachwear, vacation items and souvenirs are readily available. Special tourist services such as horse and carriage rides in the historic district, entertainment, boat tours, sailing charter opportunities, a downtown Wilmington walking tour, educational tours in the historic district, and many more enterprises continue to respond to high demand from visitors.

The Wilmington economy is heavily based on services, so there is no reliance on single industries whose futures, for better or worse, may have a significant impact on it. Service businesses account for 21.4 percent of the employment here, compared to an average of 18.7 percent for North Carolina. Wholesale and retail trade, linked strongly to tourism dollars, register more than 29 percent, compared with 22.5 percent in the state. Wilmington's retail businesses earned more than $1.63 million in June of 1993, ranking it eighth among North Carolina cities. Wilmington's retail sales are increasing at a an annual rate of 7 to 8 percent.

All of these businesses pivot on the area's natural scenic resources and on the tremendous appeal of Wilmington's beautiful architecture. Carolco Studios, home to the local film industry, opened here partly because of the scenery, period homes and varied location opportunities. The studio has eight sound stages and is a complete filming facility for motion picture, television and commercial productions. "Matlock" and "The Young Indiana Jones Chronicles" are two made-for-TV productions that regularly film around the area. More than 60 films have been made in the area to date, including *The Birds II, Stompin' at the Savoy, Crimes of the Heart, Super Mario Brothers, The Crow, Simple Justice,* and *Blue Velvet.* The studios' economic impact on the region amounted to nearly $270 million in 1993, accounting for 7 1/2 percent of the overall economy.

A major industry is just beginning to arise around the retirement population. Again, this is a matter of geography and, of course, climate. The maritime location of the area makes the climate unusually mild for its latitude. There are four discernible seasons, an important factor for northern retirees who have grown weary of Florida's almost singular season. An occasional snow and warm summers create a more interesting yearly cycle for retirees who yearn for diversity in the climate.

There are 15 domiciliary care facilities in New Hanover County alone. There are a number of planned retirement communities,

Photo: Curtis Krueger

The Henrietta II docks on the Wilmington waterfront.

and, to be sure, many more are on the way as people from more affluent economies migrate to the Cape Fear area for still reasonable housing and nursing home care options. There is also an endless variety of professional golf courses guaranteed to satisfy even the most discerning golfers who yearn to spend their golden years on the greens. The greatest benefit derived from the attraction of retirees from more prosperous locations is that these people bring their nest eggs along with them and spend several decades buying goods and services.

Health care, both for the senior population and everyone else, is coming to be big business in the region. Three hundred physicians and five regional hospitals employ large numbers of medical personnel. If advertisements for employment in local papers are an indication, skilled nurses are the most needed employ-

ees in the area. There is a high availability of a skilled work force across the boards in the area. The region seems to draw exceedingly qualified people in quantity. This is not particularly good for people looking for work, but it is very appealing to businesses that can count on a large pool of talent at a reasonable cost. This situation may not long exist; by the dawning of the 21st century, Wilmington's increasing economic diversification may shift this picture in favor of employees.

Large corporations, of which there are still relatively few in the area, deal in manufacturing and account for just over 15 percent of the local economy's base. The largest companies in the area include: Corning Glass Works, a manufacturer of optical fibers; General Electric, which manufactures aircraft engine parts, nuclear fuel and components; Carolina Power & Light, the local energy company; E. I. duPont de Nemours & Company, known widely as Dupont, which makes Dacron and polyester fibers; and Federal Paper Board, which manufactures paperboard from lumber in its Columbus County plant.

On a lower tier in the number of employees are Cape Industries, another maker of polyester; Ithaca Mills, which makes polo shirts; National Spinning Company, a manufacturer of acrylic worsted yarn; and Whiteville Apparel Corporation, a manufacturer of men's clothing.

American Crane, Applied Analytical Industries, Bedford Fair Industries, Block Industries, Takeda Chemical Products, Anvil Knitwear, Georgia-Pacific Corporation, Jasper Textiles and Stone Manufacturing Company make up the next tier.

The smallest of the major industries include Century Mills, Corbett Package Company, Dorothy's Ruffled Originals, Fox's Holsum Bakery, E. W. Godwin's & Sons, Interroll, Lousiana Pacific Corporation, Queensboro Steel, R&E Electronics, Sturdy Corporation, Wilmington Coca-Cola Bottling, Wilmington Star-News (the only local daily newspaper), Archer Daniels Midland, Exide Electronics, Atlantic Publishing Company, Myrtle Desk Company, Tabor City Products Manufacturing, Chloride Systems, Holt Hosiery Corporation, Wilmington Machinery and Oxford of Burgaw.

The University of North Carolina at Wilmington is also a significant factor in the local economy. Serving a student body of 8,000, the university is among the fastest growing universities in the 16-campus UNC system. Organized into the College of Arts and Sciences (including a marine science program that ranks seventh in the nation), the Cameron School of Business Administration, the School of Education, the School of Nursing and the Graduate School, the university offers degrees in 58 areas of concentration. The university's impact on the region is approximately $360 million, which accounts for 10 percent of the economic activity in New Hanover, Pender, Brunswick and Columbus counties.

At this point in history, it seems that Wilmington is poised perfectly in both time and space to take advantage of its natural resources, technological advances and entrepreneurial motivation in order to explore tremendous opportunities in the 21st century as it expands its economic base. The Greater Wilmington Chamber of Commerce operates a Better Business Division that promotes and develops a favorable business climate in the community. The Better Business Bureau is located in the Chamber of Commerce office beside the Coast Line Center, (919) 762-2611.

Photo: William Russ, N.C. Travel and Tourism Division

The Oak Island Lighthouse, North Carolina's newest and most powerful, was built in 1958 to replace the lighthouse on Bald Head Island. At the time of its construction, only a French light on the English Channel shone brighter than Oak Island's beacon.

Inside
Daytrips

It is beyond the scope of this insider why anyone would want to go somewhere else beyond the Cape Fear area when there is so much to do and see here. Yet, an urge comes now and then to even the most entrenched resident to go explore other places and, luckily, interesting destinations are close enough for a daytrip.

There are wonderful places within only a few hours drive or boat cruise. Travelers can enjoy the special attributes of neighboring communities without feeling too far away from home.

It is a scant two hours on Interstate 40 to Raleigh, North Carolina's Capital city. Home to the North Carolina museums of history, science and art, many outstanding restaurants, shopping opportunities, and annual events such as the State Fair in October, it is a pleasant diversion for a daytrip. Walnut Creek Amphitheater, just a few miles south of Raleigh, hosts performances by nationally-known bands. Insiders regularly take this trip for exciting entertainment on a night-tripper basis. For more information on Raleigh and surrounding areas, pick up a copy of *The Insiders' Guide to the Triangle.*

Myrtle Beach

For more than 40 years, The Grand Strand has been the standard by which all other beach resorts are measured. Its abundance of posh hotels, dining and shopping opportunities, world-class golf and profusion of amusements are only equaled by its ideal weather and magnificent beaches. The Strand stretches nearly unbroken for 60 sun-drenched miles from Little River to historic Georgetown. For the daytripper, the heart of the Strand is Myrtle Beach, the entertainment nerve center.

Myrtle is astounding, as resorts go. Its permanent resident population of about 25,000 swells to more than 350,000 each summer — and summertime tourism accounts for only 36 percent of Myrtle's annual tourist revenues. For a mile to either side of the Pavilion, Ocean Boulevard is a hotbed of endless activity. It's understandable that Wilmingtonians look upon Myrtle with equal amounts of interest and relief that their hometown is sedate by comparison. Myrtle Beach is approximately 72 miles from downtown Wilmington, a drive of little more than 90 minutes. Highway 17 is the artery stretch that gets you there. Before entering Myrtle Beach proper, the stretch of Highway 17 (here called King's Highway) is known as Restaurant Row due to the many dining establishments, particularly Calabash-style restaurants, that are built shoulder-to-shoulder at places. Highway 17 Business divides from Highway 17 Bypass and passes through Myrtle Beach's north end, a quiet, residential neighborhood of green lawns, bright gardens and tall palmettos. If you call before you go, the Myrtle Beach area code is 803.

There are more than 1,400 restaurants along the Grand Strand, most located in and around Myrtle Beach. Along with all the regional specialties available on Cape Fear, visitors will find other specialties of the "real South," such as chicken bog (chicken, seasoned rice and sausage), she crab soup, alligator stew, crawfish, and "chitlins" (deep-fried pig intestines — they're not for everyone!) All-you-can-eat buffets are ubiquitous, so bring your appetite.

Shopping is probably tied for first place with sunshine when it comes to the Grand Strand's favorite attractions. The area is replete with shops and boutiques of every description and specialty. Malls abound, and there are flea markets. Discount shopping, particularly at factory outlet stores, is what Myrtle Beach is particularly famous for.

More than at any other single location, shoppers wear their plastic thin at the mammoth Outlet Park at Waccamaw (236-4606/6152), a three-mall complex that is equal in size to five football fields and features 125 factory stores of every description. It's the home of Waccamaw Pottery (a home decor superstore) and Waccamaw Linen. Movie theaters and an enormous food court are within the complex. Outlet Park is located on Highway 501 immediately west of the Intracoastal Waterway. There's even an on-site hotel for those who live (and vacation) to shop. Free tram service between the malls is available. The mall crawl begins at 9 AM daily.

The Pavilion, on the oceanfront between Eighth and Ninth Avenues North, is the symbolic center of Myrtle Beach. Arcades, Earl's Boardwalk Cafe and live entertainment are perpetual summertime attractions. The boardwalk offers an array of shops, food stands and night life. Myrtle Beach is also home to some of the more outrageous miniature golf courses you'll see anywhere — more than 45 of them. Batting cages, go-cart tracks, arcades, water parks, amusement rides, wacky museums, souvenir shops and newcomer attractions like Beamers Laser Tag (448-1900, 1101 North Ocean Boulevard) attract thousands. Cruising the Boulevard has become so popular among swim suit-clad young folks that traffic seldom approaches the 25 mph speed limit. Don't overlook the boating and sight-seeing opportunities available among the waterways immediately to the west and the worthwhile historic attractions along the Grand Strand.

The City of Myrtle Beach provides beach wheelchairs by the hour, free of charge and provides dune crossovers at 15 locations between 28th Avenue South and 81st Avenue North. For information on beach accessibility for the handicapped, call 626-7645, ext. 129.

BROOKGREEN GARDENS
1931 Brookgreen Gardens Dr. 237-4218
Murrells Inlet

Listed on the National Register of Historic Places, Brookgreen Gardens is the first and largest permanent outdoor installation of American figurative sculpture, and it demands a visit. Within Brookgreen's 9,000 acres are manicured gardens and a rich botanical collection. Brookgreen is an arboretum, wildlife preserve, aviary and museum rolled into one, so pack a picnic lunch. Brookgreen boasts more than 500 works by hundreds of top-name sculptors and continues to expand in scope. Guided tours and lectures are offered every day. You might also want to attend some of the occasional workshops and concerts. Brookgreen Gardens is located off Highway 17, 18 miles south of Myrtle Beach (90 miles from Wilmington) between

Murrells Inlet and Pawley's Island. The gardens are open daily, except Christmas, 9:30 AM to 4:45 PM, and there is an admission charge.

MYRTLE BEACH SPEEDWAY
Hwy. 501 236-0500

For auto-racing fans, this is the real thing, a nationally-ranked track that hosts the NASCAR Winston Racing Series every Saturday (7:30 PM) from March through September. Watch for the Busch Grand National in mid-June and the 400-lap NASCAR Winston All Pro in late-November. The Speedway is located between Myrtle Beach and the town of Conway.

Nightlife

Nightlife and Myrtle Beach are practically synonymous. Live music, dancing and stage shows form the core of one of the most active seaside scenes anywhere, and there are plenty of open-air bars along the boardwalk in which to relax over a drink with the sound of the surf as backdrop. Luckily, all the fun is not reserved for adults. Nonalcoholic night spots, such as the **Magic Attic**, located at the Pavilion, cater to kids who enjoy dancing, music and socializing.

The preeminent country-music venues in the area are quite touristy and ticket prices pack a wallop, but they are all consistently well-done and entertaining. The **Carolina Opry**, located at the north junction of Highway 17 Bypass and Highway 17 Business (Restaurant Row), was twice voted the state's top tourist attraction. Its success spawned the **Dixie Jubilee** and **Southern Country Nights**. Sharing similar formats, these shows present a mix of comedy and music that may include standard country hits, bluegrass, gospel and medleys drawn from popular oldies, plus special Christmas shows. The Dixie Jubilee is located in North Myrtle Beach on Main Street, just off Highway 17. Southern Country Nights, also on Business Highway 17, is located in the town of Surfside Beach. Reservations are recommended for all three venues and can be made through one central booking service. Call 238-8888 or (800) 843-6779.

Seating only 600 people, the **Myrtle Beach Opry** offers a more intimate setting for its live stage shows and a relatively elegant take on the familiar music-and-comedy formula. Call 448-6779 or (800) 446-4110 for schedules and reservations. The Myrtle Beach Opry is located at 19th Avenue North and Business 17, in the heart of town.

In the 1970s, a then-unknown group named Alabama played for tips at The **Bowery** in downtown Myrtle Beach, earning a large, loyal following. Having since been voted Artists of the Decade (1980s) by the Academy of Country Music, Alabama returns to Myrtle Beach 20 times each year. Now they play at their own venue, the 2,200-seat **Alabama Theatre**, in Barefoot Landing. When Alabama isn't there, other major recording stars appear in conjunction with the family-oriented "American Pride Show," performed nightly. Reservations can be made by calling 272-1111 or (800) 342-2262

The **Dixie Stampede** (497-9700) is a theatrical icon of southern culture, complete with music, expert horsemanship and a colorful depiction of the conflict between the North and South. It is especially appropriate for children and comes together in a 90-minute show complemented by dinner. The Dixie Stampede is located next door to the Carolina Opry. Shows are staged from February through December at 5 PM (and 7 PM during the summer). Reservations are strongly recommended.

The shag was named the Official State Dance in 1984. It is so closely identified with old rhythm and blues (locally called "beach music") that locals contend the dance came first. One thing the dance did engender is the **Society of Stranders** (S.O.S.), an organization of the Association of Carolina Shag Clubs. The Society's Spring Safari, held annually in April, and the Autumn Migration, in October, attract thousands of shaggers doing their thing on Main Street in North Myrtle Beach, the shag's re-

In 1865 Fort Fisher, near Kure Beach, was the site of the largest land-sea battle fought until that time.

puted birthplace. In January, shaggers compete in the National Shag Dance Championships, part of the S.O.S. Mid-Winter Classic.

Studebaker's (626-3855, 2000 North Kings Highway) is a popular place to shag and attracts a relatively mature crowd. Featuring plenty of happy-days atmosphere, Studebaker's presents the Dancing Studeboppers and DJs who spin hits spanning 30 years. Discounts are offered to guests with out-of-town I.D.s. Studebaker's is open every day from 8 PM to 2 AM.

2001 (449-9434) is a 13-year-old private club for members and their guests and boasts three different clubs under one roof. Dancing to live music in a hi-tech atmosphere makes Pulsations pulse. Oldies, beach music and Motown are spun by DJ Crazy George in **Razzies Beach Club**. **Yakety Yak's Outrageous Pi-anos** is a club that features two dueling pianists who take requests — provided the person making the request gets up and sings. Yakety Yak's inevitably becomes a sing-along free-for-all. 2001 offers valet parking, plus an on-site deli for those late-night munchies. Guests may move from club to club freely. 2001 is located at 920 Lake Arrowhead Road, off Restaurant Row (Highway 17) at the north end of Myrtle Beach.

Golf

The area's self-proclaimed title as the Golf Capital of the World is well-justified. There are currently upwards of 77 world-class courses (with more in the planning) throughout the Grand Strand. Top designers have created courses of remarkable beauty, playability and variety. And although their popular-

Photo: William Russ, N.C. Travel and Tourism Division

ity sometimes translates into crowds and waiting time, prices are too competitive to ignore them. There are also plenty of driving ranges, par-3 courses and pro shops scattered up and down the Strand. Green fees are lowest from November through February and golf packages are accordingly most affordable during that time. Local Chambers of Commerce can provide the necessary details.

Among the annual golf highlights is the four-day, 72-hole DuPont World Amateur Handicap Championship. It typically draws over 3,300 contestants, each of whom is pitted against players with like handicaps, and it's played on 50 area courses. Call (203) 373-7178 for information.

Diving

Those who dive the Graveyard of the Atlantic off the Cape Fear coast can expand their explorations by diving offshore from the Grand Strand. Civil War and World War II-era wrecks litter the offshore bottoms here. Among several available, the Hurricane Fleet (249-3571) offers diving charters aboard specially-fitted boats. They also rent equipment.

For a more in-depth look at everything Myrtle Beach has to offer, check out *The Insiders' Guide to Myrtle Beach*. The South Carolina Welcome Center on Highway 17 near Little River is a convenient place for daytrippers to gather brochures about the Grand Strand (and all of South Carolina as well). Many of the publications contain discount coupons good at dozens of Grand Strand attractions and restaurants. Also, contact the Myrtle Beach Area Chamber of Commerce and Info Center, 626-7444, located at 1301 North King's Highway in Myrtle Beach (mailing address: P.O. Box 2115, Myrtle Beach, SC, 29578-2115). For brochures only, call toll-free (800) 356-3016.

The Crystal Coast

Within two hours, north by northeast up Ocean Highway 17, there are a multitude of daytripper possibilities that promise fascinating maritime themes. The Crystal Coast, featuring Bogue Banks, Morehead City, quaint Beaufort, historic New Bern, and the sprawling banks of the Neuse River as it spills into the Pamlico Sound, offers endless opportunities to enjoy the special North Carolina coastline and adjacent waters.

The Crystal Coast shares much in common with the Cape Fear Coast. Both areas boast beautiful, significant rivers; both have miles of oceanside communities; both have great opportunities for dining; and, of course, both have deep historical roots. However, they are different enough to make visiting each of them a unique experience.

If you have access to a boat — large or small, power or sail — the trip to the Crystal Coast from Wilmington will take longer than two hours. But if you enjoy beautiful coastal scenery, you will find this a very relaxing trip. A fast powerboat can transport you to Morehead City in a matter of four to five hours on the Intracoastal Waterway. A sailboat will take the better part of the day from sunrise to sunset before you are safely berthed for the night. If the weather turns foul, you should plan two days to reach Morehead City, and three to get into the Neuse River near New Bern up a section of the ICW. With the exception of this passage that connects the ocean with the Neuse River, there are many marinas along the way that welcome transient boaters.

By car simply head up Ocean Highway 17. Veer off 17 onto Highway 172 through the Marine base, Camp Lejeune, near Jacksonville. People who have never been on a military base will find this an unusual environment, with tank crossing signs, trucks filled with Marines training in artillery practice, soldiers at the gate who will issue a one-hour pass for you to drive the twenty miles through the base, and a curious feeling that this is a very different place. Should your trip be by boat on the Intracoastal Waterway beside the base, you'll be slightly startled to see a large sign warning of artillery practice. Sometimes the soldiers are

seen practicing amphibious vehicle landings or crossing the waterway.

After crossing the base (hand in your pass to the sentry at the other side, and return to the civilian world,) go east on Highway 24 to Beaufort. It is a trip of less than 100 miles from Wilmington, and there are many views of North Carolina's waters and charming coastal communities along the way.

Swansboro, an historic coastal town that dates back to the early 18th century, is a pleasant stopover after about an hour of travel from Wilmington. Situated on the White Oak River and the Intracoastal Waterway, this lovely little town is surrounded by water. It becomes quickly obvious that the town is in love with boating. The public access boat ramp is jammed with trucks and trailers; the waters teem with commercial and pleasure craft.

Swansboro has a particularly attractive downtown historic area lined with antique shops, art galleries and restaurants. Look for signs leading to the district just off Highway 24 and enter the area that is concentrated within three blocks on the shores of the White Oak River. Parking is free; the merchants are friendly; there are lots of interesting things to buy; and this is an altogether delightful spot to visit.

Back on Highway 24, travel another 20 minutes until Highway 58 appears on the right. This is the entrance to **Bogue Banks** on the southern end. Cross over a dramatic, fixed bridge that gives nearly a bird's-eye view of the Intracoastal Waterway. The communities along approximately 20 miles of the island are varied in an extreme way. **Emerald Isle** is heavily residential with attractive homes. **Indian Beach** is largely trailer parks. **Salter Path** is a jumble of commercial and residential land uses.

Pine Knoll Shores is an exclusive residential area of windswept live oaks and kudzu with attractive single-family homes and condominiums as well as hotels and the occasional restaurant. This beach also offers the North Carolina Aquarium at Pine Knoll Shores, a lively facility that includes a "Living Shipwreck," a touch tank, salt marsh explorations, and workshops on surf fishing. At the northern end of the island is Atlantic Beach, a smorgasbord of beach amenities that include an amusement park with a Ferris wheel, fishing pier, shopping opportunities, fast food places, restaurants and motels.

Cross over the bridge at the northern end of Bogue Banks and enter **Morehead City**, home to the North Carolina Port Authority and a multitude of restaurants specializing in fresh seafood. The undisputed leader in dining in Morehead City is the Sanitary Fish Market, 501 Evans Street, (919) 247-3111. The restaurant seats 600 diners and serves fresh broiled or fried seafoods, homemade chowders and Tar Heel hushpuppies. The Charter Restaurant, also on the waterfront, (919) 726-9036, serves delicious crabcakes, stuffed shrimp and flounder, prime rib, and a salad bar seven days a week.

Just a few miles from Morehead City is the magical town of **Beaufort**. Beaufort is so gorgeous that it seems more like a postcard than a real place. This little coastal community nestles up to international waters and is a gateway from the Atlantic Ocean to American waterways. Taylor's Creek, the body of water in front of the town's quaint commercial district, is filled with sailcraft and powerboats from all over the world. Even in the winter months, there are international boaters anchored in the creek cozied up alongside Snowbirds and local recreational boaters.

This daytripper's favorite pursuit is sitting at the Dock House overlooking Taylor's Creek, ordering a scrumptious shrimpburger or taco salad, listening to local music, usually live, and watching the boats at anchor or the ones that come and go in this busy maritime environment. As you munch on delicious, inexpensive food, there is excitement at suddenly noticing the wild horses that wander around on Carrot Island across Taylor's Creek. The horses are stocky steeds who pretty much care for themselves on their little windswept island. In a world where horses are rarely seen running free, this is a stirring sight.

The sheer beauty of the scenery is enough to lull a visitor into sitting in a pleasant trance for a long time, but there is also the allure of nearby shops and attractions. Within an easy walk are stores, many appealing restaurants, the North Carolina Maritime Museum, the Beaufort Restoration Grounds, and a delightful neighborhood of historic homes where the daytripper will simply enjoy strolling. The visitor who wants to stay overnight — and who

Masonboro Island offers a wildlife sanctuary.

wouldn't? — can find gracious bed and breakfast accommodations and two inns right in the heart of this area.

Shoppers will enjoy a variety of stores along the waterfront. Handscapes Gallery, Somerset Square, 400 Front Street, 762-6805, sells an attractive assortment of North Carolina pottery, jewelry, wood, glass and paintings. The nearby Fudge Factory, also in Somerset Square, 768-6202, makes delicious fudge in many flavors for sale by the slice or pound. Need something with a nautical theme? Nauticode, 300 Front Street, 728-4339, has code flags for your ship, license plates for your car, dog collars, lighthouses, and jewelry. On a nautical theme as well, Scuttlebutt, 126 Turner Street, 728-7765, sells a large selection of books about the sea and boating. NOAA charts, cruis-

ing guides, and chartbooks make this a must stop for passing boaters. Chadwick House, 119 Turner Street, 728-1815, has delightful gifts for the home and garden including lamps, prints, paintings, linens and garden ornaments. There are many more shops; you're going to enjoy strolling the streets and investigating the possibilities.

Diners will be overwhelmed with restaurant possibilities on just one daytrip. The Beaufort Grocery Co., 117 Queen Street, 728-3899, a lunch and dinner restaurant, offers fine dining and a full delicatessen. Fresh breads and desserts are baked daily. The Front Street Grill, on the Beaufort waterfront at 419 Front Street, 728-3118, has a reputation as an interesting restaurant that uses unusual spices in fresh presentations on seafood, chicken, pasta, and homemade soups. Mike's, 509 Front

Street, 728-4925, is the place to go for breakfast, especially if you've just taken your dinghy in from your boat anchored in Taylor's Creek and are starving for deeply satisfying and generous fare. The Spouter Inn, 218 Front Street, 728-5190, is a charming spot where diners enjoy a memorable clam chowder, creative seafood specialties and a great view.

New Bern

The small city of New Bern lies upriver on the Neuse, a gorgeous, deep body of water that is quite different from the Cape Fear River. The Neuse River, 3 miles wide at points, is the largest river in North Carolina. As any sailor will tell you, this is absolute sailing paradise. From New Bern down to the Pamlico Sound, sailors of virtually any level of competency enjoy the experience with little worry about running aground or bumping into the shore. The vast expanse of the river, coupled with some of the finest shoreline amenities on the entire East coast, creates a perfect environment for all boaters.

Car travelers will appreciate the lovely view of the river and will certainly enjoy the many opportunities to shop, dine, and stay in historic New Bern, settled by the Swiss in 1710. You may be interested to know that New Bern is the place where Pepsi Cola was invented. This rather sleepy little town was the site of the first public schools, the first meeting of the North Carolina Legislature and the state's first bank.

Dining is considerably less exten-sive than in Wilmington but good meals are easy to come by. The Henderson House Restaurant, 216 Pollock Street, 637-4784, is located in the vicinity of historic Tryon Palace. The menu leans toward French cooking and is well complemented by a wonderful offering of French wines. The Flame, 2303 Neuse Boulevard, 633-0262, has a gourmet salad bar, grilled seafood and chicken, as well as steak and lobster. Victorian decor creates an intimate environment for people who appreciate a gracious dining experience. For casual breakfast, lunch, or dinner, try the Pollock Street Delicatessen and Restaurant, 208 Pollock Street, 637-2480.

The biggest tourist attraction in New Bern is Tryon Palace. Built in 1770 for Colonial Governor William Tryon, the palace burned in 1798 but was reconstructed in the 1950s according to the original architectural plans. The palace is furnished with objects dating from the third quarter of the 18th century. These rare English and American antiques were selected to approximate an inventory of Governor Tryon's possessions made two years after he left New Bern to become governor of the colony of New York.

Tryon Palace and its many historic sites are open year round, with the exception of major holidays, and include tours, historical dramas and crafts demonstrations. For information, call 638-1560 or write Tryon Palace Historic Sites and Gardens, P.O. Box 1007, New Bern, 28563.

For more information on this area, pick up a copy of *The Insiders' Guide to the Crystal Coast and New Bern.*

Index of Advertisers

AuPair Care	349
Battleship North Carolina	149
Big Daddy's Restaurant	55
Blockade Runner	inside back cover
Bridge Tender Restaurant and Marina	49
Cape Fear Academy	353
Cape Fear Memorial Hospital	insert
Cape Fear Coast Convention and Visitor's Bureau	9
Coast Line Inn	81
Cotton Exchange	118
Curtis Krueger Photography	295
Drapery World Interiors	329
Echo Farms	273
Fish House Grill	49
Fisherman's Wife, The	49
Gold 104.5 FM	141, 229
Gottovi, Daniel, M.D.	379
Governor Jim Hunt	xii
Howard Johnson's Plaza Hotel and Conference Center	75
Inklings	293
James Place Bed and Breakfast	79
Jewelle on Princess	286
Jordan McColl, Inc.	308
Jungle Rapids	153
Landfall	front foldout cover
Landmark	324
McKenzie Supply	335
New Hanover Regional Medical Center	376
Nuss Strasse Cafe	38
Pellagrino Properties	341
Rucker Johns Restaurant	47
Saucepan, The	127
WAAV AM 980	21, 57, 139, 337, 403
WBMS AM 1340	221, 65
Wilmington Star News, Inc.	6,136
WMFD AM 630	29, 89
WWAY TV 3	25, 125, 383

Index

A

A & A Auto Rental, Inc. 315
A Little Class 356
AAMCO Transmissions 313
ABC Stores 315
About Time Antiques 128
Accommodations 73
   Atlantic Towers 85
   Beach Harbour Resort 85
   Blockade Runner Resort
      Hotel 83
   Cabana De Mar Motel 85
   Catherine's Inn On
      Orange 74
   Coast Line Inn 75
   Comfort Inn Executive
      Center 75
   Cooke's Inn Motel 96
   Gillies' Bed & Breakfast 86
   Gray Gull Motel 95
   Graystone Inn 76
   Hampton Inn 77
   Holiday Inn 78
   Holiday Inn Wrightsville
      Beach 78
   Howard Johnson Plaza-
      Hotel 78
   Island Motel 96
   James Place 79
   King's Motel 86
   Market Street Bed &
      Breakfast 79
   McKay-Green Inn 80
   Ocean Crest Motel 90
   Ocean Front Inn 87
   Ocean Isle Motel 96
   One South Lumina
      Motel 83
   Ramada Inn Conference
      Center 80
   Riverside Motel 97
   Savage-Bacon House 81
   Sea Captain Motor
      Lodge 97

   Sea Vista Motel 88
   Seven Seas Inn 86
   Shell Island All-Oceanfront
      Suites 84
   Shell Island Resort
      Hotel 84
   Silver Gull Motel &
      Apartments 84
   South Winds Motel 90
   St. Regis Resort 88
   Summer Sands Motel 85
   Surf Motel Suites 85
   Taylor House Inn Bed and
      Breakfast 82
   The Cricket Inn 76
   The Green Tree Inn 77
   The Inn at St. Thomas
      Court 78
   The Jolly Roger Motel 87
   The Winds Clarion
      Carriage House
      Inn 96
   The Worth House 82
   Villa Capriani Resort 89
   Wilmington Hilton 77
Acme Art 180, 289
Ad Hoc Theatre Com-
    pany 292
Adventure World 357
Aerobics Plus 253
Aeronautics 152, 254, 398
Aging, New Hanover County
    Department of 374
Air Charters 398
Air Wilmington 152, 254, 398
Airlie Gardens 152
Airlines 396
Alan Holden Realty 108, 342
Alcohol Beverage Control
    Board 315
Alcoholics Anonymous 312
Alice-E 235
AME (African Methodist
    Episcopal)
      Churches 306

American Association of
    Retired People 366
American Cancer Society
    Tournament 277
American Red Cross 318, 369
American Society of Materials
    Testing 390
American-American Eagle 397
Animal Services 312
Anna Theresa's Piasta Cafe 44
Annual Autumn with Topsail
    Beach Arts &
      Entertainment 176
Annual Chili Cookoff 177
Annual Christmas Concert 178
Annual Events 172
Annual Holiday Flotilla and Arts
    & Crafts Show 178
Annual North Carolina Oyster
    Festival 177
Antique Mall 132
Antiques 127
Aquatic Safaris & Divers
    Emporium 202
Arts 287, 375
Arts Council of the Lower
    Cape Fear 287, 374
Ashton Farm Summer Day
    Camp 262
ASK-A-NURSE Program 379
Assembly Building 137
Atlantic Coast Line 11
Atlantic Marine 243
Atlantic Marine Sales & Service,
    Inc. 251
Atlantic Telephone Membership
    Corp. 322
Atlantic Towers 85
Attractions 137, 389
Audubon Center 129
Aussie Island Surf Shop 207
Auto Spa Car Wash 314
Automotive Service 312, 313
Autumn Care of Shallotte 366
Avis Rent A Car 314

Azalea Coast Chorus of Sweet
    Adelines 290
Azalea Coast Smockers
    Guild 294

B

Back Alley Lounge 189
Bald Head Island 35
Bald Head Island Annual
    Maritime Classic Road
    Race 177
Bald Head Island Fishing
    Rodeo 224
Bald Head Island Historic Tour
    & Lunch 165
Bald Head Island Marina 246
Bald Head Island Sailing
    Regatta 177
Bald Head Island Property
    Management Office 280
Baptist Churches 302
Barbary Coast 180
Barefoots and Jackson
    Furniture 126
Barnacle Bill's Fishing Pier 228
Barnacle Bill's Grill 56
Baseball 248
Basketball 249
Battleship North Carolina 148
Baughman Toyota 312
Beach Access 211
Beach Fun Rentals 208, 318
Beach Harbour Resort 85
Beach Music Festival 175
Beaches 50
Bear Mountain 120
Beau Rivage 332
Beau Rivage Plantation Golf &
    Country Club 275
Becker Builder's Supply
    Co. 343
Belk 128
Bellamy Mansion Museum of
    Design Arts 140
Belvedere Plantation Golf &
    Country Club 276
Bert's Surf Shop 207, 208
Bessie's 182
Best 129
Bicycling 249, 250
Big Daddy's Seafood
    Restaurant 55
Bike Rentals 250
Bike Shops 250
Billiards 179
Bird Island 32
Bishop's Park 331

Bland and Associates
    Realtors 338
Blockade Runner Resort
    Hotel 83
Blue Yonder Flying
    Machines 254, 398
Blues Society of the Lower
    Cape Fear 290
B'nai Israel Synagogue 306
Boarding 312
Boat Ramps 230
Boat Rentals 251
Boathouse Marina 243
Boating 250
Boating Safety 251
Boating Services and
    Information 251
Bob King Auto Mall 312
Bobby's Garage 313
Bodyworks II 253
Bonnet, Gentleman Pirate
    Stede 7
Boot Scooters 192
Bowler's Choice 179
Bowling 179
Bowman's At the Beach 56
Boy Scouts of America, Cape
    Fear Council 373
Bradley Creek
    Boatominium 243
Brass Lantern 123
Break Time Billiards & Sports
    Bar 179
Brendle's 129
Briarwood Golf Club 264
Brick Landing Plantation 278
Brick Yard 182
Bridge Tender Marina and
    Restaurant 242
Brierwood Golf Club 278
Brigade Boy's Club 373
Bristol Books 126
Britthaven of Wilmington 365
Brookgreen Gardens 409
Brunswick Beaches 31
Brunswick Beaches
    Shopping 132
Brunswick Beacon 316
Brunswick Community
    College 387
Brunswick County
    Airport 396
Brunswick County Bowling
    Center 179
Brunswick County Department
    of Emergency
    Management 318

Brunswick County Literacy
    Council 369
Brunswick County Parks &
    Recreation 249, 261,
    265, 266, 272
Brunswick County School
    System 372
Brunswick Electric Membership
    Corporation 321
Brunswick Town 137
Bryant Real Estate 106
Buddy's Crab & Oyster
    Bar 188
Budget Rent-A-Car 314
Burrito Bob's 182
Bus and Taxi Service 314
Bushin-Kai Karate 258

C

Cabana De Mar Motel 85
Cafe Atlantique 42
Caffe Phoenix 42, 183
Calabash 33, 336
Camelot Camp-
    ground 111, 209
Camelot Stables, Inc. 255
Camp Davis Restaurant 57
Campground by the Sea 115
Camping 110, 389
Canady's Marina 241
Candy Barrel 121
Canoeing 252
CanSurvive 377
Cape Fear Academy 352
Cape Fear Area United
    Way 369
Cape Fear Area Visitor
    Information Bureau 222
Cape Fear Blues Festival 175
Cape Fear Boat Rental &
    Charters 210, 252
Cape Fear Camera Club 296
Cape Fear Coast Convention
    and Visitors Bureau 311
Cape Fear Coffee & Tea 41
Cape Fear Community
    College 350, 386
Cape Fear Council of
    Governments, Dept. of
    Aging 362
Cape Fear Filmmakers
    Accord 296
Cape Fear Ford 312
Cape Fear Hotel Apart-
    ments 364
Cape Fear Literacy
    Council 369

Cape Fear Memorial Hospital 369, 378
Cape Fear Museum 138, 143
Cape Fear Open Marlin Tournament 224
Cape Fear Optimist Club 249
Cape Fear River Rowing Club 196
Cape Fear River 7
Cape Fear Theatre Ballet 294
Cape Fear Youth Soccer Association 260
Capeside Village 363
Capt. Maffitt Sightseeing Cruise 143, 180
Capt. Willie's Restaurant 62
Captain Pete's Seafood 246
Captain Tony's Blue Marlin Restaurant & Bar 84
Capt'n Bill's Backyard Grill 265
Capt'n Pete's Seafood Market 161
Car Rentals 314, 397
Car Wash Facilities 314
Cardinal Lanes 179
Caribbean Cafe 43
Caribbean Trading Company 208, 210
Carolco Studios 16, 402
Carolina Beach 24
Carolina Beach Boardwalk 157
Carolina Beach Family Campground 112
Carolina Beach Municipal Marina 244
Carolina Beach Parks and Recreation 248
Carolina Beach Pier 227
Carolina Beach Realty 107, 340
Carolina Beach Shopping 130
Carolina Beach State Park 113, 269
Carolina Beach State Park Marina 244
Carolina Inlet Marina 243
Carolina Kite Club 258
Carolina Power & Light 321
Carolina Preschool 357
Carolina Shores 336
Carolina Telephone, 322
Carolina Yacht Club 200
Carolina Yacht Harbor 242
Carolina Yacht Yard 241
Carolinas Pro-Pro Tournament 280

Carson Cards and Gifts 133
Carter's Store 160
Castle Stables 255
Caswell Beach 31
Catherine Kennedy Home 363
Catherine's Inn On Orange 74
Catholic Churches 305
Cedar Cove Retirement and Rest Home 364
Celebration Theatre 292
Center for Marine Science Research 388, 390
Center Pier 228
Century 21 Gardner and Associates 338
Century 21 Island Realty 108, 342
Century 21 Island Realty Vacations 109
Chamber of Commerce Education Foundation 348
Champion Karate Center 258
Chandler's Wharf 120, 144
Charles Town 8
Charleston 8
Chestnut Street United Presbyterian Church 304
Child Advocacy Commission 356, 372
Child Care 347, 355
Children's Home Society 372
Christmas By-The-Sea Festival 178
Christmas By-The-Sea Flotilla 178
Christmas By-The-Sea Parade 178
Churches 301
City Pier 230
Class Action 233
Classy Bears Preschool 357
Club Astor 189
Club Rio 183
Coast Guard 311
Coast Line Inn 75
Coastal Carolina Wildlife Expo and Exhibit 172
Coastal Condo-Let 107
Coastal Fitness 254, 259
Coastal Golfaway 271
Coastal Rebuilders 313
Coastal Yellow Cab 314
Cobb's Corner Lounge 189

Coca-Cola Regatta 199
Cockle Shell 133
Coldwell Banker SeaCoast Realty 339
Coldwell Banker Southport-Oak Island Realty 108, 342
Comfort Inn Executive Center 75
Commerce and Industry 399
Community Arts Center 289
Community Boys' Club 373
Community Information 311
Compass Rose Import Company 124
Compton, Spencer (Earl of Wilmington) 8
Cooke's Inn Motel 96
Coquina Harbour 244
Cordgrass Bay 333
Cornelia Nixon Davis Health Care Center 365
Corner Kick Soccer Shop 260
Cotton Exchange 120
Cottonpatch Farms 255
Country Crafters 132
Country Vogue 129
Crabby Oddwaters Restaurant and Bar 63
Crafts 294
Creative World 357
Crew Club 197
Crisis Line 312
Crook's By the River 44, 183
Crossroads, Inc. 372
Crystal Coast 412
Crystal Pier 227
Curiosity Shop 132

D

D & E Dodge-AMC-Jeep/ Eagle 312
da Verrazano, Giovanni 7
Dallas Harris Real Estate 329
Dance 294
David Walker Day 176
Davy Jones Open Ocean Swim 209
Deborah Jamieson and Associates, Inc. 343
Del's Restaurant 61
Delta Air Lines 397
Designs on You 124
Detail Plus Appearance Center 314
Dine Ashore 56
Dineen Animal Hospital 312

Disaster Preparedness
Information 318
Discovery Place of
Wilmington 357
Dive Shops 202
Division of Marine Fisheries 223
Division of Nonpublic
Education 355
Dockside Marina 242
Doctor's In Immediate
Care 380
Doctor's Urgent Care
Clinic 381
Domestic Violence Shelter and
Services 369
Domestic Violence/Rape Crisis
(Brunswick Co.) 312
Down Island Trader 124
Downeast Rover 156, 180
Downtown Area Revitalization
Effort 12
Downtown Area Revitalization
Effort (DARE) 375
Downtown Shopping
Corridor 124
Downtown Wilmington 119
Downtown Wilmington
Association 12
Doxey's Market & Cafe 52
Drapery World Interiors 343
Drivers Licenses 309
Dune Ridge Resort 333
DuPont World Amateur
Handicap Champion-
ship 412

E

Early Childhood Learning
Center 357
East Bank Trading Co. 120
East Coast Discount Bait &
Tackle Shop 203
East Coast Got-Em-On King
Mackerel Classic 224
Easter Egg Hunt 172
Eastwood Kennel 312
Echo Farms 332
Echo Farms Golf & Country
Club 272
Eckerd Drugs 129
Eddie Romanelli's 52
El Toro 236
Elderhaus, Inc. 374
Electricity 321
Elijah's 44, 122
Elizabeth Lowe Antiques and
Interiors 127

Emergency Phone
Numbers 311
Empie Park 267
Encore Magazine 317
Entropy Dive Charters 203
Entropy Rentals 205
Episcopal Churches 305
Everhart Nissan 312
Express Care 382

F

Family Services 373
Feast of Pirates 175
Federal Bureau of Investigation
(FBI) 312
Federal Outdoor Volleyball
Association (FOVA) 265
Festival of Trees 178
Fidler's Gallery and
Framing 120, 290
Fifth Avenue United Methodist
Church 304
Figure Eight Island 31, 331
Figure Eight Realty 31, 342
Film 296
Finkelstein's Jewelry and Music
Company 126
Fire Departments 311
First Baptist Church 302
First Presbyterian
Church 303
Fish House Grill 52
Fishing 223
Fishing Licenses 223
Fishing Piers 227
Fishing Reports 227
Fishing Tournaments 224
Fitness Centers 252
Five & Dime Cultural
Productions 292
Flip's Bar-B-Que House 45
Flo-Jo 235
Flying 254
Football 254
Forest Hills 17, 328
Fort Caswell 160
Fort Fisher 28, 137
Fort Fisher Civil War
Museum 283
Fort Fisher State Historic
Site 157, 173
Fort Fisher State Recreation
Area 236, 259
Fort Fisher-Southport
Ferry 157
Fort Johnson 163
Fox Fire Farm 255

Fran Brittain Realty 107
Franklin Square Park (The
Grove) 164
Fraternal Order of The Police
Bar-B-Que 178
Frostbite Series 199
Frying Pan Shoals 7

G

Galleries 290
Gardenias 53
Gardner Realty 107, 340
Gas 321
General Longstreet's
Headquarters 182
General Rental 318
Gentleman Jim's Jazz Club 184
Gift Basket 132
Gillies' Bed & Breakfast 86
Girl Scout Council of Coastal
Carolina 373
Girls, Inc. 373
Giuseppe's Gourmet Italian
Restaurant 53
Golden Gallery 120
Golf 271
Good Shepherd House 370
Government Offices 315
Governor's Cup 199
Governor's Cup Billfishing
Conservation
Series 224
Grace Baptist Church 303
Grace United Methodist
Church 304
Grand Strand Jetport 396
Granny's Day Care Center 357
Gray Gull Motel 95
Graystone Inn 76
Greater Topsail Spring
Jubilee 173
Greater Wilmington Antique
Show 172
Greater Wilmington Chamber
of Commerce 311
Greek Orthodox Church 307
Greenfield Lake & Gardens 153
Greenfield Park 267
Greenwood Helicopters 398
Gregory School of Science,
Mathematics and
Technology 350
Greyhound Bus Lines 314
Guardian Care of
Burgaw 366

H

H. Neuwirth Men's Wear   129
Halloween Festival   177
Hampstead King Mackerel
    Tournament   224
Hampton Inn   77
Hanover Center   129
Hanover Fishing Center   233
Hanover Urological Associates,
    P.A.   382
Harbor Lite Bar & Grill   193
Harbor Masters Restaurant &
    Lounge   56, 189
Harbor View Antiques   132
Harbour Village Marina   241
Haren (Ed Pickett)   266
Harmony Belles   291
Head Boats and Charters   233
Headstart Program of New
    Hanover County   358
Health Department   312
Helicopters of Charleston,
    Inc.   398
Henrietta II   180
Herbert Bluethenthal Memorial
    Wildflower Pre-
    serve   385
Higher Education   384
Hightide Club   192
Hilda Godwin's   126
Hillhaven Rehabilitation and
    Convalescent
    Center   365
Historic Preservation and
    Community
    Development   375
Historic Wilmington
    Foundation   375
Hobie Fleet 101   199
Holden Beach Driving
    Range   282
Holden Beach Marina   246
Holden Beach Pier   230
Holden Beach Pier Family
    Campground   115
Holden Beach Rental
    Services   318
Holden Beach Surf &
    Scuba   204, 208
Holiday Flotilla   198
Holiday Inn   78
Holiday Inn Wrightsville
    Beach   83
Holland's Shelter Creek Fish
    Camp   252
Holland's Shelter Creek
    Restaurant   58

Hollingsworth American
    Country   127
Holly Shelter Game Land   256
Home & Garden Expo   176
Home Child Care   358
Homecoming Weekend   173
Hope Harbor Home
    (Domestic Violence
    Shelter)   370
Horse-drawn Carriage
    Tour   145
Horseback Riding   255
Hospice of the Lower Cape
    Fear   370
Hot Wax Surf Shop   207
Howard Johnson Plaza-
    Hotel   78
Howard's RV Center   314
Hugh MacRae Park   268
Hughes Marina   246
Hunting   256
Hunting Licenses   256

I

Independence Mall   128
Inland Greens   273
Inland Greens & Cedar
    Ridge   329
Intracoastal Marina   246
Intracoastal Realty Corpora-
    tion   107, 338
Intracoastal Waterway   2, 239
Island Chandler Delicates-
    sen   69
Island Gazette   316
Island Marina   247
Island Motel   96
Island of Lights   178
Island Passage   124, 252
Island Tackle & Hardware   131
Island Treasures   132
Island Walking Club   258
ISO Aero   152
ISO Aero Service, Inc. of
    Wilmington   254, 398

J

J. Arthur Dosher Memorial
    Hospital   380
J. Michael's Philly Deli   45
J.C. Penny   128
Jackson's Big Oak Barbe-
    cue   40
James Place   79
Jean Brown Real Es-
    tate   107, 342

Jensen's Coastal Plantation   363
Jerry Outlaw's Water Ways,
    Inc.   199
Jerry Porter Lincoln Mercury-
    Isuzu   312
Jerry's Garage   313
Jet Skis   195
Jewish Congregations   306
Jimmy's Deli   58
Jobsite   236
Jogging   257
John N. Smith Cemetery   137
Johnnie Mercer's Pier   227
Johnson Marina   241
Johnston, Governor Gabriel   8
Jolly Roger Pier   228
Jones' Seafood House   61
Jones-Onslow Electric
    Membership
    Corporation   321
Jubilee Amusement
    Park   27, 138, 157
Jungle Rapids Family Fun
    Park   153
Jung's Tae Kwon Do
    Academy   259

K

K-38 Baja Grill   45
Karate   259
Katie B. Hines Senior
    Center   366
Katy's Great Eats   185
Kiddy Korner Kinder
    Kamp   263
King Neptune   54
Kingoff's Jewelers   126, 129
King's Motel   86
Kitchen Shoppe   121
Kite Flying   258
Kites Unlimited   258
KMart   129
Kona's Coffee Beanery   41
Krazy Pizza & Subs   41
Kure Beach   28
Kure Beach Pier   228

L

Labor Day Arts & Crafts
    Fair   175
Lady Frances   236
Lake Shore Commons   362
Lake Waccamaw State
    Park   116
Lakeside Alternative
    School   350

Landfall 273, 330
Landfall Associates 339
Landmark Real Estate 339
LaQue Center for Corrosion
    Technology, Inc. 390
Larry Thomas & Associates,
    Inc. 291
Larry's Calabash Seafood
    Barn 64
Laundromats 315
Laws 310
Legion Stadium 268
Lejeune Grand Prix
    Series 257, 264
Lewis Realty 107
Libraries 315
Lifeline 379
Limousine Service 397
Linda's 132
Liquor Laws 315
Little Chapel on the
    Boardwalk 304
Little Miss & Tiny Miss North
    Carolina 4th of July
    Pagent 173
Lo-Di Farms 255
Local Call Surf Shop 208
Locals Only 188
Lockwood Golf Links 278
Long Bay Lady Anglers King
    Mackerel Tourna-
    ment 226
Long Beach Family Camp-
    ground 115
Long Beach Pier 230
Long Leaf Baptist 303
Lower Cape Fear Historical
    Society 151, 375
Lowe's 129
Lucky Fisherman 66
Lula's 185
Lutheran Churches 307

M

Magic Mountain Water
    Slide 138
Makado Gallery 120
Margaret Rudd & Associates,
    Inc., Realtors 108, 342
Marge's Restaurant & Waffle
    House 61
Maricultura, Incorporated 390
Marinas 239, 240
Marine Expo 176
Market Street Bed &
    Breakfast 79
Marsh Harbor Golf Links 279

Marsh Harbor Marina 247
Martial Arts Center 258
Masonboro Boatyard and
    Marina 243
Masonboro Island 24, 110,
    112, 166, 389
Masonboro Island Sunset
    Cruises 180
Masonboro Island Taxi & Sunset
    Cruises 113, 156
Masonboro Island Water Taxi &
    Sunset Cruises 168
Mason's Marina 241
Massachusetts Bay Colony 8
Masters Swim 209
McKay-Green Inn 80
McKenzie Supply Co. 342
Meadowsweet Kennels 312
MEDAC, Convenient Medical
    Care 381
Media Information 315
Medical Mall 378
Medieval Festival 172
Mega-Flite 235
Memorial Day 173
Mental Heath Center 312
Merritt's House of Bar-B-
    Que 40
Methodist Churches 304
Mickey Ratz 185
Mid-Summer Cruise 199
Mid-Summer Offshore
    Regatta 199
Miller-Motte Business
    College 387
Montie's Cheese Works 130
Moore Antiques 127
Morse Cemetery 137
Motions 186
Movie Theaters 187
Murrow Furniture 130
Museum of Coastal Carolina 162
Museum of the Lower Cape
    Fear 17
Music 290
MWR Recreation Division 209
Myrtle Beach 407
Myrtle Beach Speedway 409
Myrtle Grove Shopping
    Center 131

N

National Estuarine Research
    Reserve 388
National Historic
    Registry 12, 326
National Track Program 257

National Undersea Research
    Center 385, 388
NationsRealty 342
Nature of Things 312
NC Division of Coastal
    Management 385
NC Oyster Shucking
    Championship 177
NC Wildlife Resources
    Commission 224, 256
Needham Animal Hospital 312
Neuwirth Hyundai 312
New Bern 416
New Elements Gallery 290
New Hanover County
    Extension Service
    Arboretum 154
New Hanover County
    Department of Emergency
    Management 318
New Hanover County
    Fair 177
New Hanover County
    International
    Airport 12
New Hanover County Public
    Library 311
New Hanover County
    Schools 310, 347, 372
New Hanover International
    Airport 1, 396
New Hanover Regional
    BirthPlace 378
New Hanover Regional Medical
    Center 370, 377
New Hanover Regional's
    Coastal Heart
    Center 377
New Hanover Senior
    Center 367
New Hanover Youth
    Baseball 249
Night Before Christmas
    Parade 178
Nightlife 179
No-Name Island 389
North Carolina Aquarium at
    Fort Fisher 28, 283
North Carolina Aquarium at Ft.
    Fisher 158
North Carolina Azalea
    Festival 139, 173
North Carolina Festival By the
    Sea 177
North Carolina Jazz
    Festival 172
North Carolina Music
    Showcase 173

North Carolina National Estuarine Research Reserve 388
North Carolina Natural Gas 321
North Carolina Poetry Society 294
North Carolina Spot Festival 176
North Carolina Symphony 173
North Carolina Writers' Network 294
North Carolina's Artificial Reef Program 201
North Island 389
North Shore Country Club 277
North Topsail 31
Northchase 329
Northrop Mall 132
Northside Medical Center 381
Northside Park 268
Northwest District Park 269
Now and Then 130
Numero Uno 41
Nursing Homes 364
Nuss Strasse Cafe 46

O

Oak Beach Inn and Marina 246
Oak Island 31
Oak Island Golf and Country Club 277
Oak Island Senior Citizens Shop 133
Oak Winds Marina 241
Oakdale Cemetery 145
Ocean Aire Aviation, Inc. 161, 254, 398
Ocean City Fishing Pier 228
Ocean Crest Motel 90
Ocean Crest Pier 230
Ocean Front Inn 87
Ocean Isle 336
Ocean Isle Airstrip 398
Ocean Isle Beach 32
Ocean Isle Beach Water Slide 138
Ocean Isle Marina 196, 247, 252
Ocean Isle Motel 96
Ocean Isle Pier 230
Ocean Outfitters 236
Ocean Ray 203

Ocean Trail Convalescent Center 366
Oceanside Restaurant 58
Octoberfest 177
Off-Roading 259
Office Depot 129
Offshore Adventures 203
Oktoberfest Family 5K Fun Run, 257
Ol' Nep's Lounge 188
Old Baldy 285
"Old Baldy" Lighthouse 165
Old Smithville Burial Ground 137, 164
Old Town 8
Old Wilmington by Candlelight Tour 178
Old Wilmington Florist 124
Olde Point 276
Olde Wilmington Toy Company 120
One South Lumina Motel 83
Onslow County Museum Kite Festival 173, 258
Onslow County Parks & Recreation 249, 261, 266
Onslow County Parks and Recreation 248
Opera House Theatre 292
Orton Plantation Gardens 163
Osprey Charters 235
Outrigger Boutique 121

P

P.T.'s Grille 46
Paddy's Hollow 46
Parents Supporting Parents 370
Park Avenue School 358
Parks 114
Parr Antiques and Collectibles 132
Patricia's Shoes 129
Paula's Health Hut 130
Pelican Point Marina 247
Pellegrino Properties 339
Pender County School System 372
Pender Memorial Hospital 380
Penslow Medical Center 382
Perfect Golf Practice Facility 281
Permuda Island 389
Phar-mor 129

Pine Valley 329
Pine Valley Baptist Church 303
Pinewood Campground 114
Piney Woods Festival 175
Pinnacle Care Center 365
Plan B 41
Plantation Village 362
Play It Again Sports 248
Playwrights Producing Company 293
Pleasure Island Seafood & Jazz Festival 177
Pleasure Island Spring Festival 173
Pleasure Island Surf Fishing Tournament 227
Police Departments 311
Pools 209
Poor Boy Shark Tournament 224
Pop Warner Football 254
Poplar Grove Plantation 155
Port Charlie's 67
Port City Slickers 264
Porters Neck Plantation 274, 331
Presbyterian Churches 303
Pro Tee Practice Range 282
Pro-fit 253
Proper Garden 122
Pyewacket Sailing Cruises 162, 180

Q

Quarter 123
Quarterdeck Lounge 88
Quilters By the Sea 294

R

R. Bryan and Company 120
R.H. McClure Realty, Inc. 109
Rack'M Pub and Billiards 179
Racquetball 259
Radio Stations 317
Ramada Inn Conference Center 80
Rampage 191
Rape Crisis 312
RDG Real Estate 339
Re/Max 339
Real Estate 325, 362
Real Estate Companies 338
Rebecca's Lingerie, Ltd. 123
Red Carpet, Dorothy Essey & Associates, Inc., Realtors 108

Redi 132
Region O Senior Games 367
Reindeer Romp 257
Rent America 318
Rental Services 318
Rescue Squads 311
Research 384
Restaurants 39
    Anna Theresa's Piasta
        Cafe 44
    Barnacle Bill's Grill 56
    Beaches 50
    Big Daddy's Seafood
        Restaurant 55
    Bowman's At the
        Beach 56
    Cafe Atlantique 42
    Caffe Phoenix 42
    Camp Davis Restaurant 57
    Capt. Willie's Restaurant 62
    Caribbean Cafe 43
    Crabby Oddwaters
        Restaurant and Bar 63
    Crook's By the River 44
    Del's Restaurant 61
    Dine Ashore 56
    Doxey's Market &
        Cafe 52
    Eddie Romanelli's 52
    Elijah's 44
    Fish House Grill 52
    Flip's Bar-B-Que
        House 45
    Gardenias 53
    Giuseppe's Gourmet Italian
        Restaurant 53
    Harbor Masters Restaurant
        & Lounge 56
    Holland's Shelter Creek
        Restaurant 58
    Island Chandler
        Delicatessen 69
    J. Michael's Philly Deli 45
    Jimmy's Deli 58
    Jones' Seafood House 61
    K-38 Baja Grill 45
    King Neptune 54
    Larry's Calabash Seafood
        Barn 64
    Lucky Fisherman 66
    Marge's Restaurant & Waffle
        House 61
    Nuss Strasse Cafe 46
    Oceanside Restaurant 58
    P.T.'s Grille 46
    Paddy's Hollow 46
    Port Charlie's 67
    River Pilot Cafe 69

    Roberto's Pizzeria &
        Restaurant 62
    Sandfiddler Seafood
        Restaurant 68
    Sea Captain Restaurant and
        Harborside Lounge 68
    Sharky's Pizza & Deli 63
    Sims Country Bar-B-Que
        II 64
    Soundside 59
    Sunsets 60
    Szechuan 132 48
    Thai Peppers 68
    The Bald Head Island
        Club 69
    The Bridge Tender
        Restaurant 50
    The Chart House 66
    The Crow's Nest Grill 66
    The Islander Restau-
        rant 62
    The Market 60
    The Oceanic Restau-
        rant 55
    The Original Calabash
        Restaurant 65
    The Original Ella's of
        Calabash 66
    The Pharmacy 67
    The Pilot House 46
    The Round Table 67
    The Rusty Scupper 59
    Topsail View Restaurant 61
    Trails End Steak House 48
    Twin Lakes Seafood
        Restaurant 64
    Water Street Market 49
    Windjammer Restaurant &
        Lounge 62
Retired Senior Volunteer
    Program 374
Retirement 360
Rippy Cadillac-Oldsmobile-
    Mitsubishi 313
River Circle Tour 284
River Pilot Cafe 69
River Road Park 227
Riverfest 177
Riverfront Park 268
Riverside Motel 97
Robert Ruark Chili
    Cookoff 172
Robert Ruark Festival 178
Robert Strange Park 268
Roberto's Pizzeria &
    Restaurant 41, 62
Rogers Bay Family
    Campway 114

Rose's 129
Round Table Restaurant and
    Lounge 280
RSVP 367
Rugby 260
RV Repairs 313

S

S & S Water Sports,
    Inc. 196, 208
Sabra's Gifts 132
Saint Mary's Roman Catholic
    Church 305
Salon Deja Vu 123
Salty's Pier 228
Salty's Surf Shop 208
Salvation Army 370
Sam's 129
Sand 216
Sanddollar Shell Shop 120
Sandfiddler Seafood
    Restaurant 68
Sandpiper 190
Sandpiper Lounge 85
Sanitary Fish Market 414
Savage-Bacon House 81
Scentsational 123
School Registration 310
Schools 347
SCORE 367
Scotch Bonnet Fishing
    Pier 228
Scotts Hill King Mackerel
    Tournament 224
Scott's Hill Marina 241
Scruggs & Morrison
    Realty 108, 342
Scuba South Diving
    Company 204
Sea Captain Motor Lodge 97
Sea Captain Restaurant and
    Harborside Lounge 68
Sea Horse Riding Stables 255
Sea Mist Camping Resort 116
Sea Trail Plantation 264, 279
Sea Vista Motel 88
Sea Wolfe 235
Seapath Yacht
    Club 198, 199, 243
Sears 128
Seashore Weavers and
    Spinners 294
Senior Adult Retirement
    Communities 362
Senior AIDES Pro-
    gram 367, 374
Senior Services 360

Service Directory 309
Seven Seas Inn 86
Shallotte 33
Shallotte District Park 269
Shallotte Point Flounder
 Tournament 224
Shamrock Pub 193
Shandy Lane 331
Shannon's Services, Inc. 108
Sharky's Pizza & Deli 63, 266
Shaw Speakes Day Care
 Center 358
Shell Island All-Oceanfront
 Suites 84
Shell Island Resort Hotel 84
Shenanigans Beach Club Bar &
 Grill 190
Sheriff's Offices 311
Sherwin-Williams 129
SHIPP 367
Ship's Store Windsurfing and
 Sailing Center 197,
 200, 210
Shopping 119
Showroom Lighting 343
Shuckers 192
Silver Gull Motel &
 Apartments 84
Sims Country Bar-B-Que 40
Sims Country Bar-B-Que
 II 64
Sitter Network, Inc. 358
Skateboarding 260
Skaters Choice 154
Sloane Realty 108, 342
Smithville District Park 269
Sneads Ferry King Mackerel
 Tournament 226
Sneads Ferry Shrimp
 Festival 175
Snow's Cut Landing Marina 244
Snow's Cut Park 269
Soccer 260
Social Services 312
Society for Masonboro Island,
 Inc. 168
Softball 261
Soundside 59
South Brunswick Islands 32
South Brunswick Isles King
 Mackerel Tourna-
 ment 226
South Winds Motel 90
Southeastern Athletic
 Association 249
Southeastern Sickle Cell
 Association 371
Southern Bell 322

Southern Lights Festival 172
Southport 34
Southport Marina, Inc. 245
Southport Scuba and Water
 Sport 204
Southport Shopping 132
Southport Trail 164
Southport-Fort Fisher
 Ferry 283
Southport-Oak Island Masters
 Putting Tourna-
 ment 277
Spinnaker Beach Center 132
Sports 389
Sports Source 248
Sportsman's Marina 246
St. Andrews On-the-Sound
 Episcopal Church 306
St. James Episcopal
 Church 146, 305
St. John's Museum of
 Art 147, 287, 289, 374
St. Marks Episcopal
 Church 305
St. Mary Catholic School 354
St. Moritz 334
St. Nicholas Greek Orthodox
 Church 307
St. Paul's Episcopal
 Church 306
St. Paul's Evangelical Lutheran
 Church 307
St. Regis Resort 88
St. Stephen AME Church 306
St. Therese Catholic
 Church 305
Stadium Batting Cages 155
State Port Pilot 316
Steamers 192
Stemmerman's Club 186
Stepping Stone Manor 371
Sterling Edition of Wrightsville
 Dunes 333
Stillsearching 235
Storm & Hurricane
 Information 318
Stover's Martial Arts 259
Suburbs 16
Summer Camps 262
Summer Fair 173
Summer Fun Beach
 Days 161, 212
Summer Sands Motel 85
Sun & Moon Bookshop and
 Boutique 266
Sun and Moon Bookshop and
 Boutique 130
Sun-Daze Jet Ski Rentals 196

Sunset Beach 32, 336
Sunset Celebration at the
 Hilton 186
Sunset Pier 230
Sunset Properties 109, 342
Sunset Watersports 196
Sunsets 60
Surf City 31
Surf City Family Camp-
 ground 114
Surf City Pier 228
Surf City Sport Center
 Marina 241
Surf City Surf Shop 207
Surf City Water Slide 138
Surf Fishing 236
Surf Motel Suites 85
Surf Unlimited 208
Surf Unlimited at The Winds
 Clarion Inn 200
Sutton-Council Furniture 130
Swag 235
Swag II 236
Swansboro 413
Sweet Nuthin's Lingerie 120
Sweetwater Surf Shop 207
Sylvia's Pet Care Center 312
Szechuan 132 48

T

T.S. Brown Jewelers 121
Tapestry Theatre Com-
 pany 293
Tax Rates 321
Taxi Service 397
Taylor House Inn Bed and
 Breakfast 82
Taylor's Landing 246
Tee Smith Custom Golf
 Clubs 281
Tee-Times, Inc. 271
Telephone 322
Television Stations 317
Temple of Israel 306
Temptations 129
Tennis 263
Thai Peppers 68
Thalian Association 293
Thalian Hall Center for the
 Performing Arts 148,
 287
The Antique Gallery 128
The Bald Head Island Club 69
The Bald Head Island Cruise
 and Race 199
The Basin 389
The Basket Case 121

The Beat 317
The Brass Pelican 189
The Bridge Tender
    Restaurant 50
The Brunswick Hospital 380
The Cape Center for
    Alternative Programs of
    Education 387
The Cape Fear Cyclists
    Club 250
The Cape Golf & Racquet
    Club 272
The Castle Hayne Saddle
    Shop 255
The Challenger 316
The Chart House 66
The Charter Restaurant 414
The Comedy Zone 188
The Cove at Fort Fisher State
    Historic Site 269
The Cove Surf Shop 207
The Crest Fitness Cen-
    ter 254
The Cricket Inn 76
The Crow's Nest Grill 66
The Deck Entertainment
    Center 160, 209
The Fish Witch II 233
The Gallery 191
The Gauntlet Golf Club 280
The Golf Bag 281
The Greater Wilmington Tennis
    Association 263
The Green Tree Inn 77
The Hilton Hotel 245
The Ice House 184
The Inn at St. Thomas
    Court 78
The Islander Restaurant 62
The Jolly Roger Motel 87
The Julia 126
The Mad Monk 185
The Market 60
The Mermaid 190
The Oaks 378
The Oarhouse Lounge 191
The Oceanic Restaurant 55
The Odom Company 109
The Original Calabash
    Restaurant 65
The Original Ella's of
    Calabash 66
The Patio Playground 158
The Pearl Golf Links 280
The Petite Quarter 123
The Pharmacy 67
The Pilot House 46, 122

The Prudential Carolinas
    Realty 339
The Quarterdeck Lounge at St.
    Regis Resort 191
The Riverwalk 146
The Rocks 389
The Round Table 67
The Rusty Scupper 59
The Saucepan 122
The Topsail Motel 88
The Wilmington Golf
    Association 271
The Winds Clarion Carriage
    House Inn 96
The Winds Clarion Inn 208
The Wonder Shop 129
The Worth House 82
The Yellow Rose Saloon 187
Thrifty Car Rental 315
TLC Unlimited 358
Tommy's RV Storage and
    Service 314
Tom's Drug Store 126
Topsail Beach 31
Topsail Beach Assembly
    Building 159
Topsail Beach Shopping 132
Topsail Greens Country
    Club 276
Topsail Island 28
Topsail Marina 235, 241
Topsail Offshore Fishing Club
    King Mackerel
    Tourna 226
Topsail Realty 107, 340
Topsail Reef 334
Topsail Scenic Boat Tours 159
Topsail Skating Rink 159
Topsail Sound Fishing
    Pier 228
Topsail Turtle Project 29
Topsail View Restau-
    rant 61, 88
Topsail Voice 316
Topsail Water
    Sports 196, 198, 200,
    208, 251, 252
Total Child Care 358
Tour of Homes 178
Track and Field 264
Trails End Steak House 48
Trash/Recycling 322
Travelhost Magazine 317
Treasure Island Family Fun
    Park 160
Triangle Rental 314
Triathlon 264
Trinity Methodist Church 304

Trophy Hunter 236
Tropico Charters 233
Tucker Bros. Realty 340
Turtle Hall 331
Twin Lakes Seafood
    Restaurant 64

U

U.S. Open King Mackerel
    Tournament, 227
Ultimate 264
United Beach Vacations 107
United Cerebral Palsy
    Developmental
    Center 354
United Resorts 340
University of North Carolina at
    Wilmington 18, 350, 384
University Theatre, University
    of North Carolina 293
US Helicopter, Inc. 398
USAir-USAir Express 397
USS North Carolina
    Battleship 173
USTA Team Tennis Associa-
    tion 263
Utility Services 321

V

Vacation Rentals 74
Valley Golf Center & Driving
    Range 281
Vehicle Registration 309
Villa Capriani Resort 89
Virginia Jennewein Antiques
    and Appraisals 127
Visual Arts 289
Vito's Pizzeria 41
Volleyball 265
Volunteer and Information
    Center, Brunswick
    County 371
Voter Registration 310

W

Wacky Golf Cart Parade 175
Wal-Mart 129
Walk & Talk Tours 151
Walk-In Messiah Perfor-
    mance 178
Walker Realty 107, 340
Wally's Restaurant 242
Water and Sewer 322
Water Street Bakery 124
Water Street Market 49
Water Street Restaurant 126

Water Ways Charters 156
Watercraft Works, Inc. 196
Waterfront Home Tour 178
Waterfront Park 165
Waterway Campground 116
Waverunners 195
WCCA 106.3 FM 317
Wes Howell Volvo & Saab 313
Western Union 323
WGNI 102.7 FM 317
Whispering Pines 331
Whitewater Rafting 195
WHQR 93.1 FM 317
Willis Richardson Players 294
Wilmington Art
    Association 290
Wilmington Adventure Walking
    Tour 151
Wilmington and Weldon
    Railroad 11
Wilmington Athletic Club 253
Wilmington Boys
    Choir 178, 291
Wilmington Choral
    Society 291
Wilmington Christian
    Academy 353
Wilmington City Market 126
Wilmington Community
    Development
    Corporation 375
Wilmington Family
    YMCA 253, 262, 266
Wilmington Golf Course 275
Wilmington Health
    Associates 382
Wilmington Hilton 77
Wilmington Historic
    Foundation 11
Wilmington Homeschool
    Organization 355
Wilmington Honda 313
Wilmington Journal 316
Wilmington Marine
    Center 245
Wilmington Parks &
    Recreation 195, 261,
    265
Wilmington Parks and
    Recreation 248
Wilmington Pops Wind
    Ensemble 292
Wilmington Railroad
    Museum 151
Wilmington Road Runner
    Club 257
Wilmington Scuba and Water
    Sports 203

Wilmington Symphony
    Orchestra 292
Wilmington Tennis Ladder 263
Wilmington Tri-Span & City
    Circuit Run 257
Wilmington Triathlon 264
Windjammer Restaurant &
    Lounge 62
Windsurfing & Sailing
    Center 252
Wineseller 130
Wings 131
Winter Park Baptist
    Church 303
Winter Park Optimist
    Club 261
WJKA-TV 26, ABC 317
WMNX 97.3 FM 318
Women of Wilmington
    Chorale 292
Woodbury Forest 329
Woodcolt & Company 128
Worship 301
Wrestling 266
Wright, Thomas Henry Jr. 122
Wrightsville Beach 20
Wrightsville Beach Coast
    Guard 251
Wrightsville Beach King
    Mackerel Tourna-
    ment 227
Wrightsville Beach Ocean
    Racing Association 198
Wrightsville Beach Parks &
    Recreation 207, 209,
    248, 263, 265, 267
Wrightsville Beach Parks and
    Recreation 248
Wrightsville Beach Shopping 132
Wrightsville Marina Yacht
    Club, 242
Write Place 121
Writers 294
WSFX 107 FM 318
WWAY-TV 3, CBS 317
WWQQ 101.3 FM 318

Y

Yaupon Beach 32
Yaupon Pier 230
Yellow Rose Saloon 77
YMCA 209, 249, 261, 265, 373
Yoga 266
YWCA 209, 373
YWCA of
    Wilmington 253, 263

Z

Zebulon-Latimer House 151
Zeke's Island 168, 389
Zeke's Island Coastal
    Preserve 256
Zip Codes 318

ORDER FORM
Fast and Simple!

Mail to:	**Or:**
By The Sea Publications, Inc.	**for VISA or**
P.O. Drawer 860	**Mastercard orders call**
Beaufort, NC 28516	**1-800-955-1860**

Name _____

Address _____

City/State/Zip _____

Qty.	Title/Price	Shipping	Amount
	Insiders' Guide to Richmond/$12.95	$2.50	
	Insiders' Guide to Williamsburg/$12.95	$2.50	
	Insiders' Guide to Virginia's Blue Ridge/$12.95	$2.50	
	Insiders' Guide to Virginia's Chesapeake Bay/$12.95	$2.50	
	Insiders' Guide to Washington, DC/$12.95	$2.50	
	Insiders' Guide to Charlotte/$14.95	$2.50	
	Insiders' Guide to North Carolina's Triangle/$14.95	$2.50	
	Insiders' Guide to North Carolina's Outer Banks/$12.95	$2.50	
	Insiders' Guide to Wilmington, NC/$12.95	$2.50	
	Insiders' Guide to North Carolina's Crystal Coast/$12.95	$2.50	
	Insiders' Guide to Charleston, SC/$12.95	$2.50	
	Insiders' Guide to Myrtle Beach/$12.95	$2.50	
	Insiders' Guide to Mississippi/$12.95 (8/94)	$2.50	
	Insiders' Guide to Orlando/$12.95	$2.50	
	Insiders' Guide to Sarasota/Bradenton/$12.95 (8/94)	$2.50	
	Insiders' Guide to Northwest Florida/$12.95 (7/94)	$2.50	
	Insiders' Guide to Lexington, KY/$12.95	$2.50	
	Insiders' Guide to Louisville/$12.95 (12/94)	$2.50	
	Insiders' Guide to the Twin Cities/$12.95 (12/94)	$2.50	
	Insiders' Guide to Boulder/$12.95 (11/94)	$2.50	
	Insiders' Guide to Denver/$12.95 (11/94)	$2.50	
	Insiders' Guide to The Civil War (Eastern Theater)/$12.95	$2.50	
	Insiders' Guide to Western North Carolina/$12.95 (2/95)	$2.50	
	Insiders' Guide to Atlanta/$12.95 (2/95)	$2.50	

Payment in full(check or money order) must accompany this order form.
Please allow 2 weeks for delivery.

N.C. residents add 6% sales tax _____

Total _____

Who you are and what you think is important to us.

**Fill out the coupon and we'll give you
an Insiders' Guide® for half price ($6.48 off)**

Which book(s) did you buy? _____

Where do you live?_____

In what city did you buy your book? _____

Where did you buy your book? ( ) catalog ( ) bookstore ( ) newspaper ad
( ) retail shop ( ) other

How often do you travel? ( ) yearly ( ) bi-annually ( ) quarterly
( ) more than quarterly

Did you buy your book because you were ( ) moving ( ) vacationing
( ) wanted to know more about your home town ( ) other

Will the book be used by a ( ) family ( ) couple ( ) individual ( ) group

What is your annual income? ( ) under $25,000 ( ) $25,000 to $35,000
( ) $35,000 to $50,000 ( ) $50,000 to $75,000 ( ) over $75,000

How old are you? ( ) under 25 ( ) 25-35 ( ) 36-50 ( ) 51-65 ( ) over 65

How often has your family moved? ( ) never ( ) once ( ) twice
( ) three times ( ) more than three times

Did you use the book before you left for your destination? ( ) yes ( ) no

Did you use the book while at your destination? ( ) yes ( ) no

Is there anything you would like to tell us about Insiders' Guides?_____

_____

_____

Name_____ Address_____

City _____State_____Zip_____

**We'll send you a voucher for $6.48 off any Insiders' Guide® and a list of available
titles as soon as we get this card from you. Thanks for being an Insider!**

BUSINESS REPLY MAIL

FIRST CLASS   PERMIT NO. 20   MANTEO, NC

POSTAGE WILL BE PAID BY ADDREESSEE

The Insiders' Guides®, Inc.
PO Box 2057
Manteo, NC 27954